BRIAN GLANVILLE covered the 1958, 1962, 1966 and 1970 World Cup tournaments for *The Sunday Times*. His speciality has always been world soccer and he lived for several years in Italy covering football for *Corriere Dello Sport* of Rome, etc. He scripted and part-edited the well-known film on the 1966 World Cup, *Goal!*, which won the British Film Academy's Award as Best Documentary of the Year. His books *Goalkeepers are Crazy* and *The Rise of Gerry Logan* represent the first serious fiction written about professional soccer. *The Footballer's Companion* (1962) is an exhaustive anthology of the best writing on the game, both here and in Europe, while in *People in Sport* (1967) he has produced a selection of the best from his own writings. *Soccer: A Panorama* (1969) is, as its name suggests, a full and compact world history of the game. So, in a shorter way, is his *Puffin Book of Football*.

*In the same series
in Mayflower Books*

WORLD FOOTBALL HANDBOOK 1969
WORLD FOOTBALL HANDBOOK 1970
WORLD FOOTBALL HANDBOOK 1971

World Football Handbook 1972

Compiled by
Brian Glanville

Mayflower

Granada Publishing Limited
First published in 1971 by Mayflower Books Ltd
3 Upper James Street, London W1R 4BP

Copyright © Brian Glanville 1971

Made and printed in Great Britain by
C. Nicholls & Company Ltd
The Philips Park Press, Manchester
Set in Monotype Times

This book is sold subject to the condition that it shall
not, by way of trade or otherwise, be lent, re-sold, hired
out or otherwise circulated without the publisher's prior
consent in any form of binding or cover other than that
in which it is published and without a similar condition
including this condition being imposed on the
subsequent purchaser.
This book is published at a net price and is supplied
subject to the Publishers Association Standard
Conditions of Sale registered under the Restrictive
Trade Practices Act, 1956.

Table of Contents

Chapter One
European Nations Cup 1970–72 — 7

Chapter Two
European Cup 1970–71 — 20

Chapter Three
European Cupwinners' Cup 1970–71 — 33

Chapter Four
European Fairs Cup 1970–71 — 45

Chapter Five
World Club Championship 1970 — 64

Chapter Six
South American Liberators' Cup — 65

Chapter Seven
British International Championship 1971 — 67

Chapter Eight
British Internationals against Foreign Teams 1970–71 — 72

Chapter Nine
Friendly Internationals between Foreign Teams 1970/71 — 75

Chapter Ten
F.A. Cup 1970/71 — 78
Scottish Cup 1970/71 — 79
Football League Cup 1970/71 — 81

Chapter Eleven
Football League 1970/71 — 82
Scottish League 1970/71 — 84

Chapter Twelve
World Cup History 86

Chapter Thirteen
European Nations Cup History 169

Chapter Fourteen
World Club Championship History 175

Chapter Fifteen
European Cup History 181

Chapter Sixteen
European Cupwinners' Cup History 210

Chapter Seventeen
European Inter-Cities Fairs Cup History 229

Chapter Eighteen
South American Championship History 249

Chapter Nineteen
South American Libertadores Cup History 250

Chapter Twenty
Olympic Football 252

Chapter Twenty-one
England and Great Britain versus The Rest 254

Chapter One

European Nations Cup
(or European Championship) 1970-72

Qualifying Competition
Once again, the tournament has been divided into eight qualifying league groups, to produce eight quarter-finalists. The finals will again be rushed through within a week on the territory of one of the four qualifying semi-finalists, a dubious practice, as was so abundantly and depressingly shown in Italy, in 1968.

Group 1
Czechoslovakia's initial decision to suspend 20 of their leading players from international football till the end of 1971, after the scandals over German football boots in the 1970 World Cup, left them with a raw, flimsy side which even Finland held to a draw in Prague. This meant that Wales and Rumania became transitory favourites and the Rumanians began with an easy 3-0 win over the Finns.

Wales, deprived of the injured Ron Davies, then beat in vain at a massed Rumanian defence at Cardiff, in driving rain. Raducanu, in the second half, had to make two fine saves from Rees, Satmareanu headed off the line from Durban, and England, in the first half, hit the bar. But so did Dumitrache, after sinuously beating England and Powell. Still, Wales might have had a penalty when the notorious Mocanu flattened Wyn Davies, late in the game. Rumania, skilful and hard, came for a point – and got it.

By April, there'd been a change of guard and mind at the Czech Federation. The World Cup players were amnestied, though a recent collision between Migas and Petras had cost the team both players. Migas' leg was broken, Petras was suspended. Wales, meanwhile, had to forego half-a-dozen of their stars, and though their patchwork team did take the lead at Swansea (before a miserable 12,000 crowd) through Ron Davies' penalty after 49 minutes, Jan Capkovic's left wing skills brought him two goals and made another between the 79th and 85th minutes. Millington, who'd played so well in the first half, was direly at fault with the opening goal.

Wales, even more stringently depleted than they had been in the international Championship, and capping new players in Mielczarek, Page and Bryn Jones, were still good enough to beat the Finns, in Helsinki, though they owed much to Millington's goalkeeping. Toshack scored the only goal after 54 minutes, driving a free-kick into the defensive wall, then thumping in the rebound.

October 7th
    Czechoslovakia (1) 1   *Finland* (1) 1
    Albrecht   Paatalainen

October 10th
    Rumania (2) 3   *Finland* (0) 0
    Dumitrache,
    Nunweiller VI

November 11th
    Wales (0) 0   *Rumania* (0) 0
Wales: Sprake (Leeds United); Rodrigues (Sheffield Wednesday), Thomas (Swindon Town); Powell (Sheffield United), England (Spurs), Hole (Swansea City); Krzywicki (Huddersfield Town), Durban (Derby County), Davies, W. (Newcastle United), Moore (Charlton Athletic), Rees (Nottingham Forest).
Rumania: Raducanu; Satmareanu, Lupescu, Dinu (Majanuk), Mocanu, Dumitru, Neagu, Dobrin (Sub. Domide), Dumitrache, Nunweiler VI, Dumitrescu.

April 21st
    Wales (0) 1   *Czechoslovakia* (0) 3
    Ron Davies (penalty)   Jan Capkovic 2, Taborsky
Wales: Millington (Swansea City); Rodrigues (Sheffield Wednesday), Thomas (Swindon Town); Phillips (Cardiff City), James (Blackpool), Walley (Watford); Rees (Nottingham Forest), Durban (Derby County), Davies, R. (Southampton), Davies, W. (Newcastle United), Mahoney (Stoke City) (Sub.: Griffiths (Wrexham).)
Czechoslovakia: Viktor; Dobias, Hrivnak, Taborsky, Desidanik, Pollak, Vesely, Stratil, Kuna, Adamec, Jan Capkovic.

May 16th
    Czechoslovakia (0) 1   *Rumania* (0) 0
    F. Vesely

May 26th
    Finland (0) 0   *Wales* (0) 1
                              Toshack
Finland: Naesman; Kautonen, Nummelin, Rajantie, Suomalainen, Saviomaa, Heikkilae, Toivanen, Paatelainen, Tolsa, Lindholm.
Wales: Millington (Swansea City); Derrett (Cardiff City), Roberts (Arsenal), Mielczarek (Rotherham United), Page (Birmingham City), Durban (Derby County), Jones, Bryn (Bristol Rovers), Rees (Nottingham Forest), Reece (Sheffield United), Toshack (Liverpool), Krzywicki (Huddersfield Town).

Group 2

A group in which Bulgaria, France and Hungary all were in the process of reconstruction. The Hungarians, who had been playing most unconvincingly, were lucky enough in their opening match in Oslo to come up against a weak Norwegian team which presented them with a 3–1 win, thanks to defensive errors.

The French, in Lyon, beat Norway by the same score in a poor game, watched by only 10,000. With Mezy making the first two goals and scoring the third, they won easily enough, but ran out of steam towards the end.

The following Sunday, Norway made the French performance look rather better by forcing a gallant draw in Sofia. The rejuvenated Bulgarian team found that more youth didn't equal greater efficiency. They dominated the early play and, after missing several chances, went ahead finally through Atanassov. But when the Norwegians came out of their shell they were most effective. Bad marking at a corner allowed a headed equaliser by Nielsen, seven minutes from time.

An impressively successful tour of South America in January gave new life to France, who followed a draw away to Spain with another in Budapest, where they owed much to the dazzling goalkeeping of Georges Carnus. Revelli put them ahead, Kocsis eventually equalised from a penalty.

Hungary's brusque defeat by a Bulgarian side without Yakimov or Asparoukhov led to the resignation of their journalist-manager, Josef Hoffer, and an agonising reappraisal of the moribund club game with its undisciplined players.

October 7th
    Norway (0) 1   *Hungary* (2) 3
    Iversen   Bene, Fazekas, Kocsis

November 11th
    France (1) 3   *Norway* (0) 1
    Floch, Lech, Mezy   Nielsen

November 15th
    Bulgaria (1) 1   *Norway* (1) 1
    Atanassov   Nielsen

April 24th, 1971
    Hungary (0) 1   *France* (0) 1
    Kocsis (penalty)   Revelli

May 16th
    Bulgaria (1) 3   *Hungary* (0) 0
    Kolev, Petrov, Volitchkov
    Norway (0) 1   *Bulgaria* (4) 4
    Iversen   Jekov, Vassilev (A.) 2, Bonev

May 19th, 1971
Bulgaria (1) 3   *Hungary* (0) 0
Kolev, Petkov, Velichkov

Group 3

England started manifest favourites in this group, their chances looking all the better when Malta, in the first game, held Greece to a draw.

The Greeks, though their stoppers, Toskas and Kamaras, and their lively midfield half-back, Domazos, were in fine form, inevitably had great difficulty with the sandy pitch. Vassallo headed the willing but ungifted Maltese team into the lead after 66 minutes. A long shot by Kristopoulos equalised, and Lo Bello, the Italian referee, mysteriously disallowed what looked like a good goal for Greece by Antoniadis.

In December, the Swiss, under the effective managership of Louis Maurer, suddenly and unexpectedly made the running, winning, in the space of days, their matches in Greece, where they'd been thrashed in the World Cup in 1969, and Malta. Their midfield trio of Blaettler, Odermatt and Kuhn was especially successful, while the debutant "Kudi" Muller was a most effective striker, scoring a late winning goal in Athens, and making the winner for Kunzli, in Valetta.

England went to Valetta in February with a badly depleted team and won a match of dismal quality, sabotaged by the abominable pitch, through Martin Peters' goal in the 35th minute; an unexceptional long shot after Hunter's had been blocked. Bobby Moore was dropped, first caps went to Chivers, Harvey, Royle and McFarland. The withdrawal of Hurst, with stomach trouble, meant that England deployed merely a two-man spearhead of the tall Royle and Chivers, whom they failed to supply with appropriate crosses.

At home to Greece the following April, England had an easy if at first laborious passage against a Greek side which played without any Panathinaikos men, all reserved for the European Cup semi-final a week later. Inexplicably, Ramsey's full-backs were Peter Storey of Arsenal, who'd played all season in midfield, and Emlyn Hughes, who cannot cross with his left foot, thus omitting Bob McNab, who can, and who'd been picked in the initial 22.

The Greeks played cautiously, with an efficient sweeper, and Koudas lively in attack, but Banks hadn't a shot to save all evening. After 23 minutes, Chivers broke the deadlock with a typically majestic individual burst and left-footed shot. After half-time, the Greeks tired, and Hurst, generally quiescent, headed a good goal when Chivers nodded on Peters' cross, while Lee headed a spectacular third, from the effective Storey's centre. Coates, who substituted a jaded looking Ball, brought more life to the game, which drew only 55,000 spectators.

On the same day, the Swiss had no trouble in thrashing Malta 5–0 at home. The game, played at Lucerne, was absurdly one-sided; Swiss critics felt that one of their semi-professional sides could have accounted for Malta, who changed their unhappy goalkeeper, Mizzi, at half-time. He had already let through all five goals and, with the Swiss relaxing, there were no others.

On May 12th, both England and Switzerland won at home, thus maintaining the close race at the top, and making it probable that the coming matches between the two would be decisive.

England's game against Malta, at Wembley, was thoroughly tedious. The Maltese, clever ball players, useful in the air and well endowed with courage, scarcely bothered to attack; Gordon Banks touched the ball four times throughout the match. But without recognised wingers, England toiled to penetrate the packed Maltese defence, and it wasn't till midway through the first-half that the excellent Martin Chivers' headed in Peters' free-kick. Francis Lee headed a second and, after half-time, a penalty by Clarke (who missed another), a further header by Chivers and a mighty long shot by the debutant, Chris Lawler, gave England substantial but dully won victory. There was much slow hand-clapping.

Switzerland, meanwhile, defeated a Greek team still without Panathinaikos players 1–0, in Berne, with a goal by Odermatt. Coming hard on the heels of their 4–2 home defeat by Poland, this suggested that Switzerland had gone off the boil; though they are notoriously a better, fitter team in the Autumn, when England must play them. Nor can England's match in Athens be a formality.

October 11th
    Malta (0) 1   *Greece* (0) 1
    Vassallo   Antoniadis

December 16th
    Greece (0) 0   *Switzerland* (0) 1
          Muller

December 20th
    Malta (0) 1   *Switzerland* (0) 2
    Vassallo (penalty)   Quentin, Kunzli

February 3rd
    Malta (0) 0   *England* (1) 1
          Peters

Malta: Mizzi; Grima, Mallia, E. Micallef, Camilleri, Darmanin, Cocks, Vassallo, Cini, Theobald, Arpa.
England: Banks (Stoke City); Reaney (Leeds United), McFarland (Derby County), Hunter (Leeds United), Hughes (Liverpool); Mullery (Spurs), Ball (Everton), Peters (Spurs), Harvey (Everton); Chivers (Spurs), Royle (Everton).

April 21st
    England (1) 3   *Greece* (0) 0
    Chivers, Hurst, Lee

England: Banks (Stoke City); Storey (Arsenal), Hughes (Liverpool);

Mullery (Spurs), McFarland (Derby County), Moore (West Ham United); Lee (Manchester City), Ball (Everton) (Sub. Coates (Burnley),) Chivers (Spurs), Hurst (West Ham United), Peters (Spurs).
Greece: Christidis; Gaiatatzis, Stathopolous, Spyridon, Cambas (Haitas), Koudas, Synetopoulos, Dedes (Delikaris), Papoiannou, Kritikopoulos.

April 21st
>   *Switzerland* (5) 5   *Malta* (0) 0
>   Blaettler, Kunzli, Quentin,
>   Citherlet, Muller

May 12th
>   *England* (2) 5   *Malta* (0) 0
>   Chivers 2, Lee,
>   Clarke (penalty), Lawler

England: Banks (Stoke City); Lawler (Liverpool), Cooper (Leeds United); Moore (West Ham United), McFarland (Derby County), Hughes (Liverpool); Lee (Manchester City), Coates, Chivers (Spurs), Clarke (Leeds United), Peters (West Ham United), Ball (Everton).
Malta: Bonaci (Mizzi); Pace, Grima, Camilleri, Daramanin, Delia; Cocks, Vassallo, Bonnet, Theobald, Arpa.

May 12th
>   *Switzerland* (0) 1   *Greece* (0) 0
>   Odermatt

Group 4

Once again, as in the last World Cup, Russia and Northern Ireland came into conflict in a qualifying group. The presence of a recently improved Spanish team made it the more piquant.

It had little hardship, in its opening match at Seville, in beating a much depleted Irish side. For twenty minutes, Ireland were lively and good, but their troubles were compounded when Derek Dougan hurt an arm after Sol knocked him over, and was eventually forced to give way to Todd. Just before the interval, a splendid 25-yard shot from the right by Carlox Rexach gave Spain the lead. In the second half, Pirri and Luis added goals. George Best was too closely marked to give much trouble, though his free-kick early in the second-half did give Harkin the chance of a fine header – and Iribar that of a notable save.

An Irish victory came at last, after nine fruitless matches, when they won 3–0 in Cyprus the following February. They were vastly the better team on a gluepot of a pitch, with Jimmy Nicholson in splendid attacking form. Cyprus held out till the 53rd minute when Hamilton went through to hit the bar, and Nicholson put in the rebound. Dougan got a second, after Nicholson's free-kick was blocked, George Best the third, from a penalty, after Nicholson had been felled.

The return with Cyprus in Belfast, the following April, was sheer formality, a 5–0 win with three goals from George Best, the last coming straight from a corner.

November 11th
>   *Spain* (1) 3   *Northern Ireland* (0) 0
>   Rexach, Pirri, Luis

Spain: Iribar; Rife, Gallego, Sol (Hita), Violeta, Costas, Pirri, Arieta, Luis, Quini (Lora), Rexach.
Northern Ireland: McFaul (Newcastle United); Craig (Newcastle United), Nelson (Arsenal); Jackson (Nottingham Forest), Neill (Hull City), O'Kane (Nottingham Forest); Sloan (Oxford United), Best (Manchester United), Dougan (Wolves) (Sub. Todd (Sheffield Wednesday)), Harkin (Shrewsbury Town), Clements (Coventry City).

November 15th
>   *Cyprus* (1) 1   *Russia* (2) 3
>   Charalambos   Kolotov, Evrujikhin,
>   Tchevtchenko

February 3rd
>   *Cyprus* (0) 0   *Northern Ireland* (0) 3
>   Nicholson, Dougan,
>   Best (penalty)

Cyprus: Herodotus; Kattos (Lakis), Koureas, Kallis, Kavazis, Charalambous, Fokis, Stephanis, Vassiliou, Styalianou, Bomboullis.
Northern Ireland: Jennings (Spurs); Craig (Newcastle United), Nelson (Arsenal); Hunter (Blackburn Rovers), Neill (Hull City), Todd (Sheffield Wednesday); Hamilton (Linfield), McMordie (Middlesbrough), Dougan (Wolverhampton Wanderers), Nicholson (Huddersfield Town), Best (Manchester United).

April 21st
>   *Northern Ireland* (2) 5   *Cyprus* (0) 0
>   Dougan, Best 3,
>   Pashali (own goal)

Northern Ireland: Jennings (Spurs); Craig (Newcastle United), Clements (Coventry City); Harvey (Sunderland), Hunter (Blackburn Rovers), Todd (Sheffield Wednesday); Hamilton (Linfield), McMordie (Middlesbrough), Dougan (Wolves), Nicholson (Huddersfield Town), Best (Manchester United).
Cyprus: Herodotus; Kogos, Kavazis, Koureas, Pashali, Kallis, Tasos, Vassiliou, Stephanos, Papadopolous, Stylianou.

May 9th
>   *Cyprus* (0) 0   *Spain* (1) 2
>   Pirri, Violeta

May 30th
>   *Russia* (0) 2   *Spain* (0) 1
>   Kolotov, Chevtchenko,   Rexach

June 9
>   *Russia* 6   *Cyprus* 1
>   Evruzhikin 2, Fedotov 2,   Stepanos
>   Kolotov, Banichevski

Group 5

Here, eternally disappointing Scotland began with as good a chance as any team, one which looked the better when Portugal could begin with no more than a 1–0 win in Copenhagen, while the Belgians faced a revolt by Paul Van Himst and Puis. But their initial performance, at home to Denmark, was dismal indeed. On an evening of heavy rain, a Danish team bled white by the depredations of foreign clubs succumbed by only a single goal; a freak scored when O'Hare's header in the 14th minute squeezed under the goalkeeper's body. When, on when, would Scotland express their true virtues against anyone other than England?

Certainly not in Belgium, on February 3rd, where in treacherous, slippery conditions their drab team was overplayed in Liège. The first goal was unlucky, McKinnon slipping to put Van Himst's cross ball past his own goalkeeper, but Scotland, though they brought on two forwards at half-time, were scarcely in the game. Van Himst scored a second from a neatly chipped free-kick, a third from the penalty spot, after the excellent Van Moer was brought down. A humiliating night for Scotland.

Belgium, still without their excellent striker, Devrindt – now with PSV in Holland – brought in Lambert of Bruges, who scored twice against Portugal to give them another 3–0 home win. He put Belgium in the lead after 14 minutes, scored a penalty after 64, and Denul added a third, for a convincing success.

But in April the Portuguese, building on the framework of Benfica, were still good enough to beat the lustreless, poorly motivated Scottish side in Lisbon. Scotland, without the one man who might have fired them, Bremner, gave away an own goal when Stanton, after 22 minutes, deflected a cross from the lively Nene. Clark's goalkeeping kept the score down after half-time, but 10 minutes from the end the dormant Eusebio came to life and ran through for a second. Scotland's hopes seemed well and truly dead, deader still after losing in Denmark.

October 14th
Denmark (0) 0   *Portugal* (1) 1
                                Joao

November 11th
Scotland (1) 1   *Denmark* (0) 0
O'Hare

Scotland: Cruickshank (Hearts); Hay (Celtic), Greig (Rangers); Stanton (Hibernian), McKinnon (Rangers), Moncur (Newcastle United); Johnstone (Celtic), Carr (Coventry City), Stein (Rangers), O'Hare (Derby County), Johnston (Rangers).
Denmark: Poulsen; T. Nielsen, Fredericksen, Sanduad, Petersen, Hansen, Outzen, Nygard, Olsen, B. Nielsen, Peersen.

November 25th
Belgium (2) 2   *Denmark* (0) 0
Devrindt 2

February 3rd
Belgium (1) 3   *Scotland* (0) 0
McKinnon (own goal),
Van Himst 2 (1 penalty)

Belgium: Piot; Heylens, Dewalque, Plaskie, Thissen, Van Moer, Van den Daele; Semmeling, Depireux, Van Himst, Denul.
Scotland: Cruickshank (Hearts); Hay, Gemmell (Celtic); Stanton (Hibernian) (Sub. Forrest (Aberdeen)), McKinnon (Rangers), Moncur (Newcastle United); Cooke (Chelsea), Greig (Rangers), Stein (Rangers) (Sub. Green (Blackpool)), O'Hare, Gemmill (Derby County).

February 17th
Belgium (1) 3   *Portugal* (0) 0
Lambert 2 (1 penalty),
Denul

April 21st
Portugal (1) 2   *Scotland* (0) 0
Stanton (own goal),
Eusebio

Portugal: Damas; Da Silva, Humberto, Carlos, Adolfo, Rodriguas, Peres, Simoes, Nene, Eusebio, Baptista.
Scotland: Clark (Aberdeen); Hay (Celtic), Brogan (Celtic), Stanton (Hibernian), McKinnon (Rangers), Moncur (Newcastle United), McCalliog (Wolves) (Sub. Jarvie (Airdrieonians)), Henderson (Rangers), Robb (Aberdeen), Cormack (Nottingham Forest), Gilzean (Spurs).

May 12th
Portugal (2) 5   *Denmark* (0) 0.
Rodrigues, Eusebio 2,
V. Bakista 2

May 26th
Denmark (0) 1   *Belgium* (0) 2
Bjerre   Devrindt 2

June 9th
Denmark (1) 1   *Scotland* (0) 0
Laudrup

Denmark: Sorensen, T. Nielsen, Rasmussen, Berg, Arentoft, Bjerre, Bjormemose, Laudrup, Le Fevre, B. Nielsen, Kristensen.
Scotland: Clark (Aberdeen), Munro (Wolverhampton), Dickson (Kilmarnock), Stanton (Hibernian), McKinnon (Rangers), Moncur (Newcastle), McLean (Kilmarnock), Forsythe (Motherwell), Stein (Rangers), Curran (Wolverhampton), Forrest (Aberdeen).

Group 6

Italy, the Cup holders, looked much the strongest team in the group. Eire began their programme with a 1–1 draw against Sweden in Dublin before an encouragingly large 32,000 crowd. Eire dominated the first half, Dunphy keeping their attack on the move, and led after 43 minutes when Dempsey was fouled in the box and Carroll scored the penalty. In the second-half, Sweden much improved and Brzokoupil, a substitute, beat Kelly to equalise.

Two weeks later, in Stockholm, a much depleted Irish team held out against strong pressure till a quarter of an hour from time, when Tom Turesson, brought on as substitute, beat the excellent Kelly. Eamonn Dunphy also had an impressive game for the beaten Irishmen.

The following Saturday, in Vienna, Italy opened their programme with a bitterly expensive victory. Though they beat Austria 2-1, they lost Luigi Riva, their talismanic striker, with a broken right leg, after a tackle by Hof, late in the second half. Thereafter, a demoralised Italian side managed to hold out against Austria's attempts to save the game.

The first half, in which De Sisti put Italy ahead, Parits equalised and Mazzola restored the lead, had been lively and entertaining, each side's players showing much versatility. Austria hit posts and bar three times, and Albertosi saved Edtmayer's penalty – but the home defence never, while he was on, mastered Riva.

Italy's next match, against Eire in Florence, was hardly one in which Riva was likely to be missed. Eire, scarcely one of the strongest European teams at any time, were pitifully weakened by injury and the stony indifference of the Football League clubs, so that half-a-dozen players, among them Heighway, Conway and Giles, were for various reasons unavailable. They lost, 3-0.

An Italian team packed with famous and expensive players – though no Riva or Rivera – gave another of its dull but effective displays against Eire, in Dublin, winning 2-1. Boninsegna, the League's top scorer, headed a goal after 15 minutes and another header made the winner after 60 minutes, for Prati. Jimmy Conway, the most dangerous Irish forward, had himself headed an equaliser after 23 minutes. Italy were typically and drearily cautious.

October 14
    Eire (1) 1   *Sweden* (0) 1
    Carroll (penalty)   Brzokoupil

October 28th
    Sweden (0) 1   *Eire* (0) 0
    Turesson

October 30th
    Austria (1) 1   *Italy* (2) 2
    Parits   De Sisti, Mazzola

December 8th
    Italy (2) 3   *Eire* (0) 0
    De Sisti (penalty),
    Boninsegna, Prati

May 10th
    Eire (1) 1   *Italy* (1) 2
    Conway   Boninsegna, Prati
May 26th
    Sweden (0) 1   *Austria* (0) 0
    Olsson
May 30th
    Eire (0) 1   *Austria* (3) 4
    Rogers (penalty)   Schmidradner (penalty),
          Kodat, Dunne, J. (own goal),
          Starek

June 9th
    Sweden (0) 0   *Italy* (0) 0

Group 7

In a very strong and fiercely contested group, Yugoslavia got away to a good start, but Holland suffered from injuries to key players, above all to Johan Cruyff. Their home game with Yugoslavia (Cruyff absent) was a bruising one, the Slavs, taking the lead with a mighty free-kick by Dzajic, showing all the ruthlessness in defence which characterised their performance in the finals of the last European Nations Cup. Eventually, Israel equalised from a penalty, after Veenstra was brought down. Four days later, Yugoslavia won in Luxemburg.

Still without Cruyff, Holland lost 1-0 to the revitalised East German team in Dresden, Ganzera making a fine debut for the home side at left-back, Peter Ducke, the veteran centre-forward, scoring the only goal after 11 minutes. The Dutch were feeble in attack. The following Sunday, East Germany easily beat Luxemburg, away, 5-0. No fewer than four of the goals went to the Dynamo Dresden link-man, Kreische. It was Luxemburg's most disconnected performance for a long while.

Yet again without Cruyff – the phrase becomes familiar – Holland's chances disappeared when they lost 2-0 to Yugoslavia in Split, the following April. Jerkovic, a 1962 World Cup player, scored one goal, Dzajic, under suspension in the European Cup, the other.

Then East Germany, at Gera, made surprisingly heavy weather of beating Luxemburg, their second goal and Luxemburg's only one coming, respectively, after 88 and 89 minutes. 2-1 was a meagre success.

It was therefore no great surprise when the lively Yugoslavs went to East Germany and won, thus establishing themselves as almost unassailable favourites in the group. Whatever they may do in World Cups, the European Championship seems to inspire them.

October 11th
    Holland (0) 1   *Yugoslavia* (1) 1
    Israel (penalty)   Dzajic
October 14th
    Luxemburg (0) 0   *Yugoslavia* (1) 2
          Bukal 2

November 11th
    East Germany (1) 1   *Holland* (0) 0
    Ducke, P.

November 15th
    Luxemburg (0) 0   *East Germany* (4) 5
          Vogel, Kreische 4

April 4th, 1971
    Yugoslavia (1) 2   *Holland* (0) 0
    Jerkovic, Dzajic

April 25th
    East Germany (1) 2   *Luxemburg* (0) 1
    Kreische, Frenzel   Dussier

May 9th
    East Germany (0) 1   *Yugoslavia* (2) 2
    Loewe   Filipovic, Dzajic

Group 8

West Germany, who failed to reach the last European Cup finals, were favoured to win this group, with serious opposition coming only from Poland; who began with an undemanding 3-0 win over Albania. Then – of all astonishments – the Germans in their first game were held to a 1-1 draw in Cologne by the Turks, who hung on to their 15th minute lead for another quarter hour, till Gerd Muller equalised from a penalty. Would Uwe Seeler have to be recalled yet again? The Turks were very fit, strong in defence, able in the counter-attack. Metin lost a very good chance to win the match for them, after 58 minutes; Overath and Beckenbauer never won the midfield for Germany.

The following February, a goal by Gerd Muller gave the Germans an uneasy 1-0 win in Albania; where a 0-0 draw had deprived them of qualification for the Nations Cup finals, of 1968.

In April, Germany thrashed Turkey in Istanbul with unexpected ease, with another two goals from Muller and one from Koeppel; despite the absence of Overath. Clearly a game of attrition suited the Turks better than one in which they were expected to attack.

October 14th
    Poland (1) 3   *Albania* (0) 0
    Gadocha, Lubanski,
    Szoltysik

October 17th
    West Germany (1) 1   *Turkey* (1) 1
    Muller (penalty)   Kamarun

December 13th
    Turkey (2) 2   *Albania* (1) 1
    Metin, Cemil   Siu

February 2nd
    Albania (0) 0   West Germany (1) 1
                                      Muller

April 25th
    Turkey (0) 0   West Germany (1) 3
                                      Muller 2, Koeppel

May 12th
    Albania (1) 1   Poland (1) 1
    Zhega   Bene

June 12th
    West Germany 2   Albania (0) 0
    Netzer, Grabowski

GAMES TO COME
Group 1
22–9–71   *Finland* v *Rumania*
13–10–71   *Wales* v *Finland*
27–10–71   *Czechoslovakia* v **Wales**
14–11–71   *Rumania* v *Czechoslovakia*
24–11–71   *Rumania* v **Wales**

Group 2
8–9–71   *Norway* v *France*
25–9–71   *Bulgaria* v *Hungary*
9–10–71   *France* v *Hungary*
27–10–71   *Hungary* v *Norway*
10–11–71   *France* v *Bulgaria*
15–11–71   *Bulgaria* v *Norway*
11–12–71   *Bulgaria* v *France*

Group 3
13–10–71   *Switzerland* v **England**
10–11–71   **England** v *Switzerland*
1–12–71   *Greece* v **England**

Group 4
22–9–71   *Russia* v **Northern Ireland**
13–10–71   **Northern Ireland** v *Russia*
27–10–71   *Spain* v *Russia*
10–11–71   **Northern Ireland** v *Spain*
24–11–71   *Spain* v *Cyprus*

Group 5
13–10–71   Scotland v *Portugal*
10–11–71   Scotland v *Belgium*
21–11–71   *Portugal* v *Belgium*

Group 6
5–9–71	*Austria* v *Sweden*
9–10–71	*Italy* v *Sweden*
10–10–71	*Austria* v *Eire*
27–11–71	*Italy* v *Austria*

Group 7
10–10–71	*Hungary* v *East Germany*
16–10–71	*Yugoslavia* v *East Germany*
27–10–71	*Yugoslavia* v *Luxemburg*
17–11–71	*Luxemburg* v *Holland*

Group 8
22–9–71	*Poland* v *Turkey*
10–10–71	*Poland* v *West Germany*
14–11–71	*Albania* v *Turkey*
17–11–71	*West Germany* v *Poland*
5–12–71	*Turkey* v *Poland*

The winning team of each group qualifies for the quarter-finals, which will be played on a home and away basis. The semi-finals, third place match and final – one game each, though the Final may be replayed – will take place in one of the four countries surviving the quarter-finals.

Chapter Two

European Cup 1970/71

For the second consecutive year, the European Cup went to a Dutch club, proof of the astonishing progress made by Dutch football. Ajax, easily beaten by Milan in the 1969 Final, this time succeeded Feyenoord as the victors, when they comfortably defeated Panathinaikos of Athens 2–0 at Wembley, in the Final.

Nevertheless, the achievement of the Greek club, coached by Ferenc Puskas, in reaching a European Cup Final was quite remarkable. Among their victims were Everton and, in the semi-finals, Red Star, Belgrade, whom they eliminated after losing the first leg, 3–0. Celtic were beaten by Ajax in the other semi-final.

For Ferenc Puskas, the Panathinaikos manager, it was an unexpected achievement to add to his many as a player.

The preliminary round game between two such well established clubs as F.K. Austria and Levski, in which Austria prevailed after losing 3–1 in Sofia, proved the futility of the seeding process. Thus, in the First

Round proper, Everton found themselves playing the Icelandic amateur team of Keflavik, while Celtic put nine goals in their first, home leg, past the goalkeeper of the hapless Finns, Kokkola. Nor did Celtic need a full first team to do it.

Everton won easily enough in the end, but hardly covered themselves with glory. Keflavik, indeed, had the lively impertinence to take the lead at Goodison Park, when Ragnarsson beat West with a header, and Kenyon's clearance bounced into goal off the goalkeeper's back. The last word was weary Keflavik's, too, Ragnarsson scoring when West could only push out a free kick. The Icelanders held their surprising lead till late in the first half, when they rather naïvely let Alan Ball equalise from a short corner. The floodgates opened in the second half, but Olafsson, the fair haired Icelandic goalkeeper, had a finely defiant match.

Cagliari, though the Italian League season had yet to begin, were much too good for a modest St. Etienne side, winning 3-0 in their new stadium, in intense heat. Basel, short of several first team players, were three goals behind in Moscow against Spartak, eight minutes from the end, then scored twice in three minutes, to keep their chances alive. Laufenburger, the Swiss goalkeeper, admitted his culpability in the first two Spartak goals, while Sundermann, the Basel manager, praised Spartak as a better footballing side than the Russian national eleven.

Basel duly won the return match 2-1, and passed into the next round on away goals. As for Cagliari, they lost by the only goal of the game away to a revitalised St. Etienne, but their three-goal margin from the first match made it irrelevant.

The astonishment of the round, needless to say, was the elimination of the holders and world champions, Feyenoord, by the virtually unknown U.T. Arad team, champions of Rumania – this only a few weeks after the Dutchmen had beaten Estudiantes for the so-called Intercontinental Championship. Held to a draw in Rotterdam in the first match, Feyenoord had most of the play in the second but threw away their chances, could manage no more than a goalless draw, and went out, too, on away goals. The Intercontinental Championship and its taxing demands may have had much to do with this reversal.

Everton and Celtic expectedly had no trouble in increasing the margin of their lead in Iceland and Finland, respectively; only 13,400 watched the two games, all told, raising legitimate doubts about a competition which allows so many minnows through the meshes of its net.

Glentoran, however, succumbed to the surprising Waterford, who followed their 3-1 win in Belfast with a 1-0 win at home, before a mere 6,000 fans. Peter McParland returned to the field to play for Glentoran, the team the former Irish international left winger now manages, but he couldn't save them from defeat by Casey's second half goal.

Red Star of Belgrade, with Dragan Dzajic, surprisingly reversed – and more – their deficit against Ujpest of Budapest, winning 4-0 in the return, to go through on a 4-2 aggregate. Atletico Madrid, the Spanish

Champions, who had begun the season in spanking form, followed their conquest of F.K. Austria at home with an odd goal win in Vienna, frustrating Austria's hopes of a second spectacular recovery.

Cagliari were rocked on their heels by St. Etienne, in a return game they were glad, in the end, to lose by no more than a goal. Aggressive in every sense, St. Etienne played with great spirit and sometimes ruthlessly. Albertosi, the Cagliari goalkeeper, accused the spectators of throwing bottles and Keita, St. Etienne's Malian forward, of kicking him deliberately. The experienced West German referee, Schulenburg, called it "one of the hardest matches I have ever had to control". Larqué scored the only goal of the game from Keita's cross, 12 minutes from the interval. But though Luigi Riva was often the only forward Cagliari left upfield, they managed to hold out thereafter.

They themselves were strongly criticised for their wholly negative approach, with Nene used exclusively to mark Keita.

Everton, only four days after having lost 4-0 to Arsenal at Highbury, returned to their familiar team, without their new £150,000 man, Henry Newton, and commendably drew 1-1 with Borussia Munchengladbach in Germany. Bertie Vogts, Germany's famous attacking back, shot home, via an Everton defender, after Rankin had punched out, in the first half, but Howard Kendall got the equaliser, in the second, after a goalkeeping error.

Celtic thrashed Waterford in Ireland in what should have been a fraternal enough affair, but in fact was marred by fighting on the terraces; half-time lasted 16 minutes. Wallace scored for Celtic in 30 seconds and went on to a hat-trick.

U.T. Arad, surprising evictors, rather than conquerors, of Feyenoord in the previous round, crashed 3-0 in Belgrade, to Red Star.

Ajax, with Keizer irresistible, thrashed a Basel team packed in defence but far too slow and wooden to contain them. Benthaus, among several other struggling veterans, had a grim game; and Ajax were without the injured Johan Cruyff.

Everton proceeded to survive against Borussia on penalties, and by the skin of their teeth. Though they scored what looked a slightly fortuitous goal at Goodison after only 22 seconds, Johnny Morrissey's right-footed shot – or centre – drifting into the net, thereafter they were baulked by the splendid goalkeeping of young Wolfgang Kleff. With Joe Royle winning everything in the air, Kleff's one-handed prodigies alone saved his team from falling well behind. As it was, they equalised after 34 minutes, when Andy Rankin saved, but Laumen shot in the rebound.

So it came to a decision, exciting but blatantly arbitrary, on penalty kicks. Royle missed Everton's first, but at the last, Rankin's fine save from Muller took Everton, somewhat flimsily, into the next round.

Celtic, meanwhile, having thrashed Waterford in Ireland, were having all sorts of unexpected problems, under driving rain, at Celtic Park. They were actually two down at half-time, McNeill having put through his own goal, but rallied to scrape through by 3-2, in the second half.

Red Star completed an impressive double over U.T. Arad, Legia Warsaw reversed Standard Lèige's advantage to reach the last eight for the second successive season, while Slovan Bratislava beat Panathinaikos, but insufficiently to survive.

Having squeezed through 2-1 at home to Atletico Madrid in a bruising game – the Spanish defenders gave no quarter – Cagliari lost the priceless Luigi Riva five days before the return match, his leg broken in Vienna. Predictably, their demoralised team went down – and out – 3-0. Luis got all three, one from a penalty; but Atletico's ruthless methods stained the match.

Johan Cruyff returned to the Ajax attack at Basel, after long absence, and his characteristically brilliant display allowed his team to win again, this time 2-1. Both goals came from their midfield men, Rijnders and Neeskens, the first with a header which Marcel Kunz might have saved. Odermatt's penalty had given Basel the lead at the time, and the mistake was expensive.

The quarter-finals were not played till the following March, and after this long hiatus, Everton opened with an astonishing draw, at home to Panathinaikos of Athens; coached by Ferenc Puskas.

The Liverpool team, having disposed 5-0 of Colchester in the Cup, three days earlier, seemed sure to win. Instead they found themselves not only persistently frustrated in a bruising game by harsh opponents, but actually a goal behind till the last moments.

This was cleverly scored by the Greek international centre-forward, Antoniadis. Kamaras took a free-kick which he pushed to Antoniadis. The centre-forward headed the ball down to Grammos, took a return header, pivoted, and shot powerfully into the far corner. There were only nine minutes left, and it took Everton eight of them to save themselves. Then the teenaged Johnson, who had substituted Husband – hurt in a ruthless tackle – after five minutes, came to the rescue.

Ball took Everton's fourteenth corner of the match, Royle headed down, and Johnson shot home. Despite the alleged warning to the Panathinaikos players before they left by one of the sinister Greek colonels, they still managed to commit 30 of the 50 fouls given in the game.

The following day, in Amsterdam, Celtic did even worse than Everton, tumbling to Ajax 3-0, and confirming the impression that a great club team had passed its peak.

It was the brilliance of Johan Cruyff, Ajax's slender young centre-forward, finally breaking loose from the shackles of Hay, which eventually undid a Celtic team sworn to defence. After 75 minutes, Stuy kicked a long clearance out of defence, Neeskens played it on, and Cruyff spurted through to score with a low drive. Seven minutes later, McNeill brought down Cruyff on the edge of the box, and Hulshoff scored powerfully, direct from the free-kick. In the very last minute, a third goal came when Cruyff, now master of the greasy pitch, dribbled past two men and Keizer, turning sharply on his short pass, shot high into goal.

The return, played before 83,000 at Hampden Park, saw Ajax survive, deploying a massed defence and extremely dangerous breakaways, in several of which the electric Cruyff might have scored, were it not for Brogan's fine covering. Muhren, too, came close, with a shot against the post.

For all their pressure, Celtic gained only one goal. It came after 27 minutes. Following one of Ajax's many defensive fouls, Auld lobbed the free-kick into the goal area, where it rebounded to Callaghan, who lobbed in his turn for Johnstone to run in and score. Ajax's defence, statuesque on that occasion, did not relax again.

In Athens, the hard pitch, the bouncing ball and Panathinaikos' fierce, physical challenge not unexpectedly proved a match for Everton, a goalless draw putting them out of the Cup on the Greeks' solitary away goal. Indeed, the Athenian side nearly scored another, when the excellent Domazos hit the post; though against that, their own goalkeeper had to make a fine save from Howard Kendall. Joe Royle, whose header made the chance, was shadowed throughout by the tall Kapsis. Puskas' victory bonus was $12,000.

Red Star, though in due course they swept Carl Zeiss brusquely aside, lost more than their game in Jena, in the first leg; they lost the incomparable Dragan Dzajic, sent off the field, and suspended by UEFA for no less than four games. The East Germans made an excellent start, and played well enough to deserve the two-goal lead they built up in the first twenty minutes, through Strempel and Peter Ducke. Three minutes from half-time, however, Jankovic reduced the lead, and after 58 minutes, Dzajic equalised.

The Germans regained the initiative towards the end from a Red Star side apparently happy with a draw, and Peter Ducke got the winner four minutes from time, after his team had missed a penalty. It was this decision which led to a brawl between the teams, and the expulsion of Dzajic.

In the return, Red Star triumphantly proved they were no one-man team by overwhelming the East Germans, without Dzajic or, for that matter, Antonijevic, also suspended. Another four goals, with only one reply, were volleyed past Panathinaikos in the first leg of the semi-final, in Belgrade, confirming Ferenc Puskas' views, frankly and previously expressed, that Central European football was still far ahead of Greek football. Ostojic scored three.

Atletico Madrid were shipping water badly in the Spanish League by the time of the quarter-finals. They struggled to survive against Legia, scraping through by the clever Adelardo's goal at home, losing away in a match in which they also lost Orozco with a broken leg, but got the goal which counted double and qualified them. They then went on to another 1-0 home victory against Ajax, who were favoured to reach the Final, Irureta scoring the important goal. The game was ruined as a spectacle by the Dutch team's relentlessly defensive attitude, and they could well have given away other goals.

Cruyff had his moments, as always. He once made a fine chance which was missed by the talented Keizer, left alone upfield with him for almost all the match.

It was the Athenian tie, an afternoon match, which took place first when the debate was resumed, two weeks later, and it provided one of the most astounding results in the history of the European Cup. Panathinaikos, winning by an unthinkable three goals to nil, qualified again on the basis of an away goal, and became the most distant outsiders ever to reach a European Cup Final.

The Greek side, which had withheld all its men from the international team that played England the previous week, played with remarkable spirit and drive against a Red Star still unable to call on Dzajic. It was a goal in the first minute by the tall Antoniadis that gave them sudden and immediate hope, a glimpse of blinding light at the end of the tunnel.

In the second half, the astonished Yugoslavs conceded another goal to Antoniadis, and a third, to Kamaras. That night, there were frenzied celebrations and dancing in the fountains of Athens.

For Puskas, the result was a vindication of his decision to drop the experienced goalkeeper, Oeconomopoulos, who gave away two or three of the goals in Belgrade, and prefer the young Konstatinou, who had an excellent game. Indeed, with Domazos, Antoniadis and Kamaras, he was one of his team's heroes.

Ajax, wiping out their deficit against Atletico with an early goal by Piet Keizer, played the attacking game which everyone expected, but couldn't make sure of success till fourteen minutes from the end. Then Suurbier and the new, midfield star, Johan Neeskens, surging out of defence, scored twice more, to give them a convincing advantage, put them in their second Final in three years, and make them the third Dutch finalists in that period.

The Final, though a scene of cacophonous frenzy, was a disappointing game, first because Ajax were so much the stronger, secondly because of their cautious display after half-time.

That they would win became clear when they got an early goal. Barely five minutes had gone when Piet Keizer – who played despite injury, bored in from the left wing, crossed high to the near post, and Van Dijk headed neatly into the far corner. The Greek defence had been statuesque, and remained so for most of the first half in which Ajax should have had several more goals.

Inspired by the marvellous running, the glorious individual bursts, of Johan Cruyff, well supported by Keizer and Van Dijk, they created many chances. Though heavily manned, with Kapsis on Cruyff, Kamara a sort of intermittent sweeper, Panathinaikos' defence was heavy and naïve, vulnerable to the sharp diagonal ball.

It was as well for them that Oeconomopoulos, after a shaky beginning, should play so bravely and well, saving at various times from Neeskens, Van Dijk and Cruyff, twice, when his defence was breached. Yet Kamaras, three minutes from half-time, missed a good chance, made by Vlahos, to equalise.

Domazos, endlessly active, cleverly flicking and backheeling, kept the Greeks in the game, but after half-time, when Ajax played more defensively, his repertoire was limited chiefly to long, banal high balls into the area. There, the ponderous Antoniadis was generally mastered by Hulshoff.

After the interval, Ajax took off the lively Rijnders, from midfield, and their right winger, Swart, substituting the fair haired German, Blankenburg, and Haan. Van Dijk now played deeper, and tedium reigned. The Greeks had much of the field, but it seemed to be too much; nor, as Puskas admitted afterwards, did the going suit them.

When Ajax did attack, usually through the electric dashes of Cruyff, they remained dangerous. Oeconomopoulos had to make another save, from Muhren, after 64 minutes, and later Cruyff himself was only just wide, after a brilliantly elaborate move.

Not till three minutes from time, however, when a second goal seemed most unlikely, did Ajax score again. Cruyff, inevitably, provoked it, with a marvellous run, after receiving from Van Dijk. His pass found Haan, whose shot hit a Greek defender and was deflected past a helpless goalkeeper.

The Dutch were worth their victory, Cruyff above all, but it was somewhat unexcitingly gained. As for the brave Greeks, bonuses worth a reputed £100,000 a man in cash and kind had melted from their grasp.

EUROPEAN CUP 1970/71
Preliminary Round

Levski-Spartak (1) 3   *F.K. Austria* (0) 1
Mitkov, Asparoukhov 2   Redl

F.K. Austria (2) 3   *Levski-Spartak* (0) 0
Redl, Hickersberger, Foka

First Round

Everton (2) 6   *Keflavik* (1) 2
Ball 3, Kendall, Royle 2   West (own goal), F.
                                Ragnarsson

Everton: West; Wright, Newton; Kendall, Kenyon, Harvey; Husband, (Whittle), Ball, Royle, Hurst, Morrissey.
Keflavik: Olafsson; Kartisson, E. Gunnarsson, Kjartansson, A. Gunnarsson; E. Magnusson, Johansson, Torfasson; G. Magnusson, Jenssen, Ragnarsson.

Keflavik (0) 0   *Everton* (2) 3
                                Royle 2, Whittle

Kaflavik: Olafsson; Ketilsson, A. Gunarsson, E. Gunarsson, Kjartansson, E. Magnusson, Johansson, G. Magnusson, Jonsson, Farfusson, Ragnarsson.
Everton: Rankin; Wright, Newton, K.; Kendall, Labone, Harvey; Whittle, Ball, Royle, Hurst, Morrissey.

Celtic (6) 9 *Kokkola* (0) 0
Hood 3, Hughes, McNeill,
Johnstone, Wilson 2, Davidson

Celtic: Williams; McGrain, McNeill, Brogan, Hay; Murdoch, Connelly; Johnstone, Hood, Lennox, Hughes.
Kokkola: Isofais; Korhonen, Makinen, Haultala, Makela; Pankanen, A. Lamberg; Sorvisto, Raatikainen, Kallio, H. Lamberg.

Kokkola (0) 0 *Celtic* (2) 5
 Wallace 2, Callaghan,
 Davidson, Lennox

Kokkola: Isofais; Korhonen, Makinen, Haultala, Makela; Pankanen, A. Lamberg; Sorvisto, Raatikainen, Kallio, H. Lamberg.
Celtic: Fallon; Craig, Connelly, Brogan, Cattenach, Murdoch, Davidson, Wallace, Chalmers, Callaghan, Lennox.

Glentoran (0) 1 *Waterford* (0) 3
O'Neill Hall, Bryan, Casey
Glentoran: Finlay; Hill, McKeag, Coyle, McCullough, Stewart, Hutton, Weatherup, Hall, Cassidy, Lavery.
Waterford: Thomas; Bryan, Maguire; Morrissey, Brennan, McGeough; Buck, O'Neill, Casey, Hale, Matthews.

Waterford (0) 1 *Glentoran* (0) 0
Casey
Waterford: Thomas; Bryan, Maguire; Morrissey, Brennan, McGeough; Buck, Casey, Hale, O'Neill, Matthews.
Glentoran: Finlay; Hill, McKeag; Coyle, McCullough, Stewart; Macken, Weatherup, Hall, McParland (Kirk), Morrow.

Cagliari (2) 3 *St. Etienne* (0) 0
Riva 2, Nene
St. Etienne (1) 1 *Cagliari* (0) 0
Larqué
Slovan Bratislavia (1) 2 *BK 1903 (Copenhagen)* (1) 1
Josef Capkovic, Jan Andersen
Jan Zlocha (penalty)
BK Copenhagen (0) 2 *Slovan Bratislava* (1) 2
Thygessen, Josef Capkovic 2
Johansen (penalty)
Nenduri Tirana (0) 2 *Ajax Amsterdam* (1) 2
Kazanxhi, Hega Suurbier 2
Ajax (1) 2 *Nenduri* (0) 0
Keizer, Swart
IFK Gothenburg (0) 0 *Legia Warsaw* (1) 4
 Gadocha, Pieszko,
 Stachurski 2

Legia Warsaw (2) 2　　　　　*IFK Gothenburg* (1) 1
Devna, Gadocha　　　　　　Almqvist
Ujpest (0) 2　　　　　　　　*Red Star* (0) 0
Nagy, Dunai, A.
Red Star (3) 4　　　　　　　*Ujpest* (0) 0
Filipovic 2, Dzajic, Ostojic
Rosenborg (0) 0　　　　　　*Standard Liege* (1) 2
　　　　　　　　　　　　　　Kostedde, Depireux
Standard Liege (3) 5　　　　*Rosenborg* (0) 0
Pilot 2, Cvetler,
Depireux, Ostojic
Borussia Munchengladbach　*EP Larnax (Cyprus)*
　(3) 6　　　　　　　　　　　(0) 0
Laumen 2, Koeppel 2,
Netzer, Heynckes
　　　　Played at Augsburg by arrangement
EP Larnax (0) 0　　　　　　*Borussia Muchengladbach*
　　　　　　　　　　　　　　　(5) 10
　　　　　　　　　　　　　　Heynckes, Vogts, Netzer,
　　　　　　　　　　　　　　Wimmer, Koeppel 2,
　　　　　　　　　　　　　　Dietrich, Sieloff (penalty),
　　　　　　　　　　　　　　Laumen 2
　　　　Played at Munchengladbach
Spartak Moscow (1) 3　　　*Basel* (0) 2
Ossianin 2, Papaev　　　　　Odermatt, Benthaus

Basel (0) 2　　　　　　　　*Spartak Moscow* (0) 1
Siegenthaler, Balmer　　　　Khusainov

Feyenoord (1) 1　　　　　　*U.T. Arad* (1) 1
Jansen　　　　　　　　　　　Dumitrescu

U.T. Arad (0) 0　　　　　　*Feyenoord* (0) 0

Atletico Madrid (1) 2　　　*F.K. Austria* (0) 0
Luis, Garate

F.K. Austria (1) 1　　　　　*Atletico Madrid* (1) 2
Krieger (penalty)　　　　　　Luis, Garate

Jeunesse Esch (1) 1　　　　*Panathinaikos* (2) 2
Di Genova　　　　　　　　　Antoniadis, Elefterakis

Panathinaikos (3) 5　　　　*Jeunesse Esch* (0) 0
Elefterakis, Antoniadis 4

Fenerbahce (0) 0　　　　　*Carl Zeiss Jena* (1) 4
　　　　　　　　　　　　　　Krauss, Ducke 2, Vogel

Carl Zeiss Jena (1) 1   *Fenerbahce* (0) 0
Vogel

Sporting Lisbon (4) 5   *Floriana* (0) 0
Lourenco 3, Peres, Marinho
Floriana (0) 0   *Sporting Lisbon* (1) 4
                                 Nelson 2, Dinis, Tome

Second Round
Borussia Munchengladbach   *Everton* (0) 1
(1) 1
Vogts   Kendall

Borussia: Kleff; Vogts, Muller, Sieloff, Wittmann; Dietrich, Netzer, Laumen; Le Fevre (Wimmer), Koeppel, Heynckes.
Everton: Rankin; Wright, Hurst, Kendall, Newton; Harvey, Kendall, Ball; Whittle, Royle, Morrissey.

Everton (1) 1   *Borussia Munchengladbach* (1) 1
Morrisey   Laumen
After extra time: Everton won on penalty kicks.
Everton: Rankin; Wright, Newton; Kendall, Kenyon, Harvey; Whittle, Ball, Royle, Hurst, Morrissey.
Borussia: Kleff; Vogts, Muller, Sieloff, Wittmann; Dietrich, Netzer, Laumen; Le Fevre, Koeppel, Heynckes.

Waterford (0) 0   *Celtic* (4) 7
                                 Wallace 3, Murdoch 2,
                                 Macari 2
Waterford: Thomas; Bryan, Morrissey, Brennan, Maguire; McGeouch, Buck (Power); Casey, O'Neill, Hale, Matthews.
Celtic: Williams; Craig, McNeill, Quinn, Hay; Connelly, Murdoch; Macari, Wallace (Davidson), Hood (Chalmers), Lennox.

Celtic (0) 3   *Waterford* (2) 2
Hughes, Johnstone 2   McNeill (own goal),
                                 Matthews
Celtic: Williams; Craig, Gemmell; Murdoch (Brogan), McNeill, Hay; Johnstone, Lennox, Wallace (Hood), Connelly, Hughes.
Waterford: Thomas; Bryan, Brennan; McGuire, Morrissey, McGeough; Casey, Hale, Kirkby, O'Neill, Matthews.

Red Star (Belgrade) (1) 3   *U.T. Arad* (0) 0
Filipovic, Acimovic, Ostojic
U.T. Arad (0) 1   *Red Star (Belgrade)* (0) 3
Brosowski   Filipovic 2, Iankovic

Carl Zeiss (Jena) (0) 2   *Sporting Lisbon* (0) 1
Kurbjuweit, Vogel   Marinho
Sporting Lisbon (0) 1   *Carl Zeiss (Jena)* (0) 2
Goncalves   Ducke, P. Kurjuweit

Panathinaikos (1) 3   *Slovan Bratislava* (0) 0
Domazos, Antoniadis
Delyannis
Slovan Bratislava (0) 2   *Panathinaikos* (1) 1
Medvid, J. Capkovic   Antoniadis

Standard Liege (0) 1   *Legia Warsaw* (0) 0
Pilot
Legia Warsaw (2) 2   *Standard Liege* (0) 0
Pieszki, Zmijewski

Cagliari (2) 2   *Atletico Madrid* (0) 1
Riva, Gori   Luis
Atletico Madrid (1) 3   *Cagliari* (0) 0
Luis 3 (1 penalty)

Ajax Amsterdam (2) 3   *Basel* (0) 0
Keizer, Van Dijk, Hulshoff
Basel (1) 1   *Ajax Amsterdam* (0) 2
Odermatt (penalty)   Rijnders, Neeskens

Quarter-finals
Everton (0) 1   *Panathinaikos* (0) 1
Johnson   Antoniadis
Everton: Rankin; Wright, Newton (K.); Kendall, Kenyon, Harvey;
Husband, Ball, Royle, Hurst, Morrissey. Sub.: Johnson.
Panathinaikos: Oikonomopoulos; Tomaras, Vlahos, Eleytherakis,
Camaras, Sourpis, Grammos, Fylakouris, Antoniadis, Domazos,
Kapsis.
Panathinaikos (0) 0   *Everton* (0) 0
Panathinaikos: Oikonomopoulos; Tomaras, Vlahos, Athanasopoulos,
Camaras, Sourpis, Grammos, Fylakouris, Antoniadis, Domazos,
Kapsis.
Everton: Rankin; Wright, Newton (K.); Kendall, Labone, Harvey;
Whittle, Ball, Royle, Hurst, Morrissey, (Johnson).
Ajax Amsterdam (0) 3   *Celtic* (0) 0
Cruyff, Hulshoff, Keizer
Ajax: Stuy; Suurbier, Vasovic, Hulshoff, Krol, Rijnders, Neeskens,
Swart (Van Dijk), Muhren, Cruyff, Keizer.
Celtic: Williams; Craig, Gemmell; Hay, McNeill, Brogan; Connelly,
Callaghan, Johnstone, Wallace, Lennox.
Celtic (1) 1   *Ajax Amsterdam* (0) 0
Johnstone
Celtic: Williams; Hay, Gemmell; Callaghan, McNeill, Brogan;
Johnstone, Hood, Wallace (Davidson), Auld (Lennox), Hughes.
Ajax: Stuy; Suurbier, Vasovic, Hulshoff, Krol, Rijnders, Neeskens,
Blankenburg, Cruyff, Muhren, Keizer.
At Hampden Park.

Atletico Madrid (1) 1   *Legia Warsaw* (0) 0
Adelardo
Legia Warsaw (1) 2   *Atletico Madrid* (1) 1
Pieszko, Stachirski   Salcedo

Carl Zeiss (Jena) (2) 3   *Red Star (Belgrade)* (1) 2
Strempel, P. Ducke 2   Jankovic, Dzajic
Red Star (Belgrade) (2) 4   *Carl Zeiss (Jena)* (0) 0
Djoric (penalty), Filipovic,
Ostojic, Karasi

Semi-finals
Red Star (2) 4   *Panathinaikos* (0) 1
Jankovic, Ostojic 3   Kamaras
Panathinaikos (1) 3   *Red Star* (0) 0
Antoniadis 2, Kamaras

Atletico Madrid (0) 1   *Ajax* (0) 0
Irureta
Ajax (1) 3   *Atletico Madrid* (0) 0
Keizer, Suurbier, Neeskens

Final
Wembley Stadium, June 2nd, 1971
Ajax (1) 2   *Panathinaikos*
Van Dijk, Haan
Ajax: Stuy; Neeskens, Vasovic, Hulshoff, Suurbier; Rionders (Blankenburg), Muhren; Swart (Haan), Cruyff, Van Dijk, Keizer.
Panathinaikos: Oeconomopoulos; Tomaras, Vlahos, Elefterakis, Kamaras, Sourpis, Grammos, Filakouris, Antoniadis, Domazos, Kapsis.
Referee: Mr. J. K. Taylor (Wolverhampton).

FOOTBALL LEAGUE INTERNATIONALS 1970/71

The Football League internationals were again of a dullness and an irrelevance to suggest that the historical process had left them behind.

The opening game, between the Scottish League and the League of Ireland, was sheer tedium. The Scots had 80 per cent or so of play, yet could score only once, in the second half; a thirty yard drive from Celtic's tall, powerful Connelly. Ironically, Connelly had been pulled back into midfield, switching with Stanton – who played well. Only 7,654 fans bothered to watch this classical non-event.

Sir Alf Ramsey had to make seven late changes in the Football League team which played the Irish League at Norwich, but it still had an easy 5–0 win. Martin Peters, who captained the side, had a good game, and so did the West Bromwich Albion man, Tony Brown, who came on as a substitute. Both scored, Brown strongly heading in a cross by Peters for the most spectacular goal of the game, while Jeff Astle, his club mate, got two, one when the otherwise competent Nicholson dropped the ball.

In March, the usual rash of withdrawals, some occasioned by injury, some clearly "diplomatic", once again robbed the Scottish League v Football League game of much of its old relevance, and cast doubt on the persisting value of the whole competition.

The game, as it transpired, was an exciting one, decided in the Football League's favour by Ralph Coates' goal, after six minutes. The attendance of a mere and wretched 17,657, however, on Hampden's mighty slopes, was sufficient commentary in itself.

Playing at first with wingers, England quite soon withdrew the lively Coates into midfield, to play a 4–4–2 and the Scots, given the initiative, advanced the equally lively Brogan to midfield, Robb to the firing line, and put on sustained pressure. An English defence in which Bobby Moore, recalled to favour, and Jackson distinguished themselves was good enough to keep the Scots at bay.

Parkhead, September 3rd, 1970

Scottish League (0) 1   *League of Ireland* (0) 0
Connelly

Scottish League: Cruickshank (Hearts); Hay (Celtic), Dickson (Kilmarnock); Stanton (Hibernian), McKinnon (Rangers), Henry (Dundee United); Johnstone (Celtic), Connelly (Celtic), Hood (Celtic), Graham (Hibernian), Duncan (Hibernian).

League of Ireland: Thomas; Bryan, Brennan (all Waterford); O'Mahoney, Finucane (Limerick), Dunning (Shelbourne); McGeough (Waterford), Lawlor (Shamrock Rovers), Hale (Waterford), Minnock (Athlone), Matthews (Waterford).

Norwich

Football League (2) 5   *Irish League* (0) 0
Peters, Astle 2, Brown,
Hector

Football League: Shilton (Leicester City) (Jackson (Crystal Palace)); Edwards (Manchester United), Robson (Derby County); Nish (Leicester City), Sadler (Manchester United), Harvey (Everton); Coates (Burnley), Hector (Derby County), Astle (West Bromwich Albion), Peters (Spurs), Moore (Nottingham Forest), (Sub. Brown (West Bromwich Albion).)

Irish League: Nicholson (Crusaders); Patton (Glenavon), McKeag (Glentoran); Stewart (Ballymena), McCullough (Glentoran), O'Doherty (Coleraine); Humphries (Ards), Mullen (Coleraine), Millen (Linfield), Jamison (Crusaders), Cathcart (Linfield).

Hampden Park, March 17th, 1971

Scottish League (0) 0   *Football League* (1) 1
Coates

Scottish League: Clark (Aberdeen); Dickson (Kilmarnock), Hay (Celtic); Forsyth (Motherwell), McKinnon (Rangers), Brogan (Celtic); McLean (Kilmarnock), Callaghan (Celtic), Robb (Aberdeen), Jarvie (Airdrie), Ford (Hearts).
Football League: Jackson (Crystal Palace); Reaney (Leeds United), Parkin (Wolves); Hollins (Chelsea), McFarland (Derby County), Moore (West Ham United); Coates (Burnley), Brown (West Bromwich Albion), Hurst (West Ham United), O'Neill (Southampton), Storey-Moore (Nottingham Forest).

Chapter Three

European Cupwinners' Cup 1970/71

Chelsea, beating Real Madrid 2-1 in a replayed Final in Athens, became the second consecutive English club to win the tournament, the third London club to do so. Their performance was the more outstanding in that they were deprived by injuries of so many key players. Indeed, their semi-final ties against the holders, Manchester City, became something of a farce, both sides being so heavily depleted.

Chelsea's strength and fortune was that they were always able to provide the right man at the right time, so that what looked almost like an embarrassment of riches at the start of the season became a saving grace by its end. The two Final matches were a particular triumph for the highly gifted, mercurial Charlie Cooke, who had been in and out of the side earlier on, but played superbly in midfield, in Athens, deploying the whole range of his technical skills. The games were also particularly dramatic for John Dempsey, the Eire centre-half, who gave away the very late equaliser in the first match, but scored the first Chelsea goal in the second.

Manchester City, the holders, began with a surprisingly narrow 1-0 home win over the gallant part-time Ulstermen, Linfield. Only seven minutes from time did Colin Bell, who played as a spearhead throughout, exploit Oakes' through pass to score. Humphries had a fine game in goal for Linfield, well supported by Patterson and Andrews. City very seldom attained their true rhythm.

Chelsea, holders of the F.A. Cup, were set the hard task of playing Aris on an almost comically uneven pitch in Salonika. They missed a penalty, had John Dempsey, their centre-half, sent off, fell a goal behind, but managed to draw 1-1.

When Paddy Mulligan was brought down with a flying tackle, chaos ensued as the Aris players one by one kicked the ball off the penalty spot. After two and a half minutes, Peter Osgood took the kick: and Christidis parried it. Dempsey was sent off after 40 minutes, when he flew at Papoiannou, after a reckless kick at Bonetti. But after 75 minutes, the Londoners got a fine equaliser when Osgood retrieved a ball which seemed to be bouncing out of play, and Hutchinson volleyed in his pass.

Cardiff City, those veterans of the Cupwinners' Cup, easily crushed their Cypriot opponents, 8–0, and Aberdeen did well to beat Honved 3–1 at Pittodrie, after an uncertain beginning. Alas, their promising young team paid for its inexperience in Budapest, losing 3–1, and giving up the ghost, under the dubious new rule, on penalties, 5–4.

A more surprising result that evening was the defeat of Manchester City, the holders, by little Linfield, 2–1 in an ill-starred match at Belfast, when bottles were thrown at City's goalkeeper, Joe Corrigan. City had the humiliation of squeaking through on the away goal scored by Francis Lee.

Chelsea, by contrast, had no trouble with Aris, two of their first three goals being enthusiastically scored by their little right-half, Johnny Hollins; the second a fulminating left foot shot from over thirty yards. Even Marvin Hinton, an elegant centre-half, came up to score on a one-two in the second half. 5–1 was the eventual result, Aris' goal being the last of all, and looking abundantly offside. Ian Hutchinson, who scored the other two for Chelsea, was in irresistible form up front.

A goal in the last minute by Hinderyckx put Bruges through narrowly at the expense of Kickers Offenbach. Benfica had a much easier passage in Lisbon against the Yugoslavs, Olympic Ljubljana, Eusebio getting five of their eight goals.

Chelsea and Manchester City both made excellent beginnings to the Second Round with 1–0 away victories behind the Iron Curtain, Chelsea in Sofia, the holders in Budapest. Chelsea were without Ian Hutchinson, but Tommy Baldwin, his deputy, contrived to score their winning goal, two minutes from half-time. Peter Osgood, who had an excellent game, marred only by the fact that his name was taken for a foul on the goalkeeper, sent Keith Weller down the right. Weller beat his fullback, crossed, and Baldwin scored with his left foot.

The powerful CSKA side had much of the play, and Jekov, their prolific centre-forward, frequently tested Bonetti, but the nearest they came to a goal was when Penev headed in, but was given offside.

Against Honved, in Budapest, the massive Corrigan kept a very good goal for Manchester City, whose winner came in the second half, after forty minutes of dominance. Lee put in a cross by Mike Summerbee.

Cardiff City, reaffirming their prowess in the competition, positively thrashed Nantes, the French Cupholders, at Ninian Park, where John Toshack got two of their five goals. This, despite Gondet's second minute goal for Nantes. French critics were deeply impressed by Cardiff's brio.

Bruges, always formidable at home, belied their recent League form by prising open a Zurich defence with *two* sweepers! The powerful Lambert, at centre-forward, and the attacking wing-half, Carteus, were the best men on show.

The shock of the day was unquestionably Real Madrid's 1–0 defeat at the Bernabeu by Wacker Innsbruck; how, indeed, had the mighty fallen. But two weeks later, they were to retrieve themselves impressively, winning 2–0 in the return. Without Amancio, they scored two in three minutes late in the game.

Chelsea repeated their 1–0 win over CSKA in a bruising and displeasing match at Stamford Bridge. David Webb, forever surging through at dead ball situations, scored late in the first half, after Weller had headed down Houseman's corner. CSKA played a rugged *catenaccio*, but none the less had the best player on the field in the graceful Yakimov, and forced Peter Bonetti to a couple of marvellous saves. The second, the CSKA manager, Manolov, insisted, was no save at all, for the ball had crossed the line; but in the circumstances, this was academic.

Chelsea were drab in midfield and inconclusive up front, where Ian Hutchinson missed a ludicrously easy chance in the second half. In the closing minutes, Stankov of Bulgaria was sent off after a half hearted punch at Boyle.

Manchester City had no such displeasures, accounting comfortably 2–0 for Honved, Colin Bell scoring in the first half, Francis Lee in the second. Cardiff City followed their splendid home win against Nantes with a hardly less impressive one in France. Nantes seemed to be getting on top when John Toshack's goal rocked them on their heels. A national newspaper made him its footballer of the week on the strength of it.

The following week, he joined Liverpool for £110,000, and Cardiff's chances waned accordingly.

Though Bruges lost their return leg in Zurich, they played impressively, above all Thio, thrillingly fast on the right wing, scoring after five minutes a goal which made qualification all but certain, and narrowly missing a couple in the second half. If Bruges were without Lambert, they were still thoroughly resourceful in attack. Spirit rather than skill gave Zurich their unavailing victory.

By the time distant March, and the quarter-finals, came round, the picture had inevitably changed a good deal. Cardiff City had sold Toshack to Liverpool, and were unable to field, against formidable Real Madrid, their new striker, Warboys, who had scored all four goals against Carlisle, only the previous Saturday. Chelsea were severely reduced by injury to Bonetti, Harris and Hutchinson, the suspension of Osgood. Manchester City, who had been in puzzling, see-saw form all season, were in one of their troughs.

In the event, Cardiff, at home, won their first leg against Real gallantly, before the largest crowd at Ninian Park for years – 47,500 – but Chelsea and Manchester City both slumped 2–0, away.

Cardiff deserved to win by more, hammering as they did at the massed Real defence, with the 17-year-old Rees in marvellous form on the left wing – released for the occasion from a Welsh youth international against Scotland!

It was his cross from which, in the 32nd minute, Clark forcefully headed the only goal of the game. Well prompted by Ian Gibson, Cardiff's attack gave Real a chasing. They themselves settled down solidly after a couple of indecisive back passes had put them in early difficulties.

At Katowice, on a frozen pitch, Manchester City found themselves drawn against Gornik, their beaten opponents in the 1970 Final. Gornik at the last moment decided to risk their star, the brilliant Lubanski, who'd been injured, and their gamble paid. He scored a splendid first goal, and it was when Corrigan muffed his shot that Wilczek followed up, for the second. Lubanski hobbled off after an hour, his job well done.

In Bruges, Chelsea's notorious weakness in the air cost them the first goal, after only four minutes, Lambert getting up on the near post to beat Webb to Thio's corner. There were many recriminations in the Chelsea defence.

Four minutes from half-time, the tiny stadium erupted with glee again, when from another corner Houwaart's header rebounded into goal from Marmenout. Lambert, in the image of Lubanski, then went off. Meanwhile, there was some dirty work on the terraces.

Chelsea prevailed in an exciting, utterly one-sided, return game, though they needed extra time to do so. It was Peter Osgood's first match after an eight-week suspension, but he totally justified his choice with two goals, and a consistently challenging performance. Injury kept Ian Hutchinson out of the side, while though Peter Bonetti was fit, Phillips continued – impressively – in goal. Bruges, who played with the Swedish World Cup defender Axelsson as sweeper, in a packed defence, were always vulnerable to high crosses, for Sanders was an uneasy goalkeeper. They weren't helped when their striker in chief, Raoul Lambert, had to retire at half-time; but then so did Dempsey, of Chelsea, which ultimately meant that when Webb moved into attack, the propulsive force of Hollins was lost in midfield, for he had to drop back.

Peter Houseman, a splendid left winger, scored the first goal from Osgood's header, after twenty minutes. Tommy Baldwin missed a fine opportunity to head an (aggregate) equaliser, but it was not till eight minutes from time that yet another right wing cross produced it, an exultant Osgood converting Charlie Cooke's pass.

In extra time, Boyle had to clear off the line from Thio, Baldwin hit the underside of the bar, but in the second period, the reawakening of Alan Hudson brought two goals. First, a marvellous run down the left paved the way for Osgood to score, then he and Cooke set up the fourth for Baldwin.

Manchester City, on the same night, bravely retrieved their deficit against Gornik, but could do no more. Without the injured Book, Oakes and Summerbee, they brought in two raw young reserves in Donachie and Mellor, and these two combined for the first goal. On a heavy ground and a rainswept night, Donachie, just before half-time, centred for Mellor to head in. After 77 minutes, Mellor crossed for Doyle to score; then the conditions blunted the edge of City's sustained attack.

Cardiff City, after their earlier gallantry at Ninian Park, inevitably couldn't quite hold out in Madrid, though it took a couple of defensive errors to sink them. When Don Murray mistimed a header back to Eadie, in goal, there was a mêlée, from which Velazquez scored. In the next minute of the second half, Carver was unable to cut out a through pass, and Fleitas got the goal which gave Real a breathless qualification.

Manchester City qualified to play Chelsea in the semi-final with an admirable 3-1 win in Copenhagen, over Gornik – who had accused them variously of rough play and taking dope, in the Maine Road game. Since Gornik's own methods in the previous season's Final had been open to severe question, perhaps their complaints were slightly ill advised. At all events, they served to inspire rather than perturb a City team which had to play without its previous absentees, and left Arthur Mann on the tarmac at Manchester, overcome by tranquillisers and flying phobia.

The young, reshuffled City team, with Healey continuing impressively in goal for the absent Corrigan, won in a canter, dominant in midfield, where Bell was splendid, incisive up front.

On the half-hour, Lee exploited Wrazy's hesitation to make the first goal for Neil Young, now recovering confidence after a patchy season. Ten minutes later, Towers' long free kick was headed in by Tommy Booth.

Lubanski got back a goal after half-time, when Gornik at last came to life, but a fine save by Healey prevented the equaliser, and Lee made things sure with a third goal. It came after a sinuous run by Bell, a shot which Kostka couldn't hold.

The first leg of the semi-final between Chelsea and Manchester City, at Stamford Bridge, was ridiculed and devalued by injuries to key players in the Easter programme which maddeningly preceded it. As Chelsea's manager, Dave Sexton, observed, there could scarcely be a less suitable preparation for a major European game than to play two matches in three days before it, thus ruling out any tactical planning till it was seen which players were fit and which were injured.

City, most disastrously of all, lost the invaluable Colin Bell, at Newcastle, with a damaged cartilage, while Jeffries, too, was hurt. Chelsea lost the equally valuable Peter Osgood, though his injury was less serious than Bell's. They compounded their difficulties by choosing a weird side, with the blunderbuss of Webb at centre-forward, the inexperienced South African, Smethurst, beside him, to the exclusion of Weller and Baldwin, who came on only as substitutes.

As for City, they fielded a patchwork side in which yet another teenager, the 17-year-old Johnson, had to be thrown in at the deep end. But with Connor at his best at left-back, Book bravely returning after a dislocated shoulder, they gave away only one goal. Webb's pass made it early in the second-half, a through ball leftwards to Smethurst, which should have been cut out before it reached him, allowing him to score at leisure. The substitution of Weller, playing on the right wing, for Cooke, gave the team a little more purpose after half-time, but it was a shoddy game. Francis Lee's brave persistence gave it much of what distinction it had.

In Eindhoven, Real Madrid showed some of their old European form by holding PSV to a goalless draw, in a match when an Irish linesman was knocked out by a beer bottle hurled from the crowd. Junquera, Real's goalkeeper, hurt an elbow and was replaced by the veteran Betancort. The game, however, remained goalless.

Chelsea's return game with Manchester City at Maine Road was another depressing anticlimax, fittingly characterised by the absurd goal with which the London team won. Three minutes from half-time, Healey, the young City goalkeeper who was a late choice, fumbled an indirect free kick by Keith Weller over his own line; when he need not even have touched the ball.

Chelsea, strong in midfield through Boyle, Cooke and Hudson, deserved to win, but although they lacked Osgood, City's team was again a virtual reserve side.

It missed, too, the galvanic influence of the suspended Malcolm Allison.

Real Madrid maintained their reputation as extraordinary Cup fighters by beating PSV 2–1 at the Bernabeu, to reach the Final. They played some excellent football under heavy rain, and took the lead through their second stopper, the tall Zoco, after 37 minutes.

Van den Dungen equalised after 58 minutes, but eight minutes from the end, the gifted Pirri scored the winner.

The Final, staged in Athens, went to a replay, after Real Madrid equalised Osgood's goal for Chelsea at the last gasp, in injury time.

Chelsea had got Osgood and their key midfield half-back, John Hollins, fit with the utmost difficulty, and neither in fact lasted the game. Nor was the powerful and invaluable Ian Hutchinson fit for the fray.

Real, deploying their traditional morale and their high individual skills, especially through Amancio, Pirri, Velazquez and Zoco, were overall the better team. Yet it was Chelsea, with the skilful Charlie Cooke keeping them always in the race, who took the lead, ten minutes after half-time. Cooke was behind the move which finally saw Osgood, snapping up a rebound from his own header, whipping a low, left-footed shot past Borja. But his ankle was clearly troubling him, and ultimately he gave way to Baldwin while Hollins, earlier, was replaced by Paddy Mulligan.

It looked as if Chelsea had done it, against the odds and perhaps against the play, till John Dempsey suddenly and tragically miskicked. The tall Zoco, who had been moved into attack, swooped, and the score was level.

In extra-time, only the goal line clearances of an excellent Webb and the fine goalkeeping of Peter Bonetti – preferred to Phillips for this great occasion – kept Real out. And so to the replay, on the same ground, two days later.

Bravely overcoming their disappointment, and boldly switching to a 4-2-4 formation with Baldwin as an extra striker, Chelsea won the replay. Cooke, with greater support from Hudson, was again their motivating force in midfield, Dempsey atoned for his mistake, Osgood scored again before his damaged ankles forced him off the pitch, while Bonetti vindicated his inclusion with two late, marvellous saves from Zoco's header, Amancio's shot.

True, Chelsea were very lucky not to give away an early penalty when Harris blatantly shoved Amancio off the ball in a breakaway. But even by then Chelsea were obviously in command, and they scored at length when Dempsey met Houseman's corner, Borja could only punch the ball out, and Dempsey's answering, first-time shot sped past him into goal.

A fine run by Baldwin prepared the way for the second. He passed to Osgood, who ran expertly and strongly across the face of the Real defence, before shooting past Borja into the right-hand corner.

The game seemed inevitably Chelsea's till a dazzling run by the Paraguayan, Fleitas, fifteen minutes from the end, concluded with his shooting past Bonetti. Then Real, bringing on Grande and Gento, found spirit and thrust, but Bonetti denied them – and Chelsea themselves might have had a penalty when Hudson was brought down.

No small achievement with Hutchinson or Hollins – who was obliged to watch the game as a television commentator, rather than play in it. As for Gento, he, like Real, was playing in his ninth European Final. Pirri, who broke a bone in his arm in the first game, was clearly unwise to take part in the second, and played little part in midfield, where Cooke was supreme.

EUROPEAN CUPWINNERS' CUP 1970/71

Preliminary Round

Bohemians (1) 1 *Gottwaldov* (1) 2
Swan (penalty) Urban, Nehuda
Gottwaldov (2) 2 *Bohemians* (1) 2
Hojsik, Jencik O'Connell, Dunne

First Round

Aberdeen (0) 3 *Honved* (0) 1
Graham, Harper, Murray Pusztai
Aberdeen: Clarke; Hermiston, G. Murray, S. Murray, Boel, Buchan; McKay, Robb, Forrest, Harper, Graham.
Honved: Bicskei; Molnar, Ruzsinsky, Pusztai, Vari, Bagi, Jaiti, Toth, Kocsis, Kamora, Szurgent.

Honved (1) 3 *Aberdeen* (0) 1
Tajti, Kozna, Kocsis Murray
Honved won after extra time 5-4 on penalties.

Honved: Bicskai; Tajti, Ruzsinski, Vagy, Marosi, Vari, Kocsis, Pusztai, Koszma, Karakas.
Aberdeen: Clark; Bell, Young, Hermiston, Murray, G., Harper, Buchan; Robb, Forrest, Murray, S., Graham.

    Cardiff City (5) 8   *Larnaca (Cyprus)* (0) 0
    Toshack 2, Clark 2, Sutton,
    Gibson, King, Woodruff

Cardiff City: Parsons; Carver, Bell; Sutton, Murray, Harris; Gibson, Clark, Woodruff, Toshack, King.
Larnaca: Palmiris; Petrou, Paridis; Constantinou, Stellis, Thinos; Kunnidis, Karapittas, Louizou, Fillastadis, Melis.

    Larnaca (0) 0   *Cardiff City* (0) 0

Larnaca: Klyriakides; Yannakis, Paridis; Kallis, Stellis, Karapittas; Melis, Kunnidis, Stavrinos, Fillastadis (Thinos), Leonidas.
Cardiff City: Parsons; Carver, Bell; Sutton, Murray, Harris; Gibson, Clark, Woodruff, Toshack (Phillips), King.

    Aris Salonika (0) 1   *Chelsea* (0) 1
    Papoiannou   Hutchinson

Aris: Christides; Palas, Semerdzes, Spyridon, Nalbandis, Loucanaidis, Konstantinidis, Keramidas, Alexiadis, Siropoulos, Papoiannou.
Chelsea: Bonetti; Mulligan, Harris; Hollins, Dempsey, Webb; Weller, Hudson, Osgood, Hutchinson, Cooke.

    Chelsea (3) 5   *Aris Salonika* (0) 1
    Hollins 2, Hutchinson 2,   Alexiadis
    Hinton

Chelsea: Bonetti; Mulligan, Harris; Hollins, Hinton, Webb; Weller, Hudson, Osgood (Baldwin), Hutchinson, Houseman.
Aris: Christidis; Pallas (Raptopoulous), Nalbantis, Golinaris, Semertzes, Loukanidis; Mittas (Konstantinidis), Balafas, Alexiadis, Syropoulos, Papoiannou.

    Manchester City (0) 1   *Linfield* (0) 0
    Bell

Manchester City: Corrigan; Book, Pardoe; Doyle, Booth, Oakes; Summerbee, Bell, Lee, Young, Towers.
Linfield: Humphries; Frazer, Patterson; Andrews, McAllister, Bowyer; Millen, Magee, Hamilton, Sinclair, Cathcart.

    Linfield (1) 2   *Manchester City* (1) 1
    Millen 2   Lee

Linfield: Humphreys; Frazer, Patterson, Andrews, McAllister, E. Bowyer, Millen, Magee, Hamilton, Sinclair, Cathcart.
Manchester City: Corrigan; Book, Pardoe; Doyle, Jeffries, Oakes; Summerbee, Bell, Lee (Bowyer), Young, Towers.

    Hibernians Malta (0) 0   *Real Madrid* (0) 0

    Real Madrid (2) 5   *Hibernians Malta* (0) 0
    Pirri, Planelles 3, Maronon

Gottwaldov (1) 2
Urban, Nehoda
PSV Eindhoven (0) 1
Veenstra

PSV Eindhoven (0) 1
Devrindt
Gottwaldov (0) 0

Olympic Ljubljana (0) 1
Pejovic
Benfica (3) 8
Eusebio 5, Zeca, A. Jorge,
Graca

Benfica (1) 1
Eusebio
Olympic Ljubljana (0) 1

Stromsgodset (0) 0

Nantes (2) 5
Gondet, Levavasseur 2,
Arribas, Michel

Nantes (0) 2
Levavasseur, Blanchet

Stromsgodset (0) 3
I. Pettersen, S. Pettersen 2

Wacker Innsbruck (1) 3
Ettmayer (penalty), Obert,
Franceschin

Partizan Tirana (2) 2
Pano, Yangu

Partizan Tirana (1) 1
Panu
CSKA Sofia (5) 9
Yakimov 5, Nikodimov,
Zherov 2, Marashkev
Valkeakosken (0) 1
Malm

Wacker Innsbruck (1) 2
Grausam
Valkeakosken (0) 0

CSKA Sofia (0) 2
Yakimov 2

Vorwaerts (0) 0
Bologna (0) 1
Savoldi

Bologna (0) 0
Vorwaerts (0) 1
Begerad

After extra-time, Full time: 0–0.

Offenbach Kickers (0) 2
Kremers 2
Bruges (1) 2
Marmenout, Hinderyckx

Bruges (1) 1
Lambert
Offenbach Kickers (0) 0

Goeztepe Izmir (3) 5
Ertan 3, Nevzet, Nielsen
U.S. Luxemburg (1) 1

U.S. Luxemburg (0) 0

Goeztepe Izmir (0) 0

Aalborg (0) 0

Gornik (3) 8
Szarynski, Olek 2, Wilim 2,
Lubanski 2, Szoltysik

Gornik (1) 1
Lubanski
Aalborg (0) 1

Akureyri Iceland (0) 1   *Zurich* (3) 7
Armasson   Stierli, Martinelli, Volkert 3,
                                    Kunzli 2
Zurich (4) 7   *Akureyri Iceland* (0) 0
Kunzli 3, Volkert 2, Heer,
Grunig

Steaua Bucharest (0) 1   *Karpaty Lvov* (0) 0
Tataru
Karpaty Lvov (0) 0   *Steaua Bucharest* (0) 1
                                    Tataru

Second Round

CSKA Sofia (0) 0   *Chelsea* (1) 1
                                    Baldwin
CSKA: Filipov; Zakirov, Kolev, T., Yankov (Garganelov), Denev, Penev, Atanassov, Nikodimov, Jekov, Yakimov, Maraschiliev.
Chelsea: Bonetti; Mulligan, Harris; Hollins, Hinton, Webb; Weller, Hudson, Osgood, Baldwin, Houseman.
   Chelsea (1) 1   *CSKA Sofia* (0) 0
Webb
Chelsea: Bonetti; Mulligan (Boyle), Harris; Hollins, Hinton, Webb; Weller, Cooke, Osgood, Hutchinson, Houseman.
CSKA: Filipov; Zafirov, Kolev, Gaganolov, Stankov, Penev, Atanassov, Nikodimov, Jekov (Tchalev), Yakimov, Denev.

Honved (0) 0   *Manchester City* (0) 1
                                    Lee
Honved: Bicksei; Tajti, Vabi, Ruzsinszki, Marosi, Vagi (Toth); Pusztai, Kocsis, Tichy (Karakas), Komora, Kozma.
Manchester City: Corrigan; Book, Pardoe; Doyle, Heslop, Jeffries; Summerbee, Bell, Lee, Hill, Towers.
   Manchester City (1) 2   *Honved* (0) 0
Bell, Lee
Manchester City: Corrigan; Book, Pardoe; Doyle, Heslop, Oakes; Summerbee, Bell, Lee, Hill, Towers.
Honved: Bicksei; Tajti, Ruzsinszki, Marosi, Toth, Vagi, Pinter; Kocsis, Kozma, Komora, Szurgent.

Goztepe Izmir (0) 0   *Gornik* (1) 1
                                    Lubanski
Gornik (3) 3   *Goztepe Izmir* (0) 0
Lubanski 2, Banas

PSV Eindhoven (1) 4   *Steaua Bucharest* (0) 0
Veenstra, Devrindt 3
Steaua Bucharest (0) 0   *PSV Eindhoven* (1) 3
                                    Veenstra 2, Van der Kuylen

Benfica (1) 2   *Vorwaerts* (0) 0
Eusebio, Diamantino
Vorwaerts (1) 2   *Benfica* (0) 0
Wurck, Fraessdorf
    Vorwaerts win on penalties, after extra time.

Bruges (2) 2   *Zurich* (0) 0
Rensenbrink, Carteus
Zurich (1) 3   *Bruges* (1) 2
Axelsson (own goal),   Rensenbrink, Kunzli
Gruenig
Kunzli

Cardiff City (3) 5   *Nantes* (1) 1
Toshack 2, Gibson, King,   Gondet
Phillips

Cardiff City: Eadie; Carver, Harris, Murray, Bell; Sutton, Gibson, Woodruff; Clark (Phillips), Toshack, King.
Nantes: Fouché; Lemerre, Osman, Rio, De Michele; Michel, Michaelsen; Blanchet, Kervarrec, Gondet, Pech (Audiger).

Nantes (0) 1   *Cardiff City* (1) 2
Blanchet   Toshack, Clark

Nantes: Fouché; Lemerre, Rio, Gardon, De Michele; Michel, Michaelsen; Blanchet, Kervarrec, Pech, Audiger.
Cardiff City: Eadie; Carver, Harris, Murray, Bell; Sutton, Gibson; Phillips, Toshack, Woodruff, King.

Real Madrid (0) 0   *Wacker Innsbruck* (1) 1
                     Grausam

Wacker Innsbruck (0) 0   *Real Madrid* (0) 2
                     Grande, Pirri

Quarter-finals
Cardiff City (1) 1   *Real Madrid* (0) 0
Clark

Cardiff City: Eadie; Carver, Bell; Sutton, Murray, Phillips; King, Gibson, Clark, Woodruff, Rees.
Real Madrid: Borja; Zunzunegui, Sanchis; Grande, Benito, Zoco; Amancio, Pirri, Grosso, Velazquez, Perez. Subs.: De Felipe, Fleitas.

Real Madrid (0) 2   *Cardiff City* (0) 0
Velazquez, Fleitas

Bruges (2) 2   *Chelsea* (0) 0
Lambert, Marmenout

Bruges: Sanders; Bastijns, Axelsson, Van den Daele, Denaeghel, Houwaart, Carteus; Thio, Marmenout, Lambert (Deconinck), Rensenbrink.

Chelsea: Phillips; Boyle, McCreadie; Hollins, Dempsey, Webb; Smethurst, Cooke, Baldwin, Hudson, Weller.

Chelsea (1) 4   *Bruges* (0) 0
Houseman, Osgood 2,
Baldwin

After extra-time. Full time: 2–0.

Chelsea: Phillips; Harris, McCreadie; Hollins, Dempsey (Boyle), Webb; Baldwin, Cooke, Osgood, Hudson, Houseman.
Bruges: Sanders; Bastijns, Axelsson, Van den Daele, Denaeghel, Houwaart, Carteus, Thio, Marmenout, Lambert (Moeloert), Rensenbrink.

Gornik (2) 2   *Manchester City* (0) 0
Lubanski, Wilczek

Gornik: Kostka; Wrazy, Oslizlo, Latocha, Gorgon, Szoltysik, Wilczek, Skowronek, Banas, Lubanski, Wilim.
Manchester City: Corrigan; Book, Towers, Doyle, Booth, Oakes, Summerbee, Bell, Lee, Young, Jeffries.

Manchester City (0) 2   *Gornik* (0) 0
Mellor, Doyle

Manchester City: Healey; Connor, Booth, Donachie, Towers, Doyle, Jeffries, Mellor, Lee, Bell, Young.
Gornik: Gomola; Wrazy, Oslizlo, Latocha, Gorgon, Szoltysik, Wilczek, Skowronek, Banas, Lubanski, Deja.
Copenhagen: Play-Off

Manchester City (2) 3   *Gornik* (0) 1
Young, Booth, Lee   Lubanski

Manchester City: Healey; Connor, Towers, Doyle, Booth, Donachie, Jeffries, Bell, Lee, Young, Hill.
Gornik: Kostka; Wrazy, Oslizlo, Latocha, Gorgon, Szoltysik, Deja, Skowronek, Banas, Lubanski, Szarynski (Wilim).

PSV Eindhoven (0) 2   *Vorwaerts* (0) 0
Devrindt, Van den Dungen

Vorwaerts (1) 1   *PSV Eindhoven* (0) 0
Fraessdorf

Semi-finals

Chelsea (0) 1   *Manchester City* (0) 0
Smethurst

Chelsea: Phillips; Boyle, Harris; Hollins, Dempsey, Droy; Hudson, Smethurst (Baldwin), Webb, Cooke (Weller), Houseman.
Manchester City: Corrigan; Book, Connor; Towers, Booth, Mann, Donachie, Johnson, Hill, Lee, Young.

Manchester City (0) 0   *Chelsea* (1) 1
                               Healey (own goal)

Manchester City: Healey; Book, Connor, Towers, Heslop, Jeffries, Summerbee (Carter), Lee, Bowyer, Young, Johnson (Donachie).

Chelsea: Phillips; Mulligan, Harris; Cook, Dempsey, Webb; Weller, Hudson, Smethurst, Boyle, Houseman.

>*PSV Eindhoven* (0) 0   *Real Madrid* (0) 0
>*Real Madrid* (1) 2   *PSV Eindhoven* (0) 1
>Zoco, Pirri   Van den Dungen

Final
Athens, May 19th, 1971
>*Chelsea* (0) 1   *Real Madrid* (0) 1
>Osgood   Zoco

After extra time

Chelsea: Bonetti; Boyle, Harris; Hollins (Mulligan), Dempsey, Webb; Weller, Cooke, Osgood (Baldwin), Hudson, Houseman.
Real Madrid: Borja; José Luis, Benito, Zoco, Zunzunegui; Pirri, Grosso, Velazquez; Perez (Fleitas), Amancio, Gento (Grande).

Athens, May 21st, **Replay.**
>*Chelsea* (2) 2   *Real Madrid* (0) 1
>Dempsey, Osgood   Fleitas

Chelsea: Bonetti; Boyle, Harris; Cooke, Dempsey, Webb; Weller, Baldwin, Osgood (Smethurst), Hudson, Houseman.
Real Madrid: Borja; José Luis, Zunzunegui; Pirri, Benito, Zoco; Fleitas, Amancio, Grosso, Velazquez (Gento), Bueno (Grande).

Chapter Four
European Fairs Cup 1970/71

For the fourth consecutive season, an English club won the Fairs Cup. Leeds United, who'd won it already three seasons before, thus qualified to play Barcelona, the first winners, in September, 1971, for permanent possession of the trophy which Barcelona were the first to take, in 1958. In 1971/2, the European Union Cup succeeds it.

The excellent Leeds side well deserved some consolation for their hard luck and sustained disappointment over the past couple of seasons, though it was mildly absurd that they should win the Final without actually defeating Juventus! The gifted Italian side, one full of promise and fine young players, drew 2–2 with Leeds in Turin, 1–1 at Elland Road; and in these circumstances, of course, away goals count double.

Leeds United and Liverpool opened the ball for England on a September Tuesday, with 1–0 victories. Leeds, reduced by injuries to such as Giles, Clarke, Charlton and Sprake, had a rather laborious victory in Norway over Sarpsborg, thanks to a late goal by Peter

Lorimer, though they were worth a more comfortable margin. So were Liverpool, who came up against a Ferencvaros team in a state of crisis, their manager, Kalocsai, having just resigned. This was not the Ferencvaros which had won over the Kop two years before, and Bill Shankley was loud in his disdain.

Ferencvaros huddled in defence, and only the fine goalkeeping of Geczi – twice lucky, however, to be hit by attempts from Emlyn Hughes – kept the score to a single goal. This came after 17 minutes, when Alun Evans made space to centre from the left, Lawler headed back across goal, and Bobby Graham scored.

The following night, Arsenal, the holders, had an expectedly stormy passage in Rome against Lazio, managed by Juan Carlos Lorenzo, who was in charge of the Argentinian team which reduced to fiasco the 1966 World Cup quarter-final, against England. Deprived of victory by a highly dubious penalty – McLintock claimed to have headed the ball away, the West German referee insisted he had handled – Arsenal found themselves, after the match banquet, involved in a free for all outside the restaurant with Lazio players and their manager. Sport, as George Orwell once observed, is an unfailing cause of ill will.

The game, played before 60,000 in the Olympic Stadium, was on the whole well refereed by Herr Schulenburg. Arsenal went into the lead when John Radford headed in Kelly's cross, five minutes after half-time. Radford headed another goal, again from Kelly's cross, a few minutes later, and Arsenal, counter-attacking and defending cleverly, seemed well on their way. Instead, Giorgio Chinaglia, who was once on the staff of Swansea Town, scored two quick, late goals – one from the disputed penalty – to give Lazio an unexpected draw.

Coventry City, making their first venture into Europe, had a convincing 4–1 win in Sofia over Trakia, their double spearhead of John O'Rourke, who scored three, and Martin, who got a goal from 30 yards, proving far too much for the home defence.

In Munich, the inevitable Franz Beckenbauer, hammer of the British, scored the only goal of the first leg for Bayern against Rangers; their victims in the final of the Cupwinners' Cup in 1967. Rangers defended in force, giving away eight corners in the first twenty minutes, and a goal after 22, when Pumm passed back to Beckenbauer, who beat McCloy with a low 20-yard shot.

Arsenal duly beat Lazio 2–0 in a very tame return, all passion evidently spent in that street brawl. Lazio left behind one of the chief culprits, Papadopolou, and Arsenal, very much the injured parties, controlled themselves completely. An efficient if officious East German referee, Rudi Glockner, took name after Italian name and let very little escape him.

Lazio played very defensively, Wilson sweeping up, but gave away a foolish goal in each half. In the first, a feeble clearance to the right by Fortunato was snapped up and centred by Storey, for John Radford to head a very good near post goal, In the second, Pat Rice's free-kick from the right was allowed to travel across goal. Geordie Armstrong crowned an excellent match by racing in to head the ball into the opposite corner.

Newcastle United, Arsenal's predecessors as winners of the Cup, did well to hold Inter to a 1–1 draw in Milan, even if the Italians were without their fine centre-forward, Roberto Boninsegna. Wyn Davies, Newcastle's centre, had an excellent if embattled game, in which his name was taken, heading a fine goal from Robson's free-kick, a minute from half-time. Individualistic and relying overmuch on Corso's long passes, Inter could equalise only five minutes from the end through their sweeper, Cella's, long shot.

It was another long shot by a defender, this time Emlyn Hughes, which gave Liverpool an equaliser and a draw in Budapest against Ferencvaros, just when things seemed to be going gravely against them. Still another half-back, Jackie Charlton, who had previously been somewhat out of form, scored twice for Leeds in their easy success over Sarpsborg, Billy Bremner also getting a couple. Dickson, the Coleraine striker, went one better, his splendid hat-trick allowing the little Irish club to astonish Kilmarnock – veterans of the tournament – on their own ground. All three came in the second half, after Kilmarnock had held a 2–0 lead at the interval.

Newcastle duly qualified in their return with Inter, in which Italian football was further disgraced by the sending off of the celebrated international goalkeeper Lido Vieri, guilty of punching the Belgian referee, Minnoy, in the stomach. Inter, a goal down at the time – scored by Bobby Moncur, who gets so many in Fairs Cup games– pulled off an outfield player to put on their substitute goalie, Bordon, but couldn't prevent Wyn Davies from adding to the score in the second half.

Rangers, however, disappeared, at the hands or boots of Bayern. Before 70,000 at Ibrox – Newcastle had 60,000 – they could manage no better than a 1–1 draw, the inevitable Gerd Muller scoring for Bayern, Colin Stein for Rangers, an equaliser to Muller's 20-yard free-kick. Though Rangers began well, hitting the bar and having a shot cleared off the line, that was that.

Hibernian, though, duly won their return, in Malmo, by the odd goal, while Coventry completed the double over Trakia Plovdiv, who had to substitute their goalkeeper, Radenkov, after 10 minutes. Joicey – who also later went off, with rib injuries – shot the first goal; the centre-half, Blockley, headed the second.

Dundee United, holding Grasshoppers to a goalless draw in Zurich, thus retained the lead they'd built in the first match.

Hibernian opened the Second Round with a solid 2–0 victory over Vitoria Guimaraes, but the following week, poor Coventry had to face Bayern in Munich without their injured goalkeeper, Bill Glazier, and were horribly mauled. The inexperienced replacement, McManus, could be blamed for at least two of the six Bayern goals, four of which, and Coventry's one, came in the first twenty minutes. Coventry did rally after that and made some chances in the second half, but none would go in. Bayern were vastly the better team, and Franz Beckenbauer did not even have to exert his full power.

The following day – Wednesday – Arsenal most surprisingly lost 1–0 in Graz, hampered by an officious referee and Kelly's bleak match in midfield, but Newcastle, the previous winners of the Cup, deservedly beat Peczi Dosza on Tyneside, and were worth more than their two-goal win. Wyn Davies headed both of them, but desperate defence by the Hungarians prevented more than one goal in the second half.

Sturm Graz did particularly well to beat Arsenal, as they had to use a 17-year-old goalkeeper in Benko. Their goal came five minutes from half-time, from a 25-yard shot by Zamuth, their little outside-left, who beat Rice before letting fly to the far, high corner. In midfield, Graham was no more successful than Kelly in keeping the wheels turning for Arsenal.

Leeds United squeezed home 1–0 against Dynamo Dresden at Elland Road, thanks to a penalty by Peter Lorimer in the second half, after Belfitt's goal-bound header had been punched over the top. With Terry Cooper in wonderfully ebullient form, they dominated play, but badly missed Johnny Giles and Eddie Gray, Gary Sprake being another distinguished absentee.

Dundee United had a grim time of it in Prague, where their goalkeeper, Mackay, was injured, and another defender, Rolland, was sent off.

Coventry City, in their return match against Bayern, did something to redeem their standing, but nothing to retrieve a hopelessly lost cause. Perhaps they might have done more had Bayern not equalised Martin's goal through Hoeness, when the latter was allowed to run on after handling the ball. O'Rourke scored the deciding goal from a corner after 81 minutes.

The following evening, Newcastle United, too, went out of the competition – on penalty kicks – but Arsenal made rather unconvincing progress. Their game at Highbury against Sturm Graz was something of an illusionist's trick. The wonder of it was, after Ray Kennedy had headed a fine goal from Armstrong's centre, that Sturm Graz held out. They surrendered the midfield, they were under perpetual pressure, but an uncreative Arsenal side threw away its chances. It scraped through, finally, in the third minute of extra time. Reiter kept out Graham's shot with his hand, and Peter Storey scored the penalty. Phew!

Newcastle were surprisingly toppled in Hungary. Bobby Moncur, so often the goal scoring hero of their European Fairs Cup exploits, this time, alas, put through his own goal in the first half, while McNamee, the other stopper, conceded a penalty in the second. This put the teams level 2–2 after extra time – on aggregate – and Pecsi went on to win on penalties.

Liverpool's reconstructed team, a goal down at half-time in Bucharest, recovered to equalise through Boersma, and qualify. Leeds United, also behind the Iron Curtain, had a harder time of it in Dresden, where Bates was sent off and Dynamo beat them 2–1 – but Mick

Jones' "away" goal was just sufficient to take them through. Gayer of Dresden was sent off with Bates, while two other Leeds men and one from Dynamo had their names taken.

Dundee United beat Sparta Prague through a goal by Gordon in the first half; an achievement which did not save them. Coleraine lost at home 2–1 to Sparta Rotterdam, and were similarly eliminated.

Spain came out of the evening somewhat mauled, Beveren, the obscure Belgian team, drawing with and accounting for the powerful Valencia, while in Turin, Juventus put out Barcelona.

In the Third Round, doubt was cast on the significance of Beveren Was, the little Belgian club's, previous victories when Arsenal beat them with ludicrous ease at Highbury. Though they missed an early penalty, Poklepovic saving finely from Storey, Arsenal won 4–0 without really having to exert themselves. George Graham, in midfield, did virtually as he wished, and headed the first goal soon after Storey's missed penalty. All through the game, Beveren's defence was pitifully vulnerable to high crosses, and when Arsenal got round to appreciating the fact, it was simply a question of how many they would score. Ray Kennedy headed two, and Jon Sammels got a spectacular, left-footed goal from some thirty yards.

Leeds United, meanwhile, were playing superbly to demolish Sparta Prague. For twenty minutes the Czechs seemed likely to make a match of it, but when Clarke scored after confusion between Migas and Urban, the floodgates opened. Though Belfitt had to leave the field with a cut head, Billy Bremner moved up to centre-forward, Reaney came into the defence, and the bombardment continued. Reaney himself provoked the second goal, when Chovanek kicked his centre past his own goalkeeper, Kramerius, without whose excellence the score would have been much higher. Bremner and Gray, twice, added goals before half-time, Jackie Charlton headed the only one of the second half. "When we are in this form," exulted Don Revie, Leeds' manager, "I don't believe any team can live with us."

The return, in Prague, was the emptiest formality. Leeds were able to omit Charlton, Giles and Jones, go into a three-goal lead by half-time, then pull off Sprake and Hunter, into the bargain.

Brabec missed an early, skidding shot from Eddie Gray, for the first goal, Belfitt put Clarke through, for the second, taken with power and skill, while Cooper sent Belfitt in for the third. In the second half, Barton and Urban scored for Sparta, but as Revie said, "It is difficult to keep up maximum pressure when you are nine up." Indeed.

Arsenal had something of the same experience when they played their return against Beveren and drew, rather drearily, 0–0. A certain amount of life was given the proceedings when their gifted young reserves, Charlie George (who had one mighty shot) and Peter Marinello came on, in the second half, but generally they remained in an unexcitingly low gear.

Liverpool, with Tommy Smith a dominating force, Steve Heighway, their new revelation, making a good goal for Toshack fifteen minutes from the end, beat Hibernian 1–0 at Easter Road. Hibs did well, in the circumstances, for they had just changed managers in highly traumatising circumstances.

Liverpool won the return without much labour, 2–0, though Hibernian attacked spiritedly at the beginning and the end. Duncan showed pace in the Hibs attack, Brownlie overlapped well. On the quarter hour, too, Clemence made an excellent save from McBride's header. But after 24 minutes, an exhilarating burst by Heighway, almost half the length of the field, took him clean through the defence. Baines blocked his shot, but he ran the ball in. The second goal was anti-climactic, Boersma's high centre dropping over Baines' head and in by the far post.

In the quarter-finals, Juventus, after a comfortable 2–0 home win over Twente of Enschede, merely squeaked through in the return. Twente, in fact, led 2–0 at the end of normal time, but in the first eight minutes of extra time, the £440,000 centre-forward, Pietro Anastasi, got away twice, to equalise, and take Juventus narrowly through.

Arsenal made hard work of a 2–1 home victory over Cologne, though they dominated the game. Cologne's counter-attacks, however, sometimes put them in trouble and twice in the first half Wilson had to make fine saves. Ironically, the second of them led to a corner by Thielen which he allowed to curl over his head for an equaliser.

Since Thielen later cleared successive headers from McLintock and Radford off the line, he may be said to have contributed rather more than his share. McLintock had eventually given Arsenal the lead, following a long throw from the right by Radford. The winner, after long bombardment, came half way through the second period from Storey, striking his shot powerfully through a crowd of players when Radford turned the ball back to him after a corner. But Cologne suffered both from the absence of Weber, their international stopper, and Parits, who went off injured just before half-time, after playing resourcefully in Cologne's scant attack.

Graham, brought on for Sammels in the second half, gave the holders' attack more bite and method.

Liverpool, the following evening, did measurably better. The game was a personal affirmation for Alun Evans, who had returned to the team, after long absence and a cartilage operation, late in the previous Saturday's Cup-tie against Spurs, as substitute. The lively, fair-haired striker got all three goals, the first a right-foot shot into the corner after good work by the remarkable Heighway, the second soon after half-time, when Lloyd headed down Lindsay's free-kick, the third after Hughes' shot was blocked.

Bayern, highly defensive till then, woke up, and Roth shot against a post, but despite the excellence of Maier in goal, the presence of other World Cup stars in Muller and Beckenbauer, it was wholly Liverpool's night.

Leeds United, their team deprived by 'flu and injury of five men, struggled through against Vitoria Setubal. The Portuguese even had the temerity to lead with a fine goal after only 90 seconds, the formidable Baptista, his country's leading scorer, heading in at full stretch from Guerreiro's cross.

Lorimer equalised direct from a free-kick, and it took a second dead ball shot, Giles' penalty, 16 minutes from time, to give Leeds their sparse victory. Setubal bitterly objected to the decision that Cordoso had handled.

Arsenal's luck finally ran out in their return match, at Cologne. An early, somewhat contentious penalty and the extraordinary, demoralising refereeing of a Rumanian, C. Petres, were sufficient to undo them; though in the event, it might be said that Wilson's costly and uncharacteristic error put them out.

The penalty came after only four minutes, when Wilson's throw was intercepted by Kappellmann, who raced for goal, and was brought down by McNab. The referee gave the kick, from which Biskup scored. Later, he penalised not only Arsenal's straightforward tackles, but even their shouting to one another!

Reinforced by Weber's return, Cologne's defence was a strong barrier between Arsenal and their ambitions, while Overath made an increasing impact on the game in midfield.

In one of Cologne's attacks, Rupp hit the post, but as against that, George Graham had desperate ill luck with a fine shot which was somehow kept out by Manglitz and his goalposts. So Cologne's away goal, counting double in the circumstances, took them through, and Arsenal's Cup was, so to speak, dashed from their lips.

Leeds and Liverpool, the following evening, did better, each gaining a draw in Europe, and going through. Liverpool, despite their 3–0 advantage, adopted in Munich a frankly defensive posture, leaving out their graduates, Hall and Heighway, yet scoring the first goal, through Ross, after 75 minutes. An uncharacteristic mistake by Clemence, their fine young goalkeeper, gave Bayern a late but meaningless equaliser.

In Setubal, by contrast, Leeds set about Vitoria with gusto, despite the continuing absence of Billy Bremner. In a fine first half performance, they scored through Peter Lorimer, hit the post twice, and had two goals disallowed for offside.

Vitoria rallied after half-time, and scored late on when Baptista beat Sprake, who had just substituted an injured Harvey. The Welsh international goalkeeper, however, made up for it with a save from João. A fine performance by Leeds, after recent stuttering in the League.

They gave another in the first leg of their semi-final, away to Liverpool. Still faltering in the League, the return of Billy Bremner, recovered at last from a hairline fracture, galvanised them. Not only did they hold off the assaults of a Liverpool team unbeaten at home in its last thirty matches, but won the game in the second half thanks to Bremner's typically courageous goal. It was significant, too, that it should come from a free kick subtly taken by his old abettor, Johnny Giles. The ball found its way through the Liverpool defence, and Bremner flung himself to head it in. A powerful header from John Toshack was later well saved by Gary Sprake, and Leeds retained their surprising but not undeserved lead to the end.

In Cologne, the home side lost their invaluable midfield player, Wolfgang Overath, after half an hour, fell behind to a goal by Juventus' Bettega, before half-time, and equalised only three minutes from the end through the invaluable Thielen.

The return match between Leeds and Liverpool at Elland Road was tough and tight; a goalless draw. It represented a triumph of stamina and application by Leeds, obliged to play a stringent, vital League game against Arsenal two days earlier while Liverpool, in an irrelevant one, put out a reserve side. It was all the harder for Leeds as, in the course of the game, they had to replace both their strikers, Jones and Clarke, but they held on, held out, and went through to the Final.

Juventus also qualified, beating Cologne 2–0 in Turin in front of a 70,000 crowd. Clearly "Juve" and their fans were taking seriously a competition often regarded lightly by the chief Italian teams.

Helmut Haller, the West German international, was in splendid form, making both the Juventus goals. After two minutes, he beat four men and found Capello, who scored from long range, while five minutes from the end, his pass gave Anastasi the second goal. So Juventus reached their second Fairs Cup Final, Leeds their third; and it was the last Fairs Cup Final of all. In 1971/2, the Fairs Cup is to be renamed the European Union Cup.

Leeds' first attempt to play the first leg of the Final, against Juventus in Turin, was frustrated by torrential rain. The game was abandoned before half-time, though not before Eddie Gray had slipped and dislocated his shoulder, another in Leeds' endless chapter of injuries.

The following Friday, however, the game was played on a perfect pitch in pleasant conditions, and Leeds, twice behind, forced a 2–2 draw. The game was skilful and exciting, Juventus coming out on the attack, as was to be expected, Leeds counter-attacking skilfully, with Johnny Giles in splendid, co-ordinating form.

Juventus took the lead after 29 minutes against the play, when Cooper lost the ball to Haller – claiming hands – Anastasi found Juve's new young star, Causio, who in turn split the defence with a pass which Bettega touched in.

Three minutes into the second half, Leeds deservedly equalised when Lorimer won a tackle on the left and served Madeley, whose shot was deflected past Piloni, in goal, by Salvadore.

Picking up a loose clearance, Capello drove in a fine shot to the top corner from 20 yards, to give Juventus back the lead. But Leeds continued to give as good as they got, despite some highly skilful play by Juventus in attack, and a second equaliser came 13 minutes from the end. Piloni made a complete hash of a long cross from the left by Giles and Bates, now substituting Jones, put the ball in.

After 12 minutes of the return leg, at Elland Road, Leeds, going ahead, set Juventus an almost insuperable target. The goal came when Bremner took a free kick from the left, Jackie Charlton headed across goal, Peter Lorimer missed his kick, but the alert Allan Clarke, who'd already come close, swept the ball in.

Juventus equalised with a fine move, Causio dribbling fluently before finding Furino, who glided a subtle pass through the Leeds defence, Anastasi timing his run perfectly to slip it home. The second half was somewhat less interesting, it being clear enough that Leeds were home and dry. Thus the Yorkshire club took its first trophy since 1969.

Terry Cooper had a superb, attacking game for Leeds, Haller, Anastasi and Furino were splendid Juventus players, but Giles and Bremner looked, understandably, a little weary.

EUROPEAN FAIRS CUP 1970/71
First Round

AEK Athens (0) 0
Enschede (2) 3
Pahlplatz 2, Van der Kerkhof

Enschede (0) 1
AEK Athens (0) 0

Zeleznicar (1) 3
Osim, Spreco, Mujkic
Anderlecht (2) 5
Ejderstedt 3, Van Himst, Puis

Anderlecht (1) 4
Puis 2, Mulder 2
Zeleznicar (3) 4
Bukal 2, Spreco 2

La Gantoise (0) 0

Hamburg (3) 7
Dorfel 4, Honig, Zaczyk, Volkert

Hamburg (1) 1
Nogly
La Gantoise (0) 1
Bene

Liverpool (1) 1
Graham

Ferencvaros (0) 0

Liverpool: Clemence; Lawler, Lindsay; Smith, Lloyd, Hughes; Callaghan, Evans, Graham, McLaughlin, Thompson.
Ferencvaros: Geczi; Balint, Pancsics, Megyesi, Juhasz, Horvath; Fusi, Branikovics, Albert, Rakosi, Mucha.

Ferencvaros (0) 1
Mucha

Liverpool (0) 1
Hughes

Ferencvaros: Geczi; Balint, Juhasz, Pnacsics, Megyesi, Horvath (Novak), Rakosi, Szoke, Mucha, Albert, Katona.
Liverpool: Clemence; Lawler, Lindsay; Smith, Lloyd, Hughes; Hall, McLaughlin (Livermore), Evans, Graham, Thompson.

1st Round

Sarpsborg (0) 0
Sarpsborg: Nilsen; Locken, Woodruff, S. Johansen, Holt, Gjer-

Leeds United (0) 0

lrugsen, Navestad, Andresen, A. Johansen, Olsen, Spydevold, Kjoenigsen.
Leeds United: Sprake; Madeley, Cooper; Bremner, Kennedy, Gray; Lorimer, Belfitt, Jones, Bates, Hibbitt.

    Leeds United (1) 5   *Sarpsborg* (0) 0
    Charlton 2, Bremner 2,
    Lorimer
Leeds United: Sprake; Madeley, Cooper (Reaney); Bremner, Charlton, Hunter; Lorimer, Clarke, Belfitt, Bates, Gray.
Sarpsborg: Nielsen; Loeken, Johansen (F) (Holt), Woodruff, Gerlaugsen, Johansen (S.), Kjoenijsen (Melby), Andersen, Olsen, Spaydevold, Vavestead.

    Coleraine (0) 1   *Kilmarnock* (0) 1
    Mullan   Mathie
Coleraine: Crossman; McCurdy, Gordon; Campbell, Jackson, Murray; O'Doherty, Dunlop, Wilson, Dickson, Mullan.
Kilmarnock: Hunter; Arthur, Dickson; Gilmour, McGrory, Rodman; McLean (T.), Morrison, Mathie, Maxwell, Cook.

    Kilmarnock (0) 2   *Coleraine* (0) 3
    McLean, Morrison   Dickson 3
Kilmarnock: Hunter; Arthur, Dickson; Gilmour, McGrory, MacDonald; McLean, Maxwell, Morrison, McSherry, Mathie.
Coleraine: Crossan; McCurdie, Gordon, Curley, Jackson, Murray, Dunlop, Mullen, O'Docherty, Dickson, Jennings.

    Dundee United (0) 3   *Grasshoppers* (1) 2
    Reid, I., Markland, Reid, A. Grahn, Meier
Dundee United: Mackay; Rolland, Smith, Markland, Cameron; Reid, A., Henry; Traynor, Reid, I., Gordon (Gillespie), Wilson.
Grasshoppers: Deck; Staudenmann, Ruegg, Citherlet, Mocellin; Groebli, Bigi, Meyer, Ohlhauser; Meier, Grahn, Schneeberger (Noventa).

    Grasshoppers (0) 0   *Dundee United* (0) 0
Grasshoppers: Deck; Staudenmann, Ruegg, Citherlet, Mocellin; Meyer, Groebli (Noventa), Ohlhauser; Meier, Grahn, Schneeberger.
Dundee United: Mackay; Rolland, Smith, Markland, Cameron; Reid, A., Henry; Wilson, Gordon, Stevenson, Traynor.

    Lazio (0) 2   *Arsenal* (0) 2
    Chinaglia 2 (1 penalty)   Radford 2
Lazio: Sulfaro; Facco, Nanni, Governato (Fortunato), Papadopoulo, Wilson, Manservisi (Di Vincenzo), Mazzola, Chinaglia, Massa, Dolso.
Arsenal: Wilson; Rice, McNab; Kelly, McLintock, Roberts; Armstrong, Storey, Radford, Kennedy, Graham.
    Arsenal (1) 2   *Lazio* (0) 0
    Radford, Armstrong

Arsenal: Wilson; Rice, McNab; Kelly, McLintock, Roberts; Armstrong, Storey, Radford, Kennedy, Graham (Nelson).
Lazio: Sulfaro; Wilson; Nanni (Legnano), Governato, Facco, Polentes; Massa, Mazzola, Manservisi; Chinaglia, Fortunato (Morrone).

GKS (Poland) (0) 0

Barcelona (0) 3
Pujol, Filosia, Rexach

Wiener Sportklub (0) 0

Beveren (Belgium) (1) 3
Rogiers, Deraymaecker,
Janssens

Ilves (Finland) (2) 4
Lundborg, Nupponen 2,
Nouranen
Sturm Graz (2) 3
Murlsits, Albrecht, Kaiser

Juventus (5) 7
Pablowsky (own goal),
Bettega 2, Anastasi 4
Rumelange (0) 0

Seville (0) 1
Acosta
Eskisehir (Turkey) (0) 3
Fethi 3

Vitoria Guimaraes (0) 3
Bernado, Peres,
Peri (own goal)
Angouleme (2) 3
Castellan 2, Gallice

Hadjuk (2) 3
Jerkovic, Pavlica, Jovanic
Slavia (Bulgaria) (0) 1

Nykoeping (1) 2
Olsen, H. Hansen

Hertha Berlin (1) 4
Horr, Brungs 2, Gergeli

Barcelona (0) 1
Rexach
GKS (Poland) (2) 2
Rother, Nowak (penalty)

Beveren (Belgium) (0) 2
Rogiers, Janssens
Wiener Sportklub (0) 0

Sturm Graz (1) 2
Laine (own goal), Kaiser

Ilves (Finland) (0) 0

Rumelange (0) 0

Juventus (3) 4
Novellini 3, Landini

Eskisehir (Turkey) (0) 0

Seville (0) 1
Acosta

Angouleme (0) 0

Vitoria Guimaraes (0) 1
Ademis

Slavia (Bulgaria) (0) 0

Hadjuk (0) 0

Hertha Berlin (2) 4
Brungs 2, Gayer,
Steffenhagen
Nykoeping (1) 1
N. Rasmassen

Partizan Belgrade (0) 0　　*Dynamo Dresden* (0) 0
Dynamo Dresden (4) 6　　*Partizan Belgrade* (0) 0
Kreische 4, Sammer, Sachse

Barreirense (1) 2　　*Dynamo Zagreb* (0) 0
Serafim, Campora
Dynamo Zagreb (0) 6　　*Barreirense* (1) 1
Novak 4, Lalic 2　　Campora

Ruch Chorzow (0) 1　　*Fiorentina* (0) 1
Faber　　Vitali
Fiorentina (1) 2　　*Ruch Chorzow* (0) 0
Chiarugi, Mariani

Sparta Prague (1) 2　　*Atletico Bilbao* (0)
Migas (penalty), Gogh
Atletico Bilbao (0) 1　　*Sparta Prague* (0) 1
Uriarte　　Cavanev

A.B. Copenhagen (2) 7　　*Sliema Malta* (0) 0
Sultana (own goal),
F. Hansen 2, Carlsen 2,
Nielsen, Petersson
Sliema Malta (1) 2　　*A.B. Copenhagen* (2) 3
Jensen (own goal), Cini　　A. Hansen (penalty),
　　B. Neilsen 2

Dynamo Bucharest (1) 5　　*PAOK Salonika* (0) 0
PAOK Salonika (0) 1　　*Dynamo Bucharest* (0) 0
Koudas

Lausanne (0) 0　　*Vitoria Setubal* (0) 2
　　Baptista, João
Vitoria Setubal (2) 2　　*Lausanne* (1) 1
Arcanjo, Guerreiro　　Du Four

Cologne (2) 5　　*Sedan* (0) 1
Parits, Thielen, Rupp 2, Lex　　Pierron
Sedan (0) 1　　*Cologne* (0) 0
Dellamore (penalty)

Internazionale (0) 1　　*Newcastle United* (1) 1
Cella　　Davies

Internazionale: Vieri; Burgnich, Facchetti; Fabbian, Giubertoni, Cella; Pellizzaro, Mazzola, Achilli, Frustalupi, Corso.
Newcastle United: McFaul; Craig, Clark; Gibb, Burton, Moncur; Robson, Dyson, Davies, Arentoft, Young.

Newcastle United (1) 2　　*Internazionale* (0) 0
Moncur, Davies

Newcastle United: McFaul; Craig, Clark; Gibb, Burton, Moncur; Robson, Dyson, Davies, Arentoft, Young.
Internazionale: Vieri; Righetti, Facchetti; Bellugi, Giubertoni, Cella; Jair, Fabbian, Boninsegna, Achilli (Bordon), Corso.

Trnava (1) 2   *Marseilles* (0) 0
Dobias (penalty), Mazerana
Marseilles (1) 2   *Trnava* (0) 0
Couecou, Skoblar
   Trnava qualified on penalty kicks after extra time.

Bayern Munich (1) 1   *Rangers* (0) 0
Beckenbauer
Bayern: Maier; Koppenhofer, Hansen, Beckenbauer, Pumm; Brejtner (Hoeness), Roth, Zobel; Muller, Mrosko, Brenninger.
Rangers: McCloy; Jardine, Greig, McKinnon, Miller; Jackson, Fyfe, Conn; Stein (Henderson), McDonald, Johnston.
   Rangers (0) 1   *Bayern Munich* (0) 1
Stein   Muller
Rangers: McCloy; Jardine, Greig, McKinnon, Miller; Jackson, Fyfe, Conn; Stein, McDonald, Johnston.
Bayern: Maier; Koppenhofer, Hansen, Beckenbauer, Pumm, Schwarzenbeck, Roth, Zobel; Muller, Mrosko, Brenninger.

Cork Hibernian (0) 0   *Valencia* (2) 3
                                   Claramunt 2, Valdez
Valencia (2) 3   *Cork Hibernian* (1) 1
Jara, Sergio 2   Wigginton

Hibernian (2) 6   *Malmo* (0) 0
McBride 3, Duncan 2, Blair
Hibernian: Marshall; Shevlane, Schaedler; Stanton, Black, Hamilton; Duncan, Blair, McBrige, McEwan, Cropley.
Malmo: Hult; Roland Anderssen, Tristerssen, Tapper, Jacobson, Roy Anderssen, Friberg (Jonsston), Olsberg, T. Anderssen, Larsson, Svahn.
   Malmo (0) 2   *Hibernian* (0) 3
Larsson, Joensson   Duncan, McEwan, Stanton
Malmo: Hult; Jakobsson, Tapper, Kleander, Sigfrigsson, Rasmusson, Granstrom, Olsberg, Andersson, Larsson, Jonsson.
Hibernian: Marshall; R. Duncan, Schaedler, Brownlie, Stanton, McEwan, Davidson, Jones, McBride, Blair, A. Duncan.

Universitatea Craiova
   (Rumania) (0) 2   *Pecsi Dosza* (0) 1
Tzaralunga, Strimbeanu   Mahe
Pecsi Dosza (3) 3   *Universitatea Craiova* (0) 0
Kocsis 2, Mate

Trakia (Bulgaria) (0) 1   *Coventry City* (2) 4
Radkov   O'Rourke 3, Martin
Trakia: Karushkov (Radenkov); Delev, Cluchev, Apostolov, Zagdouna, Marinov, Popov, Dermendijev, Ubinov, Radkov.
Coventry City: Glazier; Coop, Smith; Machin, Blockley, Strong; Hunt, Carr, Martin, O'Rourke, Clements.

Coventry City (2) 2   *Trakia (Bulgaria)* (0) 0
Joicey, Blockley
Coventry City: Glazier; Coop, Bruck, Clements, Blockley, Strong, Hunt Carr, Joicey, O'Rourke, Alderson.
Trakia: Radenkov; Delev, Cluchev, Apostolov, Marinov, Zagdouna, Popov, Dermendijev, Hanov, Stanoev, Ubinov.

Sparta Rotterdam (3) 6   *I.A. Akranes (Iceland)* (0) 0
Venneker, Kowalik,
Kouditzer, Haijerman 2,
Walveek

I.A. Akranes (Iceland) (0) 0   *Sparta Rotterdam* (5) 9
     Klijnjan 3, Kristensen,
     Kowalik 3, Van der Veen,
     Venneker

Second Round

Sturm Graz (0) 1   *Arsenal* (0) 0
Zamuth
Sturm Graz: Benko; Solleder, Reiter, Schilsher, Russ, Fuchs, Wagner, Murlasits, Albrecht, Kaiser, Zamuth.
Arsenal: Wilson; Rice, McNab; Kelly, McLintock, Roberts; Armstrong, Storey, Radford, Kennedy, Graham.

Arsenal (1) 2   *Sturm Graz* (0) 0
Kennedy, Storey (penalty)
Arsenal: Wilson; Rice, McNab; Kelly, McLintock, Roberts; Armstrong, Storey, Radford, Kennedy, Graham.
Sturm Graz: Grloci (Benko); Solleder, Reiter, Schilscher, Russ, Fuchs, Wagner (Huberts), Murlasits, Albrecht, Kaiser, Zamut.

Sparta Rotterdam (2) 2   *Coleraine* (0) 0
Klijnjan 2
Sparta: Doesburg; Vennecker, Eijkenbroek; Vissner, Horst, Van der Veen; Heijerman, Walboek, Kowalik, Klijnjan, Kristensen.
Coleraine: Crossan; McCurdy, Gordon; O'Doherty, Jackson, Murray; Dunlop, Mullan (Curley), Wilson, Dickson, Jennings.

Coleraine (1) 1   *Sparta Rotterdam* (2) 2
Jennings   Koudijer, Kristensen
Coleraine: Crossan; McCurdy, O'Doherty, Jackson, Gordon, Wilson, Murray, Dunlop, Mullan, Dickson, Jennings (Curley).
Sparta: Doesburg; Vennecker, Eijkenbroek, Visser, Horst Van der Veen, Walboek, Heijerman, Koudijer, Klijnjan, Kristensen.

Leeds United (0) 1   *Dynamo Dresden* (0) 0
Lorimer (penalty)
Leeds United: Harvey; Davey, Cooper, Bremner, Charlton, Hunter;
Lorimer, Clarke, Jones, Belfitt (Galvin), Madeley.
Dynamo Dresden: Kallenbach; Ganzera, Dorner; Sammer, Kern,
Haustein; Zeigler, Kreische, Hemp, Heidler, Richter.
    Dynamo Dresden (1) 2   *Leeds United* (1) 1
    Hemp, Kreische   Jones
Dynamo Dresden: Kallenbach; Ganzera, Dorner, Sammer, Haustein,
Zeigler, Hemp, Kreische, Riedel (Geyer), Richter, Sachse (Heider).
Leeds United: Sprake; Davey, Madeley; Bremner, Charlton, Hunter;
Lorimer, Clarke, Jones, Giles, Bates.

    Liverpool (0) 3   *Dynamo Bucharest* (0) 0
    Lindsay, Lawler, Hughes
Liverpool: Clemence; Lawler, Yeats; Smith, Lloyd, Hughes; Hall,
Lindsay, Heighway (St. John), McLaughlin, Thompson.
Dynamo Bucharest: Constantinescu; Cheran, Deleanu, Nunweiler, N.,
Dinu, Stonescu, Lucescu, Dumitrache, Mustetea, Haidu.
    Dynamo Bucharest (1) 1   *Liverpool* (0) 1
    Salceanu   Boersma
Dynamo Bucharest: Constantinescu; Cheran, Deleanu; Nunweiler, N.,
Dinu, Stonescu; Salceanu, Popescu, Dumitrache, Nunweiler, R.,
Haidu.
Liverpool: Clemence; Lawler, Lindsay; Smith, Lloyd, Hughes; Hall,
Evans (Boersma), Heighway, McLaughlin, Thompson.

    Newcastle United (1) 2   *Pecsi Dosza* (0) 0
    Davies 2
Newcastle United: McFaul; Craig, Clark; Gibb, Young, Moncur;
Robson, Dyson, Davies, Smith, Ford.
Pecsi Dosza: Rapp; Hernadi, Maurer; Kincses, Kocsis, V., Konrad;
Berczesi, Daka, Mate, Ronai (Tuske), Toth.

    Pecsi Dosza (1) 2   *Newcastle United* (0) 0
    Moncur (own goal),
    Mate (penalty)
        Pecsi qualified after extra-time on penalties.
Pecsi Dosza: Rapp; Hernadi, Maurer; Kincses, Kocsis, V., Konrad;
Berczesi, Mate, Daka, Toth, Ronai (Koller).
Newcastle United: McFaul; Craig, Clark; Gibb, McNamee, Moncur;
Robson, Dyson (Hindson), Davies, Young, Ford (Mitchell).

    Bayern Munich (4) 6   *Coventry City* (1) 1
    Schneider 2, Schwarzenbeck,
    Muller 2, Roth
Bayern: Maier; Hansen, Schwarzenbeck, Beckenbauer, Koppenhofer,
Roth, Zobel, Mrosko (Hoeness), Schneider, Muller, Brenninger.

Coventry City: McManus; Coop, Cattlin; Machin, Blockley, Strong; Hunt, Carr, Martin, O'Rourke, Clements.

Coventry City (1) 2	*Bayern Munich* (0) 1
Martin, O'Rourke	Hoeness

Coventry City: Glazier; Coop, Smith; Mortimer, Blockley, Hill; Hunt, Carr, Martin, O'Rourke, Clements.
Bayern: Maier; Hansen, Schwarzenbeck, Beckenbauer, Koppenhofer, Pumm, Hoeness, Zobel, Muller, Mrosko, Brenninger.

Sparta Prague (1) 3	*Dundee United* (1) 1
Vrana, Jurkanin 2	Traynor

Sparta: Kramerius; Melichar, Urban; Semendax, Migas, Chovanec; Vesely, Barton, Masek (Ulicny), Jurkanin, Vrana.
Dundee United: Mackay (McAlpine); Rolland, Cameron; Markland, Smith, Henry; Wilson, Reid, Gordon (Scott), Stevenson, Traynor.

Dundee United (1) 1	*Sparta Prague* (0) 0
Gordon	

Dundee United: McAlpine; Markland, Cameron, Gillespie, Smith. Henry; Wilson, Reid, Gordon, Stevenson, Traynor.
Sparta: Kramerius; Melichar, Urban; Kessel, Migas, Chovanec; Vesely, Barton, Vrana, Jurkanin, Ulicny.

Hibernian (1) 2	*Vitoria Guimaraes* (0) 0
Duncan, Stanton	

Hibernian: Baines; Shevlane, Schaedler; Brownlie, Black, Stanton; Davidson, Blackley (McEwan), McBride, Graham, Duncan.
Guimaraes: Rodriguez; Bernardo, Silva; Peres, Costeado, Jorge; Zezinho, Augusta, Ademir, Gonçalves, Osvaldinho.

Vitoria Guimaraes (2) 2	*Hibernian* (0) 1
Gonçalves, Ademir	Graham

Guimaraes: Rodriguez; Bernardo, Silva; Peres, Costeado, Jorge; Osvaldinho, Zezinho, Ademir, Gonçalves, Artur.
Hibernian: Baines; Shevlane, Schaedler; Blackley, Black, Stanton; Hamilton (Davidson), Graham, McBride (Blair), Hunter, Duncan.

Eskisehir (2) 3	*Twente Enschede* (0)
Hahil, Fethi 2	Pahlplatz, Van der Kerkhof

Twente Enschede (3) 6	*Eskisehir* (1) 1
Jeuring 3, Van der Kerkhof, Steurer, Nagy	Fethi

A.B. Copenhagen (1) 1	*Anderlecht* (3) 3
B. Nielsen	Mulder, Ejderstedt, Nyde (own goal)

Anderlecht (2) 4	*A.B. Copenhagen* (0) 0
Van Himst, Nordahl 2, Elizeu	

Valencia (0) 0

Beveren (0) 1
Reimark

Hertha Berlin (0) 1
Horr
Spartak Trnava (2) 3
Kuna, Wild (own goal),
Martinkovic

Barcelona (0) 1
Gallego
Juventus (2) 2
Bettega, Capello

Dynamo Zagreb (2) 4
Lalic 2, Cercek, Vabec
Hamburg (1) 1
Honig

Vitoria Setubal (0) 2
José Maria, Jacinto João
Hadjuk (0) 2
Nadoveza, Hlevnjak

Fiorentina (1) 1
Mariani
Cologne (1) 1
Biskup (penalty)

Beveren (0) 1
Reymaecker
Valencia (0) 1
Forment

Spartak Trnava (0) 0

Hertha Berlin (0) 1

Juventus (1) 2
Haller, Bettega
Barcelona (0) 1
Pujol

Hamburg (0) 0

Dynamo Zagreb (0) 0

Hadjuk (0) 0

Vitoria Setubal (1) 1
José Maria

Cologne (1) 2
Flohe 2
Fiorentina (0) 0

Third Round

Arsenal (2) 4   *Beveren* (0) 0
Graham, Kennedy 2,
Sammels
Arsenal: Wilson; Rice, McNab; Graham, McLintock, Simpson; Armstrong, Storey, Radford, Kennedy, Sammels.
Beveren: Poklepovic; Verdonck, Van Genechten, Buyl, Vanderlinden, Roelandt, Mais, Van de Sompel, Rogiers, Braem, Janssens (Sub.: Debadt).

Beveren (0) 0   *Arsenal* (0) 0
Beveren: Poklepovic; Buyl, Van Genechten, Verhelst, Van der Linden, Roelandt (Debadt), Goosens, Van de Sompel, Rogiers (Maes), De-Raeymacker, Janssens.
Arsenal: Wilson; Rice, McNab; Storey, Roberts, Simpson; Armstrong (Marinello), Sammels, Radford (George), Kennedy, Graham.

Leeds United (5) 6   *Sparta Prague* (0) 0
Clarke, Chovanek (own goal),
Bremner, Gray 2, Charlton
Leeds United: Sprake; Madeley, Cooper; Bremner, Charlton, Hunter; Lorimer, Clarke, Belfitt (sub. Reaney), Giles, Gray.
Sparta: Kramerius; Melichar, Migas, Kessel, Urban, Chovanek, Vesely, Gogh, Masek, Jurkanin, Vrana.

    Sparta Prague (0) 2   *Leeds United* (2) 3
    Barton, Urban   Gray, Clarke, Belfitt
Sparta: Brabec; Melichar, Migas, Kessel, Urban, Chovanec, Vesely, Barton, Masek, Jurkanin, Vrana.
Leeds United: Sprake (Harvey); Reaney, Cooper; Bremner, Madeley, Hunter (Yorath); Lorimer, Clarke, Belfitt, Bates, Gray.

    Spartak Trnava (0) 0   *Cologne* (1) 1
    Cologne (0) 3   *Spartak Trnava* (0) 0
    Biskup (penalty),
    Hemmersbach, Rupp

    Bayern Munich (0) 2   *Sparta Rotterdam* (1) 1
    Sparta Rotterdam (0) 1   *Bayern Munich* (0) 3
    Kristensen   Muller 3

    Dynamo Zagreb (2) 2   *Twente* (1) 2

    Twente (0) 1   *Dynamo Zagreb* (0) 0

    Hibernian (0) 0   *Liverpool* (0) 1
                                    Toshack
Hibernian: Brownlie; Schaedler, Blackley, Black, Stanton, Davidson (McBride), McEwan, Stevenson, Blair, Duncan.
Liverpool: Clemence; Lawler, Lindsay; Smith, Lloyd, Hughes; Hall, McLaughlin, Heighway, Toshack, Thompson.

    Liverpool (1) 2   *Hibernian* (0) 0
    Heighway, Boersma
Liverpool: Clemence; Lawler, Evans; Smith, Lloyd, Hughes; Hall, McLaughlin, Heighway, Boersma, Callaghan.
Hibernian: Baines; Brownlie, Jones, Blackley, Black, Stanton, Duncan, McEwan, McBride, Blair, Stevenson.

    Pecsi Dosza (0) 0   *Juventus* (0) 1
    Juventus (0) 2   *Pecsi Dosza* (0) 0

Quarter-Finals
    Juventus (0) 2   *Twente* (0) 0
    Twente (0) 2   *Juventus* (0) 2
    Pahlplatz, Drost   Anastasi 2
                  After extra time.

Arsenal (1) 2   *Cologne* (1) 1
McLintock, Storey
Arsenal: Wilson; Rice, McNab; Storey, McLintock, Simpson; Armstrong, Sammels (Graham), Radford, Kennedy, George.
Cologne: Manglitz; Thielen (Kowalski), Hemmersbach, Simmet, Biskup, Cullman, Parits (Kappellmann), Flohe, Rupp, Overath, Lohr.

Cologne (1) 1   *Arsenal* (0) 0
Biskup (penalty)
Cologne: Manglitz; Thielen, Hemmersbach, Simmet, Biskup, Weber, Kappellmann, Flohe, Rupp, Overath, Lohr.
Arsenal: Wilson; Rice, McNab; Storey, McLintock, Simpson; Armstrong, Graham, Radford, Kennedy, George.

Liverpool (1) 3   *Bayern Munich* (0) 0
Evans 3
Liverpool: Clemence; Lawler, Lindsay; Smith, Lloyd, Hughes; Boersma, Evans, Heighway, Toshack, Hall.
Bayern: Maier: Hansen, Koppenhofer, Schwarzenbach, Beckenbauer, Roth, Breitner, Zobel, Muller, Hoeness, Brenninger.

Bayern (0) 1   *Liverpool* (0) 1
Schneider   Ross
Bayern: Maier; Breitner, Schwarzenbach, Beckenbauer, Koppenhofer, Roth, Zobel, Hoeness, Schneider, Muller, Brenninger.
Liverpool: Clemence; Lawler, Lindsay; Smith, Lloyd, Hughes; Callaghan, Ross, Evans, Toshack, McLaughlin.

Vitoria Setubal (0) 1   *Leeds United* (1) 1
Baptista   Lorimer
Vitoria Torres; Conceiçao (Arcanjo), Cardoso, Rebelo, Mendes, Octavio, Wagner; José Maria, Baptista, Guerreiro, Jacinto Joao.
Leeds United: Harvey (Sprake); Reaney, Cooper; Bates, Charlton, Hunter; Lorimer, Clarke, Jones, Giles, Madeley.

Leeds United (1) 2   *Vitoria Setubal* (1) 1
Lorimer, Giles (penalty)   Baptista
Leeds United: Harvey; Davey, Reaney; Bates, Charlton, Hunter; Lorimer, Belfitt, Jones, Giles, Madeley. Sub.: Jordan.
Vitoria Setubal: Torres; Rebelo, Cardoso, Mendes, Carrico, Octavio, Maria, Wagner, Baptista, Guerreiro, Joao.

Semi-Finals
Liverpool (0) 0   *Leeds United* (0) 1
                               Bremner
Liverpool: Clemence; Lawler, Lindsay; Smith, Lloyd, Hughes; Callaghan, Evans, Heighway, Toshack, Hall. Subs.: Graham, Thompson.
Leeds United: Sprake; Reaney, Cooper; Bremner, Charlton, Hunter; Bates, Clarke, Jones, Giles, Madeley.

Leeds United (0) 0   *Liverpool* (0) 0
Leeds United: Sprake; Madeley, Cooper; Bremner, Charlton, Hunter; Bates, Clarke (Reaney), Jones (Jordan), Giles, Gray.
Liverpool: Clemence; Lawler, Yeats; Smith, Lloyd, Hughes; Callaghan, Thompson, Heighway, Toshack, Hall.

Cologne (0) 1   *Juventus* (1) 1
Thielen   Bettega
Juventus (1) 2   *Cologne* (0) 0
Capello, Anastasi

Final
Turin. First Leg, May 29th, 1971
Juventus (1) 2   *Leeds United* (0) 2
Bettega, Capello   Madeley, Bates
Juventus: Piloni; Spinosi, Salvadore, Marchetti, Morini, Haller, Capello, Furino, Causio, Anastasi ((Novellini), Bettega.
Leeds United: Sprake; Reaney, Cooper; Bremner, Charlton, Hunter; Lorimer, Clarke, Jones (Bates), Giles, Madeley.

Second Leg
Elland Road, Leeds. June 3rd, 1971
Leeds United (1) 1   *Juventus* (1) 1
Clarke   Anastasi
Leeds win on "away goals".
Leeds United: Sprake; Reaney, Cooper; Bremner, Charlton, Hunter; Lorimer, Clarke, Jones, Giles, Madeley (Bates).
Juventus: Tancredi; Spinosi, Salvadore, Marchetti, Morini; Haller, Capello, Furino, Causio, Anastasi, Bettega.

Chapter Five

World Club Championships 1970

Feyenoord, European Cup holders, kept the world club championship (so called) in the Old World, by defeating Estudiantes of Argentina; runners-up for the second consecutive year. This time, however, goal difference did not have to decide, for Feyenoord drew in Buenos Aires, then won 1–0 in Rotterdam.

The first game, in Buenos Aires, was remarkable for Feyenoord's appalling start – when they gave away two goals through banal defensive errors by Treytel and Romeyn – and magnificent recovery. Kindvall headed one goal, the cool Van Hanegem got the equaliser.

Having behaved themselves with surprising restraint and success in

Buenos Aires, Estudiantes regressed unpleasantly in Rotterdam. So violent were they, in fact, that Feyenoord revealed afterwards that had a replay in Madrid become necessary, they would have ducked it, for fear of the effects on their season. They no doubt recalled how Milan had fallen to pieces the previous year; after being kicked to pieces by Estudiantes in Buenos Aires.

As it was, the replay became unnecessary. Joop Van Deale, a young, bespectacled forward who'd never played a full match in the first team, was sent on by Ernst Happel to replace the 33-year-old Coen Moulijn – fearing for his safety. And it was Van Deale who scored the decisive and only goal, with a hard, low shot into the left hand corner of the goal. The notorious Pachame, the player who so brutally kicked Bobby Charlton in Buenos Aires two years earlier, duly broke the young Dutchman's glasses, so that for the last 20 minutes he couldn't see, but Feyenoord held on for victory.

Since Estudiantes had won a South American Cup in which Brazilian teams did not compete, in which they received a bye to the semi-final, and in whose Final they beat a Penarol team (1–0 on aggregate!) deprived of all its Uruguayan World Cup men, their title to compete for a world championship was dubious, to say the least.

First Leg *Buenos Aires* August 1970
 Estudiantes (2) 2 *Feyenoord* (1) 2
 Echecopar, Veron Kindvall, Van Hanegem
Estudiantes: Errea; Pagnanini, Spadaro Togneri Malbernat Bilardo (Solari) Pachame Echecopar (Rudzki). Conigliaro, Flores, Veron.
Feyenoord: Treytel; Romeyn, Israel, Laseroms, Van Duivenbode, Hasil, Jansen, Van Hanegem (Boskamp), Wery, Kindvall, Moulijn.

Second Leg *Rotterdam* September 1970
 Feyenoord (0) 1 *Estudiantes* (0) 0
 Van Deale
Feyenoord: Treytel; Romeyn, Israel, Laseroms, Van Duivenbode, Hasil (Boskamp), Van Hanegem, Jansen, Wery, Kindvall, Moulijn (Van Deale).
Estudiantes: Pezzano; Malbernat, Spadaro, Togneri, Medina (Pagnanini), Bilardo, Pachame, Romeo, Conigliaro (Rudzki), Flores, Veron.

Chapter Six

South American Liberators' Cup

With their customary amazing resilience, Estudiantes once more reached the Final of the South American Liberators' Cup, after yet another miraculous improvement. They were at the bottom of the Argentinian League when the time came to compete in one of the two qualifying groups into which the Cup was this time divided in its penultimate stage. This made their task rather harder than usual, since in previous years it's been the custom to exempt the holders till a semi-final round which necessitated the beating of only one opponent.

Brazilian clubs at last re-entered the tournament, but to surprisingly little effect. Palmeiras comfortably eliminated their Rio opponents, Fluminense, after losing their first game against them, but they themselves were thrashed 3–0 at home in their sem-final group by Nacional of Montevideo, with Luis Artime, the Argentinian World Cup centre-forward of 1966, in fine fettle.

In the other group, Estudiantes, who had finally parted company with their unrepentant manager Zubeldia, and with a couple of their fiercer players, Poletti, once suspended for life after a brutal foul on Prati of Milan, and Manera, lost 1–0 at home to Barcelona of Ecuador. The breakaway goal was scored by a priest, the Spaniard, Father Juan Manuel Bazurko, who turned down all pleas to play on and retired, after Barcelona were finally eliminated. Despite his presence, and that of the veteran, Spencer, in attack, Estudiantes won the return, in Guayaquil, not to mention a stormy game in Santiago against Union Espanol.

The only goal was headed wide of his own keeper by Hugy Berlu of Union, in attempting to pass back. Afterward, the enraged Chilean fans remained on the terraces, wouldn't disperse, were assailed by the police, and had one of their number killed when a gas grenade exploded, poor fellow, in his face.

In the first leg of the Final, in Argentina, Estudiantes beat Nacional 1–0, the Uruguayans paying the penalty, in a dull game, for their caution. It wasn't till too late that they took off Prieto, a half-back used to reinforce the defence, and put on their international striker, Bareno. An Estudiantes defence grouped around Aguirre-Suarez – he who was suspended for elbowing Milan's Combin in the face – gave nothing away. But a pulled muscle lamed the dangerous Juan Veron in the second half, and Estudiantes' attack waned in consequence.

Final

First Leg
    Estudiantes (1) 1   *Nacional* (0) 0

Second Leg
    Nacional (0) 1   *Estudiantes* (0) 0
    Masnik

Play-off (*in Lima, Peru*)
    Nacional (1) 2   *Estudiantes* (0) 0
    Esparrago, Artime

Chapter Seven

British International Championship 1971

Once again the British International Championship was stuck on to the end of a debilitating season, to be contested by tired, jaded players. Moreover, as Sir Alf Ramsey complained, the problem of getting all those players required released by their clubs was made no easier. Success in European club competition means that club teams face the last stages of their tournaments at the very time the British Championship is in progress. Still, Scotland were at least and at last able to call on their Leeds United stars, Bremner and Gray, and on McLintock of Arsenal.

The competition began with a most contentious and unconvincing victory by England, in Belfast, and a rain-swamped goalless draw between Wales and Scotland, in Cardiff.

For the second, consecutive time in Belfast, Ireland played the football, but England won the day. The English team, deprived of an exhausted Alan Mullery, who withdrew from the reckoning, and including Paul Madeley of Leeds for the first time, owed much to Gordon Banks.

In the first half, when an Irish team inspired by the ubiquitous brilliance of George Best, the vigorous challenge of Derek Dougan, the intelligence of Jimmy Nicholson, the unexpected solidity of its back four, laid siege to England's goal, Banks twice frustrated them. He made glorious saves from McMordie and Dougan, was lucky when Hamilton headed against the bar, and perhaps marginally fortunate when George Best charged down his clearance, ran the ball into goal, but was penalised for putting his foot up.

In the second half, it was Pat Jennings' turn to make several excellent saves, while Banks tipped over a thundering drive by Sammy Nelson.

The winning goal, nine minutes from time, was a cruel injustice to Ireland. Francis Lee seemed clearly to have handled the ball before putting through an Allan Clarke who may well have been offside. Clarke went round Jennings to find the empty net, and the goal stood. But England's performance, dull in midfield and up front, owing so much to Banks in defence, was thoroughly depressing. Perhaps it was kindest to attribute its failings to a surfeit of football, a mental as well as a physical weariness. Colin Bell, injured and unavailable, might have sparked it to life.

Wales, once again decimated by injury, confirmed their fine tradition of rising above such problems by giving Scotland better than they got, on an impossible pitch. John Roberts, capped for the first time, and James, whose fine late tackle averted a late Scottish goal, were pillars in the middle; as were Moncur and Frank McLintock, Arsenal's Footballer of the Year. But ironically, the return of Bremner in such heavy conditions was not successful. Only when John Greig substituted him in the second half, 18 minutes from time, did the Scots really begin to move.

Clarke's unfortunate habit of punching corners rather than holding them twice nearly cost Scotland a goal. When, after one such incident, Davies headed in Reece's chip, the goal was disallowed only for Roberts' foul on Bremner. Later, Yorath met Clarke's inadequate clearance, and Brogan was somewhat lucky to intercept the shot. Moreover, Gray cleared off the line, and in the last minute, Reece shot straight at Clark when through on his own, and Ron Davies lobbed feebly over the top. Scotland, once again, failed to show their old, and long lacking, spirit.

The following Tuesday, Scotland's crisis of morale and talent took on still grimmer dimensions when Northern Ireland beat them 1-0 at a more than half deserted Hampden Park. It was the first Irish victory in Glasgow for 37 years, though it was only four since they beat the Scots in Belfast for their last Championship victory.

The only goal came when Derek Dougan's well-timed run to Pat Rice's long free-kick took Scotland's defenders by surprise. He headed across goal and John Greig, in the now familiar Scottish fashion, put past his own goalkeeper. Fourteen minutes had gone, but Scotland's lack of a striker made all their ensuing pressure futile. Ireland, indeed, came close to scoring a second goal near half-time, after an exchange between George Best and Hamilton, a shot by Best.

In the second half, Scotland brought on the young Jarvie of Airdrieonians for O'Hare, and continued fruitlessly battering the sturdy Irish defence. Jarvie did head a corner just outside, but the Irish survived to win.

The following evening, Alf Ramsey drastically reorganised the team which had won so luckily and limply in Belfast. Rather surprisingly, he called up four of the Liverpool defence which had recently been so unimpressive at Wembley in the Cup Final, choosing the half-back line of Smith, Lloyd (both capped for the first time) and Hughes *en bloc*. He also replaced Gordon Banks with Peter Shilton, capped for the second time, restored Geoff Hurst, and gave a first cap to the season's leading scorer, West Bromwich Albion's hard-shooting Tony Brown.

Brown, however, looked totally out of his class; his most significant contribution to the game was to nullify Lee's goal for England by being offside, just before half-time.

This followed a run and centre by the excellent Terry Cooper, whose cross also led to a header by Peters which flew, luckily for Wales, straight at Gary Sprake.

With the exception of these five lively minutes prior to the interval, and some ten early in the second half, the English performance was abysmal. Wales, in the first half hour, were much the better team, Reece playing ducks and drakes with a clumsy English defence which badly lacked Moore, and gained nothing from the presence of its Liverpool contingent. When Reece put Toshack through with a splendid pass, only a fine save by a plunging Shilton prevented a deserved Welsh goal.

Wales tired as the game wore on, but though Hurst and Lee fought well in the English attack, the power of the fine Welsh back four, the mediocrity of the England team at large, prevented goals. One began to wonder if, when Karel Capek wrote his famous and frightening RUR, it stood for Ramsey's Universal Robots.

Brown, just after he'd had his one good shot of the evening saved by Sprake, late in the game, was replaced by Clarke, while an injured Reece gave way to Ronnie Rees. Wales had long since shot their bolt in attack, but they deserved the first draw they'd ever forced at Wembley.

England recovered form to beat Scotland decisively 3–1, at Wembley, and win a Championship which Northern Ireland, conquerors of Wales, certainly deserved to share.

For this match, England threw out their half-back line of heavy Liverpool dragoons, though Ramsey hedged his bets again with the choice of Peter Storey, in midfield. What principally brought them to life, however, was the revitalisation of Alan Ball, the immense authority and power of Chivers, the deadly running of Lee. Plus, it must be admitted, the ill-balanced inadequacies of Scotland, who after a bright first twenty minutes and the encouragement of a gift of a goal, faded from view. Their back four were shaky, and despite the dazzling early running of Johnstone and the skills of Bremner and Green, there were too many mediocrities in the side.

England took the lead after nine minutes when Ball sent Lee, always the master of Brogan, down the right. Brogan blocked the centre for a corner-kick which Ball took, Chivers headed the ball on, and Peters' header beat Clark. Desperately, Greig punched the ball, but it merely struck the bar and crossed the line.

Two minutes later, a strange error by Ball led to Scotland equalising. He headed a rash, inaccurate pass to Banks, on which Curran swooped to score. Scotland, with Johnstone still running beautifully, were back in the game. But on the half hour England, following three minutes of pressure, scored again. This time, an error by Robb, always out of his depth, allowed Lee to break again. Brogan tackled him but rolled the ball straight across goal, where Chivers put it in with a rocketing left-footed shot.

Four minutes from half-time, Lawler lobbed into the area, and Chivers exploited Moncur's confusion by running on to lob, in turn, over Clark.

In the second half, Munro was brought on to look after him, McLintock moved into midfield, Robb up front, but by now the game was virtually dead; the rest was anticlimax. The bitterly disillusioned Scottish fans were singing, at the finish, "If you hate Bobby Brown, clap your hands," but it was the whole of the antique Scottish administration that they should impugn.

In Belfast, 1–0 scarcely reflected the extent of Ireland's superiority over Wales, for they missed many chances. In midfield, Jimmy Nicholson, vastly applauded when he limped off 20 minutes from time, and McMordie were in lively form, there was no holding George Best, and Dougan was again full of menace. In defence, Hunter was dominant again. Sprake, exposed by his defence, was marginally lucky to save from Clements at point blank range, the ball spinning off his body, over the top. But Wales couldn't escape indefinitely.

With 27 minutes played, Nicholson's shot was charged down, and, as he claimed a penalty, the ball reached Clements, who slipped it through the square defence for Hamilton to run on and score. There were no further goals, but Wales could count themselves a little fortunate. It was their first defeat in Belfast for twelve long years.

Belfast, May 15th
    Northern Ireland (0) 0   England (0) 1
                                  Clarke

Northern Ireland: Jennings (Spurs); Rice, Nelson (Arsenal); O'Kane (Nottingham Forest), Hunter (Blackburn Rovers), Nicholson (Huddersfield Town); Hamilton (Linfield), McMordie (Middlesbrough) Sub. Cassidy (Newcastle United), Dougan (Wolves), Clements (Coventry City), Best (Manchester United).

England: Banks (Stoke City); Madeley (Leeds United), Cooper (Leeds United); Storey (Arsenal), McFarland (Derby County), Moore (West Ham United); Lee (Manchester City), Ball (Everton), Chivers (Spurs), Clarke (Leeds United), Peters (West Ham United).

Ninian Park, May 15th
    Wales (0) 0   Scotland (0) 0

Wales: Sprake (Leeds United); Rodrigues (Sheffield Wednesday), Thomas (Swindon Town); James (Blackpool), Roberts (Arsenal), Yorath (Leeds United); Phillips (Cardiff City), Durban (Derby County), Davies, R. (Southampton), Toshack (Liverpool), Reece (Sheffield United).

Scotland: Clark (Aberdeen); Hay (Celtic), Brogan (Celtic); Bremner (Leeds United), Greig (Rangers), McLintock (Arsenal), Moncur (Newcastle United); Lorimer (Leeds United), Robb (Aberdeen), O'Hare (Derby County), Cormack (Nottingham Forest), Gray (Leeds United).

Hampden Park, May 18th
    Scotland (0) 0   Northern Ireland (1) 1
                                Greig (own goal)

Scotland: Clark (Aberdeen); Hay, Brogan (Celtic); Greig (Rangers), McLintock (Arsenal), Munro (Wolves), Moncur (Newcastle United);

Lorimer (Leeds United), Green (Blackpool), O'Hare (Derby County), Jarvie (Airdrieonians), Curran (Wolves), Gray (Leeds United).
Northern Ireland: Jennings (Spurs) Rice, Nelson (Arsenal); O'Kane (Nottingham Forest), Hunter (Blackburn Rovers), Nicholson (Huddersfield Town); Hamilton (Linfield), McMordie (Middlesbrough), Craig (Newcastle United), Dougan (Wolves), Clements (Coventry City), Best (Manchester United).

Wembley, May 19th
    England (0) 0   *Wales* (0) 0

England: Shilton (Leicester City); Lawler (Liverpool), Cooper (Leeds United); Smith, Lloyd, Hughes (Liverpool); Lee (Manchester City), Brown (West Bromwich Albion), Hurst (West Ham United), Coates (Spurs), Peters (Spurs). Sub.: Clarke (Leeds United).
Wales: Sprake (Leeds United); Rodrigues (Sheffield Wednesday), Thomas (Swindon Town); James (Blackpool), Roberts (Arsenal), Yorath (Leeds United); Phillips (Cardiff City), Durban (Derby County), Toshack (Liverpool), Davies, R. (Southampton), Reece (Sheffield United). Sub.: Rees (Nottingham Forest).

Wembley, May 22nd
    England (3) 3   *Scotland* (1) 1
    Peters, Chivers 2   Curran

England: Banks (Stoke City); Lawler (Liverpool), Cooper (Leeds United); Storey (Arsenal), McFarland (Derby County), Moore (West Ham United); Lee (Manchester City), Clarke (Leeds United), Ball (Everton), Chivers (Spurs), Hurst (West Ham United), Peters (Spurs).
Scotland: Clark (Aberdeen); Greig (Rangers), Brogan (Celtic); Bremner (Leeds United), McLintock (Arsenal), Moncur (Newcastle United); Johnstone (Celtic), Robb (Aberdeen), Curran (Wolves) (Munro (Wolves)), Green (Blackpool) (Jarvie (Airdrieonians)), Cormack (Nottingham Forest).

Belfast, May 22nd
    Northern Ireland (1) 1   *Wales* (0) 0
    Hamilton

Northern Ireland: Jennings (Spurs); Rice, Nelson (Arsenal); O'Kane (Nottingham Forest), Hunter (Blackburn Rovers), Nicholson (Huddersfield Town) (Harvey (Sunderland)); Hamilton (Linfield), McMordie (Middlesbrough), Dougan (Wolves), Clements (Coventry City), Best (Manchester United).
Wales: Sprake (Leeds United); Rodrigues (Sheffield Wednesday), Thomas (Swindon Town); James (Blackpool), Roberts (Arsenal), Yorath (Leeds United); Phillips (Cardiff City), (Rees (Nottingham Forest), Durban (Derby County), Davies, R. (Southampton), Toshack (Liverpool), Reece (Sheffield United).

FINAL TABLE

	P	W	D	L	Goals F	A	Pts
England	3	2	1	0	4	1	5
Northern Ireland	3	2	0	1	2	1	4
Wales	3	0	2	1	0	1	2
Scotland	3	0	1	2	1	4	1

Chapter Eight

British Internationals against Foreign Teams 1970/71

The need to fit in qualifying matches for the European Nations Cup and an agreement between the F.A. and the League not to have an overseas tour, the year after a World Cup, limited England's programme. Their Under 23 team opened the ball with a good 3-1 win over West Germany at Leicester, even though several of the English team withdrew, injured, while the Germans fielded several above the age limit.

The game was a particular success for the young Everton centreforward, Joe Royle, who scored a spectacular, pyrotechnical first goal from a pass by Steve Kember, another success – and a late choice. Kember started the move, with a backheel, from which Robson scored the second with a powerful long shot, and he was also involved in the final goal, by Kidd. A fine beginning for the excellent little Crystal Palace player.

Injury kept him out of the next game, against Sweden at Hull, which England Under 23 won rather less impressively. A brawny Swedish team failed to prevent Brian Kidd heading two goals in the first half, before scything him down. The lively Dave Thomas, of Burnley, was involved in both of them. It was Sweden's first defeat in six Under 23 internationals.

England's first full international of the season was refreshingly successful; a well merited 3-1 win over an East German team which arrived trailing clouds of glory. England, abandoning the sterile and misguided 4-4-2 which had doomed them in the World Cup, played an adventurous 4-3-3, in which Allan Clarke spiritedly abetted the admirable Hurst and the ebullient Lee.

East Germany's ill organised defence, weak in the air and deploying a strangely fallible version of *catenaccio*, might have given away several other goals. In the first half, Clarke and Hurst headed Lee through the defence in turn, the second occasion producing a goal.

Martin Peters got the second, when Hurst turned a high ball to him and the goalkeeper stood mysteriously still, but Vogel, the best visiting player, retorted with a fine individual goal. After a powerful run, his fine left footed shot hit Bobby Moore's foot, and curled over Shilton, the young debutant's, head.

The second half saw England dominant in midfield and creating many other chances, though the only goal was Clarke's; a left foot shot from Lee's cross which hit the goalkeeper before looping into goal. Clarke also had a left foot shot just wide of a post, a header which Croy saved, while Lee hit a post and also forced a good save from Croy.

Doubts remained about centre-half, where Sadler, a defensive wing-half by inclination and nature, was manifestly a stopgap, but the performance on the whole was most encouraging

Leicester, October 14th, 1970

England Under 23 (2) 3   *West Germany Under* 23 (1) 1
Royle, Robson, Kidd   Weist

England: Shilton (Leicester City); Edwards (Manchester United), Robson (Derby County); Todd (Sunderland), Lloyd (Liverpool), Piper (Portsmouth); Thomas (Burnley), Kember (Crystal Palace), Royle (Everton), Currie (Sheffield United) (sub. Bernard (Stoke City)), Kidd (Manchester United).
West Germany: Rynio; Bella, Kremers, Russmann, Zech, Neuberger, Koeppel, Luetkebomert, Weist (sub. Kapellmann), Scheer, Erler.

Hull, November 11th, 1970

England Under 23 (2) 2   *Sweden Under* 23 (0) 0
Kidd 2

England: Clemence (Liverpool); Edwards (Manchester United), Robson (Derby County); Todd (Sunderland), Lloyd (Liverpool), Nish (Leicester City); Piper (Portsmouth), Kidd (Manchester United) (sub. Bernard (Stoke City)), Royle (Everton), Channon (Southampton), Thomas (Burnley).
Sweden: Hellstrom; B. Andersson, Mohlberg, Nordenberg, Lind, R. Andersson, Tapper, Linderoth, Johansson, Sjostron, Nordin. Subs: Ohlsson, Mossberg, for Linderoth and Johansson.

Wembley, November 25th, 1970

England (2) 3   *East Germany* (1) 1
Lee, Peters, Clarke   *Vogel*

England: Shilton (Leicester City); Hughes (Liverpool), Cooper (Leeds United); Mullery (Spurs), Sadler (Manchester United), Moore (West Ham United); Lee (Manchester City), Ball (Everton), Hurst (West Ham United), Clarke (Leeds United), Peters (Spurs).
East Germany: Croy; Kurjuweit, Rock, Sammer, Ganzera, Strempel, Stein, Kreische, Ducker, P., Irmscher, Vogel. Sub: Frenzel.

June 14

    Russia (1) 1   *Scotland* (0) 0
    Evruzhikin

Russia: Rudakov; Istomin, Shesternev, Mativenko, Kaplichny, Kolotov, Konkov, Nodia (Dolgov), Fedotov, Shevchenko, Evruzhikin (Khmelnitsky).
Scotland: Clark; Brownley, Dickson, Munro, McKinnon, Stanton, Forrest, Watson, Stein (Curran), Robb, Scott.

OLYMPIC QUALIFYING TOURNAMENT

The unhappy, and surely avoidable, coincidence of the qualifying match against Bulgaria with the European Cup programme unhappily obscured a wonderful performance by Britain's Olympic team. With only a meagre 3,000 on the deserted terraces of Wembley, they beat a full strength Bulgarian international team, including the likes of Bonev and Yakimov, 1–0, thus raising memories of the fine 3–3 draw there with Bulgaria, in the qualifying competition for the 1956 Olympiad.

The British team, all Englishmen but for Currie, rose finely above themselves, their performance showing the benefit of Charles Hughes, their team manager's, determined preparation. In the 15th minute, Hardcastle's centre was not fully cleared, Yordanov was marooned out of his goal, and Adams headed in.

Reality, alas, firmly asserted itself on the occasion of the return, in Sofia, where Britain were trounced, 5–0. Zhekov and Mihailov wiped out the lead before half-time, and three more goals followed in the second half, Mitkov getting the last of them from a penalty.

Wembley Stadium, March 24th, 1971

    Great Britain (1) 1   *Bulgaria* (0) 0
    Adams

Great Britain: Swannell (Hendon); Fuschillo (Wycombe Wanderers), Currie (Albion Rovers), Powell (Wycombe Wanderers), Gamblin (Leatherhead), Payne (Enfield), Day (Slough Town), Haider (Hendon), Hardcastle (Skelmersdale United), (Pritchard (Wycombe Wanderers)), Gray (Enfield), Adams (Slough Town).
Bulgaria: Yordanov; Zafrov, Kolev, Aladjiev, Denev, Penev, Veselinov, Bonev (Vassiliev), Nikodimov, Yakimov, Panov.

Sofia, May 5th, 1971

    Bulgaria (2) 5   *Great Britain* (0) 0
    Zhekov 2, Mihailov,
    Vassiliev, Mitkov (penalty)

Chapter Nine

Friendly Internationals between Foreign Teams 1970/71

September 2nd, 1970
    Poland (2) 5   *Denmark* (0) 0
    Lubanski, Dejna, Marks 3

September 5th
    France (3) 3   *Czechoslovakia* (0) 0
    Gondet, Loubet, Bosquier

September 6th
    East Germany (1) 5   *Poland* (0) 0
    Strempel, Stein, Kreische 2,
    Vogel (penalty)

September 9th
    West Germany (2) 3   *Hungary* (1) 1
    Sieloff, Muller 2   Fazekas

September 10th
    Austria (0) 0   *Yugoslavia* (1) 1
                                          Bajevic

September 13th
    Norway (2) 2   *Sweden* (1) 4
    Nielsen, Thorfugltet   Danielsson, Trochokopil,
                                          Svensson, T. 2

September 23rd
    Eire (0) 0   *Poland* (2) 2
                                            Anczok, Szoltysik

September
    Denmark (0) 0   *Norway* (0) 1
                                            Iversen

September 27th
    Hungary (1) 1   *Austria* (1) 1
    Vidats   Redl

September 30th
    Brazil (1) 2   *Mexico* (0) 1
    Jairzinho, Tostao   Valdivia

October 4th
    Chile (0) 1   *Brazil* (1) 5
    Messen   Pelé, Roberto,
                                            Jairzinho 2, Paulo Cesar

October 7th
> *Austria* (0) 1 *France* (0) 0
> Kreuz

October 20th
> *Switzerland* (1) 1 *Italy* (0) 1
> Blaettler Mazzola

October 25th
> *Czechoslovakia* (0) 2 *Poland* (2) 2
> Stratil 2 Kozierski, Blaut

October 29th
> *Russia* (2) 4 *Yugoslavia* (0) 0
> Schevtschenko, Fedotov,
> Koltov, Nodia

October 29th
> *Spain* (1) 2 *Greece* (0) 1
> Luis, Quini Papoiannou

November 10
> *Israel* (0) 0 *Australia* (0) 1

November 11th
> *Switzerland* (0) 0 *Hungary* (0) 1
>   Fazekas

November 11th
> *Belgium* (0) 1 *France* (0) 2
> Van Moer Molitor 2

November 17th
> *Greece* (1) 1 *Australia* (2) 3
> Eleftherakis Alston, Blue, Panton

November 18
> *Yugoslavia* (0) 2 *West Germany* (0) 0
> Dzajic, Bukal

November 22nd
> *Greece* (0) 1 *West Germany* (2) 3
> Youtsos Netzer, Grabowski,
>   Beckenbauer

December 2nd
> *Holland* (1) 2 *Rumania* (0) 0
> Cruyff 2

December 9th
> *Mexico* (1) 3 *Australia* (0) 0
> Valdivia 2, Gomez

December 10th
> *Algeria* (1) 3 *Morocco* (1) 1
> Khalem 3 Maati
> (*African Nations Cup*)

December 27th
    Morocco (2) 3   *Algeria* (0) 0
    Bamous, Petchou, Boujemaa
           (*African Nations Cup*)

January 8th
    Argentina XI (0) 3   *France* (1) 4
    Brindisi, Nicolau,   Loubet, Djorkaeff (penalty),
    Laraignée (penalty)   Lech, Revelli

January 13th
    Argentina XI (1) 2   *France* (0) 0
    Laraignée, Madurga

February 9th
    Uruguay (0) 0   *East Germany* (2) 3
                              Stein 2, Richter

February 11th
    Uruguay (0) 1   *East Germany* (1) 1
    Zubia   Richter

February 18th
    Mexico (0) 0   *Russia* (0) 0

March 2nd
    Israel (2) 2   *Sweden* (0) 1
    Faygenbaum, Spiegel   Eklund

March 14th
    Morocco (1) 3   *Egypt* (0) 0
    Petchou, Bamouss, Silali
           (*African Nations Cup*)

April 4th
    Austria (0) 0   *Hungary* (0) 2
                              Bene 2

April 7th
    Greece (0) 0   *Bulgaria* (0) 1
                              Vasiliev

April 16th
    Egypt (2) 3   *Morocco* (0) 2
    Chazli 2, Bassari   Bamouss, El Arabi
           (*African Nations Cup*)

April 21st
    Yugoslavia (0) 0   *Rumania* (0) 1
                              Dembrowski

May 5th
    Switzerland (1) 2   *Poland* (1) 4
    Kunzli, Kuhn   Szoltysik, Banas, Dejna,
                              Lubanski

May 19th
    Belgium (2) 4   *Luxemburg* (0) 0
    Denul, Van Himst (penalty),
    Semmeling, Van Moer

May 23rd
    Russia (4) 7   *Algeria* (0) 0

Chapter Ten
F.A. Cup 1970/71

Arsenal, like Spurs ten years before them, did the double; only the second team to accomplish it, this century.

Intriguingly, history repeated itself when the Cup Final turned out to be between Arsenal and Liverpool, who met at Wembley in 1950, the Londoners winning, 2–0. This time, the margin was 2–1, but there was no question of Arsenal's great superiority, of the fact that they should never have required extra time; let alone fallen a surprising goal behind.

As always, the Cup had its surprises, none greater than the brave elimination of Leeds United by Colchester United, of the Fourth Division, in the Fifth Round. Though the absence of Billy Bremner had much to do with Leeds' defeat, it was certainly no fluke. Scoring midfield subtleties, the little Essex team banged the ball hard and high into a Leeds goalmouth where Charlton and Sprake had a dismal day. Ray Crawford, the former English international centre-forward, now a 36-year-old veteran retrieved from the Southern League, was the hero of the day, heading one goal, sweeping in another while on the ground, the third coming from an error by Sprake, in the second half. 3–2 was the final score, but it slightly flattered Leeds. Colchester then went up to Everton – and lost, 5–0.

But Everton were themselves defeated in a semi-final against their city rivals, Liverpool. Again, history was repeating itself, for Liverpool had beaten Everton at this stage in 1950. In the first half, when Alan Ball scored, Everton looked good for Wembley, but when Brian Labone hobbled off soon afterwards, their defence collapsed, Heighway making a goal for Evans, Evans one for Hall.

At Sheffield, meanwhile, Arsenal were surviving precariously against Stoke. Two freakish goals gave Stoke the lead, Storey's clearance rebounding home off Smith, George's ridiculous back pass giving Ritchie an easy second. But Storey's shot was deflected past Banks just after half-time, Stoke threw away several good chances, and in the last seconds of injury time, Mahoney punched out McLintock's header from a corner (was Banks impeded when Arsenal gained it?) and Storey completed an eventful match by scoring the penalty.

At Villa Park, four days later, Arsenal made no such mistake, rolling over Stoke with some ease, Graham and Kennedy getting their goals.

So the the Final, which Arsenal were obliged to play while still nursing the aches and pains of their fine performance at Tottenham only five days earlier, when they made sure of the League. Their superiority on the day was manifest; seldom can the Liverpool defence have looked so heavy and square.

John Radford, who'd lately been out of form, played ducks and drakes with Smith and Lloyd, and made a plentitude of chances for his side. It was from his cross that Armstrong might have headed a goal in the first half, when Clemence finely saved; his long throw from which Graham headed against the bar, in the second, his hook which Kelly and Graham forced into goal for the equaliser, his return pass which Charlie George powerfully thumped home for the winner.

Till Peter Thompson substituted Alun Evans, midway through the second half – soon after Kelly replaced Peter Storey – Liverpool's mid field was overplayed by Arsenal's.

With Kennedy missing a fine chance in each half – George made one for him in the first, Radford a still easier one in the second – Graham's headers twice going so close, Liverpool were fortunate to survive normal time. Then, two minutes into the extra period, Thompson found Steve Heighway, who at last exploited his acceleration, leaving the defence standing, and beating Wilson, who had come too far off his line, perhaps expecting a centre.

Arsenal had the morale and the energy to fight back, Eddie Kelly now turning the ball into Clemence's goal, nine minutes after Liverpool scored, the excellent George getting the winner, with nine minutes left. It was finely appropriate that this goal, the goal which gave Arsenal the double, should be scored by their only locally born player.

F.A. CUP FINAL. *Wembley*, May 8th, 1971
Arsenal (0) 2   *Liverpool* (0) 1
Kelly, George   Heighway
(after extra time)
Arsenal: Wilson; Rice, McNab; Storey (Kelly), McLintock, Simpson; Armstrong, Graham, Radford, Kennedy, George.
Liverpool: Clemence; Lawler, Lindsay; Smith, Lloyd, Hughes; Callaghan, Evans (Thompson), Heighway, Toshack, Hall.

SCOTTISH CUP 1970/71
Though the competition moved, at last, to the familiar Rangers v Celtic conclusion, its semi-finals were anything but a formality, and emphasised the waning of the Old Firm's powers. Both teams had need of a replay to defeat opponents given, in advance, little hope. Rangers

were held to a draw by a Hibernian team forced, in recent seasons, to transfer one after another of its most gifted players – Stein to Rangers themselves, not to mention Cormack and Marinello.

In an ill tempered, goalless draw, Hibs were worthy of survival, though there was a moment near the end when Rangers broke away with a numerical advantage, which they threw away. The replay they won by a couple of goals, without overmuch difficulty, Jardine playing a fine and versatile game at right-back, often joining in or initiating attacks.

As for Celtic, the great invincibles till a season or so ago, they were caught, remarkably, by little Airdrieonians, after enjoying a 2-0 lead at half-time. This Airdrie reduced and, nothing daunted when the score reached 3-1, hit back again, and again, to equalise. But they, too, had shot their bolt, and Celtic sailed through in the replay.

So, in the Final, there was yet another meeting of the Old Firm; a reprise of the League Cup Final, in which Rangers had surprisingly beaten Celtic late in the game with a goal by Johnstone, a precocious, 16-year-old substitute.

History duly repeated itself; or very nearly; for it was Johnstone, again, who came on as substitute and got the equaliser four minutes from the end. Billy Johnston lobbed high into the penalty area, and Derek Johnstone leaped above Williams and Connelly to send the ball bouncing into goal.

Yet Rangers, very much the underdogs, might well have been three up at half-time, so thoroughly was the biter bit, so embarrassed were Celtic by Rangers' infernal rhythm. Greig, Penman and McDonald dominated midfield, Henderson and his colleagues had the Celtic defence in confusion. Five minutes from half-time, Wallace beat Jackson in the air – a rare event – Hood flicked on, and Lennox ran in to score.

In the second half, the pendulum swung Celtic's way, Brogan, Callaghan, Hay and Johnstone setting the pace; yet Rangers pulled themselves round, to equalise. There were 188 arrests, 117 fans treated in hospital.

In the replay, Celtic took their twenty-first Cup and the double to boot, when they beat Rangers, 2-1. Rangers brought in the young, inexperienced Denny at right-back to replace Miller, who'd fractured his jaw on the previous Saturday.

Celtic won on merit, largely dominating the final half-hour, but getting both their goals in a two minute period, midway through the first half. Lou Macari scored the first, when Lennox's corner was allowed to run to him. Then Jimmy Johnstone, who was in irresistible form, was brought down when clean through by McKinnon. Hood converted the penalty.

In the second half, Rangers again brought on their own young Johnstone as substitute; and again he provoked a goal. His shot from close in struck Williams' legs, and Callaghan put through his own goal.

Six minutes from time, Colin Stein had two attempts cleared from the Celtic line; but Jock Stein's men held out.

FINAL, *Hampden Park,* May 8th, 1971
    Rangers (0) 1   *Celtic* (1) 1
    Johnstone, D.   Lennox

Rangers: McCloy; Miller, Mathieson; Greig, McKinnon, Jackson; Henderson, Penman (Johnstone, D.), Stein, McDonald, Johnston.
Celtic: Williams; Craig, Brogan; Connelly, McNeill, Hay; Johnstone, Lennox, Wallace, Callaghan, Hood.

REPLAY, *Hampden Park,* May 12th, 1971
    Celtic (2) 2   *Rangers* (0) 1
    Macari, Hood (penalty)   Callaghan (own goal)

Celtic: Williams; Craig, Brogan; Connelly, McNeill, Hay; Johnstone, J., Macari, Hood, (Wallace), Callaghan, Lennox.
Rangers: McCloy; Denny, Mathieson; Craig, McKinnon, Jackson; Henderson, Penman (Johnstone, D.), Stein, McDonald, Johnston.

FOOTBALL LEAGUE CUP 1970/71

For the third time in five seasons, the Football League Cup produced the exciting if rather unconvincing phenomenon of a Final between First and Third Division clubs. It was tempting to suggest that in the future, much time and trouble might be saved by simply putting all the First Division clubs in one hat, all the Third in another, and drawing one finalist from each.

In the event Aston Villa, playing marvellously above themselves, as they had to beat Manchester United, but in accordance with their great tradition, gave Spurs a tremendous run for their money. For most of the game, Villa, with Chico Hamilton showing marvellous brio and acceleration on the right wing, called the tune. They gave the Spurs defence, in which Phil Beal was forever stopping gaps and plugging holes, a severe chasing; and they did it with skilful football, not simply by using the tactic which had served them so well against Manchester United in the semi-final, using the heading powers of Andy Lochhead.

But alas for Villa, superiority must be translated into goals, and in the closing minutes, it was not they but the powerful Martin Chivers, hitherto subdued, who got them. 70 minutes had gone when a fast move down the left ended with Gilzean putting the little, lively Neighbour through. Dunn blocked the shot, Chivers scored.

Three minutes later, Chivers, powerfully holding off Tiler and Turnbull, swivelled on the ball to beat Dunn again, with a cracking low shot. It was a fine goal, but a cruel injustice to the Villa.

FOOTBALL LEAGUE CUP FINAL, *Wembley,* February 27th, 1971
    Tottenham Hotspur (0) 2   *Aston Villa* (0) 0
    Chivers 2

Tottenham Hotspur: Jennings; Kinnear, Knowles; Mullery, Collins, Beal; Gilzean, Perryman, Chivers, Peters, Neighbour.
Aston Villa: Dunn, Bradley, Aitken; Godfrey, Turnbull, Tiler; McMahon, Rioch, Lockhead, Hamilton, Anderson.

Chapter Eleven

Football League 1970/71

In an immensely dramatic finish, Arsenal won their eighth title, their first since 1953, when they beat Spurs at Tottenham in their final game, two days after Leeds had completed their programme.

It was, for most of its length, the most blatant of two horse races, Leeds and Arsenal utterly outstripping the field. Arsenal, carrying on from their success of 1970 in the Fairs Cup, fulfilled the ambition of their manager, Bertie Mee, by achieving a fine, solid, if slightly uninspired, consistency. He himself conceded that his young team had yet to reach its peak. Stronger critics condemned its lack of originality, its persistent reliance on the high cross to its two tall strikers, Radford and a powerfully built new star, the 19-year-old Ray Kennedy, from the North East.

But there was also, when he was recalled in mid season, the wayward brilliance of Charlie George, that rarity, an Arsenal player actually born on the doorstep, in Islington. Tall and strong, George's ball control and imagination were exceptional for so large, and young (20), a man, though his temperament sometimes betrayed him.

Also to be applauded was the endless industry of George Armstrong, on both wings, the brave goalkeeping of Bob Wilson, and the versatility of Frank McLintock, converted from right-half to centre-half, scoring vital goals as well as preventing them. Peter Storey, converted from fullback, was used successfully, if somewhat uninventively, in midfield.

Leeds, after an imposing beginning, suffered badly from the prolonged absence of Billy Bremner, the dynamo of the team, not to mention the gifted young Scot, Eddie Gray. This took the edge off a team already handicapped by the inconsistent goalkeeping of Gary Sprake and the waning at centre-half of the veteran Jackie Charlton. Yet Leeds still managed to build, till the closing weeks of the season, a big lead over every club but Arsenal, who then started winning their games in hand.

The season was also notable for the failure of the experiment of Wilf McGuinness, at Manchester United. At the turn of the season, the young McGuinness, once a Manchester United junior, later an international, was replaced by the club's father figure, Sir Matt Busby, and went back, acquiescently, to being the second team coach. The task of revitalising an ageing team had not unexpectedly been too much for him.

Everton surprisingly waned, though they spent another thumping £150,000 on Forest's Henry Newton, but Liverpool, after losing a whole attack through injury, rallied wonderfully, thanks to their fine young replacements. Outstanding among them was the 22-year-old Warwickshire University Graduate Steve Heighway, still an amateur at the end of the previous season. With his pace, his courage and his initiative, he became a force in the land, and above all demonstrated that the old myth – that a professional must turn to the game at 15 or, at the latest, 17 – was absurd.

Further, corroboratory, evidence was provided by his Liverpool colleague and fellow graduate, the lively Brian Hall, a Scot, and Blackpool's Oxford blue, the half-back, Peter Suddaby.

Though Blackpool went down, they were rallied when Bob Stokoe took them over, at the turn of the year, and showed enough spirit and talent – Suddaby, Green, Ramsbottom, Craven – to suggest all was not lost.

Burnley, too, though they never recovered from a dreadful start, itself partly the product of injuries, had many gifted young players, including Coates, (sold to Spurs in May), Thomas, Dobson and Kindon.

In its last paroxysms, the duel between Leeds and Arsenal centred on a couple of contentious offside decisions at Elland Road, the first of which went against Leeds – and brought a fusillade of peevish protest – the second, for them. Playing against West Bromwich, when a goal down, a careless square pass by Hunter put Brown clear and led to a goal. Suggett was standing in a plainly offside position but Mr.Tinkler clearly decided he wasn't interfering with play. An invasion of the pitch followed. There was no such extenuation of the goal Jackie Charlton scored to beat Arsenal 1–0 in injury time, in the "summit meeting" nine days later. He looked to many people four or five yards offside before he received the ball and put it in at the second attempt, though McNab may well have narrowly played him on. Unlike Leeds, Arsenal did *not* immediately squeal for "professional" referees. In each case, there was sufficient ground for believing the goal was good to obviate certainty.

Thus on the Monday that Arsenal went to White Hart Lane to play, poetically, their nearest London rivals, the only team so far to have won the double this century, they needed either victory or a goalless draw to be Champions. They won, on the whole deservedly, in a fast, exciting, vigorously contested game, in which Kinnear's late error exposed the Spurs goal, Kennedy eventually and firmly heading in Armstrong's cross. The stadium, besieged before the game, became the scene of wild jubilation.

The Second Division, closely contested all the way, but lacking in quality, was won at the end by Leicester City, Sheffield United's promising young side producing a late spurt to come up with them. For much of the way, Luton and Hull looked as though they might do it, Luton having a prolific scorer in Macdonald, at centre-forward, Hull cleverly player-managed by Terry Neill. But they, and Cardiff City, faltered at the last. At the bottom, it was again a bad year for Lancashire clubs, two illustrious names in Bolton and Blackburn sinking to the Third Division.

Still, a nearby team won the Championship of that section, Preston North End, under the ebullient managership of Alan Ball, father of the England star, beating Fulham away in their last game but one, then winning at home, for the title. Fulham, under Bill Dodgin, junior, were talented but inconsistent, and shipped a lot of water before limping finally into port. Villa's good young team, astoundingly well supported, fell badly away after the League Cup Final.

In Division Four, Notts County, buying back their original discovery, Tony Hateley, led almost all the way.

The overall impression was, once again, that power is being concentrated in fewer and fewer hands, and that the gap between First and Second Divisions grows ever greater.

SCOTTISH LEAGUE 1970/71

With Aberdeen, winners of the Scottish Cup in 1970, setting a brave pace at the top of the League for most of the season, it was hard to decide which was the salient feature of the tournament; the emergence of their good young side, or the decline of Celtic. If you like, the Celtic Twilight. Celtic's sixth consecutive victory was historic rather than impressive.

Those of us who had questioned Celtic's claims to true greatness in previous seasons, on the grounds that they relied too much on sheer pace and stamina (a most un-Scottish trait, in football at least) were surely borne out. Even the club's shrewdest apologists traced their falling off to a flagging of morale, the readiness and ability to run as they had run before. Coupled with the insistent but unfounded, rumours, from early in the New Year, that their remarkable manager, Jock Stein, was bound for Manchester United, this appeared to spell the end of the club's protracted supremacy. Well beaten by Ajax, another Dutch team, in the European Cup, its players largely overlooked by Scotland, the Celtic era had sadly and seemingly passed. They might continue to win titles, but it would plainly be some time before they won them, and strode across Europe, with the same proud prowess.

Faltering at the last stride when they lost by a penalty at Falkirk, Aberdeen allowed Celtic to pass them in the home straight, though there was the consolation of having their young skipper, Martin Buchan, named Player of the Year.

The season as a whole, however, was brutally overshadowed by the horrible disaster at Ibrox in January at the Rangers–Celtic match, when

66 died on a stairway which had at least twice previously led to alarming incidents. The subsequent inquiry did nothing to reassure the uncommitted.

FIRST DIVISION

	P	W	D	L	F	A	Pts
Arsenal	42	29	7	6	71	29	65
Leeds United	42	27	10	5	72	30	64
Tottenham H.	42	19	14	9	54	33	52
Wolves	42	22	8	12	64	54	52
Liverpool	42	17	17	8	42	24	51
Chelsea	42	18	15	9	52	42	51
Southampton	42	17	12	13	56	44	46
Man. United	42	16	11	15	65	66	43
Derby County	42	16	10	16	56	54	42
Coventry City	42	16	10	16	37	38	42
Man. City	42	12	17	13	47	42	41
Newcastle Utd.	42	14	13	15	44	46	41
Everton	42	12	13	17	54	60	37
Stoke City	42	12	13	17	44	48	37
Huddersfield T.	42	11	14	17	40	49	36
Notts. Forest	42	14	8	20	42	61	36
West Brom. A.	42	10	15	17	58	75	35
Crystal Palace	42	12	11	19	39	57	35
Ipswich Town	42	12	10	20	42	48	34
West Ham U.	42	10	14	18	47	60	34
Burnley	42	7	13	22	29	63	27
Blackpool	42	4	15	23	34	66	23

SECOND DIVISION

	P	W	D	L	F	A	Pts
Leicester City	42	23	13	6	57	30	59
Sheffield Utd.	42	21	14	7	73	39	56
Cardiff City	42	20	13	9	64	41	53
Carlisle United	42	20	13	9	65	43	53
Hull City	42	19	13	10	54	41	51
Luton Town	42	18	13	11	62	43	49
Middlesbrough	42	17	14	11	60	43	48
Millwall	42	19	9	14	59	42	47
Birmingham City	42	17	12	13	58	48	46
Norwich City	42	15	14	13	54	52	44
Queen's Park R.	42	16	11	15	58	53	43
Swindon Town	42	15	12	15	61	51	42
Sunderland	42	15	12	15	52	54	42
Oxford United	42	14	14	14	41	48	42
Sheffield Wed.	42	12	12	18	51	69	36
Portsmouth	42	10	14	18	46	61	34
Leyton Orient	42	9	16	17	29	51	34
Watford	42	10	13	19	38	60	33
Bristol City	42	10	11	21	46	64	31
Charlton Athletic	42	8	14	20	41	65	30
Blackburn Rov.	42	6	15	21	37	69	27
Bolton W.	42	7	10	25	35	74	24

THIRD DIVISION

	P	W	D	L	F	A	Pts
Preston N. E.	46	22	17	7	63	39	61
Fulham	46	24	12	10	68	41	60
Halifax Town	46	22	12	12	74	55	56
Aston Villa	46	19	15	12	54	46	53
Chesterfield	46	17	17	12	66	38	51
Bristol Rovers	46	19	13	14	69	50	51
Mansfield Town	46	18	15	13	64	62	51
Rotherham Utd.	46	17	16	13	64	60	50
Wrexham	46	18	13	15	72	65	49
Torquay United	46	19	11	16	54	57	49
Swansea City	46	15	16	15	59	56	46
Shrewsbury T.	46	16	13	17	58	62	45
Barnsley	46	17	11	18	49	52	45
Brighton	46	14	16	16	50	47	44
Plymouth Arg.	46	12	19	15	63	63	43
Rochdale	46	14	15	17	61	68	43
Port Vale	46	15	12	19	52	59	42
Tranmere Rov.	46	10	22	14	45	55	42
Bradford City	46	13	14	19	49	62	40
Walsall	46	14	11	21	51	57	39
Reading	46	14	11	21	48	85	39
Bury	46	12	13	21	52	60	37
Doncaster Rov.	46	13	9	24	45	66	35
Gillingham	46	10	13	23	42	67	33

FOURTH DIVISION

	P	W	D	L	F	A	Pts
Notts. County	46	30	9	7	89	36	69
Bournemouth	46	24	12	10	81	46	60
Oldham Athletic	46	24	11	11	88	63	59
York City	46	23	10	13	78	54	56
Chester	46	24	7	15	69	55	55
Colchester Utd.	46	21	12	13	70	54	54
Northampton T.	46	19	13	14	63	59	51
Southport	46	21	6	19	63	57	48
Workington T.	46	18	12	16	48	49	48
Exeter City	46	17	14	15	67	68	48
Stockport C.	46	16	14	16	49	65	46
Darlington	46	17	11	18	58	57	45
Aldershot	46	14	17	15	66	71	45
Brentford	46	18	8	20	66	62	44
Crewe Alex.	46	18	8	20	75	76	44
Peterborough U.	46	18	7	21	70	71	43
Scunthorpe Utd.	46	15	13	18	56	61	43
Southend Utd.	46	14	15	17	53	66	43
Grimsby Town	46	18	7	21	57	71	43
Cambridge Utd.	46	15	13	18	51	66	43
Lincoln City	46	13	13	20	70	71	39
Newport County	46	10	8	29	55	85	28
Hartlepool Utd.	46	8	12	26	34	74	28
Barrow	46	7	8	31	51	90	22

85

SCOTTISH LEAGUE – DIVISION ONE

	P	W	D	L	F	A	Pts
Celtic	34	25	6	3	89	23	56
Aberdeen	34	24	6	4	68	18	54
St. Johnstone	34	19	6	9	59	44	44
Rangers	34	16	9	9	58	34	41
Dundee	34	14	10	10	53	45	38
Dundee United	34	14	8	12	53	54	36
Falkirk	34	13	9	12	46	53	35
Morton	34	13	8	13	44	44	34
Motherwell	34	13	8	13	43	47	34
Aidrieonians	34	13	8	13	60	65	34
Hearts	34	13	7	14	41	40	33
Hibernian	34	10	10	14	47	53	30
Kilmarnock	34	10	8	16	43	67	28
Ayr United	34	9	8	17	37	54	26
Clyde	34	8	10	16	33	59	26
Dunfermline	34	6	11	17	44	56	23
St. Mirren	34	7	9	18	38	56	23
Cowdenbeath	34	7	3	24	33	77	17

SCOTTISH LEAGUE – DIVISION TWO

	P	W	D	L	F	A	Pts
Partick Thistle	36	23	10	3	78	26	56
East Fife	36	22	7	7	86	44	51
Arbroath	36	19	8	9	80	52	46
Dumbarton	36	19	6	11	87	46	44
Clydebank	36	17	8	11	57	43	42
Montrose	36	17	7	12	88	64	41
Albion Rovers	36	15	9	12	53	52	39
Raith Rovers	36	15	9	12	62	62	39
Stranraer	36	14	8	14	54	52	36
Stenhousemuir	36	14	8	14	64	70	36
Queen of South	36	13	9	14	50	56	35
Stirling Albion	36	12	8	16	61	61	32
Berwick Rangers	36	10	10	16	42	60	30
Queens Park	36	13	4	19	51	72	30
Forfar Athletic	36	9	11	16	63	75	29
Alloa Athletic	36	9	11	16	56	86	29
East Stirling	36	9	9	18	57	86	27
Hamilton A.	36	8	7	21	50	79	23
Brechin City	36	6	7	23	30	73	19

Chapter Twelve

World Cup History

The World Cup – or to give it its proper name, the Jules Rimet Trophy was first played in Montevideo in 1930, but the principle of it was agreed by FIFA, the federation of international football associations, at their Antwerp Congress of 1920. No man did more to further the idea than Jules Rimet, President of the French Football Federation, who was elected FIFA President in Antwerp, and it was thus that the attractive gold cup came to be given his name.

By 1930 the four British associations had withdrawn from FIFA, and it was not for another twenty years that British teams competed for a World Cup. Whether they would have won it between the wars is open to question. The fact that they did not undergo the test allowed the myth of British superiority in football to last a generation longer than it might otherwise have done. In 1934, just before the Italian version of the World Cup, Hugo Meisl, the brilliant manager of the Austrians, expressed the view that England, had they competed, would not even have reached the semi-final.

Four years later, England were invited to compete in the Finals without qualifying, to take the place of Austria, overrun by the Nazis. But the invitation was refused.

In 1930 the competing countries were divided into four pools, the qualifiers going into the semi-finals, which were played on the normal Cup tie basis of "sudden death". In 1934 and 1938 the World Cup finals were played as a straight knock-out tournament, but in 1950 the four pools were reconstituted, with one main difference. The four winners went into a further pool, to contest the title. It was thus only a matter of chance that the last match between Brazil and Uruguay, one of the most passionate and exciting in the history of the tournament, should also turn out to be the decider.

In 1958 and 1962 four groups were again constituted, but on these occasions, two teams from each went into the quarter-finals after which, as in 1930, the tournament followed the pattern of a straight knock-out contest. In 1966, when the World Cup was played in England, the same dubious formula applied. In 1970, goal "difference" replaced goal average. In 1974, two further qualifying groups replace the quarter and semi-finals, and produce the finalists.

WORLD CUP, 1930 – Montevideo

Though the tournament was won by a very fine team – Uruguay had previously come to Europe to take the Olympic titles of 1924 and 1928 – it hardly drew a representative entry.

In the 1926 FIFA Congress Henri Delaunay, the French Federation's excellent secretary, expressed the view that football could no longer be confined to the Olympics: "Many countries where professionalism is now recognised and organised cannot any longer be represented there by their best players." In 1928, FIFA passed his resolution to hold a World Cup tournament at once. Only the Scandinavian block, and Esthonia, voted against it! Odd that Sweden should eventually stage a World Cup and play in the Final.

Uruguay got the competition for a variety of reasons: their Olympic success, their promise to pay every competing team's full expenses and to build a new stadium, and the fact that 1930 was their centenary.

But distance and the need to pay their players for a couple of months, led to most of the big European powers withdrawing: Italy, Spain, Austria, Hungary, Germany, Switzerland, Czechoslovakia, Britain, of course, were out of FIFA. It was only thanks to King Carol himself that Rumania entered; he not only picked the team but got time off for the players from their firms. France, Belgium and Yugoslavia were the other three: lower middle-class European teams of that era. The stage was set for a South American domination.

It was the United States who provided the surprise. Their team, made up largely of ex-British professionals jokingly christened "the shot putters" by the French, because of their massive physique, showed great stamina and drive, and actually qualified for the semi-finals. There, an excellent Argentinian eleven – beaten 2–1 in the replayed 1928 Olympic Final, by Uruguay – brushed them aside.

Uruguay, however, again proved irresistible. They prepared with the dedication one has come to expect over the past fifteen years from leading South American teams; but then, it was quite new. For two months, their players were "in concentration" at an expensive hotel in the middle of the Prado park. When Mazzali, the brilliant goalkeeper, sneaked home late one night, he was thrown out of the team.

A splendid half-back line (playing in the old attacking centre-half-back style) was Uruguay's strength: José Andrade, Lorenzo Fernandez and Alvaro Gestido. José Nasazzi, the captain and right-back, was a great force, and in the forward-line Scarone and Petrone (now slightly over the hill) were superb technicians and dangerous goalscorers.

The tournament began on July 13, 1930. France surprised Argentina in an early match, losing only 1-0, after the crowd had invaded the pitch, when the referee blew for time six minutes early – then had to clear the pitch and restart the game. The Argentinians, who had the ruthless but effective Monti at centre-half, and the clever Stabile at centre-forward, duly won that group. Their match with Chile included a violent free-for-all, provoked by Monti.

Yugoslavia, beating Brazil 2-1 in their first match, also qualified. The brave Americans won their pool without conceding a goal, while Uruguay, too, kept their defence intact, though Peru ran them very close. This was the first match to be played at the new Centenary Stadium, which still wasn't ready when the competition started.

In the semi-finals, Argentina and Uruguay both had 6-1 wins, against the U.S.A. and Yugoslavia respectively. In the final, Uruguay had to take the field without their new star, the young centre-forward Anselmo, who was unfit. But Argentina's new man, Stabile, first capped in their opening game, was able to lead their attack.

The match took place on July 30, 1930. Uruguay deservedly won, but their team seemed to lack the confidence it had shown in the two Olympic successes. An argument about the ball led to each side playing one half with a ball of native manufacture. Argentina survived an early goal by Pablo Dorado, the Uruguayan outside-right, to lead 2-1 at half-time, through Peucelle and Stabile. But a splendid dribble by Pedro Cea was crowned by the equaliser, after which Iriarte and Castro made it 4-2. Montevideo went wild – the following day was a national holiday.

DETAILS

POOL I

France (3) 4, *Mexico* (0) 1
France: Thépot; Mattler, Capelle; Villaplane (capt.), Pinel, Chantrel; Liberati, Delfour, Maschinot, Laurent, Langiller.
Mexico: Bonfiglio; Guitierrez, R. (capt.), Rosas, M.; Rosas, F., Sanchez, Amezcua; Perez, Carreno, Mejia, Ruiz, Lopez.
Scorers: Laurent, Langiller, Maschinot (2) for France, Carreno for Mexico.

Argentina (0) 1, *France* (0) 0
Argentina: Bossio; Della Torre, Muttis; Suarez, Monti, Evaristo, J.;
Perinetti, Varallo, Ferreira (capt.), Cierra, Evaristo, M.
France: Thépot; Mattler, Capelle; Villaplane (capt.), Pinel, Chantrel;
Liberati, Delfour, Maschinot, Laurent, Langiller.
Scorer: Monti for Argentina.

Chile (1) 3, *Mexico* (0) 0
Chile: Cortes; Morales, Poirier; Torres, A., Saavedra, Helgueta; Ojeda,
Subiabre, Villalobos, Vidal, Schneeberger (capt.).
Mexico: Sota; Guitierrez, R. (capt.), Rosas, M.; Rosas, F., Sanchez,
Amezcua; Perez, Carreno, Ruiz, Gayon, Lopez.
Scorers: Vidal, Subiabre (2) for Chile.

Chile (0) 1, *France* (0) 0
Chile: Cortes; Ciaparro, Morales; Torres, A., Saavedra, Torres, C.;
Ojeda, Subiabre, Villalobos, Vidal, Schneeberger (capt.).
France: Thépot; Mattler, Capella; Chantrel, Delmer, Villaplane (capt.);
Liberati, Delfour, Pinel, Veinantie, Langiller.
Scorer: Subiabre for Chile.

Argentina (3) 6, *Mexico* (0) 3
Argentina: Bossio; Della Torre, Paternoster; Cividini, Zumelzu (capt.),
Orlandini; Peucelle, Varallo, Stabile, Demaria, Spadaro.
Mexico: Bonfiglio; Guitierrez, R. (capt.), Gutierrez, F.; Rosas, M.,
Sanchez, Rodriguez; Rosas, F., Lopez, Gayon, Carreno, Olivares.
Scorers: Stabile (3), Varallo (2), Zumelzu for Argentina, Lopez, Rosas,
F., Rosas, M., for Mexico.

Argentina (2) 3, *Chile* (1) 1
Argentina: Bossio; Della Torre, Paternoster; Evaristo, J., Monti,
Orlandini; Peucelle, Varallo, Stabile, Ferreira, Evaristo, M.
Chile: Cortes; Ciaparro, Morales; Torres, A., Saavedra, Torres, C.;
Arellanc, Subiabre (capt.), Villalobos, Vidal, Aguilera.
Scorers: Stabile (2), Evaristo, M. for Argentina, Subiabre for Chile.

POOL II
Yugoslavia (2) 2, *Brazil* (0) 1
Yugoslavia: Yavocic; Ivkovic (capt.), Milhailovic; Arsenievic, Stefan-
ovic, Djokic; Tirnanic, Marianovic, Beck, Vujadinovic, Seculic.
Brazil: Montiero; Costa, Gervasoni; Fonseca, Santos, Guidicelli;
Ribeiro, Braga, Patsuca, Neto, Pereira.
Scorers: Tirnanic, Beck for Yugoslavia, Neto for Brazil.

Yugoslavia (0) 4, *Bolivia* (0) 0
Yugoslavia: Yavocic; Ivkovic (capt.), Milhailovic; Arsenievic, Stefan-
ovic, Djokic; Tirnanic, Marianovic, Beck, Vujadinovic, Naidanovic.
Bolivia: Bermudez; Durandal, Civarria; Argote, Lara, Valderama;
Gomez, Bustamante, Mendez (capt.), Alborta, Fernandez.
Scorers: Beck (2), Marianovic, Vujadinovic for Yugoslavia.

Brazil (1) 4, *Bolivia* (0) 0
Brazil: Velloso; Gervasoni, Oliveira; Fonseca, Santos, Guidicelli; Meneses, Quieroz, Leite, Neto (capt.), Visintainer.
Bolivia: Bermudez; Durandal, Civarria; Sainz, Lara, Valderama; Oritiz, Bustamante, Mendez (capt.), Alborta, Fernandez.
Scorers: Visintainer (2), Neto (2) for Brazil.

POOL III
Rumania (1) 3, *Peru* (0) 1
Rumania: Lapuseanu; Steiner, Burger; Rafinski, Vogl (capt.), Eisembeisser; Covaci, Desu, Wetzer, Staucin, Barbu.
Peru: Valdivieso; De las Casas (capt.), Soria; Galindo, Garcia, Valle; Flores, Villanueva, Denegri, Neira, Souza.
Scorers: Staucin (2), Barbu for Rumania, Souza for Peru.

Uruguay 1, *Peru* 0 (0–0)
Uruguay: Ballesteros; Nasazzi (capt.), Tejera; Andrade, Fernandez, Gestido; Urdinaran, Castro, Petrone, Cea, Iriarte.
Peru: Pardon; De las Casas, Maquilon (capt.); Denegri, Galindo, Astengo; Lavalle, Flores, Villanueva, Neira, Souza.
Scorer: Castro for Uruguay.

Uruguay (4) 4, *Rumania* (0) 0
Uruguay: Ballesteros; Nasazzi (capt.), Mascheroni; Andrade, Fernandez, Gestido; Dorado, Scarone, Anselmo, Cea, Iriarte.
Rumania: Lapuseanu; Burger, Tacu; Robe, Vogl (capt.), Eisembeisser; Covaci, Desu, Wetzer, Rafinski, Barbu.
Scorers: Dorado, Scarone, Anselmo, Cea for Uruguay.

POOL IV
United States (2) 3, *Belgium* (0) 0
United States: Douglas; Wood, Moorhouse; Gallacher, Tracey, Brown; Gonsalvez, Florie (capt.), Patenaude, Auld, McGhee.
Belgium: Badjou; Nouwens, Hoydonckx; Braine (capt.), Hellemans, De Clercq; Diddens, Moeschal, Adams, Voorhoof, Versijp.
Scorers: McGhee (2), Patenaude for U.S.A.

United States (2) 3, *Paraguay* (0) 0
United States: Douglas; Wood, Moorhouse; Gallacher, Tracey, Auld; Brown, Gonsalvez, Patenaude, Florie (capt.), McGhee.
Paraguay: Denis; Olmedo, Miracca; Etcheverri, Diaz, Aguirre; Nessi, Romero, Dominguez, Gonzales, Carceres, Pena (capt.).
Scorers: Patenaude (2), Florie for U.S.A.

Paraguay (1) 1, *Belgium* (0) 0
Paraguay: Benitez, P.; Olmedo, Flores; Benitez, S., Diaz, Garcete; Nessi, Romero, Gonzales, Carceres, Pena (capt.).

Belgium: Badjou; De Deken, Hoydonckx; Braine (capt.), Hellemans, Moeschal; Versijp, Delbeke, Adams, Nouwens, Diddens.
Scorer: Pena for Paraguay.

Placings	Pool I						Goals
	P	W	D	L	F	A	Pts.
Argentina	3	3	0	0	10	4	6
Chile	3	2	0	1	5	3	4
France	3	1	0	2	4	3	2
Mexico	3	0	0	3	4	13	0
	Pool II						
Yugoslavia	2	2	0	0	6	1	4
Brazil	2	1	0	1	5	2	2
Bolivia	2	0	0	2	0	8	0
	Pool III						
Uruguay	2	2	0	0	5	0	4
Rumania	2	1	0	1	3	5	2
Peru	2	0	0	2	1	4	0
	Pool IV						
United States	2	2	0	0	6	0	4
Paraguay	2	1	0	1	1	3	2
Belgium	2	0	0	2	0	4	0

SEMI-FINALS

Argentina (1) 6, *United States* (0) 1
Argentina: Botasso; Della Torre, Paternoster; Evaristo, J., Monti, Orlandini; Peucelle, Scopelli, Stabile, Ferreira (capt.), Evaristo, M.
U.S.A.: Douglas; Wood, Moorhouse; Gallacher, Tracey, Auld; Brown, Gonsalvez, Patenaude, Florie (capt.), McGhee.
Scorers: Monti; Scopelli, Stabile (2), Peucelle (2) for Argentina. Brown for U.S.A.

Uruguay (3) 6, *Yugoslavia* (1) 1
Uruguay: Ballesteros; Nasazzi (capt.), Mascheroni; Andrade, Fernandez, Gestido; Dorado, Scarone, Anselmo, Cea, Iriarte.
Yugoslavia: Yavocic; Ivkovic (capt.), Milhailovic; Arsenievic, Stefanovic, Djokic; Tirnanic, Marianovic, Beck, Vujadinovic, Seculic.
Scorers: Cea (3), Anselmo (2), Iriarte for Uruguay, Seculic for Yugoslavia.

FINAL

Uruguay (1) 4, *Argentina* (2) 2
Uruguay: Ballesteros; Nasazzi (capt.), Mascheroni; Andrade, Fernandez, Gestido; Dorado, Scarone, Castro, Cea, Iriarte.

Argentina: Botasso; Della Torre, Paternoster; Evaristo, J., Monti, Suarez; Eucelle, Varallo, Stabile, Ferreira (capt.), Evaristo, M.
Scorers: Dorado, Cea, Iriarte, Castro for Uruguay, Peucelle, Stabile for Argentina.
Leading scorer: Stabile (Argentina) 8.

WORLD CUP, 1934 – Italy

The 1934 World Cup was altogether more representative and better attended, even though Uruguay, piqued by the way the European powers had snubbed them, stayed away and Argentina, fearful to lose more of their stars to Italian clubs, did not take part at full strength. Eight FIFA conferences were needed before Italy was chosen as the host. It had been realised that future World Cups could no longer be played in a single city nor could they be put on by any but a wealthy football federation. Italy, whose Fascist government looked on the powerful national team as a fine instrument of propaganda, eagerly put forward her claims. "The ultimate purpose of the tournament," said General Vaccaro, a political appointment as President of the Italian federation (FIGC), "was to show that Fascist sport partakes of a great quality of the ideal."

"Italy wanted to win," wrote the Belgian referee, John Langenus, "it was natural. But they allowed it to be seen too clearly."

Italy's remarkable team manager, Vittorio Pozzo, drew from the inflated, martial spirit of the times the authority and inspiration to build a fine team. It contained three Argentinians – Monti, Guaita and Orsi – of Italian extraction, whose inclusion Pozzo justified on the grounds that they would have been eligible to fight for Italy in the first world war. "If they were able to die for Italy, they could certainly play for Italy."

His team pivoted round a strong, attacking centre-half in Monti; had a splendid goalkeeper in Combi; a powerful defence, and a clever attack in which Meazza, one of the most gifted Italian forwards of all time, figured as a "striking" inside-right.

Austria, Italy's great rivals, were a tired team, and their equally gifted manager, Hugo Meisl, was convinced they could not win the tournament. Nevertheless in Seszta, their rugged left-back, Smistik, the roving centre-half, and Sindelar, the brilliantly elusive, ball-playing centre-forward, they had players of world class. The previous February Austria's *wunderteam* had beaten Italy 4–2, in Turin.

Hungary and Spain were the strongest "outsiders". Hungary had a fine centre-forward in Dr. Georges Sarosi, later to become an attacking centre-half. Their technique was brilliant, but their finishing poor. Both they and the Czechs had beaten England 2–1, on England's May tour of Europe. Spain had their great veteran, Ricardo Zamora, in goal, and the excellent Quincoces at left-back. The Czechs had an equally famous and experienced goalkeeper in Planicka and a smooth, clever forward-line.

Then there was Germany, playing a rigid third-back game, captained by the blond and versatile Franz Szepan.

Italy kicked off in Rome with an easy win against the U.S.A., fielding only three of their 1930 team. The surprise of the first round was France's excellent performance against Austria in Turin. As in 1930, the French rose to the occasion. They nearly scored in the first minute when Seszta's mistake was brilliantly retrieved by Peter Platzer, Austria's goalkeeper, and would probably have won, had it not been for an injury to Nicolas, their captain and centre-forward, who had to go on the wing. He scored almost at once, but that was virtually his last contribution. Despite the handicap, France dominated the second half, and it was only a doubtful goal by Schall, in extra-time – he looked offside – which really beat them. In later years, Schall himself said it was offside.

Germany, beating Belgium in Florence, looked uninspired; only Szepan, at centre-half, rose above mediocrity. The Czechs were another disappointment, needing two fine saves by Planicka to survive against the Rumanians, in Trieste, Egypt gave Hungary a fright at Naples, going down 4–2, and both South American challengers went out at once, Brazil to Spain, Argentina to Sweden.

In the second round in Florence, a marvellous exhibition of goalkeeping by Zamora enabled Spain to hold Italy to a 1–1 draw, but so roughly was he handled in a feebly refereed match that he could not take part in the replay. This was still more lamentably refereed, so much so that the Swiss official, Mercet, was suspended by his own Federation. Italy got through, thanks to a goal by Meazza, in a game that left a very nasty aftertaste.

The other match of the second round was that which opposed the classical Danubian rivals, Hungary and Austria. "It was a brawl," said Meisl, "not an exhibition of football." He brought the lively Horwath into his attack, and Horwath rewarded him with a goal after only seven minutes. Markos, Hungary's outside-right, was sent off, soon after Sarosi (on a poor day) had got Hungary's only goal from a penalty. The Austrians just about deserved their 2–1 win. Germany beat a Swedish team reduced for most of the match to ten men, and the Czechs beat Switzerland 3–2 in Turin, in the most thrilling match of the round. Nejedly got the winning goal seven minutes from the end.

The semi-finals pitted Italy against Austria in Milan, Germany against Czechoslovakia in Rome. Italy deservedly got through, on a muddy ground, thanks to a goal by Guaita after 18 minutes, showing amazing stamina after their hard replay against Spain, only two days before. Austria did not have a shot until the 42nd minute.

The Czechs, surviving the trauma of a ridiculous equalising goal, when Planicka inexplicably let the ball sail over his head, were much too clever for the Germans, and beat them 3–1. Thus, they would meet Italy in the Final.

Meanwhile, in the third place match, a dejected Austrian team surprisingly went down 3–2 at Naples to the plodding Germans, who scored in 24 seconds.

Fortified by gargantuan presents of food, the Czechs gave Italy a tremendous run for their money in the Final. Short passing cleverly, making use of Puc's thrust on the left wing, with Planicka at his best in goal, they had slightly the better of the first half. Twenty minutes from time, Puc took a corner, and when the ball came back to him, drove it past Combi for the first goal.

Czechoslovakia should have clinched it, then. Sobotka missed a fine chance, Svoboda hit the post. Then Guaita and Schiavio switched, the Italian attack began to move better, and a freak goal by Orsi equalised. His curling, right-footed shot swerved in the air, and went over Planicka's hands. Next day, in practice, he tried twenty times, without success, to repeat it.

In the seventh minute of extra time, the injured Meazza got the ball on the wing, centred to Guaita, and the ball was moved on to Schiavio, who scored. Italy had done it, with little to spare. Neutral experts believed that home ground, frenzied support, the consequent intimidation of referees, may have been decisive. Nevertheless, theirs was a fine splendidly fit and dedicated team.

FIRST ROUND

Italy (3) 7, *U.S.A.* (0) 1. *Rome*
Italy: Combi; Rosetta (capt), Allemandi; Pizziolo, Monti, Bertolini; Guarisi, Meazza, Schiavio, Ferrari, Orsi.
U.S.A.: Hjulian; Czerchiewicz, Moorhouse (capt.); Pietras, Gonsalvez, Florie, Ryan, Nilsen, Donelli, Dick, Maclean.
Scorers: Schiavio (3), Orsi (2), Meazza, Ferrari for Italy, Donelli for U.S.A.

Czechoslovakia (0) 2, *Rumania* (1) 1. *Trieste*
Czechoslovakia: Planicka (capt.); Zenisek, Ctyroky; Kostalek, Cambal, Krcil; Junek, Silny, Sobotka, Nejedly, Puc.
Rumania: Zambori; Vogl, Albu; Deheleanu, Cotormani (capt.), Moravet; Bindea, Covaci, Depi, Bodola, Dobai.
Scorers: Puc, Nejedly for Czechoslovakia, Dobai for Rumania.

Germany (1) 5, *Belgium* (2) 2. *Florence*
Germany: Kress; Haringer, Schwarz; Janes, Szepan (capt.), Zielinksi; Lehner, Hohmann, Conen, Siffling, Kobierski.
Belgium: Van de Weyer; Smellinckx, Joacim; Peeraer, Welkenhuyzen (capt.), Klaessens; Devries, Voorhoof, Capelle, Grimmonprez, Herremans.
Scorers: Voorhoof (2) for Belgium, Conen (3), Kobierski (2) for Germany.

Austria (1) 3, *France* (1) 2 (1–1) after extra time. *Turin*
Austria: Platzer; Cisar, Seszta; Wagner, Smistik (capt.), Urbanek; Zischek, Bican, Sindelar, Schall, Viertel.

France: Thépot; Mairesse, Mattler; Delfour, Verriest, Llense; Keller, Alcazar, Nicolas (capt.), Rio, Aston.
Scorers: Nicolas, Verriest (penalty) for France, Sindelar, Schall, Bican for Austria.

Spain (3) 3, *Brazil* (1) 1. *Genoa*
Spain: Zamora (capt.); Ciriaco, Quincoces; Cillauren, Muguerza, Marculeta; Lafuente, Iraragorri, Langara, Lecue, Gorostiza.
Brazil: Pedrosa; Mazzi, Luz; Tinoco, Zaccone, Canilli; Oliviera, De Britto, Leonidas, Silva, Bartesko.
Scorers: Iraragorri (penalty), Langara (2) for Spain, Silva for Brazil.

Switzerland (2) 3, *Holland* (1) 2. *Milan*
Switzerland: Sechehaye; Minelli, Weiler (capt.); Guinchard, Jaccard, Hufschmid; Von Kaenel, Passello, Kielholz, Abegglen III, Bossi.
Holland: Van der Meulen; Weber, Van Run; Rellikaan, Andeniesen (capt.), Van Heel; Wels, Vente, Bakhuijs, Smit, Van Nellen.
Scorers: Kielholz (2), Abegglen III for Switzerland, Smit, Vente for Holland.

Sweden (1) 3, *Argentina* (1) 2. *Bologna*
Sweden: Rydberg; Axelsson, Andersson, S.; Carlsson, Rosen (capt.), Andersson, E.; Dunker, Gustafsson, Jonasson, Keller, Kroon.
Argentina: Freschi; Pedevilla, Belis; Nehin, Sosa-Urbieta, Lopez; Rua, Wilde, De Vincenzi (capt.), Galateo, Iraneta.
Scorers: Bellis, Galateo for Argentina, Jonasson (2), Kroon for Sweden.

Hungary (2) 4, *Egypt* (1) 2. *Naples*
Hungary: Szabo, A.; Futo, Sternberg; Palotas, Szucs, Lazar; Markos, Vincze, Teleky, Toldi, Szabo, F.
Egypt: Moustafa Kamel; Ali Caf, Hamitu; El Far, Refaat, Rayab; Latif, Fawzi, Muktar (capt.), Masoud Kamel, Hassan.
Scorers: Teleky, Toldi (2), Vincze for Hungary, Fawzi (2) for Egypt.

SECOND ROUND

Germany (1) 2, *Sweden* (0) 1. *Milan*
Germany: Kress; Haringer, Busch; Gramlich, Szepan (capt.), Zielinski; Lehner, Hohmann, Conen, Siffling, Kobierski.
Sweden: Rydberg; Axelsson, Andersson, S.; Carlsson, Rosen (capt.), Andersson, E.; Dunker, Jonasson, Gustafsson, Keller, Kroon.
Scorers: Hohmann (2) for Germany, Dunker for Sweden.

Austria (1) 2, *Hungary* (0) 1. *Bologna*
Austria: Platzer; Disar, Seszta; Wagner, Smistik (capt.), Urbanek; Zischek, Bican, Sindelar, Horwath, Viertel.
Hungary: Szabo, A.; Vago, Sternberg; Palotas, Szucs, Szalay; Markos, Avar, Sarosi, Toldi, Kemeny.
Scorers: Horwarth, Zischek for Austria, Sarosi (penalty) for Hungary.

Italy (0) 1, *Spain* (1) 1 after extra time. *Florence*
Italy: Combi (capt.); Monzeglio, Allemandi; Pizziolo, Monti, Castellazzi; Guaita, Meazza, Schiavio, Ferrari, Orsi.
Spain: Zamora (capt.); Ciriaco, Quincoces; Cillauren, Muguerza, Fede; Lafuente, Iraragorri, Langara, Regueiro, Gorostiza.
Scorers: Regueiro for Spain, Ferrari for Italy.

Italy (1) 1, *Spain* (0) 0. Replay. *Florence*
Italy: Combi (capt.); Monzeglio, Allemandi; Ferraris IV, Monti, Bertolini; Guaita, Meazza, Borel, De Maria, Orsi.
Spain: Noguet; Zabalo, Quincoces (capt.); Cillauren, Muguerza Lecue, Ventolra, Regueiro, Campanal, Chacho, Bosch.
Scorer: Meazza for Italy.

Czechoslovakia (1) 3, *Switzerland* (1) 2. *Turin*
Czechoslovakia: Planicka; Zenisek, Ctyroky; Kostalek, Cambal, Krcil; Junek, Svoboda, Sobotka, Nejedly, Puc.
Switzerland: Sechehaye; Minelli, Weiler; Guinchard, Jaccard, Hufschmid; Von Kaenel, Jaeggi IV, Kielholz, Abegglen III, Jaeck.
Scorers: Kielholz, Abegglen III for Switzerland, Svoboda, Sobotka, Nejedly for Czechoslovakia.

SEMI-FINALS

Czechoslovakia (1) 3, *Germany* (0) 1. *Rome*
Czechoslovakia: Planicka (capt.); Burger, Ctyroky; Kostalek, Cambal, Krcil; Junek, Svoboda, Sobotka, Nejedly, Puc.
Germany: Kress; Haringer, Busch; Zielinski, Szepan (capt.), Bender; Lehner, Siffling, Conen, Noack, Kobierski.
Scorers: Nejedly (2) Krcil for Czechoslovakia, Noack for Germany.

Italy (1) 1, *Austria* (0) 0. *Milan*
Italy: Combi (capt.); Monzeglio, Allemandi; Ferraris IV, Monti, Bertolini; Guaita, Meazza, Schiavio Ferrari, Orsi.
Austria: Platzer; Disar, Seszta; Wagner, Smistik (capt.), Urbanek; Zischek, Bican, Sindelar, Schall, Viertel.
Scorer: Guaita for Italy.

THIRD PLACE MATCH

Germany (3) 3, *Austria* (1) 2. *Naples*
Germany: Jakob; Janes, Busch; Zielinski, Muenzenberg, Bender; Lehner, Siffling, Conen, Szepan (capt.), Heidemann.
Austria: Platzer; Disar, Seszta; Wagner, Smistik (capt.), Urbanek; Zischek, Braun, Horwath, Viertel.
Scorers: Lehner (2), Conen for Germany, Horwath, Seszta for Austria.

FINAL

Italy (0) 2, *Czechoslovakia* (0) 1 after extra time. *Rome*
Italy: Combi (capt.); Monzeglio, Allemandi; Ferraris IV, Monti, Bertolini; Guaita, Meazza, Schiavio, Ferrari, Orsi.
Czechoslovakia: Planicka (capt.); Zenisek, Ctyroky; Kostalek, Cambal, Krcil; Junek, Svoboda, Sobotka, Nejedly, Puc.
Scorers: Orsi, Schiavio for Italy, Puc for Czechoslovakia.
Leading Scorers: Schiavio (Italy), Nejedly (Czechoslovakia), Conen (Germany) each 4.

WORLD CUP 1938 – France

Italy were the winners again, but this time their win was more convincing. For the first time, indeed, a host nation failed to take the World Cup. Pozzo himself has said that on grounds of pure football, his 1938 side was superior to the team of 1934. Only the inside-forwards, Meazza and Ferrari, survived from that eleven. Monti's place at centre-half had been taken by another South American, Andreolo, from Uruguay. Foni and Rava, full-backs in the successful Italian Olympic side of 1936, were now in the full national side. Olivieri, an excellent goalkeeper, was a fitting successor to Combi. At centre-forward, the tall, powerful Silvio Piola rivalled Meazza (and overhauled him in 1951!) as the most prolific Italian goalscorer of all time.

Argentina wanted to put on this World Cup, but the claims of France were preferred. Austria and Spain had to withdraw for political reasons, Uruguay, still worried by the crisis of professionalism (another factor in their refusal to compete in 1934) refused again to take part. So did Argentina – whose fans demonstrated their displeasure outside the offices of the Federation.

But Brazil, a much improved side, were there again, with the great Leonidas at centre-forward, and Da Guia at full-back. Sarosi was in great form for Hungary, who had not long since beaten the Czechs 8–3 – he had fine support from Szengeller, the 22-year-old inside-left. Planicka, Nejedly and Puc survived from the Czechs' 1934 team, and Germany, now under Sepp Herberger, was still recovering from a 6–3 home defeat by England. The Swiss looked strong.

In the first round, the hardest fought tie was that between Germany – England's victims – and Switzerland, who had beaten England 2–1 a few days later, in Zurich. The Germans fielded four Austrians in the first match, one of whom, the outside-left, Pesser, was sent off in extra time. Gauchel gave Germany the lead from Pesser's centre. Abegglen headed an equaliser, and extra time brought no more goals. The teams had a good five days to gird themselves for the replay. This time, Germany fielded three Austrians, and brought back their talented 1934 captain, Szepan, to play at inside-left. They went into a 2–0 lead – one from Hahnemann, an unlucky own goal by Loertscher, the Swiss left-half – at half-time. Wallasshek made it 1–2 early in the second half, but when the Swiss left-winger Aebi went off injured, the die seemed cast.

Not a bit of it. The Swiss held out till Aebi came back, Bickel equalised and Abegglen, the star of the match, rounded it off with two fine goals.

The greatest surprise was Cuba's defeat of Rumania, after a 3–3 draw in Toulouse. Half the Rumanian side had previous World Cup experience, three had played in Uruguay. But the Cubans played with great speed and *brio*, and were 3–2 ahead in extra time, when the Rumanians equalised. In the replay, they surprisingly dropped their star goalkeeper, Carvajales, who was brilliantly replaced by Ayra, and won, after being a goal down. The winner, according to the French linesman, was offside, but the German referee allowed it. What has happened to Cuban football since 1938? Obscurely, it has sunk without trace.

The Czechs, with four 1934 men, beat Holland 3–0 in Le Havre, but then needed extra time to do it, and were fortunate that Holland lacked Bakhuijs, their leading scorer. Two of the Czech goals came from their half-backs; the celebrated Nejedly got the other.

At Strasbourg, a marvellous match between Brazil and Poland ended at 4–4. Poland had had a fine season, culminating with a 6–1 win over Ireland, and victory by 4–1 aggregate over Yugoslavia, in the eliminators for the World Cup. Their inside-forward, Ernest Willimowski, was one of the most talented in Europe, and a notable goalscorer. Brazil had six players making their international début. Their magnificent centre-forward Leonidas, the Black Diamond, did the hat-trick for them in the first half, but in the second, the Polish half-backs took control, and ordinary time ended at 4–4. In extra time, Leonidas and Willimowski each got his fourth goal, but another by Romeo, for Brazil, was decisive – 6–5.

In Marseilles, Italy got the shock of their lives from little Norway. Within two minutes, Ferrari had given Italy the lead, but Norway tightened their grip on Piola and their own centre-forward, the powerful Brunyldsen, gave Andreolo a terrible time of it. Three times the Italian posts and bar were hit; at others Olivieri saved them. In the second half, Brustand, an excellent left-winger, made it 1–1, but Piola eventually got the winner from a rebound.

Pozzo, however, revived his team's morale, and in the next round they won comfortably, 3–1 against France in Paris, before 58,000 spectators, the biggest crowd of that World Cup. Foni replaced Monzeglio at right-back, and Biavati, the winger with the fluttering foot, took over from Paserati.

For France, Delfour and Mattler were playing their third World Cup, the star was Piola. His two goals in the second half won the game, after France had rashly thrown themselves into attack.

Sweden, exempt from the first round, managed by Nagy, a Hungarian, and smarting from their humiliation by Japan in the last

Olympiad, put an end to the Cuban illusion, winning 8–0. Torre Keller, their 35-year-old right-half and captain, was celebrating fourteen years of international competition. The fair-haired right-winger, Gustav Wetterstroem, was, however, the chief destroyer. Four of the goals were his.

In Lille, a tired Swiss team lost 2–0 to a technically superior Hungary; the Swiss felt the lack of Minelli and Aebi.

In Bordeaux, where the new municipal stadium was inaugurated, Czechoslovakia, 1934 finalists, played Brazil the now joint favourites with Italy. It was a holocaust; three players sent off, two Brazilians and a Czech while Planicka with a broken arm, and Nejedly, with a broken leg, finished in hospital. Zeze, violently kicking Nejedly, for no apparent reason – and getting himself sent off – began it. Leonidas gave Brazil the lead, Nejedly equalised from a penalty in the second half, and the depleted Czechs held out against the nine-man Brazilians, in extra time.

Curiously enough, the replay was conducted in the mildest of climates. The Brazilians made nine changes, the Czechs six. The Czechs led at half-time through the energetic Kopecky, moved up to the attack, but they badly missed the passing of Nejedly. Worse, Kopecky had to leave the field injured, a shot by Senecky seemed to be over the line before the Brazilian 'keeper cleared it – and Leonidas was at his best. He it was who equalised and Roberto got the winning goal.

In the semi-finals, Brazil paid the penalty for over-confidence, inexplicably omitting Leonidas and the brilliant Tim, against the Italians at Marseilles, and Colaussi scored the opening goal and Meazza clinched the game from a penalty after Domingas had rashly fouled Piola. Thus it was 2–0, and Romeo's goal for Brazil had no real significance. For all his folly, Domingas had impressed Pozzo as "one of the greatest defenders one is likely to meet."

In the other semi-final, Hungary thrashed Sweden 5–1 in Paris. Nyberg got a 35-second goal for Sweden, but the Hungarians took it in their stride. They were 3–1 up by half-time – two for Szengeller – and he and Sarosi added goals in the second half. There could have been many more.

Sweden again took the lead in the third place match, at Bordeaux, and led 2–1 against Brazil at half-time. Then Leonidas turned it on, scored two goals, and Brazil won 4–2.

On June 19, at the Stade Colombes, the Hungarians played graceful, short-passing football, the Italians showed rhythm and bite. Again, Colaussi got the first goal. Sarosi equalised within a minute – he was Hungary's great hope – but Meazza, getting too much room all the while, made one for Piola, and Italy led 2–1. By half-time Colaussi, put through by Meazza, had scored again – 3–1.

In the second half, Sarosi got another in a scramble, but the Italian defence was in control. Colaussi was too fast for Polgar, while Biavati and Piola were too quick for the whole defence when Piola scored from Biavati's ultimate back-heel. A swift, strong, ruthless team had kept Italy the World Cup.

FIRST ROUND

Switzerland (1) 1, *Germany* (1) 1 after extra time. *Paris*
Switzerland: Huber; Minelli (capt.), Lehmann; Springer, Vernati, Loertscher; Amado, Wallaschek, Bickel, Abegglen III, Abei.
Germany: Raftl; Janes, Schnaus; Kupfer, Mock (capt.), Kitzinger; Lehner, Gellesch, Geuchel, Hahnemann, Pesser.
Scorers: Gauchel for Germany, Abegglen III for Switzerland.

Switzerland (0) 4, *Germany* (2) 2 Replay. *Paris* (Parc des Princes)
Switzerland: Huber; Minelli (capt.), Lehmann; Springer, Vernati, Loertscher; Amado, Abegglen III, Bickel, Wallaschek, Abei.
Germany: Raftl; Janes, Strietel; Kupfer, Goldbrunner, Skoumal; Lehner, Stroh, Hahnemann, Szepan (capt.), Haumer.
Scorers: Hahnemann, Loertscher own goal for Germany, Wallaschek, Bickel, Abegglen III (2) for Switzerland.

Cuba (0) 3, *Rumania* (1) 3 after extra time. *Toulouse*
Cuba: Cavajeles; Barquin, Chorens (capt.); Arias, Rodriquez, Berges; Maquina, Fernandez, Socorro, Tunas, Sosa.
Rumania: Palovici; Burger, Chiroiu; Vintila, Rasinaru (capt.), Rafinski; Bindea, Covaci, Baratki, Bodola, Dobai.
Scorers: Covaci, Baratki, Dobai for Rumania, Tunas, Maquina, Sosa for Cuba.

Cuba (0) 2, *Rumania* (1) 1 Replay. *Toulouse*
Cuba: Ayra; Barquin, Chorens (capt.); Arias, Rodriquez, Berges; Maquina, Fernandez, Socorro, Tunas, Sosa.
Rumania: Sadowski; Burger, Felecan; Barbulescu, Rasinaru, Rafinski; Bogden, Moldoveanu, Baratki, Pranzler, Dobai.
Scorers: Dobai for Rumania, Socorro, Maquina for Cuba.

Hungary (4) 6, *Dutch East Indies* (0) 0. *Reims*
Hungary: Hada; Koranyi, Biro; Lazar, Turai, Balogh; Sas, Szengeller, Sarosi (capt.), Toldi, Kohut.
Dutch East Indies: Mo Heng; Hu Kom, Samuels; Nawir, Meng (capt.), Anwar; Hang Djin, Soedarmadji, Sommers, Pattiwael, Taihuttu.
Scorers: Kohut, Tolid, Sarosi (2), Szengeller (2) for Hungary.

France (2) 3, *Belgium* (1) 1. *Paris, Colombes*
France: Di Lorto; Czenave, Mattler (capt.); Bastien, Jordan, Diagne; Aston, Heisserer, Nicolas, Delfour, Vienante.
Belgium: Badjou; Pavrick (capt.), Sayes; Van Alphen, Stynen, De Winter; Van de Wouwer, Voorhoof, Isemborghs, Braine, R., Byle.
Scorers: Vienante, Nicolas (2) for France, Isemborghs for Belgium.

Czechoslovakia (0) 3, *Holland* (0) 0 after extra time. *Le Havre*
Czechoslovakia: Planicka; Berger, Daucik; Kostalek, Boucek (capt.), Kopecky; Riha, Simunek, Zeman, Nejedly, Puc.

Holland: Van Male; Weber, Caldenhove; Pawae, Anderiesen, (capt.), Van Heel; Wels, Van der Veen, Smit, Vente, De Harder.
Scorers: Kostalek, Boucek, Nejedly for Czechoslovakia.

Brazil (3) 6, *Poland* (1) 5 after extra time. *Strasbourg*
Brazil: Batatoes; Domingas Da Guia, Machados; Zeze, Martin (capt.), Alfonsinho; Lopez, Romeo, Leonidas, Peracio, Hercules.
Poland: Madejski; Szcepaniak, Galecki; Gora, Nytz (capt.), Dytko; Piec I, Piontek, Szerfke, Willimowski, Wodarz.
Scorers: Leonidas (4), Peracio, Romeo for Brazil, Willimowski (4), Piontek for Poland.

Italy (1) 2, *Norway* (0) 1 after extra time. *Marseilles*
Italy: Olivieri; Monzeglio, Rava; Serantoni, Andreolo, Locatelli; Paserati, Meazza (capt.), Piola, Ferrari, Ferraris.
Norway: Johansen, H.; Johansen, R. (capt.), Holmsen; Henriksen, Eriksen, Homberg; Frantzen, Kwammen, Brunylden, Isaksen, Brustad.
Scorers: Ferrari, Piola for Italy, Brustad for Norway.

SECOND ROUND

Sweden (4) 8, *Cuba* (0) 0. *Antibes*
Sweden: Abrahamson; Eriksson, Kjellgren; Almgren, Jacobsson. Svanstroem; Wetterstroem, Keller, Andersson H., Jonasson, Nyberg.

Cuba: Carvajeles; Barquin, Chorens; Arias, Rodriquez, Berges; Ferrer, Fernandez, Socorro, Tunas, Alonzo.
Scorers: Andersson, Wetterstroem (4), Jonasson, Nyberg, Keller for Sweden.

Hungary (1) 2, *Switzerland* (0) 0. *Lille*
Hungary: Szabo; Koranyi, Biro; Szalay, Turai, Lazar; Sas, Vincze, Sarosi (capt.), Szengeller, Kohut.
Switzerland: Huber; Stelzer, Lehmann (capt.); Springer, Vernati, Loertscher; Amado, Wallaschek, Bickel, Abegglen III, Grassi.
Scorers: Szengeller (2) for Hungary.

Italy (1) 3, *France* (1) 1. *Paris, Colombes*
Italy: Olivieri; Foni, Rava; Serantoni, Andreolo, Locatelli; Biavati, Meazza (capt.), Piola, Ferrari, Colaussi.
France: Di Lorto; Czenave, Mattler (capt.); Bastien, Jordan, Diagne; Aston, Heisserer, Nicolas, Delfour, Vienante.
Scorers: Colaussi, Piola (2) for Italy, Heisserer for France.

Brazil (1) 1, *Czechoslovakia* (1) 1 after extra time. *Bordeaux*
Brazil: Walter; Domingas Da Guia, Machados; Zeze, Martin (capt.) Alfonsinho; Lopez, Romeo, Leonidas, Peracio, Hercules.
Czechoslovakia: Planicka; Berger, Daucik; Kostalek, Bocek (capt.), Kopecky; Riha, Simunek, Ludl, Nejedly, Puc.
Scorers: Leonidas for Brazil, Nejedly (penalty) for Czechoslovakia.

Brazil (0) 2, *Czechoslovakia* (1) 1 replay. *Bordeaux*
Brazil: Walter; Jahu, Nariz; Britto, Brandao (capt.), Algemiro; Roberto, Luisinho, Leonidas, Tim, Patesko.
Czechoslovakia: Burkert; Berger, Daucik; Kostalek, Bocek (capt.), Ludl; Horak, Senecky, Kreutz, Kopecky, Rulc.
Scorers: Kopecky for Czechoslovakia, Leonidas, Roberto for Brazil.

SEMI-FINALS

Italy (2) 2, *Brazil* (0) 1. *Marseilles*
Italy: Olivieri; Foni, Rava; Serantoni, Andreolo, Locatelli; Biavati, Meazza (capt.), Piola, Ferrari, Colaussi.
Brazil: Walter; Domingas, Da Guia, Machados; Zeze, Martin (capt.), Alfonsinho; Lopez, Luisinho, Peracio, Romeo, Patesko.
Scorers: Colaussi, Meazza (penalty) for Italy, Romeo for Brazil.

Hungary (3) 5, *Sweden* (1) 1. *Paris, Colombes*
Hungary: Szabo; Koranyi, Biro; Szalay, Turai, Lazar; Sas, Szengeller, Sarosi (capt.), Toldi, Titkos.
Sweden: Abrahamson; Eriksson, Kjellgren; Almgren, Jacobsson, Svanstroem; Wetterstroem, Keller (capt.), Andersson H., Jonasson, Nyberg.
Scorers: Szengeller (3), Titkos, Sarosi for Hungary, Nyberg for Sweden.

THIRD PLACE MATCH

Brazil (1) 4, *Sweden* (2) 2. *Bordeaux*
Brazil: Batatoes; Domingas Da Guia, Machados; Zeze, Brandao, Alfonsinho; Roberto, Romeo, Leonidas (capt.), Peracio, Patesko.
Sweden: Abrahamson; Eriksson, Nilssen; Almgren, Linderholm, Svanstroem (capt.); Berssen, Andersson H., Jonasson, Andersson, A., Nyberg.
Scorers: Jonasson, Nyberg for Sweden, Romeo, Leonidas (2), Peracio for Brazil.

FINAL

Italy (3) 4, *Hungary* (1) 2. *Paris, Colombes*
Italy: Olivieri; Foni, Rava; Serantoni, Andreolo, Locatelli; Biavati, Meazza (capt.), Piola, Ferrari, Colaussi.
Hungary: Szabo; Polgar, Biro; Szalay, Szucs, Lazar; Sas, Vincze, Sarosi (capt.), Szengeller, Titkos.
Scorers: Colaussi (2), Piola (2) for Italy, Titkos, Sarosi for Hungary.

WORLD CUP 1950 – Brazil

The first World Cup for twelve years, the first since the outbreak of war, was in many ways the most vivid and impassioned yet. If Brazil were the moral victors, Uruguay's success was a marvellous anticlimax, emphasising the uncertainties of the game. Certainly the Uruguayans were most fortunate to have their qualifying pool reduced to a single, ludicrous match against Bolivia – but in the Final the defensive prowess of Varela, Andrade and Maspoli, and the counter-attacking of Schiaffino and Ghiggia, were worthy of success.

For the first – and so far last – time the competition was organised on the curious basis of four qualifying pools and a final pool. Again, there were several distinguished absentees; Austria, Hungary, Czechoslovakia, Argentina. The Austrians, who seem to suffer from a periodic inferiority complex (they were to withdraw again in 1962) said quaintly that their team was too inexperienced – and then proceeded to beat Italy in Vienna. Russia stayed out, and Germany were still excluded from FIFA. But the British countries took part for the first time, their own International Championship charitably being recognised as a qualifying group, in which the first two would go through to the finals. Scotland, with baffling insularity and pique, decided that if they did not win the title they would not go to Brazil. England beat them 1–0 at Hampden – and they stayed at home to sulk.

England and Brazil were the favourites; Brazil as talented hosts, England for, presumably, historical reasons. Their chances were diminished by the withdrawal of Neil Franklin, their gifted centre-half, who flew off to play in Bogota, Colombia, then unregistered with FIFA. Injuries had blunted the edge of the gallant Mortensen, a splendid opportunist, but there were still such giants as Matthews, Finney, Williams, Ramsey, Mannion. In retrospect, the team looks better than one felt it to be in prospect.

Brazil approached the tournament with all the intense dedication shown by Uruguay in 1930 – and Italy in 1934. Managed by Flavio Costa, a lean, intense man with the inevitable South American moustache, they took up monastic residence in a house just outside Rio, with vitamin drinks, ten o'clock curfew and a ban on wives. Local firms accoutred the house for nothing. There were two doctors, two masseurs, three chefs.

The massive Maracana Stadium – shades of Uruguay in 1930 – was still being completed (capacity 200,000) when the teams arrived – and when they left. Its seats had been painted blue; allegedly a pacifying colour.

France, angered by the amount of travelling they would have to do, withdrew at the last moment; this, after having been eliminated, then invited to take the place of Turkey, another country that withdrew. Though the French attitude was hardly defensible, there's no doubt that the travelling arrangements strongly favoured Brazil. So did the thin air of Rio.

Brazil kicked off against Mexico in a stadium that was still no more than an ambitious shambles. Brazil won 2–0, both goals coming from their lithe and brilliant centre-forward, Ademir. In São Paulo, a brave Swedish team sprang the first surprise of the competition by beating Italy. George Raynor, their clever little Yorkshire coach, had brilliantly rebuilt an Olympic winning team pillaged of its stars by – the Italians. In Nacka Skoglund and Kalle Palmer, he had unearthed two delicate and subtle inside-forwards, flanking a powerful leader in the fair-haired Hasse Jeppson who completely mastered the great Carlo Parola. Italy had picked a strange team with Campatelli, a veteran left-half, at inside-left – after three years out of the national side. Carapallese, the Italian captain and outside-left, gave them the lead before a crowd that was full of Italo-Brazilians, but the hefty Knud Nordahl dominated Gino Cappello, their centre-forward. Jeppson equalised, Andersson gave Sweden the lead with a long shot, and a mistake in the second half by Sentimenti IV, in goal, allowed Jeppson to clinch it. Muccinelli pulled back a goal, Carapellese hit the bar – but that was as near as Italy could get.

In the other matches, the United States roused echoes of 1930 by leading Spain at half-time, fighting gallantly, and going down only by 3–1. Spain, with fine wingers in Basora and Gainza, and a tough centre-forward in Zarra, were greatly surprised. At the hard little Belo Horizonte ground, Yugoslavia easily beat Switzerland, with Cjaicowski, at right-half, Mitic and Bobek, at inside-forward, standing out for their skill.

England's win against Chile, in Rio, was laboured, but in their next match they suffered one of the greatest humiliations in world football history; they were beaten 1–0 by the United States in Belo Horizonte. So casually did the Americans take the game that most of them were up till the small hours. Everything seemed set for England; crisp mountain air; a British mining firm to put them up; a forward line of stars. But gallant defence by Borghi, in goal, Colombo at centre-half, and Eddie McIlvenny, a Scotsman discarded eighteen months earlier by Third Division Wrexham on a free transfer, held them out; and after 37 minutes America scored. Gaetjens got his head to a cross by Bahr, to beat Williams; and all England's pressure could not bring an equaliser. Did Mullen's header from Ramsey's free kick cross Borghi's line? Perhaps; but America deserved their win for their courage.

In São Paulo, Brazil, too, faltered; held to a 2–2 draw by little Switzerland, who equalised two minutes from the end. Costa had picked a team full of *paulistas*, to flatter São Paulo, and the gesture had very nearly been expensive.

Italy beat Paraguay, who had drawn with Sweden, but the die was cast. Brazil, who had to beat Yugoslavia, conquerors of Mexico, in Rio, to qualify, got through by the skin of their teeth. Indeed, had it not been for a wretchedly unlucky head injury to Mitic, on a steel girder outside the dressing-room, who knows what might have happened?

In the third minute, Ademir took a pass from the splendid right-half, Bauer, and opened the score. Yugoslavia, however, gave as good as they got. Cjaicowski II missed a fine chance to equalise, Bauer found the inimitable Zizinho – playing his first game of the tournament – and the inside-right wriggled through to clinch a difficult game. The Brazilians, playing "diagonal" defence with a wandering centre-half and half-backs on the flanks, had made heavy weather of qualifying. Uruguay, 8–0 conquerors of Bolivia, had no trouble at all.

As for England, they went down 1–0 to Spain (a goal headed by Zarra) in Rio, and that was the end of them. Changes brought in Eddie Baily of Spurs at inside-left, Stanley Matthews on the right wing, Jackie Milburn at centre-forward, but the forward-line was still dogged by bad luck, and when Milburn did get the ball in the net, he was very dubiously given offside. Chile, winning 5–2 against the United States, emphasised England's shame.

In their first matches of the final pool, Brazil played some of the finest football that has ever graced the World Cup. Their inside-forward trio of Zizinho, Ademir and Jair, with its pyrotechnical ball play, its marvellous understanding, was practically unstoppable, and Bauer gave it marvellous support. Raynor planned for Sweden to get an early goal, but two early chances went begging, and after that Brazil swept them aside. It was sheer execution. A second-half penalty by Andersson was the most Sweden could do against seven Brazilian goals, four of them Ademir's.

Spain went the same way, giving one goal less away. This time Jair and Chico got two each, Ademir did not score. Meanwhile Spain had held Uruguay to a bad-tempered 2–2 draw, Basora getting two more goals, despite the marking of Andrade. It seemed doubtful indeed whether the Uruguayans, bogeys of Brazil though they were, could hold them this time, when they were under full sail.

Against Sweden, in São Paulo, the Uruguayans scraped through 3–2, after being a goal down at half-time. Skoglund's off day and a bad foul by M. Gonzales on Johnsson – not to mention Uruguay's far easier programme – weighed against Sweden in the second half.

Thus to the deciding match, played before 200,000 impassioned fans at the Maracana; a match which Brazil had only to draw to take the World Cup. For three-quarters of an hour they pounded a superb Uruguayan defence, brilliantly marshalled by their veteran centre-half, Obdulio Varela. Not till two minutes after half-time did Friaça meet a cross from the left to beat the astonishing Maspoli. Then Uruguay began to hit back, Varela turned to the attack, and after 20 minutes sent the fragile Ghiggia away on the right. Tall, pale, slender Juan Schiaffino controlled his centre, unmarked, advanced, shot – and scored. Eleven minutes from time, Ghiggia took a return from Perez, ran on, and scored the winner.

Sweden, beating Spain 3–1 with a sudden late show of life, bravely took third place. And Brazil had to wait another eight years for ultimate satisfaction.

POOL I

Brazil (1) 4, *Mexico* (0) 0. *Rio*
Brazil: Barbosa; Augusto (capt.), Juvenal; Eli, Danilo, Bigode; Meneca, Ademir, Baltazar, Jair, Friaça.
Mexico: Carbajal; Zetter, Montemajor; Ruiz, Ochoa, Roca; Septien, Ortis, Casarin, Perez, Velasquez (capt.).
Scorers: Ademir (2), Jair, Baltazar for Brazil.

Yugoslavia (3) 3, *Switzerland* (0) 0. *Belo Horizonte*
Yugoslavia: Mrkusic; Horvat, Stankovic; Cjaicowski I (capt.), Jovanovic, Djaic; Ognanov, Mitic, Tomasevic, Bobek, Vukas.
Switzerland: Corrodi; Gyger, Rey; Bocquet, Eggimann, Neury; Bickel (capt.), Antenen, Tamini, Bader, Fatton.
Scorers: Tomasevic (2), Ognanov for Yugoslavia.

Yugoslavia (2) 4, *Mexico* (0) 1. *Porto Alegre*
Yugoslavia: Mrkusic; Horvat, Stankovic; Cjaicowski I (capt.), Jovanovic, Djaic; Mihailovic, Mitic, Tomasevic, Bobek, Cjaicowski II
Mexico: Carbajal; Gutierrez, Ruiz; Gomez, Ochao, Ortiz; Flores, Naranjo, Casarin, Perez, Velasquez (capt.).
Scorers: Bobek, Cjaicowski II (2), Tomasevic for Yugoslavia, Casarin for Mexico.

Brazil (2) 2, *Switzerland* (1) 2. *São Paulo*
Brazil: Barbosa; Augusto (capt.), Juvenal; Bauer, Ruy, Noronha; Alfredo, Maneca, Baltazar, Ademir, Friaça.
Switzerland: Stuber; Neury, Bocquet; Lasenti, Eggimann, Quinche; Tamini, Bickel (capt.), Antenen, Bader, Fatton.
Scorers: Alfredo, Baltazar for Brazil, Fatton, Tamini for Switzerland.

Brazil (1) 2, *Yugoslavia* (0) 0. *Rio*
Brazil: Barbosa; Augusto (capt.), Juvenal; Bauer, Danilo, Bigode; Maneca, Zizinho, Ademir, Jair, Chico.
Yugoslavia: Mrkusic; Horvat, Brokela; Cjaicowski I (capt.), Jovanovic, Djaic; Vukas, Mitic, Tomasevic, Bobek, Cjaicowski II.
Scorers: Ademir, Zizinho for Brazil.

Switzerland (2) 2, *Mexico* (0) 1. *Porto Alegre*
Switzerland: Hug; Neury, Bocquet; Lusenti, Eggimann (capt.), Kerner; Tamini, Antenen, Friedlander, Bader, Fatton.
Mexico: Carbajal; Gutierrez, Gomez; Roca, Ortiz, Vuburu; Flores, Naranjo, Casarin, Borbolla, Velasquez (capt.).
Scorers: Bader, Fatton for Switzerland, Velasquez for Mexico.

POOL II

Spain (0) 3, *United States* (1) 1. *Curitiba*
Spain: Eizaguirre; Asensi, Alonzo; Gonzalvo III, Gonzalvo II, Puchades; Basora, Hernandez, Zarra, Igoa, Gainza.

U.S.A.: Borghi; Keough, Maca; McIlvenny (capt.), Colombo, Bahr; Craddock, Souza, J., Gaetjens, Pariani, Valentini.
Scorers: Souza, J. for U.S.A. Basora (2), Zarra for Spain.

England (1) 2, *Chile* (0) 0. *Rio*
England: Williams; Ramsey, Aston; Wright (capt.), Hughes, Dickinson; Finney, Mortensen, Bentley, Mannion, Mullen.
Chile: Livingstone; Faerias, Roldon; Alvarez, Busquez (capt.) Carvalho; Malanej, Cremaschi, Robledo, Munoz, Diaz.
Scorers: Mortensen, Mannion for England.

United States (1) 1, *England* (0) 0. *Belo Horizonte*
U.S.A.: Borghi; Keough, Maca; McIlvenny (capt.), Colombo, Bahr; Wallace, Pariani, Gaetjens, Souza, J., Souza, E.
England: Williams; Ramsey, Aston; Wright (capt.), Hughes, Dickinson; Finney, Mortensen, Bentley, Mannion, Mullen.
Scorer: Gaetjens for U.S.A.

Spain (2) 2, *Chile* (0) 0. *Rio*
Spain: Eizaguirre; Alonzo, Pana; Gonzalvo III, Antunez, Purchades; Basora, Igoa, Zarra, Panizo, Gainza.
Chile: Livingstone; Faerias, Roldon; Alvarez, Brusquez (capt.), Valho, Prieto, Cremaschi, Robledo, Munoz, Diaz.
Scorers: Basora, Zarra for Spain.

Spain (0) 1, *England* (0) 0. *Rio*
Spain: Ramallets; Asensi, Alonzo; Gonzalvo III, Antunez, Puchades; Basora, Igoa, Zarra, Panizo, Gainza.
England: Williams; Ramsey, Eckersley; Wright (capt.), Hughes, Dickinson; Matthews, Mortensen, Milburn, Baily, Finney.
Scorer: Zarra for Spain.

Chile (2) 5, *United States* (0) 2. *Recife*
Chile: Livingstone; Machuca, Roldon; Alvarez, Busquez (capt.), Faerias; Munoz, Cremaschi, Robledo, Prieto, Ibanez.
U.S.A.: Borghi; Keough, Maca; McIlvenny (capt.), Colombo, Bahr; Wallace, Pariani, Gaetjens, Souza, J., Souza, E.
Scorers: Robledo, Cremaschi (3), Prieto for Chile, Pariani, Souza, J. (penalty) for U.S.A.

POOL III

Sweden (2) 3, *Italy* (1) 2. *São Paulo*
Sweden: Svennsson; Samuelsson, Nilsson, G. (capt.); Andersson, Nordahl, K., Gard; Sundqvist, Palmer, Jeppson, Skoglund, Nilsson, S.
Italy: Sentiment IV; Giovannini, Furiassi; Annovazzi, Parola, Magli; Muccinelli, Boniperti, Cappello, Campatelli, Carapallese (capt.).

Scorers: Jeppson (2), Andersson for Sweden, Carapellese, Muccinelli for Italy.

Sweden (2) 2, *Paraguay* (1) 2. *Curitiba*
Sweden: Svensson; Samuelsson, Nilsson, E. (capt.); Andersson, Nordahl, K., Gard; Johnsson, Palmer, Jeppson, Skoglund, Sundqvist.
Paraguay: Vargas; Gonzalito, Cespedes; Gavilan, Lequizamon, Cantero; Avalos, Lopez, A., Jara, Lopez, F., Unzaim.
Scorers: Sundqvist, Palmer for Sweden, Lopez, A., Lopez, F. for Paraguay.

Italy (1) 2, *Paraguay* (0) 0. *São Paulo*
Italy: Moro; Blason, Furiassi; Fattori, Remondini, Mari; Muccinelli, Pandolfini, Amadei, Cappello, Carapellese.
Paraguay: Vargas; Gonzalito, Cespedes; Gavilan, Lequizamon Cantero; Avalos, Lopez, A., Jara, Lopez, F., Unzaim.
Scorers: Carapellese, Pandolfini for Italy.

POOL IV

Uruguay (4) 8, *Bolivia* (0) 0. *Recife*
Uruguay: Maspoli; Gonzales, M., Tejera; Gonzales, W., Varela (capt.), Andrade; Ghiggia, Perez, Miguez, Schiaffino, Vidal.
Bolivia: Gutierrez I; Achs, Bustamente; Greco, Valencia, Ferrel; Alganaraz, Ugarte, Caparelli, Gutierrez II, Maldonado.
Scorers: Schiaffino (4), Miguez (2), Vidal, Ghiggia for Uruguay.

Placings

Pool I

	P	W	D	L	F	A	Pts.
Brazil	3	2	1	0	8	2	5
Yugoslavia	3	2	0	1	7	3	4
Switzerland	3	1	1	1	4	6	3
Mexico	3	0	0	3	2	10	0

Pool II

	P	W	D	L	F	A	Pts.
Spain	3	3	0	0	6	1	6
England	3	1	0	2	2	2	2
Chile	3	1	0	2	5	6	2
United States	3	1	0	2	4	8	2

Pool III

	P	W	D	L	F	A	Pts.
Sweden	2	1	1	0	5	4	3
Italy	2	1	0	1	4	3	2
Paraguay	2	0	1	1	1	4	1

Pool IV

	P	W	D	L	F	A	Pts.
Uruguay	1	1	0	0	8	0	2
Bolivia	1	0	0	1	0	8	0

FINAL POOL

Uruguay (1) 2, *Spain* (2) 2. *São Paulo*
Uruguay: Maspoli; Gonzales, M., Tejera; Gonzales, W., Verela (capt.), Andrade; Ghiggia, Perez, Miguez, Schiaffino, Vidal.
Spain: Ramallets; Alonzo, Gonzalvo II; Gonzalvo III, Parra, Puchades; Basora, Igoa, Zarra, Molowny, Gainza.
Scorers: Ghiggia, Varela for Uruguay, Basora (2) for Spain.

Brazil (3) 7, *Sweden* (1) 1. *Rio*
Brazil: Barbosa; Augusto (capt.), Juvenal; Bauer, Danilo, Bigode; Maneca, Zizinho, Ademir, Jair, Chico.
Sweden: Svensson; Samuelsson, Nilsson, E.; Andersson, Nordahl, K., Gard; Sundqvist, Palmer, Jeppson, Skoglund, Nilsson, S.
Scorers: Ademir (4), Chico (2), Maneca for Brazil, Andersson (penalty) for Sweden.

Uruguay (1) 3, *Sweden* (2) 2. *São Paulo*
Uruguay: Paz; Gonzales, M., Tejera; Gambetta, Varela (capt.), Andrade; Ghiggia, Perez, Miguez, Schiaffino, Vidal.
Sweden: Svensson; Samuelsson, Nilsson, E.; Andersson, Johansson, Gard, Johnsson, Palmer, Melberg, Skoglund, Sundqvist.
Scorers: Palmer, Sundqvist for Sweden, Ghiggia, Miguez (2) for Uruguay.

Brazil (3) 6, *Spain* (0) 1. *Rio*
Brazil: Barbosa; Augusto (capt.), Juvenal; Bauer, Danilo, Bigode; Friaça, Zizinho, Ademir, Jair, Chico.
Spain: Eizaguirre; Alonzo, Gonzalvo II; Gonzalvo III, Parra, Puchades; Basora, Igoa, Zarra, Panizo, Gainza.
Scorers: Jair (2), Chico (2), Zizinho, Parra (own goal) for Brazil, Igoa for Spain.

Sweden (2) 3, *Spain* (0) 1. *São Paulo*
Sweden: Svensson; Samuelsson, Nilsson, E.; Andersson, Johansson, Gard; Sundqvist, Mellberg, Rydell, Palmer, Johnsson.
Spain: Eizaguirre; Asensi, Alonzo; Silva, Parra, Puchades; Basora, Fernandez, Zarra, Panizo, Juncosa.
Scorers: Johansson, Mellberg, Palmer for Sweden, Zarra for Spain.

Uruguay (0) 2, *Brazil* (0) 1. *Rio*
Uruguay: Maspoli; Gonzales, M., Tejera; Gambetta, Varela (capt.), Andrade; Ghiggia, Perez, Miguez, Schiaffino, Moran.
Brazil: Barbosa; Augusto (capt.), Juvenal; Bauer, Danilo, Bigode; Friaça, Zizinho, Ademir, Jair, Chico.
Scorers: Friaça for Brazil, Schiaffino, Ghiggia for Uruguay.

FINAL POSITIONS

	P	W	D	L	Goals F	A	Pts.
Uruguay	3	2	1	0	7	5	5
Brazil	3	2	0	1	14	4	4
Sweden	3	1	0	2	6	11	2
Spain	3	0	1	2	4	11	1

Leading Scorers: Ademir (Brazil) 7, Schiaffino (Uruguay), Basora (Spain) 5.

WORLD CUP 1954 – Switzerland

The 1954 World Cup, which rolled over little, under-organised Switzerland like a tidal wave over some peaceful village, was another instance of the Cup being won, at the last gasp, by the "wrong" team. This time, the "wrong" team was Sepp Herberger's cunningly managed Germany, the "wronged" team, the brilliant Hungarians.

Hungary, who had smashed England's unbeaten home record against foreign teams 6–3 at Wembley the previous November, then beaten them again 7–1 in Budapest, as an aperitif to the World Cup, had the finest team the world had seen since the 1950 Brazilians; and probably the best Europe has ever seen.

The organisation of the tournament settled down into the somewhat hybrid and equally unsatisfactory form it has retained ever since. Four qualifying groups provided two qualifiers each, which then met in the quarter-finals, those which had finished first playing those which had finished second. Again, the British Championship was charitably designated as a qualifying group, and this time, Scotland, again runner-up to England, deigned to enter. Their team paid a heavy penalty for the insularity of their Association in 1950.

Uruguay at last entered a European World Cup; they had yet to lose a match in the competition. Of the victorious 1950 team, still playing with a roving centre-half and "bolt" defence, Maspoli, Andrade, Varela, Miguez and Schiaffino all remained. There were splendid new wingers in Abbadie and Borges, and a powerful stopper in the fair-haired Santamaria, later to become a bulwark of Real Madrid.

Even so, Hungary remained favourites, with their marvellous attack, pivoting on Boszik, the right-half, and Nandor Hidegkuti, the deep-lying centre-forward; most of their goals scored from the remarkable head of Sandor Kocsis or the matchlessly powerful left foot of the captain, Ferenc Puskas, whose injury was probably to decide the series.

Austria, whose European dominance was ended by Hungary, had the remains of a fine team, a superb half-back in the tall, dark, strong Ernest Ocwirk, formerly their roving centre-half, now a wing-half. Austria had at last abandoned the classic Vienna School for the third back game which Meisl would have loathed.

Sweden, robbed of their stars by Italian clubs and eliminated by

Belgium, were not there. Italy, under the management of the Hungarian Lajos Czeizler, basing their defence on the Inter (Milan) block, had a good recent record. Brazil had largely rebuilt their side. The great inside-forward trio had disappeared *en bloc*. Only Bauer and Baltazar remained, but the black Djalma Santos and his elegant namesake Nilton, were fine backs, and Julinho came with a forbidding reputation for power and brilliance on the right wing. The defence still clung to the old, "diagonal" system and had not mastered the third-back game. Costa had given way to Zeze Moreira, as the manager.

Yugoslavia, with the experience of Mitic, Bobek and Cjaicowski I, the acrobatic goalkeeping of Beara, the skill and finishing power of the excellent Zebec and Vukas, were obviously good outsiders. One should add that an absurd omission in the rules made it necessary for extra time to be played *whenever* two teams were level at full-time. Each pool included two "seeded" teams.

The tournament began with France losing by a single goal to Yugoslavia – a goal scored by the young Milutinovic, who was later to play for Racing Club de Paris. Brazil, with Didi directing operations, gobbled up Mexico. Hungary had an even easier task against little Korea in Pool II. Germany disposed of Turkey without trouble.

Scotland played well against the talented Austrian side in Zürich, and their remodelled defence, with new backs in Willy Cunningham and Aird, looked promisingly solid. In attack, they missed the punch of Lawrie Reilly, who had been ill. Scotland gave Schmied in the Austrian goal much more to do than had their own goalkeeper; their half-backs were excellent, and it was only Schmied's late, daring save from centre-forward Mochan, which allowed them to hang on to Probst's first-half goal.

England, still tottering from the travesty of Budapest, threw away all Matthews' brilliant work, in a 4–4 draw with Belgium. Pol Anoul, the fair-haired inside-forward, gave Belgium the lead after only five minutes, fifteen minutes from time England were 3–1 in the lead thanks to the finishing of Ivor Broadis and Nat Lofthouse, who divided the goals between them. Over-complacent, they allowed Belgium to wipe out the lead through Anoul again, and their talented compact centre-forward, the unpredictable Rik Coppens. That meant – under the farcical rules of the competition – extra time.

For half an hour, England were dominant, but Matthews, the inspiration of the side, here, there and everywhere, pulled a muscle, and two minutes after Lofthouse had crowned a fine inter-passing movement between Broadis and Manchester United's Tommy Taylor, Dickinson headed Dries' free kick past Merrick, for the Belgian equaliser.

In the meantime, Italy surprisingly came a cropper at Lausanne against Switzerland. The days of Pozzo, present only in his capacity of journalist, were distant indeed. Bad refereeing by Viana of Brazil unsettled the players and led to a holocaust of fouls and bad temper. Italy had the play, Switzerland got the goals, Hugi, who had switched to outside-right, scoring the winner twelve minutes from time. Two Swiss players were kicked in the stomach, and the Italians chased Viana off the field after he had dubiously ruled out a goal by Benito Lorenzi, who had persistently argued with him. Not for nothing was Lorenzi nicknamed "*Veleno*" – Poison.

The next round of matches included what was perhaps the decisive moment of the competition; the kick, accidental perhaps, with which Germany's centre-half Werner Liebrich injured Ferenc Puskas, and put him out of action till a Final in which he should not really have taken part. Sepp Herberger cleverly decided to throw away this match, fielding a team which consisted largely of reserves, convinced that Germany would easily dispose of Turkey in the play-off. The Hungarians tore Germany apart, getting eight goals, four of them by Kocsis, whose heading was remarkable. The fact that a team could be thus overwhelmed and still come back to win a *cup* competition was as good a comment on the organisation of this World Cup as one could require. Three of Hungary's goals came in the last fifteen minutes, when Puskas was off the field.

Uruguay, who had conquered the mud in Berne to beat an uninspired Czech team, now exploited the firmer going in Basel to humiliate Scotland 7–0. Schiaffino, tall, pale, lean, a wonderful ball-player and strategist, with a splendid understanding with his centre-forward, Miguez, tore Scotland's defence to pieces. Borges and Abbadie, the wingers, got five of the goals between them against a wretched Scottish team, which had not been helped by dissension among its officials. Andy Beattie, the team manager, had resigned after the Austrian game.

Austria, meanwhile, showed dazzling form in thrashing the Czechs 5–0, Ocwirk and the polished Gerhard Hanappi cleverly supporting an attack in which inside-forwards Probst and Stojaspal divided the goals.

But the finest match of all, perhaps the best of the whole tournament, with the exception of the Hungary–Uruguay semi-final, was Brazil's draw with Yugoslavia in Pool I.

On the pretty Lausanne ground overlooking Lake Geneva, the Yugoslavs gave a splendid exhibition, Cjaicowski and Boskov dominating midfields, with Beara superb in goal. But the only goal was by Zebec, three minutes from half-time. In the second half Brazil came to life and Didi, after sustained pressure, got an equaliser with a spectacular drive. There were no more goals in extra time.

In the play-offs, Germany, with a full team again, swamped Turkey while Italy, who had revived to beat Belgium 4–1, lost by the same score to Switzerland; a bafflingly inconsistent team. England, who had beaten the Swiss 2–0 in a dull game in Berne, were already through. They had strengthened their defence by moving Wright to centre-half in place of the injured Owen, a move which would bear abundant fruit in the years to come.

In the quarter-finals, England's 4–2 defeat by Uruguay has subsequently been put down to the goalkeeping of Merrick, as though

England really deserved to win. In fact, the Uruguayans did remarkably well to defeat England, with both Varela and Andrade pulling muscles and Abbadie limping for much of the game.

England, with Matthews back in the side and shining again, did well, Lofthouse rubbing out Borges' fifth-minute goal. Varela's long-distance volley gave Uruguay a lead they did not deserve on the play – Merrick might have saved it; then after Varela had taken a free kick "from hand", Schiaffino made it 3–1; again with a shot that could have been saved. Schiaffino's later excellence at left-half saw to it that England did not save the game. Finney's goal made it 2–3, Matthews hit the post, but at last Ambrois slipped through for the fourth, and England were eliminated.

In Lausanne, Austria, again on form, won an astonishing twelve-goal match with the Swiss; a score unthinkable two World Cups later! Using the speed of the Koerners down the wings and shooting, untypically, from long range, Austria had the star of the match in the classical Ocwirk. The best Swiss player was their dark inside-right, Roger Vonlanthen, who was behind most of their goals.

Meanwhile, the Brazilians met the Hungarians in what has come to be known as the Battle of Berne; a potentially great match which degenerated into a shocking display of violence.

Hungary made one of their spectacular starts, Hidegkuti scoring from a corner in the third minute, and getting his shorts ripped off for his pains. Then, five minutes later, he centred for Kocsis to head in. As the rain poured down, tackling grew ferocious. Buzansky knocked Indio down, big Djalma Santos scored from the penalty and Hungary, without Puskas, were faltering.

A quarter of an hour after half-time, they too scored from a penalty – by Lantos, after Pinheiro had handled – but a marvellous run and shot by Julinho made it 3–2. Nilton Santos and Boszik came to blows, and Arthur Ellis, the Halifax referee, sent both off the field. Hostilities were well and truly open. Four minutes from time, when the field resembled a boxing ring, Ellis sent off Humberto Tozzi, Brazil's inside-left, for kicking at an opponent, and in the last minute, Koscis headed the fourth for Hungary. Then the battle was transferred to the dressing-rooms. . . .

In Geneva, Yugoslavia dominated Germany for an hour without being able to score. But the towering Horvat put past his own goalkeeper. The Slav forwards again finished poorly; Kohlmeyer kicked off the German line three times, and at last a breakaway goal by the bull-like Helmut Rahn, Germany's splendid outside-right, settled matters.

The Lausanne Hungary–Uruguay semi-final was unforgettable, though Hungary missed Puskas, Czibor gave Hungary a fifteen-minute lead, from Kocsis' header, and Hidegkuti's head made it 2–0 just before half-time.

That seemed to be that but with only a quarter of an hour left Schiaffino put the Argentinian-born Hohberg through to make it 2–1 – and repeated the move three minutes from the end.

In the first half of extra time, Hohberg was through a third time, but his shot hit the post and Hungary survived. Two splendid headers from Kocsis in the last fifteen minutes gave them a wonderful match.

Germany, meanwhile, to the general astonishment, routed Austria, not least because goalkeeper Walter Zeman had a tragic game. The Germans, splendidly marshalled by their captain, Fritz Walter, backed up by his Kaiserslautern "block", scored twice from corners, twice from centres, twice from penalties. Germany's switching, Walter's scheming and his cunning corners gave Austria a nightmare second-half, in which they conceded five goals.

In the third place match, in Zürich, Austria gained consolation. Unlike the equivalent game of 1934, they started underdogs, yet won – against a tired, demoralised Uruguay. A first-half injury to Schiaffino put the lid on it; Stojaspal emerged as the game's cleverest forward, and Ocwirk was magisterial. It was Ocwirk who shot the third goal from 25 yards, in a tepid second-half.

And so to Berne, and the dramatic, unexpected Final.

Hungary, with Puskas insisting that he play, might have demoralised Germany with their opening attack. After six minutes Boszik put Koscis through, his shot was blocked, but Puskas followed up to score. Two minutes more and Czibor, on the right wing, made it 2–0.

What saved Germany was their swift reply – Morlock putting in Fritz Walter's fast centre. Rahn scored from a corner – and the game was open again. Turek, in Germany's goal, made save after dazzling save, Hidegkuti hit a post, Kocsis the bar, and Kohlmeyer kicked off the line. Then Eckel and Mai got a tighter grip on the Hungarian inside-forwards, Fritz Walter brought his wingers into the game and at last Boszik mispassed. Schaefer found Fritz Walter, the cross was pushed out – and Rahn smashed the ball in. Germany had won. When Puskas, coming to life again, raced on to Toth's pass to score, the goal was flagged offside. And when Czibor shot Turek made another marvellous save.

Hungary, tired in body and spirit by their battles with the South Americans, may have been the moral victors, but Germany's success was none the less a memorable one.

POOL I

Yugoslavia (1) 1, *France* (0) 0. *Lausanne*
Yugoslavia: Beara; Stankovic, Crnkovic; Cjaicowski I (capt.), Horvat, Boskov; Milutinovic, Mitic, Vukas, Bobek, Zebec.
France: Remetter; Gianessi, Kaelbel; Penverne, Jonquet (capt.), Marcel; Kopa, Glovacki, Strappe, Dereuddre, Vincent.
Scorer: Milutinovic for Yugoslavia.

Brazil (4) 5, *Mexico* (0) 0. *Geneva*
Brazil: Castilho; Santos, D., Santos, N.; Brandaozinho, Pinheiro (capt.), Bauer; Julinho, Didi, Baltazar, Pinga, Rodriguez.

Mexico: Mota; Lopez, Gomez; Cardenas, Romo, Avalos; Torres, Naranjo (capt.), Lamadrid, Balcazar, Arellano.
Scorers: Baltazar, Didi, Pinga (2), Julinho for Brazil.

France (1) 3, *Mexico* (0) 2. *Geneva*
France: Remetter; Gianessi, Marche (capt.); Marcel, Kaelbel, Mahjoub; Kopa, Dereuddre, Strappe, Ben Tifour, Vincent.
Mexico: Carbajal; Lopez, Romo; Cardenas, Avalos, Martinez; Torres, Naranjo (capt.), Lamadrid, Balcazar, Arellano.
Scorers: Vincent, Cardenas (own goal), Kopa (penalty) for France Naranjo, Balcazar for Mexico.

Brazil (0) 1, *Yugoslavia* (0) 1 after extra time. *Lausanne*
Brazil: Cartilho; Santos, D., Santos, N.; Brandaozinho, Pinheiro (capt.), Bauer; Julinho, Didi, Baltazar, Pinga, Rodriguez.
Yugoslavia: Beara; Stankovic, Crnkovic; Cjaicowski I (capt.), Horvat, Boskov; Milutinovic, Mitic, Zebec, Vukas, Dvornic.
Scorers: Zebec for Yugoslavia, Didi for Brazil.

POOL II

Hungary (4) 9, *Korea* (0) 0. *Zürich*
Hungary: Grosics; Buzansky, Lantos; Boszik, Lorant, Szojka; Budai, Kocsis, Palotas, Puskas (capt.), Czibor.
Korea: Hong; Park, K., Kang; Min (capt.), Park, Y., Chu; Chung, Park, I., Sung, Woo, Choi.
Scorers: Czibor, Kocsis (3), Puskas (2), Lantos, Palotas (2) for Hungary.

Germany (1) 4, *Turkey* (1) 1. *Berne*
Germany: Turek; Laband, Kohlmeyer; Eckel, Posipal, Mai; Klodt, Morlock, Walter, O., Walter, F. (capt.), Schaefer.
Turkey: Turgay (capt.); Ridvan, Basti; Mustafa, Cetin, Rober; Erol, Suat, Feridun, Burhan, Lefter.
Scorers: Suat for Turkey; Klodt, Morlock, Schaefer, Walter for Germany.

Hungary (3) 8, *Germany* (1) 3. *Basel*
Hungary: Grosics; Buzansky, Lantos; Boszik, Lorant, Zakarias; Toth, J., Kocsis, Hidegkuti, Puskas (capt.), Czibor.
Germany: Kwiatowski; Bauer, Kohlmeyer; Posipal, Liebrich, Mebus; Rahn, Eckel, Walter, F. (capt.), Pfaff, Herrmann.
Scorers: Hidegkuti (2), Kocsis (4), Puskas, Toth for Hungary, Pfaff, Herrmann, Rahn for Germany.

Turkey (4) 7, *Korea* (0) 0. *Geneva*
Turkey: Turgay (capt.); Ridvan Basri; Mustafa, Cetin, Rober; Erol, Suat, Necmettin, Lefter, Burhan.

Korea: Hong; Park, K. (capt.), Kang; Han, Lee, C.K., Kim; Choi, Lee, S., Lee, G. C., Woo, Chung.
Scorers: Burhan (3), Erol, Lefter, Suat (2) for Turkey.

PLAY-OFF

Germany (3) 7, *Turkey* (1) 2, *Zürich*
Germany: Turek; Laband, Bauer; Eckel, Posipal, Mai; Klodt, Morlock, Walter, O., Walter, F. (capt.), Schaefer.
Turkey: Sukru; Ridvan, Basri; Mehmet, Cetin (capt.), Rober; Erol, Mustafa, Necmettin, Soskun, Lefter.
Scorers: Morlock (3), Walter, O., Schaefer (2), Walter, F. for Germany, Mustafa, Lefter for Turkey.

POOL III

Austria (1) 1, *Scotland* (0) 0. *Zürich*
Austria: Schmied; Hanappi, Barschandt; Ocwirk (capt.), Happel, Koller; Koerner, R., Schleger, Dienst, Probst, Koerner, A.
Scotland: Martin; Cunningham (capt.), Aird; Docherty, Davidson, Cowie; McKenzie, Fernie, Mochan, Brown, Ormond.
Scorer: Probst for Austria.

Uruguay (0) 2, *Czechoslovakia* (0) 0. *Berne*
Uruguay: Maspoli; Santamaria, Martinez; Andrade, Varela (capt.), Cruz; Abbadie, Ambroid, Miguez, Schiaffino, Borges.
Czechoslovakia: Reiman; Safranek, Novak (capt.); Trnka, Hledik, Hertl; Hlavacek, Hemele, Kacani, Pazicky, Krauss.
Scorers: Miguez, Schiaffino for Uruguay.

Austria (4) 5, *Czechoslovakia* (0) 0. *Zürich*
Austria: Schmied; Hanappi, Barschandt; Ocwirk (capt.), Happel, Koller; Koerner, R., Wagner, Stojaspal, Probst, Koerner, A.
Czechoslovakia: Stacho; Safranek, Novak (capt.); Trnka, Pluskal, Hertl; Hlavacek, Hemele, Kacani, Pazicky, Krauss.
Scorers: Stojaspal (2), Probst (3) for Austria.

Uruguay (2) 7, *Scotland* (0) 0. *Basel*
Uruguay: Maspoli; Santamaria, Martinez; Andrade, Varela (capt.), Cruz; Abbadie, Ambrois, Miguez, Schiaffino, Borges.
Scotland: Martin; Cunningham (capt.). Aird; Docherty, Davidson, Cowie; McKenzie, Fernie, Mochan, Brown, Ormond.
Scorers: Borges (3), Miguez (2), Abbadie (2) for Uruguay.

POOL IV

England (2) 4, *Belgium* (1) 4. after extra time. *Basel*
England: Merrick; Staniforth, Byrne; Wright (capt.), Owen, Dickinson; Matthews, Broadis, Lofthouse, Taylor, Finney.

Belgium: Gerneay; Dries (capt.), Van Brandt; Huysmans, Carré, Mees; Mermans, Houf, Coppens, Anoul, Van den Bosch (P.).
Scorers: Anoul (2), Coppens, Dickinson (own goal) for Belgium, Broadis (2), Lofthouse (2) for England.

England (1) 2, *Switzerland* (0) 0. *Berne*
England: Merrick; Staniforth, Byrne; McGarry, Wright (capt.), Dickinson; Finney, Broadis, Wilshaw, Taylor, Mullen.
Switzerland: Parlier; Neury, Kernen; Eggimann, Bocquet (capt.), Bigler; Antenen, Vonlanthen, Meier, Ballaman, Fatton.
Scorers: Mullen, Wilshaw for England.

Switzerland (1) 2, *Italy* (1) 1. *Lausanne*
Switzerland: Parlier; Neury, Kernen; Flueckiger, Bocquet (capt.), Casali; Ballaman, Vonlanthen, Hugi, Meier, Fatton.
Italy: Ghezzi; Vincenzi, Giacomazzi; Neri, Tognon, Nesti; Muccinell Boniperti (capt.), Galli, Pandolfini, Lorenzi.
Scorers: Ballaman, Hugi for Switzerland, Boniperti for Italy.

Italy (1) 4, *Belgium* (0) 1. *Lugano*
Italy: Ghezzi; Magnini, Giacomazzi (capt.); Neri, Tognon, Nesti; Frignani, Cappello, Galli, Pandolfini, Lorenzi.
Belgium: Gernaey; Dries (capt.), Van Brandt; Huysmans, Carré, Mees; Mermans, Van den Bosch, H., Coppens, Anoul, Van den Bosch, P.
Scorers: Pandolfini (penalty), Galli, Frignani, Lorenzi for Italy, Anoul for Belgium.

PLAY-OFF

Switzerland (1) 4, *Italy* (0) 1. *Basel*
Switzerland: Parlier, Neury, Kernan; Eggimann, Bocquet (capt.), Casali; Antenen, Vonlanthen, Hugi, Ballaman, Fatton.
Italy: Viola; Vincenzi, Giacomazzi (capt.), Neri, Tognon, Nesti; Muccinelli, Pandolfini, Lorenzi, Segato, Frignani.
Scorers: Hugi (2), Ballaman, Fatton for Switzerland, Nesti for Italy.

Placings	Pool I				Goals		
	P	W	D	L	F	A	Pts.
Brazil	2	1	1	0	6	1	3
Yugoslavia	2	1	1	0	2	1	3
France	2	1	0	1	3	3	2
Mexico	2	0	0	2	2	8	0
	Pool II						
Hungary	2	2	0	0	17	3	4
Germany	2	1	0	1	7	9	2
Turkey	2	1	0	1	8	4	2
Korea	2	0	0	2	0	16	0

Placings

	Pool III				Goals		
	P	W	D	L	F	A	Pts.
Uruguay	2	2	0	0	9	0	4
Austria	2	2	0	0	6	0	4
Czechoslovakia	2	0	0	2	0	7	0
Scotland	2	0	0	2	0	8	0

	Pool IV						
England	2	1	1	0	6	4	3
Italy	2	1	0	1	5	3	2
Switzerland	2	1	0	1	2	3	2
Belgium	2	0	1	1	5	8	1

QUARTER-FINALS

Germany (1) 2, *Yugoslavia* (0) 0. *Geneva*
Germany: Turek; Laband, Kohlmeyer; Eckel, Liebrich, Mai; Rahn, Morlock, Walter, O., Walter, F. (capt.), Schaefer.
Yugoslavia: Beara; Stankovic, Crnkovic; Cjaicowski I, Horvat, Boskov; Milutinovic, Mitic (capt.), Vukas, Bobek, Zebec.
Scorers: Horvat (own goal), Rahn for Germany.

Hungary (2) 4, *Brazil* (1) 2. *Berne*
Hungary: Grosics; Buzansky, Lantos; Boszik (capt.), Lorant, Zakarias; Toth, M., Kocsis, Hidegkuti, Czibor, Toth, J.
Brazil: Castilho; Santos, D., Santos, N.; Brandaozinho, Pinheiro (capt.), Bauer; Julinho, Didi, Indio, Tozzi, Maurinho.
Scorers: Hidegkuti (2), Kocsis, Lantos (penalty) for Hungary, Santos, D. (penalty), Julinho for Brazil.

Austria (2) 7, *Switzerland* (4) 5. *Lausanne*
Austria: Schmied; Hanappi, Barschandt; Ocwirk (capt.), Happel, Koller; Koerner, R., Wagner, Stojaspal, Probst, Koerner, A.
Switzerland: Parlier; Neury, Kernen, Eggimann, Bocquet (capt.), Casali; Antenen, Vonlanthen, Hugi, Ballaman, Fatton.
Scorers: Ballaman (2), Hugi (2), Hanappi (own goal) for Switzerland, Koerner, A. (2), Ocwirk, Wagner (3), Probst for Austria.

Uruguay (2) 4, *England* (1) 2. *Basel*
Uruguay: Maspoli; Santamaria, Martinez; Andrade, Varela (capt.), Cruz; Abbadie, Ambrois, Miguez, Schiaffino, Borges.
England: Merrick; Staniforth, Byrne; McGarry, Wright (capt.), Dickinson; Matthews, Broadis, Lofthouse, Wilshaw, Finney.
Scorers: Borges, Varela, Schiaffino, Ambrois for Uruguay, Lofthouse, Finney for England.

SEMI-FINALS

Germany (1) 6, *Austria* (0) 1. *Basel*
Germany: Turek; Posipal, Kohlmeyer; Eckel, Liebrich, Mai; Rahn, Morlock, Walter, O., Walter, F. (capt.), Schaefer.
Austria: Zeman; Hanappi, Schleger; Ocwirk (capt.), Happel, Koller; Koerner, R., Wagner, Stojaspal, Probst, Koerner, A.
Scorers: Schaefer, Morlock, Walter, F. (2 penalties), Walter. O, (2) for Germany, Probst for Austria.

Hungary (1) 4, *Uruguay* (0) 2, after extra time. *Lausanne*
Hungary: Grosics; Buzansky, Lantos; Boszik (capt.), Lorant, Zakarias; Budai, Kocsis, Palotas, Hidegkuti, Czibor.
Uruguay: Maspoli; Santamaria, Martinez; Andrade (capt.), Carballo, Cruz; Souto, Ambrois, Schiaffino, Hohberg, Borges.
Scorers: Czibor, Hidegkuti, Kocsis (2) for Hungary, Hohberg (2) for Uruguay.

THIRD PLACE MATCH

Austria (1) 3, *Uruguay* (1) 1. *Zürich*
Austria: Schmied; Hanappi, Barschandt; Ocwirk (capt.), Kollmann Koller; Koerner, R., Wagner, Dienst, Stojaspal, Probst.
Uruguay: Mospoli; Santamaria, Martinez; Andrade (capt.), Carballo, Cruz; Abbadie, Hohberg, Mendez, Schiaffino, Borges.
Scorers: Stojaspal (penalty), Cruz (own goal), Ocwirk for Austria, Hohberg for Uruguay.

FINAL

Germany (2) 3, *Hungary* (2) 2. *Berne*
Germany: Turek; Posipal, Kohlmeyer; Eckel, Liebrich, Mai; Rahn, Morlock, Walter, O., Walter, F., Schaefer.
Hungary: Grosics; Buzansky, Lantos; Boszik, Lorant, Zakarias; Czibor, Kocsis, Hidegkuti, Puskas, Toth, J.
Scorers: Puskas, Czibor for Hungary, Morlock, Rahn (2) for Germany.
Leading Scorer: Kocsis (Hungary) 11.

WORLD CUP 1958 – Sweden

At long last, after the disappointment of 1950, and the violent elimination of 1954, Brazil carried off the World Cup in spectacular fashion, with a performance, in the Final against Sweden, which rivalled the greatest ever seen. There, on the rain-soaked stadium of Rasunda, the Brazilian forwards juggled, gyrated and, above all, finished with marvellous, gymnastic skill. There, Garrincha, the outside-right, and Pelé, the 17-year-old inside-left, together with the incomparable Didi, wrote themselves indelibly into the history of the game.

It was a World Cup which began greyly, and built up to an ultimate crescendo; a World Cup heavy with nostalgia, thanks to the return of Sweden's stars. Professionals now, the Swedes could recall Nacka Skoglund, a hero of their 1950 World Cup team – and Nils Liedholm and Gunnar Gren, from their great 1948 Olympic team. They could also bring back from Italy Julli Gustavsson, their splendid centre-half, and Kurt Hamrin, a dazzling little outside-right. To begin with, their supporters were pessimistic, but as round succeeded round and George Raynor's elderly team marched on to the Final, nationalist feeling mounted alarmingly, culminating in the Gothenburg semi-final.

Brazil had toured Europe in 1956 without much success, but they had learned from their tour. Now they brought with them the 4–2–4 formation which was soon to sweep the world. Four defenders in line, two pivotal players in midfield, four forwards up to strike. They were established, if a little precariously, as the favourites.

England's chances had been gravely affected by the tragic air disaster at Munich, in which their Manchester United stars, Tommy Taylor, Roger Byrne and the mighty Duncan Edwards, had perished.

The Russians, included with England, Brazil and Austria in quite the most powerful qualifying group of all (this time, all three teams would play one another), had just drawn 1–1 with England in Moscow. This was their first World Cup, but they had won the Olympic tournament in Australia two years before, while in Lev Yachin they had one of the finest goalkeepers in the game.

Italy and Uruguay were out; Uruguay thrashed 5–0 in Asuncion by Paraguay, Italy eliminated by brave little Northern Ireland. The Irish, brilliantly captained by their elegant right-half Danny Blanchflower, generalled in attack by Jimmy McIlroy, were the surprise of the eliminators. After a black game of violence in Belfast, when the referee, Hungary's Zsolt, was fog bound, and the World Cup game was turned into a friendly, Chiappella of Italy was sent off and the crowd swarmed on to the pitch. The rematch saw Ireland victorious 2–1. But the Munich crash deprived them of Jackie Blanchflower, a key man at centre-half.

Wales was there on the most fragile grounds. Already eliminated, they were given a second chance when FIFA decided Israel could not qualify by forfeit alone after Uruguay had refused to come back into the competition. So Wales had the fairly easy task of eliminating Israel, which they did surprisingly well.

Scotland, who had eliminated Spain, were in mediocre form, and had been humiliated by England in Glasgow 4–0. Germany, the holders, captained again by Fritz Walter, had the burly Helmut Rahn on the right wing, but had turned Hans Schaefer into an inside-forward. A new star was the powerful, ruthless wing-half, Horst Szymaniak. Clearly they would take some beating.

Sweden opened the tournament on June 8 in Stockholm, with an easy 3–0 win over Mexico. Two of the goals were scored by their strong, fair-haired centre-forward, Ange Simonsson. Nils Liedholm got the other goal from a penalty. Bror Mellberg, a 1950 World Cup man, played at inside-right.

In the same group, Hungary, shorn of Puskas, Kocsis and Czibor, who had stayed in the West after the 1956 Revolution, were held to a 1–1 draw by Wales. Jack Kelsey, Wales' calm, strong goalkeeper, a hero of the tournament, was dazzled by the sun when Boszik scored after four minutes, but the massive John Charles, recalled from Italy, headed the equaliser from a corner.

In Gothenburg, England and Russia had an exciting battle in which England rallied for a somewhat lucky draw. The power of Voinov and Tsarev (left-half and captain Igor Netto was injured) plus the skill of Salnikov, in midfield, the goalkeeping of Yachin and the domination of Krijevski, enabled Russia to take a 2–0 lead. But Kevan headed in a free kick and at last Tom Finney, injured in a ruthless tackle and destined to take no further part in the competition, equalised with a penalty.

The Brazilians accounted for Austria 3–0 in Boras, but their team was still in the melting-pot. Pelé, canvassed as their *wunderkind*, was injured, and some wanted the unorthodox Garrincha on the right wing. Team manager Feola himself preferred Vavà to Mazzola at centre-forward, despite the fact that Mazzola (real name José Altafini) scored two of the three goals.

In Group I, the brave Irish at once showed their quality by defeating the Czechs 1–0 at Halmstad, tough little Wilbur Cush, their versatile inside-right, getting the goal. Harry Gregg had a fine game in goal, but the absence of Jackie Blanchflower forced his brother, Danny, much deeper into defence.

At Malmö, Germany were too strong and efficient for an Argentine side which, having brilliantly won the South American Championship the previous year, at once lost its chief stars to Italy. Their style looked old-fashioned, and they had no answer to Rahn, who added two more to his tally of World Cup goals.

No one had expected anything from the French, yet here they were in Norrköping, thrashing Paraguay 7–3, their inside-forward trio of Fontaine (who had expected to be a reserve), Kopa, back from Real Madrid and playing deep, and Piantoni doing remarkable things. Three of the goals were from Kopa. In fact the weeks in training camp at Kopparberg, under Paul Nicolas, had transformed the French morale.

Scotland, meanwhile, undeterred by the fact that Yugoslavia had recently beaten England 5–0, held them to a 1–1 draw at Vasteras. Stamina and determination saved the game after an anxious first half and a seven-minute goal by Petakovic. At right-half, the 35-year-old Eddie Turnbull was in splendid form for the Scots.

The second "round" was full of surprises. In Gothenburg, an English defence cleverly organised to the prescription of Bill Nicholson, the team coach, held up Brazil's forwards. Howe, the right-back, played in the middle, Clamp, the right half, on the flank, while Slater marked

Didì out of the game. Brazil were rather lucky not to give away a penalty in the second half when Bellini felled Kevan, but England, on the other hand, owed much to the cool elegance in goal of Colin McDonald of Burnley. There was no score.

At Boras, Russia, too, accounted for an ageing Austria.

In Group I, Ireland had a shock from the Argentinians, who brought back 40-year-old Angel Labruna at inside-left, and gave them a casual lesson in the skills of the game, to beat them 3–1. The stars were Labruna and another veteran, the roving centre-half Nestor Rossi.

Germany, two down, rallied to draw with the Czechs, both goals going to the rejuvenated Helmut Rahn, who'd been written off between the two World Cups.

Yugoslavia, who had Branko Zebec, their Rest of Europe left-winger, at centre-half, surprised France to win with a breakaway goal three minutes from time. At Norrköping, a tired-looking Scottish team went down to Paraguay, inspired by Silvio Parodi, from inside-forward. Bobby Evans, the red-haired Celtic centre-half, laboured in vain against a thrustful Paraguayan attack.

Wales, feeble in attack, were held to a draw by Mexico, in Stockholm, and the following day, again at Rasunda, the Swedes rather unconvincingly beat Hungary. Hungary, with Boszik of all people at deep centre-forward, were laboured in attack, with only the ferocious shooting of Tichy to keep them in the game. Did Tichy score in the fifty-fifth minute with a shot that beat Svensson and hit the underside of the bar? The referee thought not, and half a minute later Hamrin's lob was deflected past Grosics to make it 2–0. Tichy's goal, when it did come, was irrelevant.

The shock of the final round was Czechoslovakia's 6–1 crushing of Argentina at Halsingborg, the sequel to which was a bombardment of rubbish for the Argentine players when they got back to Buenos Aires airport. The Czechs were altogether too fast, with Borovicka and Molnar unstoppable.

Ireland and Germany drew 2–2 in one of the best matches of the competition, with Gregg superb in goal, and Rahn having a superb first half but fading in the second. Peter McParland, Ireland's tough outside-left, twice gave them the lead, but Uwe Seeler, a new young star at centre-forward, equalised 11 minutes from time; so Ireland had to play off against the Czechs.

England, in Boras, stubbornly unchanged by their manager, Walter Winterbottom, toiled to a mediocre draw with Austria, so they too had to replay. Haynes, the general, and Douglas, on the right wing, were plainly exhausted after the effort they had made to drag their respective clubs out of Division II; Kevan remained a blunt instrument; Finney was still injured. In Gothenburg, meanwhile, Brazil, at the plea of their own players, at last gave a chance to Garrincha, who mesmerised the Russian defence. Pelé had his first game, and the clever Zito replaced Dino as linking right-half. Russia used Netto to shadow Didì, but Didì was the dominant player of the match. Vavà, replacing

Mazzola at centre-forward, scored in the 3rd and 77th minutes, but the 2–0 score flattered Russia. Brazil had found their team, and their form.

In Group II, France just got home against a Scottish team well served by Bill Brown, making his début in goal, while Paraguay held the Yugoslavs to a draw. Sweden, fielding five reserves, were satisfied with a goalless draw with Wales, who thus had to meet Hungary (easy conquerors of Mexico) in the play-off.

This they bravely and surprisingly won 2–1 with John Charles back in defence. Tichy opened the score; Ivor Allchurch equalised with a superb forty-yard volley, and, five minutes later, Terry Medwin intercepted Grosics' short goal kick to win the game. Sipos was sent off for kicking Hewitt, and Wales hung on to win and to qualify. A famous victory.

Equally famous was Ireland's defeat of the Czechs. Peter Doherty, once a great Irish inside-forward, now an inspirational team manager, had expressed his confidence that what they had done once, they could do again; and so they did. Injuries to Uprichard, in goal, and to Bertie Peacock did not hold them back. A goal down and forced to play half an hour's extra time, they won in the 100th minute, when McParland converted Blanchflower's free kick. Again, the winger scored both goals.

England, at last making changes, throwing Peter Broadbent and Peter Brabrook in the deep end, unluckily went down to Russia in Gothenburg. Twice Brabrook hit the post, but when Russia's Ilyin hit the post, the ball went in. England were eliminated.

In the quarter-finals, the weary, depleted Irish went down 4–0 to France at Nörrkoping, Casey playing despite just having had four stitches in his shin and Gregg keeping goal on one leg. But theirs had been a glorious achievement.

Wales too went out, defending superbly against Brazil, but falling at last to a goal by Pelé, deflected past the splendid Kelsey by the equally splendid Williams. John Charles was unfit to play, but his brother, Mel, was a superb centre-half and Hopkins cleverly contained Garrincha.

Sweden, with Hamrin irresistible, knocked out the Russians. The little winger headed the first goal, and made the second for Simonsson. Finally, a ruthless German team knocked out the Yugoslavs in Malmö with Rahn, inevitably getting the goal. As in Switzerland, four years earlier, the Slavs dominated the game, but just could not score.

In the semi-finals, France's luck deserted them. For 37 minutes, at the Rasunda, they held Brazil, but with the score 1–1, Jonquet, their elegant centre-half, was hurt, and that was that. Didi's thirty-yard swerver gave Brazil the lead, and Pelé, at last showing his quality, got three more in the second half.

In Gothenburg, a chanting, nationalistic crowd mustered by official cheer leaders, was urging Sweden on to victory against the Germans. It was rather an unsatisfactory match in many ways. Schaefer brilliantly volleyed Germany into the lead – but Sweden equalised after Liedholm had handled with impunity. In the second half, the game turned on Juskowiak's flash of temper. He kicked Hamrin, was sent off, and the way was clear for Gren, nine minutes from time, and Hamrin himself – a wonderfully impertinent, dribbling goal – to take Sweden into the Final.

France thrashed Germany 6-3 on that same ground, in the third-place match, four of the goals going to the rampant Fontaine, brilliantly combining with Kopa. This was one of the finest partnerships the World Cup has seen, giving Fontaine a new scoring record for the competition.

It rained in Stockholm on the day of the Final, but the crowd, its cheer leaders now properly banned, was quiet, and even Liedholm's fine, early goal, as he picked his way through the Brazilian penalty area, did not decide the game. The Brazilians, scornful of George Raynor's forecast that if they gave away an early goal, "they'd panic all over the show," stubbornly held on. Six minutes later, Garrincha, with marvellous swerve and acceleration, left Axbom and Parling standing, and made the equaliser for Vavà. Pelé hit a post; Zagalo, always ready to drop deep, cleared from under his own bar; but it was clear that the two full-backs Santos (with Djalma playing his first game of the tournament) had the measure of Sweden's little wingers.

After thirty-two minutes Garrincha repeated his astonishing *tour de force*, and Vavà scored again. In the second half, he gave way to the incredible Pelé, who coolly juggled the ball to smash in a third. Zito and Didì were immaculate now in midfield, while Zagalo had sandwiched a goal of his own between Pelé's and the Swedes' second, making it 4-2. Then came the final goal, a brilliant header from Pelé, with the Brazilian fans shouting, "*Samba, samba!*" It had been a dazzling exhibition of the arts of the game, and victory, at last, for the team which morally deserved it.

POOL I

Germany (2) 3, *Argentina* (1) 1. *Malmö*
Germany: Herkenrath; Stollenwerk, Juskowiak; Eckel, Erhardt, Szymaniak; Rahn, Walter, Seeler, Schmidt, Schaefer.
Argentina: Carrizo; Lombardo, Vairo; Rossi, Dellacha, Varacka; Corbatta, Prado, Menendez, Rojas, Cruz.
Scorers: Rahn (2), Schmidt for Germany, Corbatta for Argentina.

Ireland (1) 1, *Czechoslovakia* (0) 0. *Halmstad*
Ireland: Gregg; Keith, McMichael; Blanchflower, Cunningham, Peacock; Bingham, Cush, Dougan, McIlroy, McParland.
Czechoslovakia: Dolejsi; Marz, Novak; Pluskal, Cadek, Masopust; Hovorka, Dvorak, Borovicka, Hartl, Kraus.
Scorer: Cush for Ireland.

Germany (1) 2, *Czechoslovakia* (0) 2. *Halsingborg*
Germany: Herkenrath; Stollenwerk, Juskowiak; Schnellinger, Erhardt, Szymaniak; Rahn, Walter, Seeler, Schaefer, Klodt.
Czechoslovakia: Dolejsi; Mraz, Novak; Pluskal, Popluhar, Masopust; Hovorka, Dvorak, Molnar, Feureisl, Zikan.

Scorers: Rahn (2) for Germany, Dvorak (penalty), Zikan for Czechoslovakia.

Argentina (1) 3, *Ireland* (1) 1. *Halmstad*
Argentina: Carrizo; Lombardo, Vario; Rossi, Dellacha, Varacka; Corbatta, Avio, Menendez, Labruna, Boggio.
Ireland: Gregg; Keith, McMichael; Blanchflower, Cunningham, Peacock; Bingham, Cush, Casey, McIlroy, McParland.
Scorers: Corbatta (2) (one penalty), Menendez for Argentina, McParland for Ireland.

Germany (1) 2, *Ireland* (1) 2. *Malmö*
Germany: Herkenrath; Stollenwerk, Juskowiak; Eckel, Erhardt, Szymaniak; Rahn, Walter, Seeler, Schaefer, Klodt.
Ireland: Gregg; Keith, McMichael; Blanchflower, Cunningham, Peacock; Bingham, Cush, Casey, McIlroy, McParland.
Scorers: Rahn, Seeler for Germany, McParland (2) for Ireland.

Czechoslovakia (3) 6, *Argentina* (1) 1. *Halsingborg*
Czechoslovakia: Dolejsi; Mraz, Novak; Dvorak, Popluhar, Masopust; Hovorka, Borovicka, Molnar, Feureisl, Zikan.
Argentina: Carrizo; Lombardo, Vario; Rossi, Dellacha, Varacka; Corbatta, Avio, Menendez, Labruna, Cruz.
Scorers: Dvorak, Zikan (2), Feureisl, Hovorka (2) for Czechoslovakia, Corbatta for Argentina.

Qualifying Match

Ireland (1) 2, *Czechoslovakia* (1) 1 after extra time. *Malmö*
Ireland: Uprichard; Keith, McMichael; Blanchflower, Cunningham, Peacock; Bingham, Cush, Scott, McIlroy, McParland.
Czechoslovakia: Dolejsi; Mraz, Novak; Bubernik, Popluhar, Masopust; Dvorak, Borovicka, Feureisl, Molnar, Zikan.
Scorers: McParland (2) for Ireland, Zikan for Czechoslovakia.

POOL II

France (2) 7, *Paraguay* (2) 3. *Norrköping*
France: Remetter; Kaelbel, Lerond; Penverne, Jonquet, Marcel; Wisnieski, Fontaine, Kopa, Piantoni, Vincent.
Paraguay: Mayeregger; Arevalo, Miranda; Achucarro, Lezcano, Villalba; Aguero, Parodi, Romero, Re, Amarilla.
Scorers: Fontaine (3), Piantoni, Wisnieski, Kopa, Vincent for France, Amarilla (2) (1 penalty), Romero for Paraguay.

Yugoslavia (1) 1, *Scotland* (0) 1. *Vasteras*
Yugoslavia: Beara; Sijakovic, Crnkovic; Krstic, Zebec, Boskov; Petakovic, Veselinovic, Milutinovic, Sekularac, Rajkov.

Scotland: Younger; Caldow, Hewie; Turnbull, Evans, Cowie; Leggat Murray, Mudie, Collins, Imlach.
Scorers: Petakovic for Yugoslavia, Murray for Scotland.

Yugoslavia (1) 3, *France* (1) 2. *Vasteras*
Yugoslavia: Beara; Tomic, Crnkovic; Krstic, Zebec, Boskov; Petakovic, Veselinovic, Milutinovic, Sekularac, Rajkov.
France: Remetter; Kaelbel, Marche; Penverne, Jonquet, Lerond; Wisnieski, Fontaine, Kopa, Piantoni, Vincent.
Scorers: Petakovic, Veselinovic (2) for Yugoslavia, Fontaine (2) for France.

Paraguay (2) 3, *Scotland* (1) 2. *Norrköping*
Paraguay: Aguilar; Arevalo, Enhague; Achucarro, Lezcano, Villalba; Aguero, Parodi, Romero, Re, Amarilla.
Scotland: Younger; Parker, Caldow; Turnbull, Evans, Cowie; Leggat, Collins, Mudie, Robertson, Fernie.
Scorers: Aguero, Re, Parodi for Paraguay, Mudie, Collins for Scotland.

France (2) 2, *Scotland* (0) 1. *Cerebro*
France: Abbes; Kaelbel, Lerond; Penverne, Jonquet, Marcel; Wisnieski, Fontaine, Kopa, Piantoni, Vincent.
Scotland: Brown; Caldow, Hewie; Turnbull, Evans, Mackay; Collins, Murray, Mudie, Baird, Imlach.
Scorers: Kopa, Fontaine for France, Baird for Scotland.

Yugoslavia (2) 3, *Paraguay* (1) 3. *Ekilstuna*
Yugoslavia: Beara; Tomic, Crnkovic; Boskov, Zebec, Krstic; Petakovic, Veselinovic, Ognjanovic, Sekularac, Rajkov.
Paraguay: Aguilar; Arevalo, Echague; Villalba, Lezcano, Achucarro; Aguero, Parodi, Romero, Re, Amarilla.
Scorers: Ognjanovic, Veselinovic, Rajkov for Yugoslavia, Parodi, Aguero, Romero for Paraguay.

POOL III

Sweden (1) 3, *Mexico* (0) 0. *Stockholm*
Sweden: Svensson; Bergmark, Axbom; Liedholm, Gustavsson, Parling; Hamrin, Mellberg, Simonsson, Gren, Skoglund.
Mexico: Carbajal; Del Muro, Gutierrez; Cardenas, Romo, Flores; Hernandez, Reyes, Calderon, Gutierrez, Seema.
Scorers: Simonsson 2, Liedholm (penalty) for Sweden.

Hungary (1) 1, *Wales* (1) 1. *Sandviken*
Hungary: Grosics; Matray, Sarosi; Boszik, Sipos, Berendi; Sandor Tichy, Hidegkuti, Bundzsak, Fenyvesi.
Wales: Kelsey; Williams, Hopkins; Sullivan, Charles, M., Bowen; Webster, Medwin, Charles, J., Allchurch, Jones.
Scorers: Boszik for Hungary, Charles, J., for Wales.

Wales (1) 1, *Mexico* (1) 1. *Stockholm*
Wales: Kelsey; Williams, Hopkins; Baker, Charles, M., Bowen; Webster, Medwin, Charles, J., Allchurch, Jones.
Mexico: Carbajal; Del Muro, Gutierrez; Cardenas, Romo, Flores; Belmonte, Reyes, Blanco, Gonzales, Sesma.
Scorers: Allchurch for Wales, Belmonte for Mexico.

Sweden (1) 2, *Hungary* (0) 1. *Stockholm*
Sweden: Svensson; Bergmark, Axbom; Liedholm, Gustavsson, Parling; Hamrin, Melberg, Simonsson, Gren, Skoglund.
Hungary: Grosics; Matray, Sarosi; Szojka, Sipos, Berendi; Sandor, Tichy, Boszik, Bundzsak, Fenyvesi.
Scorers: Hamrin 2 for Sweden, Tichy for Hungary.

Sweden (0) 0, *Wales* (0) 0. *Stockholm*
Sweden: Svensson; Bergmark, Axbom; Boerjesson, Gustavsson, Parling; Berndtsson, Kaelgren, Lofgren, Skoglund.
Wales: Kelsey; Williams, Hopkins; Sullivan, Charles, M., Bowen; Vernon, Hewitt, Charles J., Allchurch, Jones.

Hungary (1) 4, *Mexico* (0) 0. *Sandviken*
Hungary: Ilku; Matray, Sarosi; Boszik, Sipos, Kotasz; Budai, Bencsics, Tichy, Bundzsak, Fenyvesi.
Mexico: Carbajal; Del Muro, Gutierrez; Cardenas, Sepulvedo, Flores; Belmonte, Reyes, Blanco, Gonzales, Sesma.
Scorers: Tichy 2, Sandor, Bencsics for Hungary.

Play-off
Wales (0) 2, *Hungary* (1) 1. *Stockholm*
Wales: Kelsey; Williams, Hopkins; Sullivan, Charles, M., Bowen; Medwin, Hewitt, Charles, J., Allchurch, Jones.
Hungary: Grosics; Matray, Sarosi; Boszik, Sipos, Kotasz; Budai, Bencsics, Tichy, Bundzsak, Fenyvesi.
Scorers: Allchurch, Medwin for Wales, Tichy for Hungary.

POOL IV

England (0) 2, *Russia* (1) 2. *Gothenburg*
England: McDonald; Howe, Banks; Clamp, Wright, Slater; Douglas, Robson, Kevan, Haynes, Finney.
Russia: Yachin; Kessarev, Kuznetsov; Voinov, Krijevski, Tsarev; Ivanov, A., Ivanov, V., Simonian, Salnikov, Ilyin.
Scorers: Simonian, Ivanov, A., for Russia, Kevan, Finney (penalty) for England.

Brazil (1) 3, *Austria* (0) 0. *Boras*
Brazil: Gilmar; De Sordi, Santos, N.; Dino, Bellini, Orlando; Joel, Dida, Mazzola, Didì, Zagalo.

Austria: Szanwald; Halla, Swoboda; Hanappi, Happel, Koller; Horak, Senekowitsch, Buzek, Koerner, Schleger.
Scorers: Mazzola (2), Santos for Brazil.

England (0) 0, *Brazil* (0) 0. *Gothenburg*
England: McDonald; Howe, Banks; Clamp, Wright, Slater; Douglas, Robson, Kevan, Haynes, A'Court.
Brazil: Gilmar; De Sordi, Santos, N.; Dino, Bellini, Orlando; Joel, Didi, Mazzola, Vavà, Zagalo.

Russia (1) 2, *Austria* (0) 0. *Boras*
Russia: Yachin; Kessarev, Kuznetsov; Voinov, Krijevski, Tsarev; Ivanov, A., Ivanov, V., Simonian, Salnikov, Ilyin.
Austria: Schmied; Kozlicek, E., Swoboda; Hanappi, Stotz, Koller; Horak, Hozlicek, P., Buzek, Koerner, Senekowitsch.
Scorers: Ilyin, Ivanov, V., for Russia.

Brazil (1) 2, *Russia* (0) 0. *Gothenburg*
Brazil: Gilmar; De Sordi, Santos, N.; Zito, Bellini, Orlando; Garrincha, Didì, Vavà, Pelé, Zagalo.
Russia: Yachin; Kessarev, Kuznetsov; Voinov, Krijevski, Tsarev; Ivanov, A., Ivanov, V., Simonian, Netto, Ilyin.
Scorer: Vavà (2) for Brazil.

England (0) 2, *Austria* (1) 2. *Boras*
England: McDonald; Howe, Banks; Clamp, Wright, Slater; Douglas, Robson, Kevan, Haynes, A'Court.
Austria: Szanwald; Kollmann, Swoboda; Hanappi, Happel, Koller; Kozlicek, E., Kozlicek, P., Buzek, Koerner, Senekowitsch.
Scorers: Koller, Koerner for Austria, Haynes, Kevan for England.

PLAY OFF

Russia (0) 1, *England* (0) 0. *Gothenburg*
Russia: Yachin; Kessarev, Kuznetsov; Voinov, Krijevski, Tsarev; Apoukhtin, Ivanov, V., Simonian, Falin, Ilyin.
England: McDonald; Howe, Banks; Clayton, Wright, Slater; Brabrook, Broadbent, Kevan, Haynes, A'Court.
Scorer: Ilyin for Russia.

Placings	Pool I				Goals		
	P	W	D	L	F	A	Pts.
Germany	3	1	2	0	7	5	4
Czechoslovakia	3	1	1	1	8	4	3
Ireland	3	1	1	1	4	5	3
Argentina	3	1	0	2	5	10	2

Arsenal captain Frank McLintock holds the FA Cup aloft after his team had beaten Liverpool 2-1 after extra-time in the 1971 final.
(*United Press International*)

Liverpool full back Chris Lawler shoots over the bar during the FA Cup Final against Arsenal.
(*London Express News and Feature Service*)

Peter Simpson of Arsenal (light shirt) flicks the ball clear as Brian Hall of Liverpool prepares to shoot during the 1971 FA Cup Final.
(*London Express News and Feature Service*)

Malta goalkeeper Mizzi saves from England's Roy McFarland (5) and Martin Chivers in the first leg of their European Championship match in Malta. England won 1-0. (*London Photo Agency*)

Celtic number 8 Macari shows his delight after scoring his side's first goal in the Scottish Cup replay at Hampden Park. Celtic beat Rangers 2-1. (*United Press International*)

Northern Ireland's disallowed goal against England in the
Home International Championship. George Best, after flicking the ball
away from Gordon Banks, heads into an empty net but the
referee ruled Best had fouled Banks. (*Syndication International*)

John O'Hare (left) of Scotland loses possession to John Roberts (centre)
and Rod Thomas of Wales during the 1971 Home International
Championship. (*Syndication International*)

Arsenal striker Ray Kennedy fails to score against FC Cologne in the Fairs Cup. The Cologne players are goalkeeper Manglitz and Kolmer. (*United Press International*)

Living up to his name is Stuart Jump of Stoke City (white shirt) during a match against Arsenal at Highbury. Arsenal won 1-0 and clinched the League Championship in their next game versus Tottenham Hotspur at White Hart Lane. (*United Press International*)

Chelsea skipper Ron Harris with the European Cup Winners Cup trophy after his team had beaten Real Madrid 2-1 in the replayed final in Athens. The first match ended 1-1. (*United Press International*)

England goalkeeper Peter Shilton finishes in the back of the net after making a spectacular save against Wales during the 1971 Home International Championship. (*United Press International*)

England's Alan Ball evades a Maltese defender during an international match in Valletta. (*Syndication International*)

Jimmy Greaves – the player who has scored more goals in the English first division than any other player – announced his retirement at the end of the 1970-71 campaign. (*Syndication International*)

England and Leeds United left back Terry Cooper – rated the best attacking full back in the world. (*Syndication International*)

Placings

	P	W	D	L	F	A	Pts.
Pool II							
France	3	2	0	1	11	7	4
Yugoslavia	3	1	2	0	7	6	4
Paraguay	3	1	1	1	9	12	3
Scotland	3	0	1	2	4	6	1
Pool III							
Sweden	3	2	1	0	5	1	5
Hungary	3	1	1	1	6	3	3
Wales	3	0	3	0	2	2	3
Mexico	3	0	1	2	1	8	1
Pool IV							
Brazil	3	2	1	0	5	0	5
England	3	0	3	0	4	4	3
Russia	3	1	1	1	4	4	3
Austria	3	0	1	2	2	7	1

QUARTER-FINALS

France (1) 4, *Ireland* (0) 0. *Norrköping*
France: Abbes; Kaelbel, Lerond; Penverne, Jonquet, Marcel; Wisnieski Fontaine, Kopa, Piantoni, Vincent.
Ireland: Gregg; Keith, McMichael; Blanchflower, Cunningham, Cush; Bingham, Casey, Scott, McIlroy, McParland.
Scorers: Wisnieski, Fontaine (2), Piantoni for France.

Germany (1) 1, *Yugoslavia* (0) 0. *Malmö*
Germany: Herkenrath; Stollenwerk, Juskowiak; Eckel, Erhardt Szymaniak; Rahn, Walter, Seeler, Schmidt, Schaefer.
Yugoslavia: Krivocuka; Sijakovic, Crnkovic; Kristic, Zebec, Boskov; Petakovic, Veselinovic, Milutinovic, Ognjanovic, Rajkov.
Scorer: Rahn for Germany.

Sweden (0) 2, *Russia* (0) 0. *Stockholm*
Sweden: Svensson; Bergmark, Axbom; Boerjesson, Gustavsson, Parling; Hamrin, Gren, Simonsson, Liedholm, Skoglund.
Russia: Yachin; Kessarev, Kuznetsov; Voinov, Krijevski, Tsarev; Ivanov, A., Ivanov, V., Simonian, Salnikov, Ilyin.
Scorers: Hamrin, Simonsson for Sweden.

Brazil (0) 1, *Wales* (0) 0. *Gothenburg*
Brazil: Gilmar; De Sordi, Santos, N.; Zito, Bellini, Orlando; Garrincha Didì, Mazzola, Pelé, Zagalo.
Wales: Kelsey; Williams, Hopkins; Sullivan, Charles, M., Bowen; Medwin, Hewitt, Webster, Allchurch, Jones.
Scorer: Pelé for Brazil.

SEMI-FINALS

Brazil (2) 5, *France* (1) 2. *Stockholm*
Brazil: Gilmar; De Sordi, Santos, N.; Zito, Bellini, Orlando; Garrincha Didì, Vavà, Pelé, Zagalo.
France: Abbes; Kaelbel, Lerond; Penverne, Jonquet, Marcel; Wisnieski Fontaine, Kopa, Piantoni, Vincent.
Scorers: Vavà, Didì, Pelé (3) for Brazil, Fontaine, Piantoni for France.

Sweden (1) 3, *Germany* (1) 1. *Gothenburg*
Sweden: Svensson; Bergmark, Axbom; Boerjesson, Gustavsson, Parling; Hamrin, Gren, Simonsson, Liedholm, Skoglund.
Germany: Herkenrath; Stollenwerk, Juskowiak; Eckel, Erhardt, Szymaniak; Rahn, Walter, Seeler, Schaefer, Cieslarczyk.
Scorers: Schaefer for Germany, Skoglund, Gren, Hamrin for Sweden.

THIRD PLACE MATCH

France (0) 6, *Germany* (0) 3. *Gothenburg*
France: Abbes; Kaelbel, Lerond; Penverne, Lafont, Marcel; Wisnieski, Douis, Kopa, Fontaine, Vincent.
Germany: Kwiatowski; Stollenwerk, Erhardt; Schnellinger, Wewers, Szymaniak; Rahn, Sturm, Kelbassa, Schaefer, Cieslarzcyk.
Scorers: Fontaine (4) Kopa (penalty), Douis for France, Cieslarczyk, Rahn, Schaefer for Germany.

FINAL

Brazil (2) 5, *Sweden* (1) 2. *Stockholm*
Brazil: Gilmar; Santos, D., Santos, N.; Zito, Bellini, Orlando; Garrincha, Didì, Vavà, Pelé, Zagalo.
Sweden: Svensson; Bergmark, Axbom; Boerjesson, Gustavsson, Parling; Hamrin, Gren, Simonsson, Liedholm, Skoglund.
Scorers: Liedholm, Simonsson for Sweden, Vavà (2), Pelé (2), Zagalo for Brazil.
Leading Scorer: Fontaine (France) 13 (present record total).

WORLD CUP 1962 – Chile

The selection of Chile as host to the 1962 World Cup was a surprising one, determined largely by sentiment and by the pressures of Chile's representative to FIFA, the late Carlos Dittborn: "We have nothing, that is why we must have the World Cup." Chile had recently suffered a disastrous earthquake, but Dittborn promised all would be ready in time. Argentina, the logical choice, had a poor record in terms of loyalty to the tournament and, in fact, Chile made a good enough job of the organisation, though the insanely high prices kept out an impoverished working class, and there was flagrant profiteering by hotels and agencies.

Once again, the four-pool qualifying system was employed, this time with such disastrous effects (goal average was counted) as to cast doubt not only on the system but on the whole future of the game. Manic defence, eight men in the penalty box, reduced many of the qualifying matches to farce.

Brazil and Russia were the favourites, Russia because, on their recent South American tour, they had beaten Argentina, Uruguay and Chile. Otherwise, the field looked a mediocre one. England had just lost to Scotland in Glasgow for the first time for twenty-five years; Hungary, Argentina and Italy were in decline; Germany as tough as ever, but lacking a Fritz Walter, Chile had the great advantage of playing at home, and the experienced managership of Fernando Riera, but nobody much favoured them.

In their opening match, at the fine new Santiago stadium, they easily beat the Swiss 3–1. Brazil, kicking off at the beautiful little seaside ground at Viña del Mar – also especially constructed – beat Mexico 2–0, but with great difficulty. Their team, rather to the general surprise, showed but two changes from 1958; Mauro (Santos) replacing Bellini as centre-half and captain, and Zozimo coming in for Orlando, now in Argentina. Vavà, back from Spain, displaced Santos' Coutinho at centre-forward, and Zagalo, destined to be used deep in a virtual 4–3–3 formation, had regained his position on the left wing. Pelé, making the first goal for Zagalo, and scoring the second himself, saved a Brazilian team which seemed to be hardening in its arteries.

The following day, the Czechs surprised Helenio Herrera's Spain 1–0, although they were lacking their star finisher, Rudolf Kucera, left at home for a cartilage operation. The great Di Stefano, suffering from a pulled muscle, did not play for Spain at all.

In the Rancagua stadium, Argentina scored the only goal of a tedious, defensive match against the destructive Bulgarians, who had eliminated France. The following day, Hungary, much more relaxed, surprised an uninspired England team, feeble and straightforward in attack. A long-range goal by Tichy, a penalty equaliser by Flowers, then the game was decided by a brilliant individual goal by Florian Albert, the young Hungarian centre-forward. Right-half Solymosi, tall, fair-haired, infinitely relaxed, was perhaps the best player on the field.

Up in the far north, at Arica, Uruguay squeezed home 2–1 against Colombia. Sanchez played splendidly in goal for the Colombians, who were to spring yet another great surprise.

Next day Russia won a violent game against the Yugoslavs 2–0; nevertheless it was the best game played in the group, and the only one in which Yachin, in goal, justified his mighty reputation. A serious foul by Mujic put Dubinski out of the game, and the tournament, with a broken leg. Both Russian goals in the second half were owed to their powerful centre-forward, Victor Ponedelnik. For the first, Ponedelnik hit the bar with a free kick, and Ivanov beat Soskic to the ball. For the second, four minutes from time and soon after Dubinski's injury, Ponedelnik both began and finished the movement.

Netto, back in the team again as captain, had a fine match, as did Ivanov, while Dragoslav Sekularac showed his immense class for the impassioned Yugoslav team.

In Pool II, Germany and Italy drew goallessly in Santiago. Both teams played with an extra man in defence. The Italians, admirably marshalled by their pivot, Maldini, stood up well to the Germans' physical power but were lucky when Uwe Seeler hit the bar.

The second "round" saw tragedy afflict Brazil. Playing against the Czechs, Pelé severely pulled a muscle, and that was the last of him we saw in the tournament. A left-footed shot against the foot of the post after twenty-five minutes provoked the injury. Both sides closed up in defence; the Czechs, with Schroiff excellent in goal, and Popluhar a strapping centre-half, gave nothing away, and there was not a goal.

Spain, thanks to a goal by Perió of Madrid Athletic, a minute from the end, squeezed home against the gallant Mexicans, for whom the veteran Carbajal was a splendid goalkeeper.

In Rancagua, England found better form, and deservedly beat the Argentinians, Alan Peacock making an excellent début at centre-forward. The tall, slim, blond Sacchi and Marzolini, in Argentine's defence, were their only stars; Sanfilippo's goal came too late to matter.

Hungary thrashed the Bulgars 6–1, with Albert scoring a brilliant hat-trick. The Bulgarians, without their best forwards, Diev and Iliev, looked vulnerable indeed.

Group II, in Santiago, also produced the notorious and distasteful match between Italy and Chile. At the root of the trouble was a couple of foolish, inflammatory articles written by Italian journalists in Chile; the first, and more offensive, was the work of a non sports-writer. Later, the Italians alleged that the Chileans had deliberately used these articles to create an atmosphere hostile to their team. Certainly that atmosphere existed. The Italian players claimed that the Chileans were, from the start, spitting in their faces and insulting them. When Leonel Sanchez, the Chilean left-winger, felled Maschio, Italy's Argentinian inside-forward, with a left hook, Mr. Ken Aston, the English referee, had his back to the incident; his linesmen claimed they had seen nothing and play went on, with Maschio nursing a broken nose. It was somewhat ironic that the two players eventually sent off in a vicious, brawling travesty of a game should both be Italian; Ferrini for a scything tackle on Landa, and David for allegedly kicking an opponent.

The Italians, who had made wholesale and somewhat ill-advised changes, were thus reduced to nine men, and Chile duly scored in the 75th and 89th minutes through Ramirez and their strong impressive inside-right, Jorge Toro. To this day, the Italians bitterly blame Mr. Aston for their defeat. He himself said the game was literally uncontrollable; the French, neutral parties, felt he was weak, and lacked authority. In the circumstances it would have required the authority of a Hercules.

Germany, meanwhile, beat the Swiss 2–1 in a thoroughly tedious match, during which a ruthless tackle by Szymaniak put Eschmann,

Switzerland's inside-left, off with a broken leg. The Germans did not look impressive. In their final qualifying match against Chile, they were an offence to the eye; negative, destructive winners thanks to an early penalty and a late breakaway goal, headed by Seeler. The Chileans, faced by a defence reinforced by Szymaniak, nominally an inside-right attacked with naive enthusiasm, but were limited to long drives from outside the box, often by their strong left-half, Eladio Rojas.

Germany thus qualified, with Chile, and Italy's 3–0 win over the Swiss was of mere academic value.

In Viña del Mar, a brave last-ditch rally by Spain, fielding a lively young experimental side, nearly accounted for Brazil. Indeed, it was only two goals late in the game by Pelé's excellent young substitute, Amarildo, which won it for Brazil. Adelardo's 34th-minute goal for Spain stood for nearly 40 minutes. One bright spot for Brazil was the improved form of Garrincha late in the game; form which was to be brilliantly maintained.

As for the Czechs, they went down 3–1 to a Mexican side which was one of the revelations of the tournament, this, despite the fact that Masek put the Czechs ahead in the very first minute. Not a bit perturbed, the Mexicans hit back with three goals, the second of which was scored after a superb individual run by their outside-right, Del Aguila. They had gone out – but with much more honour than in their previous World Cup disappointments.

There were no goals at all in the concluding matches at Rancagua, between Hungary and Argentina, and England and Bulgaria. The latter game was of infinite tedium, Bulgaria massing in defence for no obvious reason – they had already been eliminated – and England growing content with a draw, as the game wore wearily on. This they were rather lucky to get, when Kolev, his side's one star, eluded Armfield near the end, and put across a centre which should surely have been exploited.

Up at Arica, there had been high jinks. Russia, in the second round, had been held to a most unexpected 4–4 draw by the undervalued Colombians. It was a bad day for Yachin, a very good one for the gifted little black Colombian inside-left Klinger. A French critic described the match, in retrospect, as "one of the great surprises of modern football." Russia led 3–0 after a quarter of an hour. With twenty-two minutes left it was 4–1; then the Colombians hit back. Yachin, explicably, let the ball in straight from Coll's corner. Galvanised, Colombia added two more goals; and two fine saves by Yachin prevented others. But the French claim that the match signified "the end of the greatest goalkeeper of modern times" was ridiculed by Yachin's memorable display for FIFA at Wembley in 1963.

The draw with Russia seemed to exhaust Colombia, who crashed 5–0 in their last match, against Yugoslavia. The Slavs, inspired by Sekularac, had ridden a goal by Cabrera to beat Uruguay 3–1. At the end of the match, the sporting Uruguayans carried the little inside-forward off in triumph. He set far too deep a problem for Colombia.

As for the Russians, they beat Uruguay 2–1 and were lucky to do so, the Uruguayans being depleted by injury to Eliseo Alvarez. Yet they dominated the second half, hitting the post three times. Ivanov's winning goal came in the last minute.

In the quarter-finals, Brazil "at home" in Viña del Mar, won a curious match against England, who had to take the field without the injured Peacock. Garrincha was in unstoppable form, his swerve and acceleration as irresistible as in Sweden. After 31 minutes, he showed another talent, getting up splendidly to head in a corner. England should have been two down when Flowers unaccountably passed across his own goal to Amarildo, but Springett saved brilliantly, and Hitchens equalised after Greaves' header came back from the bar.

Alas for Springett, however, he allowed Garrincha's second-half free kick to come back off his chest, for Vavà to score easily, and later he was tricked by Garrincha's clever swerving long shot. Brazil were through, but they had been a little lucky.

In Arica, Chile, whose fans were growing more and more crazily excited, put out Russia. Again, Yachin had a poor game, badly placed for Leonel Sanchez's goal straight from a free kick after ten minutes; still more at fault with Eladio Rojas' 35-yard second. Chislenko replied a couple of minutes later, but the 4–2–4 Chilean team held on to a narrow success.

Surprisingly, the Czechs beat the Hungarians 1–0 in Rancagua. For 80 minutes they were penned in their own half, while Hungary beat a tattoo on their goalposts. Schroiff, in goal, was unbeatable, and Scherer's breakaway goal in the 13th minute won the match. Tichy's "equaliser" was ruled, disputably, offside.

In Santiago, the much more creative Yugoslavs beat Germany 1–0, at last revenging themselves for previous World Cup defeats at the hands of Germany. Radakovic, a head injury bandaged, smashed in Galic's pass four minutes from the end, to win a match which seemed bound for extra time.

In the semi-finals, Garrincha dashed Chile's hopes, with another marvellous display. A magnificent 20-yard left-footer after nine minutes put Brazil ahead; a header from a corner doubled the lead. Toro, with a mighty free kick, made it 2–1, but just after half-time, Vavà headed a vital goal from Garrincha's dropping corner-kick: 3–1. Leonel Sanchez made it 3–2, from a penalty, but Vavà tied up the match, heading in Zagalo's centre. Zagalo had worked with boundless stamina and decisive effect.

In a displeasing finale, Landa, Chile's centre-forward, and Garrincha were in turn sent off the field. Garrincha for kicking Rojas, Landa for a foul on Zito. As he made his way round the track, Garrincha had his head cut by a missile thrown from a frantically partisan crowd.

The Czechs, to everyone's amazement, prevailed again – over the talented Yugoslavs. At Viña del Mar, watched by a mere and miserable 5,000, Schroiff was again the determining player. The Slavs had most of the game but, weak on the wings, could not turn their domination into more than Jerkovic's equalising goal. A breakaway allowed Scherer to give the Czechs the lead again; a silly handling offence by Markovic allowed the same player to decide the match from the penalty spot.

A tired Yugoslav team, with Sekularac even so the best player on the field, lost 1–0 to Chile in the third place game. Rojas' long shot, deflected, beat an excellent Soskic for the only goal of a dreary match.

In the Final, Brazil once more had to play without Pelé. Playing at a slow, steady rhythm, with Kvasniak tireless and long-legged in midfield, the Czechs cleverly took the lead when Masopust ran on to Scherer's through pass. But alas for the Czechs, this was not to be a good day for Schroiff. He should have stopped Amarildo's equaliser from the narrowest of angles. In the second half, Amarildo whiplashed past his man to make a headed goal, under the bar, for Zito, and, 13 minutes from time, poor Schroiff dropped a high lob into the sun by Djalma Santos, and that was number three. Not a Brazilian victory to be compared with Stockholm; this was an older, more cautious team, without Pelé, with a slower Didì, with Garrincha well controlled by the experienced Czech defence. The Czechs had been distinguished losers. With Kucera, who knows how much better they might have done?

GROUP I *Arica*

Uruguay (0) 2, *Colombia* (1) 1
Uruguay: Sosa; Troche, Em. Alvarez; El. Alvarez, Mendez, Goncalves; Rocha, Perez, Langon, Sasia, Cubilla.
Colombia; Sanchez; Zaluaga, Gonzalez, Lopez, Etcheverri; Silva, Coll; Aceros, Klinger, Gamboa, Arias.
Scorers: Zaluaga for Colombia, Cubilla, Sasia for Uruguay.

Russia (0) 2, *Yugoslavia* (0) 0
Russia: Yachin; Dubinski, Ostrovski; Voronin, Maslenkin, Netto; Metreveli, Ivanov, Ponedelnik, Kanevski, Meschki.
Yugoslavia: Soskic; Durkovic, Jusufi; Matus, Markovic, Popovic; Mujic, Sekularac, Jerkovic, Galic, Skoblar.
Scorers: Ivanov, Ponedelnik for Russia.

Yugoslavia (2) 3, *Uruguay* (1) 1
Yugoslavia: Soskic; Durkovic, Jusufi; Radakovic, Markovic, Popovic; Melic, Sekularac, Jerkovic, Galic, Skoblar.
Uruguay: Sosa; Troche, Em. Alvarez, El. Alvarez, Mendez; Goncalves, Rocha; Cubilla, Cabrera, Sasia, Perez.
Scorers: Cabrera for Uruguay, Skoblar, Galic, Jerkovic for Yugoslavia.

Russia (3) 4, *Colombia* (1) 4
Russia: Yachin; Tchokelli, Ostrovski; Netto, Maslenkin, Voronin; Chislenko, Ivanov, Ponedelnik, Kanevski, Meschki.

Colombia: Sanchez; Gonzalez, L., Lopez, Alzate, Etcheverri; Serrano, Coll; Aceros, Rada, Klinger, Gonzalez, C.
Scorers: Ivanov (2), Chislenko, Ponedelnik for Russia, Aceros, Coll, Rada, Klinger for Colombia.

Russia (1) 2, *Uruguay* (0) 1
Russia: Yachin; Tchokelli, Ostrovski; Netto, Maslenkin, Voronin; Chislenko, Ivanov, Ponedelnik, Mamikin, Hussainov.
Uruguay: Sosa; Troche, El. Alvarez, Em. Alvarez, Mendez; Goncalves, Cortes; Cubilla, Carera, Sasia, Perez.
Scorers: Mamikin, Ivanov for Russia, Sasia for Uruguay.

Yugoslavia (2) 5, *Colombia* (0) 0
Yugoslavia: Soskic; Durkovic, Yusufi; Radakovic, Markovic, Popovic; Ankovic, Sekularac, Jerkovic, Galic, Melic.
Colombia: Sanchez; Alzate, Gonzalez, O., Lopez, Etcheverri; Serrano, Coll; Aceros, Klinger, Rada, Gonzalez, C.
Scorers: Galic, Jerkovic (3), Melic for Yugoslavia.

GROUP II *Santiago*

Chile (1) 3, *Switzerland* (1) 1
Chile: Escuti; Eyzaguirre, Sanchez, R., Contreras, Navarro; Toro, Rojas; Ramirez, Landa, Fouilloux, Sanchez, L.
Switzerland: Elsener; Morf, Schneiter, Tacchella; Grobety, Weber; Allemann, Pottier, Eschmann, Wuthrich, Antenen.
Scorers: Wuthrich for Switzerland, Sanchez, L. (2), Ramirez for Chile.

Germany (0) 0, *Italy* (0) 0
Germany: Fahrian; Novak, Schnellinger; Schulz, Erhardt, Szymaniak; Sturm, Haller, Seeler, Brulls, Schaefer.
Italy: Buffon; Losi, Robotti; Salvadore, Maldini, Radice; Ferrini, Rivera, Altafino, Sivori, Menichelli.

Chile (0) 2, *Italy* (0) 0
Chile: Escutti; Eyzaguirre, Contreras, Sanchez, R., Navarro; Toro, Rojas; Ramirez, Landa, Fouilloux, Sanchez, L.
Italy: Mattrel; David, Robotti; Salvadore, Janich, Tumburus; Mora, Maschio, Altafini, Ferrini, Menichelli.
Scorers: Ramirez, Toro for Chile.

Germany (1) 2, *Switzerland* (0) 1
Germany: Fahrian; Novak, Schnellinger; Schulz, Erhardt, Szymaniak; Koslowski, Haller, Seeler, Brulls, Schaefer.
Switzerland: Elsener; Schneiter, Tacchella, Groberty; Wuthrich, Weber; Antenen, Vonlanthen, Allemann, Eschmann, Durr.
Scorers: Brulls, Seeler for Germany, Schneiter for Switzerland.

Germany (1) 2, *Chile* (0) 0
Germany: Fahrian; Novak, Schnellinger; Schulz, Erhardt, Giesemann; Krauss, Szymaniak, Seeler, Schaefer, Brulls.
Chile: Escutti; Eyzaguirre, Contreras, Sanchez, R., Navarro; Tobar, Rojas; Moreno, Landa, Sanchez, L., Ramirez.
Scorers: Szymaniak (penalty), Seeler for Germany.

Italy (1) 3, *Switzerland* (0) 0
Italy: Buffon; Losi, Robotti; Salvadore, Maldini, Radice; Mora, Bulgarelli, Sormani, Sivori, Pascutti.
Switzerland: Elsener; Schneiter, Meier, Tacchella; Grobety, Weber; Antenen, Vonlanthen, Wuthrich, Allemann, Durr.
Scorers: Mora, Bulgarelli (2) for Italy.

GROUP III *Vina del Mar*

Brazil (0) 2, *Mexico* (0) 0
Brazil: Gilmar; Santos, D., Mauro, Zozimo, Santos N.; Zito, Didi; Garrincha, Vavà, Pelé, Zagalo.
Mexico: Carbajal; Del Muro, Cardenas, Sepulveda, Villegas; Reyes, Najera; Del Aguila, Hernandez, Jasso, Diaz.
Scorers: Zagalo, Pelé for Brazil.

Czechoslovakia (0) 1, *Spain* (0) 0
Czechoslovakia: Schroiff; Lala, Novak; Pluskal, Popluhar, Masopust; Stibranyi, Scherer, Kvasniak, Adamec, Jelinck.
Spain: Carmelo; Rivilla, Reija; Segarra, Santamaria, Garay; Del Sol, Martinez, Puskas, Suarez, Gento.
Scorer: Stibranyi for Czechoslovakia.

Brazil (0) 0, *Czechoslovakia* (0) 0
Brazil: Gilmar; Santos, D., Mauro, Zozimo, Santos, N.; Zito, Didì; Garrincha, Vavà, Pelé, Zagalo.
Czechoslovakia: Schroiff; Lala, Novak; Pluskal, Popluhar, Masopust; Stibranyi, Scherer, Kvasniak, Adamec, Jelinek.

Spain (0) 1, *Mexico* (0) 0
Spain: Carmelo; Rodri, Garcia; Verges, Santamaria, Pachin; Del Sol, Pieró, Puskas, Suarez, Gento.
Mexico: Carbajal; Del Muro, Cardenas, Sepulveda, Jauregui; Reyes, Najera; Del Aguila, Hernandez, H., Jasso, Diaz.
Scorer: Peiró for Spain.

Brazil (0) 2, *Spain* (1) 1
Brazil: Gilmar; Santos, D., Mauro, Zozimo, Santos, N., Zito, Didì; Garrincha, Vavà, Amarildo, Zagalo.
Spain: Araquistain; Rodri, Gracia; Verges, Echevarria, Pachin; Collar, Adelardo, Puskas, Peiró, Gento.
Scorers: Adelardo for Spain, Amarildo (2) for Brazil.

Mexico (2) 3, *Czechoslovakia* (1) 1
Mexico: Carbajal; Del Muro, Cardenas, Sepulveda, Jauregui; Reyes, Najera; Del Aguila, Hernandez, A., Hernandez, H., Diaz.
Czechoslovakia: Schroiff; Lala, Novak; Pluskal, Popluhar, Masopust; Stibranyi, Scherer, Kvasniak, Adamec, Masek.
Scorers: Masek for Czechoslovakia, Diaz, Del Aguila, Hernandez, H. (penalty) for Mexico.

GROUP IV *Rancagua*

Argentina (1) 1, *Bulgaria* (0) 0
Argentina: Roma; Navarro, Baez, Sainz, Marzolini; Sacchi, Rossi; Facundo, Pagani, Sanfilippo, Belen.
Bulgaria: Naidenov; Rakarov, Kotov; Kostov, Dimitrov, Kovatchev; Diev, Velitchkov, Iliev, Yakimov, Kolev.
Scorer: Facundo for Argentina.

Hungary (1) 2, *England* (0) 1
Hungary: Grosics; Matrai, Sarosi; Solymosi, Meszoly, Sipos; Sandor, Rakosi, Albert, Tichy, Fenyvesi.
England: Springett; Armfield, Wilson; Moore, Norman, Flowers; Douglas, Greaves, Hitchens, Haynes, Charlton.
Scorers: Tichy, Albert for Hungary, Flowers (penalty) for England.

England (2) 3, *Argentina* (0) 1
England: Springett; Armfield, Wilson; Moore, Norman, Flowers; Douglas, Greaves, Peacock, Haynes, Charlton.
Argentina: Roma; Capp, Baez, Navarro, Marzolini; Sacchi, Rattin; Oleniak, Sosa, Sanfilippo, Belen.
Scorers: Flowers (penalty), Charlton, Greaves for England, Sanfilippo for Argentina.

Hungary (4) 6, *Bulgaria* (0) 1
Hungary: Ilku; Matrai, Sarosi; Solymosi, Meszoly, Sipos, Sandor, Rakosi, Albert, Tichy, Fenyvesi.
Bulgaria: Naidenov; Rakarov, Kotov; Kostov, Dimitrov, Kovatchev; Sokolov, Velitchkov, Asparoukhov, Kolev, Dermendiev.
Scorers: Albert (3), Tichy (2), Solymosi for Hungary, Sokolov for Bulgaria.

Argentina (0) 0, *Hungary* (0) 0
Argentina: Dominguez; Capp, Aainz, Delgado, Marzolini; Sacchi, Pando; Facundo, Pagani, Oleniak, Gonzales.
Hungary: Grosics; Matrai, Sarosi; Solymosi, Meszoly, Sipos; Kuharszki, Gorocs, Monostroi, Tichy, Rakosi.

England (0) 0, *Bulgaria* (0) 0
England: Springett; Armfield, Wilson; Moore, Norman, Flowers; Douglas, Greaves, Peacock, Haynes, Charlton.

Bulgaria: Naidenov; Rakarov, Jetchev; Kostov, D., Dimitrov, Kovatchev; Kostov, A., Velitchkov, Iliev, Kolev, Yakimov.

Placings

	Group I				Goals		
	P	W	D	L	F	A	Pts.
Russia	3	2	1	0	8	5	5
Yugoslavia	3	2	0	1	8	3	4
Uruguay	3	1	0	2	4	6	2
Colombia	3	0	1	2	5	11	1

	Group II				Goals		
	P	W	D	L	F	A	Pts.
Germany	3	2	1	0	4	1	5
Chile	3	2	0	1	5	3	4
Italy	3	1	1	1	3	2	3
Switzerland	3	0	0	3	2	8	0

	Group III				Goals		
	P	W	D	L	F	A	Pts.
Brazil	3	2	1	0	4	1	5
Czechoslovakia	3	1	1	1	2	3	3
Mexico	3	1	0	2	3	4	2
Spain	3	1	0	2	2	3	2

	Group IV				Goals		
	P	W	D	L	F	A	Pts.
Hungary	3	2	1	0	8	2	5
England	3	1	1	1	4	3	3
Argentina	3	1	1	1	2	3	3
Bulgaria	3	0	1	2	1	7	1

QUARTER-FINALS

Yugoslavia (0) 1, *Germany* (0) 0. *Santiago*
Yugoslavia: Soskic; Durkovic, Jusufi; Radakovic, Markovic, Popovic; Kovacevic, Sekularac, Jerkovic, Galic, Skoblar.
Germany: Fahrian; Novak, Schnellinger; Schulz, Erhardt, Giesemann; Haller, Szymaniak, Seeler, Brulls, Schaefer.
Scorer: Radakovic for Yugoslavia.

Brazil (1) 3, *England* (1) 1. *Viña del Mar*
Brazil: Gilmar; Santos, D., Mauro, Zozimo, Santos, N.,; Zito, Didì; Garrincha, Vavà, Amarildo, Zagalo.
England: Springett; Armfield, Wilson; Moore, Norman, Flowers; Douglas, Greaves, Hitchens, Haynes, Charlton.
Scorers: Garrincha (2), Vavà for Brazil, Hitchens for England.

Chile (2) 2, *Russia* (1) 1. *Arica*
Chile: Escutti; Eyzaguirre, Contreras, Sanchez, R., Navarro; Toro, Rojas; Ramirez, Landa, Tobar, Sanchez, L.
Russia: Yachin; Tchokelli, Ostrovski; Voronin, Maslenkin, Netto; Chislenko, Ivanov, Ponedelnik, Mamikin, Meshki.
Scorers: Sanchez, L., Rojas for Chile, Chislenko for Russia.

Czechoslovakia (1) 1, *Hungary* (0) 0. *Rancagua*
Czechoslovakia: Schroiff; Lala, Novak; Pluskal, Popluhar, Masopust; Pospichal, Scherer, Kvasniak, Kadraba, Jelinek.
Hungary: Grosics; Matrai, Sorisi; Solymosi, Meszoly, Sipos; Sandor, Rakosi, Albert, Tichy, Fenyvesi.
Scorer: Scherer for Czechoslovakia.

SEMI-FINALS

Brazil (2) 4, *Chile* (1) 2. *Santiago*
Brazil: Gilmar; Santos, D., Mauro, Zozimo, Santos, N.; Zito, Didì; Garrincha, Vavà, Amarildo, Zagalo.
Chile: Escutti; Eyzaguirre, Contreras, Sanchez, R., Rodriguez; Toro, Rojas; Ramirez, Landa, Tobar, Sanchez, L.
Scorers: Garrincha (2), Vavà (2) for Brazil, Toro, Sanchez, L. (penalty) for Chile.

Czechoslovakia (0)3, *Yugoslaiva* (0) 1. *Viña del Mar*
Czechoslovakia: Schroiff; Lala, Novak; Pluskal, Popluhar, Masopust; Pospichal, Scherer, Kvasniak, Kadraba, Jelinek.
Yugoslavia: Soskic; Durkovic, Jusufi; Radakovic, Markovic, Popovic; Sujakovic, Sekularac, Jerkovic, Galic, Skoblar.
Scorers: Kadraba, Scherer (2), for Czechoslovakia, Jerkovic for Yugoslavia.

THIRD PLACE MATCH

Chile (0) 1, *Yugoslavia* (0) 0. *Santiago*
Chile: Godoy; Eyzaguirre, Cruz, Sanchez, R., Rodriguez; Toro, Rojas; Ramirez, Campos, Tobar, Sancez, L.
Yugoslavia: Soskic; Durkovic, Svinjarevic; Radakovic, Markovic, Popovic; Kovacevic, Sekularac, Jerkovic, Galic, Skoblar.
Scorer: Rojas for Chile.

FINAL

Brazil (1) 3, *Czechoslovakia* (1) 1. *Santiago*
Brazil: Gilmar; Santos, D., Mauro, Zozimo, Santos, N.; Zito, Didì; Garrincha, Vavà, Amarildo, Zagalo.
Czechoslovakia: Schroiff; Tichy, Novak; Pluskal, Popluhar, Masopust; Pospichal, Scherer, Kvasniak, Kadraba, Jelinek.

Scorers: Masopust for Czechoslovakia, Amarildo, Zito, Vavà for Brazil.
Leading Scorers: Albert (Hungary), Ivanov (Russia), Sanchez (Chile), Garrincha, Vavà (Brazil), Jerkovic (Yugoslavia) each 4.

WORLD CUP 1966 – England

England, as Alf Ramsey had promised, won the World Cup. They won it, in the end, deservedly, with two fine performances in semi-final and final, won it without Jimmy Greaves, won it despite a brutal setback, in the last minute of the Final itself.

Starting painfully and laboriously, their attack terribly unimpressive in the three qualifying games, the ill-tempered quarter-final against Argentina (when the Argentinians went virtually berserk in the tunnel, at the end) England "came good" when it was most necessary. Geoff Hurst, the West Ham United player, who had looked sadly out of form as recently as the tour match against Denmark in Copenhagen, came back into the team against Argentina to become, perhaps, the decisive force in England's success. His three goals in the Final established a new record.

In general terms, it was a disappointing World Cup, with no team to match the Brazilians of 1958 and 1962, or the Hungarians of 1954. England had a superb defence, but their 4–3–3 formation, generally without specialised wingers, was by no means as impressive in attack. What saved them was the eruption of Hurst, the sudden blossoming of Bobby Charlton, in semi-final and Final, the energy of Alan Ball against Portugal, followed by his astonishing, all-round performance against the West Germans.

Brazil were shown to be clearly in decline. This time, they and their manager, Feola, paid the penalty for an exaggerated reliance on old names, old faces. An injury to Pelé in the first game had an effect on them which it never had in Chile. Good young players had, it's true, been left behind, but obviously a period of retrenchment was needed.

The surprise of the tournament were the lively little North Koreans, who astonished and humiliated the listless Italians. Quick, intelligent, learning from game to game, wonderfully popular with the Middlesbrough crowd, they made one wonder just how good they'll be, with more international experience.

The Hungarians, with a novel tactical formation, played superbly against Brazil, but were betrayed by poor goalkeeping. Portugal, with Eusebio the leading scorer and perhaps the outstanding player of the whole tournament, might have done better still had their defence in any way matched their attack. As for the West Germans, the runners-up, their powerful, well-balanced side, though it never lived up to its opening flourish against Switzerland, was full of talent.

Fittingly, the tournament started with that epitome of modern World Cups, a goalless draw. Uruguay went out to stop England from scoring, massed eight and nine men in defence, and succeeded with little trouble.

An ingenuously chosen England team, with Ball as a pseudo-winger and the essentially destructive Stiles at linking wing-half, played into their hands. The strikers and schemers alike were impotent against the tough, rhythmic, immensely professional Uruguayans, responding as always to the challenge of a World Cup.

It was Pelé, appropriately, who scored the first goal of the tournament next day – the player who, above all others, was expected to dominate the tournament. After 14 minutes of Brazil's match at Everton with Bulgaria, he smashed in a phenomenal right-footed free kick. In the second half, an equally remarkable free kick by Garrincha gave Brazil a second, but they were not over impressive. Pelé dazzlingly apart, the team often stuttered. He himself was ruthlessly marked by Zhechev, Yakimov followed him as the best player on the field. Ankle trouble blunted the edge of the much praised Bulgarian centre-forward, Asparoukhov. Brazil gave a first cap as a – largely destructive – midfield player to Edilson, taking the place of an injured Gerson.

At Sheffield, in Group II, the Germans annihilated a Swiss side which dropped two key men, Kuhn and Leimgruber, at the last moment, for breaking curfew. The Germans played splendidly powerful, intelligent football, Beckenbauer, Haller and Held, being especially good. No one but the bookmakers was surprised; they'd been widely favoured.

North Korea, the "mystery" side which had qualified by beating Australia twice in Cambodia, after the mass withdrawal of the Afro-Asian bloc, played bravely against a rough Soviet team at Middlesbrough, but still went down. They looked fit, but their finishing was poor, their small physique against them. The years they had spent monastically in barracks clearly weren't, on their own, enough.

On the Wednesday, in Group I, Mexico, after a lamentably unsuccessful tour of Europe, surprised a disappointing French side at Wembley. Both sides played 4-3-3, the fashionable pattern. Mexico took the lead through Borja, after he'd first miskicked, just after halftime. Hausser equalised. Guérin, the French manager, said his team was "paralysed by nervousness".

At Villa Park, in Group II, Argentina, inspired by Onega, beat Spain in an untidy game, with two goals by Artime, to one sandwiched in between, by Pirri. Spain's attack, though Suarez did some clever things was most disappointing, especially on the wings.

At Sunderland, Italy won without glory against a Chilean team reduced for most of the second half to ten men; but at least there wasn't a second Battle of Santiago. Barison's fine, but late, second goal was one of the few features of a dullish match. Yet again, as many had feared, Italy, away from home, looked cautious. This, despite some splendid pre-tournament results . . . at home.

At Old Trafford, Hungary, with two bad goalkeeping errors, were rather unlucky to go down to Portugal. Their new tactics, with three link-men breaking frequently to support two strikers, were most effective. But Szentmihalyi let a corner escape him, for Augusto to score and, late in the game, he should have had either the centre from which Torres scored, or the actual header, Graça was in excellent form for Portugal, in midfield.

Three days later, Hungary confirmed their quality with a spectacular win against Brazil; Brazil's first defeat in the World Cup since they lost 4–2 in Berne in 1954: to Hungary. Played under steady rain, it was a game largely and brilliantly dominated by Hungary, for whom Bene scored a fine individual goal after three minutes. Brazil without Pelé severely felt the lack of him – and the burden of years carried by Djalma Santos, Bellini and Garrincha. They did equalise when Lima's free kick came out to Tostao, making his World Cup début. But with Florian Albert more irresistible by the minute, Alcindo limping, Hungary dominated the second half. Albert and Bene made a glorious goal for Farkas, then Moszoly scored from a penalty.

At Hillsborough, the Swiss, with eight changes, took the lead against Spain, who rallied in the second half to squeeze home by the odd goal. Uruguay, much more enterprising now, deservedly beat France at the White City, despite giving away an early penalty goal. North Korea fought bravely against a depleted Chilean side, to equalise with Pak Seung Jin's 20-yard drive, three minutes from time. Chile had wasted their first-half dominance.

Saturday's surprise was the defeat of Italy by Russia, at Sunderland. Leaving out Rivera, off form against Chile, Fabbri surprisingly brought in a half-back, Leoncini. The team as a whole fell badly below its individual potential and a hard, uninspired Russian side won with a splendid goal by outside-right Chislenko, in the second half.

England, bringing in Paine and Peters (as a link-man) beat a nervous ultra-defensive Mexico with difficulty. A superb right-footed shot by Bobby Charlton gave them the lead before half-time; Charlton's fine pass sent Greaves through near the end, for Hunt to put in the rebound. Moore was an impressive half-back, but the game was virtually a non-contest. Mexico barely tried to score.

Portugal, helped by defensive errors – an own goal, a silly pass-back – easily beat Bulgaria at Old Trafford. In Group 2, the most unpleasant match of the tournament so far saw Albrecht of Argentina sent off, both sides massing cautiously in defence. A great anti-climax after Germany's bright beginning.

So to the following Tuesday, the elimination of Brazil, the traumatic shock of North Korea beating Italy.

At Everton, Brazil made nine desperate changes, brought in seven men having their first World Cup game. But with Manga, Gilmar's deputy, unsafe in goal, Portugal quickly went two ahead, each a rather soft goal. After 14 minutes, Manga weakly punched out Eusebio's cross. Lively little Simoes, who'd started the move, headed in. Then Torres headed Coluna's free kick across for Eusebio to head another.

A brutal foul by Morais on the clearly half-fit Pelé then crippled him; and Brazil's last hope of recovery. Late in the game, Rildo came up to score a consolation goal, but when a right-wing corner was only half headed clear, the superb Eusebio whipped the ball in, to decide the match. Portugal, who played with Augusto as a deep inside-left, had always been the more impressive. An era had ended.

At Middlesbrough, Italy missed two good chances, lost Bulgarelli with an injury after 34 minutes, a goal (Pak Doo Ik) seven minutes later – and never recovered. Running fast and hard, the Koreans were worth their astonishing success against a flaccid, demoralised side.

In Group II, an unenterprising Argentina made heavy weather of beating Switzerland, while Uruguay, deplorably negative, allowed Mexico the initiative at Wembley. Still, their goalless draw was enough to qualify them.

Next day, England took the field to win a laboured 2–0 victory over France; reduced to ten fit men after Herbin's early injury. Roger Hunt scored a goal in each half, but the midfield build-up was again poor while the defence had two sustained bad periods.

Russia, with nine reserves, defended much of the game, but still beat Chile, after the injured Marcos had equalised. Bulgaria shocked Hungary with Asparoukhov's early goal (Gelei was stranded outside the penalty area) but Bulgaria's second own goal of the tournament helped Hungary to come back, and join Portugal in the quarters.

In the quarter-finals, the four "first" teams in their groups knocked out the four "seconds". North Korea, playing wonderfully lively football, astonished Portugal with a goal in the first minute, followed by two more. Their attack in this period was mobile, inventive and incisive. Then Eusebio brilliantly took over, scoring twice before half-time – the second a penalty – two more (including another penalty) after the interval. A fifth goal from a corner, by Augusto, ended Korea's brave fight, but they had won the hearts of the Everton crowd.

At Wembley, England scraped through by 1–0 against a lamentably undisciplined Argentina. Rattin, the captain, was sent off shortly before half-time by the German referee, Herr Kreitlein; and wouldn't go. It took eight minutes' wrangling and a narrowly averted exodus by the whole Argentinian team before play re-started. Previously, Argentina's policy of cynical, deliberate fouling had led Kreitlein to put name after name in his notebook. Rattin's was one of them; soon afterwards, his angry protests led to his expulsion.

Geoff Hurst, brought in to replace the injured Greaves, beautifully headed the goal, 13 minutes from time, but England made awfully heavy weather of it against 10 men.

Gelei's feeble goalkeeping was largely responsible for Hungary going down to Russia, at Sunderland. Chislenko tapped in the first goal, after he fumbled a shot. Porkujan – kept in the side after his two mid-week goals – scored the second after he and Meszoly had failed to deal with a corner. If Rakosi had taken advantage of an open goal, all might have been different. As it was, there was only Bene's goal to console the Hungarians for the fact they'd lost, while playing much the better football.

At Sheffield, where Uruguay should have taken an early lead, Germany took it instead. Held's shot being deflected past the goalkeeper by

Haller. Infuriated when they thought Schnellinger had handled with impunity on the line, some of the Uruguayans lost their heads. Troche went off for kicking Emmerich in the stomach, Silva for badly fouling Haller; and the Germans added three more goals.

Germany's semi-final with Russia, at Goodison, was a travesty of the game. Russia paid the penalty for their ruthless methods when, after only ten minutes, Sabo attempted to trip Beckenbauer, but succeeded only in injuring his ankle so badly that he was a passenger for the rest of the game.

In the early stages, only the astonishing goalkeeping of Yachin kept Germany from taking the lead. It was a minute from half-time when Schnellinger powerfully tackled – and lamed – Chislenko, sending Haller a perfect crossfield ball on to which he ran and scored spectacularly. When Chislenko limped back, he lost the ball at once to a fair tackle by Held, pursued him, kicked him, and was sent off by Lo Bello, the Italian referee.

Germany, then, should have overrun the nine fit Russians, in the second half. Instead, they played cautious, obvious, laborious football, which produced only one goal – a marvellous left-footed shot from outside the box, by Beckenbauer.

Russia fought bravely, with Khusainov and Voronin outstanding, Banichevski and Malafeev willingly chasing everything. A couple of minutes from time, they shamed the Germans with a goal, when Tilkowski dropped a cross from the left, under pressure, and Porkujan headed in. But, to the jeers of a disenchanted crowd, Germany held on, to reach their second Final.

Wembley's semi-final, by contrast, was a delight, one of the most attractive, and sporting, of the competition. England's defence, with Stiles capably looking after Eusebio, was as perfectly compact as ever, while for the first time, Bobby Charlton brilliantly struck his true form. Not only did he get both goals, he distributed the ball with an imaginative subtlety which should have gained a better response. Portugal's attack looked desperately for a way through the fine English defence, pressed for 15 minutes at the start of the second half, without making chances, and dominated the closing minutes, always at their most dangerous when the ball floated to Torres' head.

England led after 30 minutes when Wilson admirably put through Hunt, Pereira could only block the shot, and Charlton coolly scored. Eleven minutes from time, Hurst powerfully shook off a tackle near the right-hand post, and pulled the ball back for Charlton's right foot to strike the second.

Three minutes later, Torres headed in Simoes' centre, Jackie Charlton fisted it out, Eusebio scored handsomely from the penalty. In the last stages, Stiles' fine tackle thwarted Simoes, through alone, Banks, excellent throughout, turned over the bar a right-foot shot from the splendid Coluna. But sandwiched between these incidents was a fine left-footer from Bobby Charlton which Pereira blocked but, again, couldn't hold. England were more than worth a famous victory.

The third place match was a dismal contrast; two disappointed teams playing jaded football. A ridiculous, quite unnecessary handling by Khurtsilava after 13 minutes, when jumping with Torres, allowed Eusebio to give Portugal the lead with yet another penalty. This made his personal total for the competition nine.

Two minutes from half-time, Pereira botched an uncomplicated shot from the lively Metreveli, allowing Malafeev to rush in the equaliser. Two minutes from the end, we were spared extra time when the two Russian centre-backs failed to head away a cross by Simoes from the right. Augusto nodded it down for Torres to score.

England won the Final, maintaining a 65-year unbeaten record against Germany, despite a contentious last-minute equaliser after Emmerich had sent a free kick of doubtful origin into the goalmouth. Weber scored, and the Final went into extra time for the first occasion since 1934.

It was a dramatic, unpredictable game, which produced a vast amount of incident. Germany led after 13 minutes, when Ray Wilson, most untypically, headed a cross weakly down to Haller – who scored. England equalised six minutes later, when Hurst perfectly met Moore's free kick in the air, to head past Tilkowski.

There might well have been other goals. After a German corner, Banks made a double save from Overath, then Emmerich. Three minutes from half-time, Roger Hunt, who'd been preferred to a now fit Jimmy Greaves, should have converted Hurst's fine header. Instead, he shot straight at Tilkowski.

The second half woke up after 18 dull minutes. England being inspired by the splendid control, tireless running and subtle passing of the electrified Ball. Twelve and a half minutes from the end, Hurst's shot, after a half-cleared corner, bobbed up in the goalmouth from the German defence for Peters to score from point blank range. England seemed to have the match won; but then came Weber's goal, and extra time. It was the more ironical as England, 3 minutes earlier, had wasted a marvellous chance, when Ball put through Hunt. With a three to one numerical advantage, Hunt passed so inaccurately, Bobby Charlton shot so hastily, that Germany escaped.

One hundred minutes had gone when Ball got away yet again, for a cross which Hurst thumped in off the underside of the bar. After a breathless hiatus, a conversation with his linesman, Herr Diens allowed it. And in the closing seconds, Hurst ran through a stationary, demoralised German defence to get the fourth.

England's defence had again played splendidly, while Ball, Hurst and Bobby Charlton were the stars of the attack. For Germany, Schulz, the sweeper-up, Beckenbauer, in midfield, Uwe Seeler and the perpetually dangerous Held had been the most impressive.

There can have been no more dramatic World Cup Final.

GROUP I
London – Wembley, White City

England (0) 0, *Uruguay* (0) 0. *Wembley*
England: Banks (Leicester City); Cohen (Fulham), Wilson (Everton); Stiles (Manchester United), Charlton, J. (Leeds United), Moore (West Ham United); Ball (Blackpool), Greaves (Spurs), Charlton, R. (Manchester United), Hunt (Liverpool), Connelly (Manchester United).
Uruguay: Mazurkiewicz; Troche, Ubinas; Gonçalves, Manicera, Caetano; Cortes, Viera, Silva, Rocha, Perez.

France (0) 1, *Mexico* (0) 1. *Wembley*
France: Aubour; Djorkaeff, Budzinski, Artelesa, De Michele; Bosquier, Herbin, Bonnel; Combin, Gondet, Hausser.
Mexico: Calderon; Chaires, Pena, Nunez, Hernandez; Diaz, Mercado, Reyes; Borja, Fragoso, Padilla.
Scorers: Borja for Mexico, Hausser for France.

Uruguay (2) 2, *France* (1) 1. *White City*
Uruguay: Mazurkiewicz; Troche, Ubinas; Gonçalves, Manicera, Caetano; Viera, Cortes, Rocha, Sacia, Perez.
France: Aubour; Djorkaeff, Artelesa, Budzinski, Bosquier; Bonnel, Simon; Herbet, Gondet, De Bourgoing, Hausser.
Scorers: De Bourgoing (penalty) for France, Rocha, Cortes for Uruguay.

England (1) 2, *Mexico* (0) 0. *Wembley*
England: Banks (Leicester City); Cohen (Fulham), Wilson (Everton); Stiles (Manchester United), Charlton, J. (Leeds United), Moore (West Ham United); Paine (Southampton), Greaves (Spurs), Charlton, R. (Manchester United), Hunt (Liverpool), Peters (West Ham United).
Mexico: Calderon; Del Muro; Chaires, Pena, Nunez, Hernandez; Diaz, Jauregui, Reyes; Borja, Padilla.
Scorers: Charlton, R., Hunt for England.

Uruguay (0) 0, *Mexico* (0) 0. *Wembley*
Uruguay: Mazurkiewicz; Troche; Ubinas, Gonçalves, Manicera, Caetano; Viera, Rocha, Cortes, Sacia, Perez.
Mexico: Carbajal; Chaires, Pena, Nunez, Hernandez; Diaz, Mercado; Reyes, Cisneros, Borja, Padilla.

England (1) 2, *France* (0) 0. *Wembley*
England: Banks (Leicester City); Cohen (Fulham), Wilson (Everton); Stiles (Manchester United), Charlton, J. (Leeds United), Moore (West Ham United); Callaghan (Liverpool), Greaves (Spurs), Charlton, R. (Manchester United), Hunt (Liverpool), Peters (West Ham United).
France: Aubour; Djorkaeff, Artelesa, Budzinski, Bosquier; Bonnel, Herbin, Simon; Herbet, Gondet, Hausser.
Scorer: Hunt (2) for England.

GROUP II
Birmingham, Sheffield
West Germany (3) 5, *Switzerland* (0) 0. *Sheffield*
West Germany: Tilkowski; Hottges, Schulz, Weber, Schnellinger; Beckenbauer, Haller; Brulls, Seeler, Overath, Held.
Switzerland: Elsener; Grobety, Schneiter; Tachella, Fuhrer, Bani; Durr, Odermatt, Kunzli, Hosp, Schindelholz.
Scorers: Held, Haller 2 (1 penalty), Beckenbauer 2 for West Germany.

Argentina (0) 2, *Spain* (0) 1. *Villa Park*
Argentina: Roma; Perfumo, Marzolini; Ferreiro, Rattin, Albrecht; Solari, Gonzalez, Artime, Onega, Mas.
Spain: Iribar; Sanchis, Eladio; Pirri, Gallego, Zoco; Ufarte, Del Sol, Peiro, Suarez, Gento.
Scorers: Artime 2 for Argentina, Pirri for Spain.

Spain (0) 2, *Switzerland* (1) 1. *Sheffield*
Spain: Iribar; Sanchis, Reija; Pirri, Gallego, Zoco; Amancio, Del Sol, Peiro, Suarez, Gento.
Switzerland: Elsener; Brodmann, Fuhrer; Leimgruber, Armbruster, Stierli; Bani, Kuhn, Gottardi, Hosp, Quentin.
Scorers: Quentin for Switzerland, Sanchis, Amancio for Spain.

Argentine (0) 0, *West Germany* (0) 0. *Villa Park*
Argentina: Roma; Perfumo, Marzolini; Ferreiro, Rattin, Albrecht; Solari, Gonzalez, Artime, Onega, Mas.
Germany: Tilkowski; Hottges, Schulz, Weber, Schnellinger; Beckenbauer, Haller; Brulls, Seeler, Overath, Held.

Argentina (0) 2, *Switzerland* (0) 0. *Villa Park*
Argentina: Roma; Perfumo, Marzolini; Ferreiro, Rattin, Calics; Solari, Gonzalez, Artime, Onega, Mas.
Switzerland: Eichmann; Fuhrer, Brodmann; Kuhn, Armbruster, Stierli; Bani, Kunzli, Gottardi, Hosp, Quentin.
Scorers: Artime, Onega for Argentina.

West Germany (1) 2, *Spain* (1) 1. *Villa Park*
West Germany: Tilkowski; Hottges, Schulz, Weber, Schnellinger; Beckenbauer, Overath; Kramer, Seeler, Held, Emmerich.
Spain: Iribar; Sanchis, Reija; Glaria, Gallego, Zoco; Amancio, Adelardo, Marcelino, Fuste, Lapetra.
Scorers: Fuste for Spain, Emmerich and Seeler for West Germany.

GROUP III
Liverpool, Manchester
Brazil (1) 2, *Bulgaria* (0) 0. *Everton*
Brazil: Gilmar; Djalma Santos, Bellini, Altair, Paolo Henrique;

Edilson, Lima; Garrincha, Pelé, Alcindo, Jairzinho.
Bulgaria: Naidenov; Shalamanov, Vutzov, Ganganelov, Penev; Kitov, Zhechev, Yakimov; Dermendjiev, Asparoukhov, Kolev.
Scorers: Pelé, Garrincha for Brazil.

Portugal (1) 3, *Hungary* (0) 1. *Old Trafford*
Portugal: Carvalho; Morais, Baptista, Vicente, Hilario; Graça, Coluna; Augusto, Eusebio, Torres, Simoes.
Hungary: Szentmihalyi; Matrai, Kaposzta; Sovari, Meszoly, Sipos; Bene, Nagy, Albert, Farkas, Rakosi.
Scorers: Augusto 2, Torres for Portugal, Bene for Hungary.

Hungary (1) 3, *Brazil* (1) 1. *Everton*
Hungary: Gelei; Kaposzta, Matrai, Sipos, Szepesi; Mathesz, Meszoly; Bene, Albert, Farkas, Rakosi.
Brazil: Gilmar; Djalma Santos, Bellini, Altair, Paolo Henrique; Lima, Gerson; Garrincha, Alcindo, Tostao, Jairzinho.
Scorers: Bene, Farkas, Meszoly (penalty) for Hungary, Tostao for Brazil.

Portugal (2) 3, *Bulgaria* (0) 0. *Old Trafford*
Portugal: José Pereira; Festa, Germano, Vicente, Hilario; Graça, Coluna; Augusto, Eusebio, Torres, Simoes.
Bulgaria: Naidenov; Shalamanov, Vutzov, Gaganelov, Penev; Zhechev, Yakimov; Dermendjiev, Zhekov, Asparoukhov, Kostov.
Scorers: Vutzov (own goal), Eusebio, Torres for Portugal.

Portugal (2) 3, *Brazil* (0) 1. *Everton*
Portugal: José Pereira; Morais, Baptista, Vicente, Hilario; Graça, Coluna, Augusto; Eusebio, Torres, Simoes.
Brazil: Manga; Fidelis, Brito, Orlando, Rildo; Denilson, Lima; Jair, Silva, Pelé, Parana.
Scorers: Simoes, Eusebio 2 for Portugal, Rildo for Brazil.

Hungary (2) 3, *Bulgaria* (1) 1. *Old Trafford*
Hungary: Gelei; Kaposzta, Matrai, Meszoly, Sipos, Szepesi; Mathesz, Albert, Rakosi; Bene, Farkas.
Bulgaria: Simenov; Penev, Largov, Vutzov, Gaganelov; Zhechev, Davidov; Kotkov, Asparoukhov, Yakimov, Kolev.
Scorers: Asparoukhov for Bulgaria; Davidov (own goal), Meszoly, Bene for Hungary.

GROUP IV

Sunderland, Middlesbrough
Russia (2) 3, *North Korea* (0) 0. *Middlesbrough*
Russia: Kavazashvili; Ponomarev, Chesternjiev, Khurtsilava, Ostrovski; Sabo, Schinava; Chislenko, Malafeev, Banichevski, Khusainov.
North Korea: Li Chan Myung; Pak Li Sup, Shin Yung Kyoo, Lim

Zoong Sun, Kang Bong Chil; Pak Seung Din, Im Seung Hwi; Han Bong Jin, Pak Doo Ik, Kang Ryong-Woon, Kim Seung II.
Scorers: Malafeev 2, Banichevski for Russia.

Italy (1) 2, *Chile* (0) 0. *Sunderland*
Italy: Albertosi; Burgnich, Facchetti; Rosato, Salvadore, Lodetti; Perani, Bulgarelli, Mazzola, Rivera, Barison,
Chile: Olivares; Eyzaguirre, Cruz, Figueroa, Villanueva; Prieto, Marcos, Araya, Tobar, Fouilloux, Sanchez.
Scorers: Barison, Mazzola for Italy.

Chile (1) 1, *North Korea* (0) 1. *Middlesbrough*
Chile: Olivares; Valentini, Cruz; Figueroa, Villanueva, Prieto; Marcos, Fouilloux, Landa, Araya, Sanchez.
North Korea: Li Chan Myung; Pak Li Sup, Shin Yung Kyoo, Kim Joon Sun, O Yoon Kyung; Pak Seung Jin, Im Sung Hwi; Han Bong Jin, Pak Doo Ik, Ri Dong Woon, Kim Seung II.
Scorers: Marcos (penalty) for Chile, Pak Sung Jin for North Korea.

Russia (0) 1, *Italy* (0) 0. *Sunderland*
Russia: Yachin; Ponomarev, Chesternjiev, Khurtsilava, Danilov; Sabo, Voronin; Chislenko, Malafeev, Banichevski, Khusainov.
Italy: Albertosi; Burgnich, Facchetti; Rosato, Salvadore, Leoncini; Meroni, Lodetti, Mazzola, Bulgarelli, Pascutti.
Scorer: Chislenko for Russia.

North Korea (1) 1, *Italy* (0) 0. *Middlesbrough*
North Korea: Li Chan Myung; Lim Zoong Sun, Shin Yung Kyoo; Ha Jung Won, O Yoon Kyung, Im Seun Hwi; Han Bong Jin, Pak Doo Ik, Pak Seung Zin, Kim Bong Hwan, Yan Sung Kook.
Italy: Albertosi; Landini, Facchetti; Guarneri, Janich, Fogli; Perani, Bulgarelli, Mazzola, Rivera, Barison.
Scorer: Pak Doo Ik for North Korea.

Russia (1) 2, *Chile* (1) 1. *Sunderland*
Russia: Kavazashvili; Getmanov, Chesternjiev, Afonin, Ostrovski; Voronin, Korneev; Metreveli, Serebrianikov, Markarov, Porkujan.
Chile: Olivares; Valentini, Cruz, Figueroa, Villanueva; Marcos, Prieto; Araya, Landa, Yavar, Sanchez.
Scorers: Porkujan 2 for Russia, Marcos for Chile.

Placings

	Group I				Goals		
	P	W	D	L	F	A	Pts.
England	3	2	1	0	4	0	5
Uruguay	3	1	2	0	2	1	4
Mexico	3	0	2	1	1	3	2
France	3	0	1	2	2	5	1

Placings

	Group II			Goals		
	P	W	D	L	F	A	Pts.
W. Germany	3	2	1	0	7	1	5
Argentina	3	2	1	0	4	1	5
Spain	3	1	0	2	4	5	2
Switzerland	3	0	0	3	1	9	0

	Group III					
	P	W	D	L	F	A	Pts.
Portugal	3	3	0	0	9	2	6
Hungary	3	2	0	1	7	5	4
Brazil	3	1	0	2	4	6	2
Bulgaria	3	0	0	3	1	8	0

	Group IV					
	P	W	D	L	F	A	Pts.
Russia	3	3	0	0	6	1	6
N. Korea	3	1	1	1	2	4	3
Italy	3	1	0	2	2	2	2
Chile	3	0	1	2	2	5	1

QUARTER-FINALS

England (0) 1, *Argentina* (0) 0. *Wembley*
England: Banks (Leicester City); Cohen (Fulham), Wilson (Everton); Stiles (Manchester United), Charlton, J. (Leeds United), Moore (West Ham United); Ball (Blackpool), Hurst (West Ham United), Charlton, R. (Manchester United), Hunt (Liverpool), Peters (West Ham United).
Argentina: Roma; Ferreiro, Perfumo, Albrecht, Marzolini; Gonzalez, Rattin, Onega; Solari, Artime, Mas.
Scorer: Hurst for England.

West Germany (1) 4, *Uruguay* (0) 0. *Sheffield*
West Germany: Tilkowski; Hottges, Weber, Schulz, Schnellinger; Beckenbauer, Haller, Overath; Seeler, Held, Emmerich.
Uruguay: Mazurkiewicz; Troche; Ubinas, Gonçalves, Manicera, Caetano; Salva, Rocha; Silva, Cortez, Perez.
Scorers: Held, Beckenbauer, Seeler, Haller for West Germany.

Portugal (2) 5, *North Korea* (3) 3. *Everton*
Portugal: José Pereira; Morais, Baptista, Vicente, Hilario; Graça, Coluna; Augusto, Eusebio, Torres, Simoes.
North Korea: Li Chan Myung; Rim Yung Sum, Shin Yung Kyoo, Ha Jung Won, O Yoon Kyung; Pak Seung Jin, Jon Seung Hwi; Han Bong Jin, Pak Doo Ik, Li Dong Woon, Yang Sung Kook.
Scorers: Pak Seung Jin, Yang Sung Kook, Li Dong Woon, for North Korea, Eusebio 4 (2 penalties), Augusto, for Portugal.

Russia (1) 2, *Hungary* (0) 1. *Sunderland*
Russia: Yachin; Ponomarev, Chesternjiev, Voronin, Danilov; Sabo, Khusainov; Chislenko, Banichevski, Malafeev, Porkujan.
Hungary: Gelei; Matrai, Kaposzta, Meszoly, Sipos, Szepesi; Nagy, Albert, Rakosi; Bene, Farkas.
Scorers: Chislenko, Porkujan for Russia, Bene for Hungary.

SEMI-FINALS

West Germany (1) 2, *Russia* (0) 1. *Everton*
West Germany: Tilkowski; Hottges, Weber, Schulz, Schnellinger; Beckenbauer, Haller, Overath; Seeler, Held, Emmerich.
Russia: Yachin; Ponomarev, Chesternjiev, Voronin, Danilov; Sabo, Khusainov; Chislenko, Banichevski, Malafeev, Porkujan.
Scorers: Haller, Beckenbauer for Germany, Porkujan for Russia.

England (1) 2, *Portugal* (0) 1. *Wembley*
England: Banks (Leicester City); Cohen (Fulham), Wilson (Everton); Stiles (Manchester United), Charlton, J. (Leeds United), Moore (West Ham United); Ball (Blackpool), Hurst (West Ham United), Charlton, R. (Manchester United), Hunt (Liverpool), Peters (West Ham United).
Portugal: José Pereira; Festa, Baptista, Carlos, Hilario; Graça, Coluna, Augusto; Eusebio, Torres, Simoes.
Scorers: Charlton, R. 2 for England, Eusebio (penalty) for Portugal.

THIRD PLACE MATCH

Portugal (1) 2, *Russia* (1) 1. *Wembley*
Portugal: José Pereira; Festa, Baptista, Carlos, Hilario; Graça, Coluna, Augusto; Eusebio, Torres, Simoes.
Russia: Yachin; Ponomarev, Khurtsilava, Korneev, Danilov; Voronin, Sichinava; Metreveli, Malafeev, Banichevski, Serebrianikov.
Scorers: Eusebio (penalty), Torres for Portugal, Malafeev for Russia.

FINAL

England (1) 4, *W. Germany* (1) 2 after extra time. *Wembley*
England: Banks; Cohen, Wilson; Stiles, Charlton, J., Moore; Ball, Hurst, Hunt, Charlton, R., Peters.
West Germany: Tilkowski; Hottges, Schulz, Weber, Schnellinger; Haller, Beckenbauer, Overath; Seeler, Held, Emmerich.
Scorers: Hurst (3), Peters for England, Haller, Weber for Germany.
Leading Scorer: Eusebio 9.

WORLD CUP 1970

For the third time in four tournaments, Brazil won the World Cup, and very properly retained the Jules Rimet trophy in consequence. There was no doubt at all of the merits of their success, even if the Italian team they crushed 4–1 in the Final could scarcely claim to be the competition's second best. Brazil won every one of their matches, including a narrow and slightly fortunate win against England – thus condemned to play their quarter final in Leon, against West Germany.

Most teams seemed to solve the problem of altitude, but that of heat was simply insoluble. Goodness knows how much the temperatures in Guadalajara, which sometimes rose as high as 98° in a match, affected the England players. In the circumstances they acquitted themselves with honour especially Bobby Moore, rising superbly above the dingy and unfounded charges of theft brought against him in Colombia.

From an objective point of view, the success of a Brazilian team so wholeheartedly committed to attack – and definitely porous in defence – was a splendid sign in a grey footballing world. For the next four years, one was entitled to hope, the future might at long last lie with creative rather than negative football.

Brazil's triumph was the more remarkable in that they had changed horses, or managers, rather further than mid-stream, Zagalo, a hero of their 1958 and 1962 teams, succeeding the controversial Joao Saldanha.

The tournament opened, as it did in 1966, with a dull 0–0 draw; this time in the torrid heat of the Azteca Stadium, between Mexico and Russia. The Mexicans, who had lost one of their best young players, Onofre, with a broken leg, a few days earlier, and unwisely left out their most thrustful forward, Enrique Borja, who had very nearly been omitted from the 22 for "political reasons", had rather the better of things. At least they obliged the sound Russian goalkeeper, Kavazashvili, to make saves from the lively Horacio Lopez and Guzman, in the first and second halves respectively. Lopez, in the second half, received the ball in a surprisingly unmarked position, but was too slow to score.

Evriuzhikin was lively on Russia's left wing in the opening stages, but by the last twenty minutes, their cautious side had manifestly run out of steam. Asatiani made occasional promising breaks from midfield, and Bychevetz had his moments, but all in all it was a dull Russian display.

On Tuesday, in Guadalajara, England deservedly beat Rumania 1–0, playing an efficient, disciplined game, in which they were given no protection by a Belgian referee, M. Loraux, who did not even caution Mocanu, Rumania's left-back, after three dreadful fouls on Newton (whom he put out of the game), Lee and Wright, Newton's substitute. The only goal came after twenty minutes of the second half when Ball crossed from the right, and the ball reached Geoff Hurst, via the head of Francis Lee. Very calmly, Hurst controlled the ball, beat his man, and pivoted to hit a low, left-footed cross shot into the far corner of goal.

The Rumanians attacked briskly in the opening minutes, but later settled down to what Alan Ball termed scornfully "keep ball". They did have two powerful long range shots in the second half, by Dembrowski and Nunweiller VI, but Banks got to them both. Moore had an excellent game in the England defence, Terry Cooper was superbly adventurous, and Bobby Charlton showed more fire and drive than for many an international.

In Leon, on the same day, in Group IV, an extraordinary and fascinating game between Peru and Bulgaria saw the Bulgarians go two ahead, cleverly exploiting free kicks, only for the Peruvians to recover superbly and score three times, to win.

There was a minute's silence at the start for victims of the appalling Peruvian earthquake, and it was small wonder that the Peruvians started badly. Dermendijev scored the first goal after 13 minutes, when he ran over the ball and on, to convert a cleverly taken free kick. Perhaps the Peruvians expected the same tactic in the second half when, after 4 minutes, Bulgaria were awarded another free kick on the edge of the box. But Bonvev drove the ball straight past a goalkeeper who might have had it.

The Peruvians had changed their right-back Campos for Javier Gonzalez, thus tightening a porous defence. But it was the substitution of the young centre-forward, Hugo Sotil, for the fast coloured winger, Baylon, just after Gallardo had scored with a cross shot just after Bonev's goal, which was decisive. The Peruvian 4-2-4 formation really began to move, and when Sotil was fouled, it was Chumpitaz's turn to surprise a goalkeeper directly from a free kick. With 65 minutes played, Cubillas ran on to a long ball from Mifflin and beat Chalamanov to shoot home again; the winning goal.

At Puebla, in Group II, Uruguay won unimpressively, 2-0, against a stalwart Israeli team. The Uruguayans' poor performance was not unconnected with the fact that they lost their key midfield player, Pedro Rocha, with a serious injury, after only 12 minutes.

The following day, in Guadalajara, Brazil took the field and charmed everybody with an effervescent 4-1 win over the Czechs. The Mexicans, who had long since decided to cheer Brazil and jeer England, were particularly pleased, but there was a touch of unreality about it all. Having shown up the obvious holes in the Brazilian defence and taken an early lead through Petras, the Czechs conceded an equaliser directly from Rivelino's ferocious left-footed free kick; and fell to pieces.

They conceded a second goal, early in the second half when Pelé, in splendid form, was allowed to catch Gerson's long left footed pass on his chest, control it and score. Kvasniak, who had come on as substitute after the interval, to play at a snail's pace, missed the easiest of equalising chances from a corner; and away went Brazil immediately to make it 3-1. The powerful Jairzinho looked offside when he strode on to Gerson's pass, lobbed the goalkeeper, and ran the ball in, but the goal stood.

Desperate now to score, the Czechs left larger gaps than ever, and Jairzinho forced his way admirably past three men to get a fourth. He Gerson, Pelé and Rivelino had looked formidable; but the England players were unperturbed. After all, the Czech marking had been scandalously slack.

In Group I, Belgium had no great trouble in beating El Salvador 3-0 at the Azteca in an undistinguished game. Magana, the Salvador goalkeeper, kept the score down, but Belgium, who went ahead through a long shot by Van Moer after only two minutes, were anything but effective in attack. Their third goal came from the tournament's first penalty, converted by Lambert.

The great surprise of the day, and of the tournament so far, came at Leon in Group IV, where Morocco gave West Germany the fright of their lives. Playing with skill and spirit, Morocco deservedly led after 20 minutes when Hottges headed weakly back to Maier, in goal, and the ball dropped at the feet of Houmane – who coolly scored.

Morocco stayed ahead till the 56th minute, when Uwe Seeler converted Muller's pass with a strong ground shot. 12 minutes from time, Grabowski got away on the right wing, Loehr headed against the bar, and Muller put it in. It had been an awfully close call and a splendid riposte by the Moroccans to their many detractors.

In Group II, at Toluca, Italy squeezed through against Sweden with a goal scored from long range after 11 minutes by Domenghini, after Giacinto Facchetti had played the ball back to him from his corner. Thereafter, an Italian team which had been shaken by a contretemps between Rivera and its officials, was content to hold on to its lead. It may be said in passing that England and Bobby Moore had shown no adverse reactions at all to his misadventures in Bogota, where he'd been held in custody for several days on a manifestly absurd charge of stealing a bracelet.

The next round of matches, the following Saturday, saw Russia come most powerfully and unexpectedly out of their shells. Before a huge crowd in Mexico City, they showed the other, offensive side of their Jekyll and Hyde personality, demolishing Belgium with superb attacking football, in which Asatiani, Muntijan, Bychevetz and Evriuzhikin were outstanding, while Albert Chesternijev, that ever faithful bird dog, was massive in defence, and excellent in distribution.

Belgium might have led after 14 minutes, when Kavazashvili made a fine save from Van Moer's header, but from that point, Russia took over the game. A minute later, Bychevetz went through to open the score. Piot's saves kept Russia at bay till 12 minutes into the second half, then Asatiani, tall and strong, broke through to beat Piot with a ground shot. Two minutes more, and Bychevetz scored again, this time a right footed shot, and Khmelnitzki headed the fourth from an exchange with Evriuzhikin. Belgium's consolatory goal was scored by Lambert, after Kavazashvili had blocked Van Himst's drive.

In Puebla, Italy, interested only in survival, played a dreary draw against Uruguay without Pedro Rocha. Italy's plan to put all their eggs in the basket of Gigi Riva had certainly not borne fruit so far.

In Group III, at Guadalajara, the Czechs again took an early lead through the blond Petras, this time heading in Bohumil Vesely's right wing centre, but again were betrayed by their lack of condition. In the second half, Neagu wriggled through on the left to equalise, and when 31 minutes into the second half, Neagu was brought down by Zlocha

Dumitrache converted the penalty to keep Rumanian hopes alive, and end those of the Czechs. The win was just about deserved.

In Leon, the Peruvians were held by the brave Moroccans till the 65th minute, but then the storm broke, and Sotil, Challe and Cubillas scored goals in a comfortable win.

Next day came the clash all Mexico, and the football world, awaited; England against Brazil. Till three o'clock in the morning, Brazilians and Mexicans deliberately laid siege to the Hilton Hotel where England were staying, with chants and motor horns, doing their best – and not without success – to keep the players awake. The police played an ominously passive role. Despite this, and the fact that the match was played at high noon, in 98 degrees of heat, England put up a magnificent performance, against splendid opponents. Had the World Cup committee not prostituted the tournament to European television, fixing all kick off times in the afternoon, who knows what might have happened? As it was, the rain broke in the afternoon, so that a 4 p.m. kick off might have made all the difference to England. But as Bobby Moore, who played another superlative game, said, "We couldn't have come any nearer. They made one chance, and took it."

This was after 14 minutes of the second half, when brilliant control by Tostao, on the left, took out three England players. Pelé, well policed by Mullery but always dangerous, rolled the ball across goal to Jairzinho, who scored at leisure.

England, however, missed chances aplenty. In the first half, Geoff Hurst stopped, believing himself in an offside position, then shot feebly, when he might have run on. Late in the second half, when Jeff Astle and Colin Bell had replaced Bobby Charlton and Francis Lee, Astle nodded down a chance which Ball should have exploited, while Astle himself missed parlously, when a defender played the ball to his feet. Later, Alan Ball clipped the bar with Felix, Brazil's uncertain goalkeeper, beaten.

But the finest save of the match was made after 10 minutes by Gordon Banks, when Jairzinho eluded Terry Cooper, crossed, and Pelé headed ferociously to the left-hand corner. Somehow Banks got across his goal to turn the ball over the top with one hand. In the second half, he made other fine saves from Paulo Cesar, twice, Rivelino and Jairzinho. Brazil clearly and badly missed their injured general, Gerson.

In Group I, Mexico made an easy meal of El Salvador, while in Leon, West Germany suddenly and devastatingly came to life, ripping apart what had once been considered a tough Bulgarian defence, to score five.

Libuda, the gifted but inconsistent right winger, had one of his most devastatingly effective games. After slack marking had allowed Nikodimov to give Bulgaria the lead from Bonev's free kick, he rounded Gaganelov and shot past Simeonov to equalise. He then beat the left-back again to make a furiously volleyed goal for Muller; then, when Nikodimov brought him down early in the second half, Muller converted the penalty. Seeler got the fourth, but Libuda was again involved in the fifth. Fouled on the edge of the box, he placed his free kick expertly for Muller to head a fine goal.

In Toluca, Israel surprised the disappointing Swedes in a very tough game, watched by only 3,000. Turesson put Sweden ahead after 54 minutes, but three minutes later, Spiegler shot the equaliser.

Brazil won their third and final qualifying game in Guadalajara in intense afternoon heat, the next Wednesday, though the Rumanians, after a bad beginning, gave them quite a game of it. Pelé, who once more had some jewelled moments, scored the first goal from a sizzling right footer after 19 minutes, Tostao jumping over the ball, and also scored the third Brazilian goal, 21 minutes into the second half, stretching out an elastic leg to push in Tostao's square pass – from Jairzinho's centre. The winger himself scored the second, in the 22nd minute, after Paulo Cesar had beaten his back and gone to the line.

But Dumitrache exploited Brazil's central defensive weaknesses to get back a goal, and Dembrowski, heading in Satmareanu's cross, scored a second, seven minutes from the end. Weak goalkeeping was again a clear Brazilian failing, though it's true that the lack of Rivelino and Gerson deprived the team of strength in attack.

In Leon, Gerd Muller scored a hat trick, bringing his total to seven, and West Germany beat Peru 3–1, to lead their group. Playing with Schnellinger as sweeper, Uwe Seeler in midfield, two wingers lying wide and sending in high crosses, Germany riddled Peru's weak defence in the first half. Muller seldom moved out of the middle, but he exploited those chances he had splendidly; one of his goals was a superb header. In the second half, Germany seemed to run out of steam in the heat and altitude, and the Peruvians got one goal back and might have had more, were it not for the fine goalkeeping of Maier.

In Group II, there was a small scandal. The Uruguay v Sweden game should have been refereed by the Brazilian, Moraes, but he was replaced owing to rumours that there had been attempts to "buy" him. The Uruguayans denied them violently, played under protest – and lost to an 89th minute goal headed from a right wing cross by Grahn. Nevertheless, they squeezed through the the quarter-finals on goal difference.

In Mexico City, El Salvador defended to the death against Russia, but couldn't hold out in the second half, when the Russians scored twice through Bychevetz, exploiting a fine pass by Muntijan, and repeated the combination after 73 minutes.

Mexico then proceeded to qualify on the Thursday, beating the disappointing Belgians 1–0, thanks to a strongly disputed penalty, converted by Pena.

In Toluca, Italy disgraced themselves again in Group II, easily the poorest and most disappointing of the four, by allowing themselves to be held to a goalless draw by Israel, despite the presence of millions of lire worth of stars.

England, in Group III, were scarcely much better. They qualified thanks to their meagre 1–0 victory over Czechoslovakia, but their performance was wretched in the extreme. The changes made by Ramsey may have rested star players, but they decisively weakened the side. Jackie Charlton looked clumsily unhappy against the quick Petras, while Jeff Astle, till he was replaced in the second half by Peter Osgood, was totally inept. Bobby Charlton, equalling Billy Wright's record by playing in his 105th international, was also replaced; by Alan Ball – and things did improve a little. The one goal came early in the second half, when Kuna tackled Colin Bell, then fell on the ball and handled it. The handling may or may not have been intentional; afterwards, the French referee, M. Machin, indicated that he'd given it for a trip. Be that as it may, Allan Clarke coolly converted it – and England were sonorously whistled till the end of play. Three balls went into the crowd, and were not thrown back.

Cooper, the superb Moore, Newton and Mullery could look back on the game with satisfaction, but the Czechs were the smoother, more intelligent team, and were several times unlucky not to score – not least when Dobias' fine shot tore through Banks' hands and struck the crossbar, late in the second half – not long after Alan Ball had struck the bar for England. This apart, Banks had another excellent game.

In Leon, the Moroccans again distinguished themselves, and the Bulgarians once more disappointed gloomily, in a drawn match. Though Bulgaria took the lead with a soft goal from Jetchev's long range ground shot, Morocco fought back well, to equalise through Chazouani.

The eight quarter finalists were thus Mexico, Russia, Italy, Uruguay, Brazil, England, West Germany and Peru, with Brazil and West Germany looking much the best propositions, on form.

England went out in the quarter-finals, in Leon, to West Germany; in a match they seemed to have well won, and virtually in their pockets It may well have been that the vicissitudes, the physical strain, of Group III took its toll in the end, it may well have been that to substitute Bobby Charlton and Martin Peters with Colin Bell and Norman Hunter was a mistake. Be that as it may, they would probably have kept their 2–0 lead had Gordon Banks not been taken ill the day before the match and forced to withdraw. His place went to Peter Bonetti, who played well enough till he was beaten by a long, diagonal shot from the edge of the area by Franz Beckenbauer. Banks, one felt, would have had that shot, and at least one of the other German goals.

For more than an hour, England played superbly, and they well deserved their two, excellent goals. The first – his own first goal in international football – was brilliantly engineered and scored by Alan Mullery. Midway through the first half, he exchanged passes with Lee, hit a fine crossfield pass to Keith Newton, then raced to the far post to smash in the responding centre.

Five minutes after half-time, Newton crossed for another fine goal, after receiving from the excellent Geoff Hurst. This time, it was Peters, much sharper in this game, who ran the ball in.

The substitution of Grabowski for Libuda on Germany's right wing was of decisive value. Where Libuda had been mastered, Grabowski was irresistible, and the balance tipped in the hot sunshine. Beckenbauer scored his goal, Hurst almost made it 3–1 with a glorious low header which beat Maier but skimmed the far post – then Schnellinger's high centre caused chaos in the tired England defence and Uwe Seeler back-headed the equaliser.

So the game, like the 1966 Final, went to extra time. Lee wriggled past Schnellinger on the line and pushed the ball across for Hurst to score; but the goal was mysteriously disallowed. Lee wasn't offside, nor had he fouled Schnellinger. So, in the second period of extra time, Grabowski beat Cooper again and crossed, Loehr returned the ball and Muller, who had been kept quiet for most of the game, banged it home, in the goalmouth. The holders were out; in a game they should have won.

Bobby Moore had another superlative game, while Bobby Charlton, in impressive form till he was substituted, beat Billy Wright's record by winning his 106th England cap.

Perhaps the largest surprise of the quarter finals was that both Group II teams, Italy and Uruguay should get through, despite their previous drab form. The Italians played Mexico in Toluca and crushed them with a splendid second half, in which Luigi Riva, with two goals, finally justified the Messianic campaign there had been in his favour throughout Italy, while Gianni Rivera substituted Mazzola at half time and splendidly organised the Italian forward line. This was deeply satisfying to a player who had been dropped from the first match, and very nearly sent home after outspokenly criticising the team's officials. Mexico opened the score after only 12 minutes when Munguia and Fragoso set up a goal for Gonzalez, but once Italy had equalised through a deflected shot by Domenghini, they lost their grip on the game. Italy's vastly superior skills asserted themselves; as they should have done in previous games.

In Mexico City, the Uruguayans, still without Rocha, most un-expectedly beat Russia with a disputed goal in the last moments of extra time, thus justifying their astonishing record in the World Cup. Esparrago got it, after Cubilla, a very active striker, had beaten Chesternijev and crossed from the goal line. The Russians bitterly pro-tested that the ball had gone out of play; but though they had some near misses, they'd only themselves to blame for a lack of flair and punch in attack.

In Guadalajara, Brazil beat Peru 4–2 in an expectedly high scoring game, full of goal scoring errors. With Gerson and Rivelino back in the six, Brazil took the lead through the latter and increased it through Tostao. Gallardo made it 1–2 after 27 minutes, Tostao restored the two goal margin after 52, Gallardo scored again after a rebound from Brito, but a splendid individual goal by Jairzinho made the game safe for Brazil.

The semi-finals were won, respectively, by Italy in Mexico City and Brazil in Guadalajara. Italy's victory over West Germany was achieved in a match of extraordinary ups and downs, which will long be the source of argument. Should West Germany have had one, or even two penalty kicks? Would they have won if Franz Beckenbauer had not been injured, and forced to play extra time with his arm strapped to his chest? Would the Germans have been favoured by a stronger, better referee than the ineptly permissive Yamasaki?

On the other hand, it must be confessed that in the second half, when they dominated an over-cautious Italy, they missed chances in superabundance. It was in the third minute of injury time that Grabowski, from the left, crossed the ball, and Karl Heinz Schnellinger banged it home for Germany's belated equaliser.

Italy had taken the lead with a good left-footed goal by Boninsegna, hit from the edge of the box after a lucky rebound from two German defenders. Only seven and a half minutes had gone, and with Italy's *catenaccio* subduing the German attack, the Italians seemed firmly entrenched.

In the second half, they brought on Gianni Rivera for Mazzola, as they'd so successfully done against Mexico. But now they lost control of midfield, went back too cautiously into defence, and surrendered their initiative to a German team which proceeded to bombard them. Seeler missed a fine chance when Cera allowed the ball to pass him, then Grabowski and Overath missed fine opportunities. Beckenbauer raced through with marvellous fluency, only to be ruthlessly chopped down on the edge of the box; an incident which cost Germany not only a probable goal but the later services of Beckenbauer.

Desperate, they took off Patzke, brought on Siggi Held – full of fire and running – and abandoned their own *catenaccio*. Held's tremendous shot was stopped on the line, Albertosi made a fine save from Seeler's header; and at last came the equaliser.

Extra time brought a flurry of goals. Germany went ahead after five minutes when Poletti ran the ball almost over his own line, and Gerd Muller provided the finishing touch. Burgnich materialised to score after Rivera's free kick, Riva pivoted to beat Schnellinger and score with a splendid left foot cross shot, and the first period ended. In the second, Seeler had another header saved by Albertosi. From the corner, however, he nodded across goal for Muller to fling himself to head an equaliser. The winner came after six minutes, Boninsegna breaking on the left, then pulling the ball back for Gianni Rivera to score.

In Guadalajara, Uruguay, still without Rocha, embarrassed Brazil by taking the lead with a somewhat ludicrous goal. Coming in from the right, along the goal line, Cubilla was confronted by Wilson Piazza. His shot, if that is what it was, went by Piazza, bounced past Felix, and ended in the goal.

It was only late in the first half that Brazil equalised through a fine goal by Clodoaldo, running through on the blind side. From that point, their superiority manifested itself. This, though Felix was obliged to make one glorious save from a header by Cubilla.

Despite the various ingenuities of Pelé, however, the second Brazilian goal did not arrive till 14 minutes from time, after a marvellous run down the right wing and shot into the far corner, by Jairzinho. A left-footed shot by Rivelino, in the very last minute, made it 3–1. Uruguay had resisted nobly against the highly gifted Brazilian team.

The third place match, which lacked Rocha, Beckenbauer and Grabowski, was a curious, paradoxical, entertaining affair, won 1–0 by a West German team which, manifestly weary, could have given away four or five goals. Twice, in the closing stages of the first half, Schnellinger made remarkable saves from Montero-Castillo.

The only goal, scored after 27 minutes, was a splendid one. Libuda, always the master of Mujica, beat him once again and crossed. Seeler, astonishing as always in the air, headed back across goal to Muller, who played the ball backwards to Overath. Overath, who had been spreading some glorious passes around, now produced an equally glorious shot, which flew wide of Mazurkiewicz's left hand.

From that point, most of the pressure was Uruguay's, but Mazurkiewicz, in the second half, still had to make a couple of thrilling saves from sharp German attacks. In the event, however, it was Horst Wolter, who had been scrambling sadly for high crosses throughout the game, who saved it for Germany, brilliantly parrying Ancheta's header.

Brazil, overwhelming favourites to win the Final against Italy, won it . . . overwhelmingly. This, though they did let Italy back into the game late in the first half, with a silly defensive mistake. Their football, throughout, was wonderfully assured, technically adroit, calm and deadly. For Italy, only the stout-hearted, incisive Sandro Mazzola and the lively Boninsegna – who was mysteriously substituted – reached the same high plateau attained by so many of the Brazilians. Gerson, who was given a bewildering amount of room by Italy, was once more his team's chief orchestrator, and restored their lead in the second half with a marvellous left-footed shot on the turn from outside the penalty box.

Pelé may have had more spectacular games, but what can one say about a player who heads one goal and makes two others? Tostao bravely laid off fine balls throughout the match, under formidable pressure, Jairzinho ran with his usual insistent power, Clodoaldo recovered from his mistake to play with high skill and resilience in midfield.

Brazil took the lead after 18 minutes when Pelé leaped gymnastically to Rivelino's high cross from the left and headed it in. With Carlos Alberto finding infinite space on the right – his ultimate goal was a long time a-looming – Brazil seemed to have the game well in hand. But with seven minutes left till half-time, Clodoaldo's foolish backheel threw his defence into tatters, Felix rushed hastily out of goal, and Boninsegna had only to kick the ball into an empty net, after a spirited burst.

Italy, with Mazzola running and dribbling and passing beautifully, seemed to be back in the game. But Gerson's goal stunned them after 21 minutes, and from that point, Brazil took charge again. Five minutes later, they scored a third when Gerson took a free kick, Pelé touched the ball on to Jairzinho and the outside-right ran it in, on the left hand post.

Italy substituted Juliano for Bertini, Rivera inexplicably for Boninsegna, but it made no difference, other than to diminish their thrust up front. Three minutes from time, another finely articulated Brazilian movement concluded with Jairzinho finding Pelé, who laid the ball off perfectly for Carlos Alberto to come thundering in to score his captain's goal. It was, all in all, a fine day for football.

GROUP I. Mexico City

Mexico (0) 0, *Russia* (0) 0
Mexico: Calderon; Vantolra, Pena, Guzman, Perez; Hernandez Pulido, Velarde (Munguia); Valdivia, Fragoso, Horacio Lopez.
Russia: Kavazashvili; Lovchev, Chesternijev, Kaplichni, Logofet, Serebrianikov (Pusacs), Muntijan, Asatiani; Nodia (Porjujan), Bychevetz, Evriuzhikin.

Belgium (1) 3, *El Salvador* (0) 0
Belgium: Piot; Heylens, Thissen; Dewalque, Dockx, Semmeling, Van Moer, Devrindt, Van Himst, Lambert, Puis.
El Salvador: Magaña, Rivas, Mariona, Osorio, Manzano; Quintanilla, Vazquez, Cabezas; Rodriguez, Martinez, Aparicio.
Scorers: Van Moer (2), Lambert, penalty for Belgium.

Russia (1) 4, *Belgium* (0) 1
Russia: Kavazashvili; Dzodzuashvili (Kiselev), Chesternijev, Khurtsilava, Afonin, Kaplichni (Lovchev); Asatiani, Muntijan; Bychevetz, Evriuzhikin, Khmelnitzki.
Belgium: Piot; Heylens, Thissen, Dewalque, Jeck, Dockx, Semmeling, Van Moer, Van Himst, Puis, Lambert.
Scorers: Bychevetz 2, Asatiani, Khmelnitzki for Russia, Lambert for *Belgium.*

Mexico (1) 4 *El Salvador* (0) 0
Mexico: Calderon; Vantolra, Pena, Guzman, Perez; Gonzalez, Munguia; Valdivia, Borja (Basaguren, then Lopez), Fragoso, Padilla.
El Salvador: Magana; Rivas, Mariona, Osorio, Cortez, (Monge); Quintanilla, Vazquez, Cabezas; Rodriguez, Martinez, Aparicio (Mendez.)
Scorers: Valdivia 2, Fragoso, Basaguren, for Mexico.

Russia (0) 2, *El Salvador* (0) 0
Russia: Kavazashvili; Dzodzuashvili, Khurtsilava, Chesternijev, Afonin; Kiselev (Asatiani), Serebrianikov, Muntijan; Pusacs, (Evriuzhikin), Bychevetz, Khmelnitzki.
El Salvador: Magana; Rivas Mariona, Castro, Osorio, Vazquez;

Portillo, Cabezas (Aparicio), Rodriguez (Sermeno), Mendez, Monge.
Scorers: Bychevetz 2 for Russia.

Mexico (1) 1, *Belgium* (0) 0
Mexico: Calderon; Vantolra, Guzman, Pena, Perez; Gonzalez, Munguia, Pulido; Padilla, Fragoso, Valdivia (Basaguren).
Belgium: Piot; Heylens, Jeck, Dockx, Thissen, Dewalque, Polleunis (Devrindt), Semmeling, Van Moer, Van Himst, Puis.
Scorer: Pena (penalty) for Mexico.

Placings

	P	W	D	L	F	A	Pts
Mexico	3	2	1	0	5	0	5
Russia	3	2	1	0	6	1	5
Belgium	3	1	0	2	4	5	2
El Salvador	3	0	0	3	0	9	0

GROUP II. Puebla, Toluca

Uruguay (1) 2, *Israel* (0) 0
Uruguay: Mazurkiewicz; Ubinas, Mujica; Montero Castillo, Ancheta, Matosas; Cubilla, Esparrago, Maneiro, Rocha (Cortes), Lozado.
Israel: Vissoker; Bello, Rosen, Daniel, Talbi (Bar), Schwager (Vollach), Rosenthal, Shum, Spiegler, Spiegel, Faygenbaum.
Scorers: Maneiro, Mujica for Uruguay.

Italy (1) 1, *Sweden* (0) 0
Italy: Albertosi; Burgnich, Facchetti; Cera, Niccolai (Rosato), Bertini; Domenghini, Mazzola, Boninsegna, De Sisti, Riva.
Sweden: Hellstrom; Nordqvist, Grip, Svensson, Axelsson, Larsson, B.; Grahn, Eriksson (Ejderstedt), Kindvall, Kronqvist, Olsson.
Scorer: Domenghini for Italy.

Uruguay (0) 0, *Italy* (0) 0
Uruguay: Mazurkiewicz; Ubinas, Ancheta, Matosas, Mujica; Cortes, Montero Castillo, Maniziro; Cubilla, Esparrago, Bareno (Zubia).
Italy: Albertosi; Burgnich, Cera, Rosato, Facchetti; De Sisti, Bertini, Mazzola, Domenghini (Furino), Boninsegna, Riva.

Sweden (0) 1, *Israel* (0) 1
Sweden: G. Larsson; Selander, Axelsson, Grip, Svensson, Bo Larsson, Nordahl, Turesson, Kindvall, Persson, Olsson.
Israel: Vissoker; Primo, Rosen, Bar, Rosenthal, Shum, Schwager, Spiegel, Vollach, Spiegler, Faygenbaum.
Scorers: Turesson for Sweden, Spiegler for Israel.

Sweden (0) 1, *Uruguay* (0) 0
Sweden: G. Larsson; Selander, Nordqvist, Axelsson, Grip, Svensson,

Larsson, B., Eriksson, Kindvall, Nicklasson (Grahn), Persson (Turesson).
Uruguay: Mazurkiewicz; Ubinas, Ancheta, Matosas, Mujica; Montero Castillo, Maneiro, Cortes; Esparrago (Fontes), Zubia, Losada.
Scorer: Grahn for Sweden.

Italy (0) 0, *Israel* (0) 0
Italy: Albertosi; Burgnich, Facchetti; Cera, Rosato, Bertini; Domenghini (Rivera), Mazzola, Boninsegna, De Sisti, Riva.
Israel: Vissoker; Primo, Bello, Bar, Rosenthal, Rosen, Shum, Spiegel, Faygenbaum (Daniel), Spiegler, Schwager.

Placings

	P	W	D	L	F	A	Pts
Italy	3	1	2	0	1	0	4
Uruguay	3	1	1	1	2	1	3
Sweden	3	1	1	1	2	2	3
Israel	3	0	2	1	1	3	2

GROUP III. Guadalajara

England (0) 1, *Rumania* (0) 0
England: Banks (Stoke City); Newton (Everton, (sub. Wright (Everton)), Cooper (Leeds United); Mullery (Spurs), Labone (Everton) Moore (West Ham United); Lee (Manchester City), (sub. Osgood (Chelsea)), Ball (Everton), Charlton (Manchester United), Hurst (West Ham United), Peters (Spurs).
Rumania: Adamache; Satmareanu, Lupescu, Dinu, Mocanu; Dumitru Nunweiller VI; Dembrowski, Tataru (sub. Neagu), Dumitrache Lucescu.
Scorer: Hurst for England.

Brazil (1) 4, *Czechoslovakia* (1) 1
Brazil: Felix; Carlos Alberto, Piazza, Brito, Everaldo; Clodoaldo, Gerson (Paulo Cesar), Jairzinho, Tostao, Pelé, Rivelino.
Czechoslovakia: Viktor; Dobias, Migas, Horvath, Hagara; Hrdlicka (Kvasniak), Kuna; Frantisek Vesely (Bohumil Vesely), Petras, Adamec, Jokl.
Scorers: Petras for Czechoslovakia, Rivelino, Pelé, Jairzinho 2, for Brazil.

Rumania (0) 2, *Czechoslovakia* (1) 1
Rumania: Adamache; Satmareanu, Lupescu, Dinu, Mocanu; Dumitru (Tataru), Nunweiller VI; Dembrowski, Neagu, Dumitrache, Lucescu (Ghergheli).
Czechoslovakia: Vencel; Dobias, Migas, Horvath, Zlocha; Kuna, Kvasniak; Vesely, B., Petras, Jurkanin (Adamec), Jokl (Vesely, F.).
Scorers: Petras for Czechoslovakia, Neagu, Dumitrache (penalty) for Rumania.

Brazil (0) 1, *England* (0) 0
Brazil: Felix; Carlos Alberto, Brito, Piazza, Everaldo; Clodoaldo Rivelino, Paulo Cesar; Jairzinho, Tostao (Roberto), Pelé.
England: Banks (Stoke City); Wright (Everton), Cooper (Leeds United) Mullery (Spurs), Labone (Everton), Moore (West Ham United); Lee (Manchester City), (Astle (West Bromwich Albion)), Ball (Everton), Charlton (Manchester United, (Bell (Manchester City)), Hurst (West Ham United), Peters (Spurs).
Scorer: Jairzinho for Brazil.

Brazil (2) 3, *Rumania* (1) 2
Brazil: Felix; Carlos Alberto, Brito, Fontana, Everaldo (Marco Antonio); Clodoaldo, Piazza; Jairzinho, Tostao, Pelé, Paulo Cesar.
Rumania: Adamache (Raducanu); Satmareanu, Lupescu, Dumitru Mocanu; Neagu, Dinu, Nunweiller VI; Dembrowski, Dumitrache (Tataru), Lucescu.
Scorers: Jairzinho, Pelé 2 for Brazil, Dumitrache, Dembrowski for Rumania.

England (0) 1, *Czechoslovakia* (0) 0
England: Banks (Stoke City); Newton (Everton), Cooper (Leeds United), Mullery (Spurs), Charlton, J. (Leeds United), Moore (West Ham United); Bell (Manchester City), Clarke (Leeds United), Astle (West Bromwich Albion), (Osgood (Chelsea)), Charlton, R. (Manchester United) (Ball (Everton)), Peters (Spurs).
Czechoslovakia: Viktor; Dobias, Migas, Hrivnak, Hagara; Pollak, Kuna; F. Vesely (Jokl), Petras, Adamec, Jan Capkovic.
Scorer: Clarke (penalty) for England.

Placings

	P	W	D	L	F	A	Pts
Brazil	3	3	0	0	8	3	6
England	3	2	0	1	2	1	4
Rumania	3	1	0	2	4	5	2
Czechoslovakia	3	0	0	3	2	7	0

GROUP IV. Leon

Peru (0) 3, *Bulgaria* (1) 2
Peru: Rubiños; Campos (J. Gonzalez), De La Torre, Chumpitaz, Fuentes; Cubillas, Mifflin, Challe, Baylon (Sotil), Perico Leon, Gallardo.
Bulgaria: Simeonov; Chalamanov, Dimitrov, Davidov, Aladjiev, Bonev (Asparoukhov), Penev, Yakimov, Popov (Maraschliev), Jekov, Dermendjiev.
Scorers: Dermendjiev, Bonev for Bulgaria; Chumpitaz, Gallardo, Cubillas for Peru.

West Germany (0) 2, *Morocco* (1) 1
West Germany: Maier; Vogts, Schulz, Fichtel, Hottges (Loehr); Haller (Grabowski), Beckenbauer, Overath; Seeler, Muller, Held.
Morocco: Allal Abdallah; Lamrani, Moulay, Slimani; Boujema, Bamous (Faras), Maaroufi, Filali; Said, Houmane, Ghazouani (Abdelkader).
Scorers: Houmane for Morocco, Seeler, Muller for West Germany.

Peru (0) 3, *Morocco* (0) 0
Peru: Rubiños; P. Gonzalez, De La Torre, Chumpitaz, Fuentes; Challe, Mifflin (Cruzado), Cubillas; Sotil, Perico Leon, Gallardo (Ramirez).
Morocco: Allal Abdallah; Lamrani, Khanoussi, Slimani, Boujema (Fadili); Maaroufi, Bamous, Filali; Ghandi (Allaqui), Houmane, Ghazouani.
Scorers: Cubillas 2, Challe for Peru.

West Germany (2) 5, *Bulgaria* (1) 2
West Germany: Maier; Vogts, Schnellinger, Fichtel, Hottges; Beckenbauer, Overath; Libuda, Seeler, Muller, Loehr (Grabowski). (sub. Weber).
Bulgaria: Simeonov; Gaydarski, Penev, Jetchev, Gaganelov; Kolev, Bonev, Nikodimov; Dermendjiev, Asparoukhov, Maraschliev.
Scorers: Libuda, Muller 3 (1 penalty), Seeler for West Germany, Nikodimov, Kolev for Bulgaria.

West Germany (3) 3, *Peru* (1) 1
West Germany: Maier; Vogts, Fichtel, Schnellinger, Hottges (Patzke), Beckenbauer, Seeler, Overath; Libuda (Grabowski), Muller, Loehr.
Peru: Rubiños; P. Gonzalez, De La Torre, Chumpitaz, Fuentes; Mifflin, Challe (Cruzado); Sotil, Perico Leon (Ramirez), Gallardo.
Scorers: Muller (3) for West Germany; Perico Leon for Peru.

Bulgaria (1) 1, *Morocco* (0) 1
Bulgaria: Yordanov; Chalamanov, Gaydarski, Jetchev, Penev (Dimitrov), Popov, Kolev, T., Yakimov (Bonev), Mitkov, Asparoukhov, Nikodimov.
Morocco: Hazzaaz; Khanoussi, Slimani, Benkrif, Fadili; Maaroufi, Bamous (Choukhri), Filali; Ghandi, Allaqui (Faras), Ghazouani.
Scorers: Jetchev for Bulgaria; Ghazouani for Morocco.

Placings

	P	W	D	L	F	A	Pts
West Germany	3	3	0	0	10	4	6
Peru	3	2	0	1	7	5	4
Bulgaria	3	0	1	2	5	9	1
Morocco	3	0	1	2	2	6	1

QUARTER-FINALS
Leon
>West Germany (0) 3   England (1) 2
after extra time.

West Germany: Maier; Schnellinger, Vogts, Hottges (Schulz); Beckenbauer, Overath, Seeler; Libuda (Grabowski), Muller, Loehr.
England: Bonetti (Chelsea); Newton (Everton); Cooper (Leeds United); Mullery (Spurs), Labone (Everton), Moore (West Ham United); Lee (Manchester City), Ball (Everton), Hurst (West Ham United), Charlton (Manchester United) (Bell (Manchester City)), Peters (Spurs) (Hunter (Leeds United)).
Scorers: Mullery, Peters for England; Beckenbauer, Seeler, Muller for West Germany.

Guadalajara
>Brazil (2) 4   Peru (1) 2

Brazil: Felix; Carlos Alberto, Brito, Piazza, Marco Antonio; Clodoaldo, Gerson (Paulo Cesar); Jairzinho (Roberto), Tostao, Pelé, Rivelino.
Peru: Rubiños; Campos, Fernandez, Chumpitaz, Fuentes; Mifflin, Challe; Baylon (Sotil), Perico Leon (Eladio Reyes), Cubillas, Gallardo.
Scorers: Rivelino, Tostao 2, Jairzinho for Brazil; Gallardo, Cubillas for Peru.

Toluca
>Italy (1) 4   Mexico (1) 1

Italy: Albertosi; Burgnich, Cera, Rossato, Facchetti; Bertini, Mazzola (Rivera), De Sisti; Domenghini (Gori), Boninsegna, Riva.
Mexico: Calderon; Vantolra, Pena, Guzman, Perez; Gonzales (Borja), Pulido, Munguia (Diaz); Valdivia, Fragoso, Padilla.
Scorers: Domenghini, Riva 2, Rivera for Italy; Gonzalez for Mexico.

Mexico
>Uruguay (0) 1   Russia (0) 0
after extra time

Uruguay: Mazurkiewicz; Ubinas, Ancheta, Matosas, Mujica; Maneiro, Cortes, Montero Castillo; Cubilla, Fontes (Gomez), Morales (Esparrago).
Russia: Kavazashvili; Dzodzuashvili, Afonin, Khurtsilava (Logofet), Chesternijev; Muntijan, Asatiani (Kiselev), Kaplichni; Evriuzhkinzin, Bychevetz, Khmelnitzki.
Scorer: Esparrago for Uruguay.

SEMI-FINALS
Mexico City
>Italy (1) 4   West Germany (0) 3
after extra time

Italy: Albertosi; Cera; Burgnich, Bertini, Rosato, (Poletti) Facchetti; Domenghini, Mazzola (Rivera), De Sisti; Boninsegna, Riva.
West Germany: Maier; Schnellinger; Vogts, Schulz, Beckenbauer, Patzke (Held); Seeler, Overath; Grabowski, Muller, Loehr (Libuda).
Scorers: Boninsegna, Burgnich, Riva, Rivera for Italy; Schnellinger, Muller 2 for West Germany.

Guadalajara
    Brazil (1) 3   *Uruguay* (1) 1
Brazil: Felix; Carlos Alberto, Brito, Piazza, Everaldo; Clodoaldo, Gerson; Jairzinho, Tostao, Pelé, Rivelino.
Uruguay: Mazurkiewicz; Ubinas, Ancheta, Matosas, Mujica; Montero Castillo, Cortes, Fontes; Cubilla, Maneiro (Esparrago), Morales.
Scorers: Cubilla for Uruguay; Clodoaldo, Jairzinho, Rivelino for Brazil.

THIRD PLACE MATCH: *Mexico City*
    West Germany (1) 1   *Uruguay* (0) 0
West Germany: Wolter; Schnellinger (Lorenz); Patzke, Fichtel, Weber, Vogts; Seeler, Overath; Libuda (Loehr), Muller, Held.
Uruguay: Mazurkiewicz; Ubinas, Ancheta, Matosas, Mujica; Montero Castillo, Cortes, Fontes; (Sandoval); Cubilla, Maneiro (Esparrago), Morales.
Scorer: Overath for West Germany.

FINAL
Mexico City
    Brazil (1) 4   *Italy* (1) 1
Brazil: Felix; Carlos Alberto, Brito, Piazza, Everaldo; Clodoaldo, Gerson; Jairzinho, Tostao, Pelé, Rivelino.
Italy: Albertosi; Cera; Burgnich, Bertini, (Juliano), Rosato, Facchetti; Domenghini, Mazzola, De Sisti; Boninsegna (Rivera), Riva.
Scorers: Pelé, Gerson, Jairzinho, Carlos Alberto for Brazil. Boninsegna for Italy.

Leading Scorer: Muller (West Germany) 10.

Chapter Thirteen

The European Nations Cup History

This was initiated in 1958 as a home and away knock-out tournament, with the semi-finals and Final to be played on neutral soil. It dragged on till 1960 and a somewhat anti-climactic finish in Paris. Russia won it, but they had been favoured by the withdrawal of Spain, whom they were due to meet in the quarter-final. No British country competed. The final rounds were notable for the superb form of Russia's goalkeeper, Lev Yachin.

EUROPEAN NATIONS CUP 1958-60

Preliminary Round
Eire 2, Czechoslovakia 0
Czechoslovakia 4, Eire 0

First Round
France 7, Greece 1
Greece 1, France 1
Russia 3, Hungary 1
Hungary 0, Russia 1
Rumania 3, Turkey 0
Turkey 2, Rumania 0
Norway 0, Austria 1
Austria 5, Norway 2
Yugoslavia 2, Bulgaria 0
Bulgaria 1, Yugoslavia 1
Portugal 2, East Germany 0
East Germany 2, Portugal 3
Denmark 2, Czechoslovakia 2
Czechoslovakia 5, Denmark 1
Poland 2, Spain 4
Spain 3, Poland 0

Quarter-finals
Portugal 2, Yugoslavia 1
Yugoslavia 5, Portugal 1
France 5, Austria 2
Austria 2, France 4
Rumania 0, Czechoslovakia 2
Czechoslovakia 3, Rumania 0
Russia beat Spain who withdrew

Semi-finals
Yugoslavia 5, *France* 4 in Paris
Russia 3, *Czechoslovakia* 0 in Marseilles

Final *Paris*, July 10, 1960
Russia 2, *Yugoslavia* 1 after extra time
Russia: Yachin; Tchekeli, Kroutikov; Voinov, Maslenkin, Netto; Metreveli, Ivanov, Ponedelnik, Bubukin, Meshki.
Yugoslavia: Vidinic; Durkovic, Jusufi; Zanetic, Miladinovic, Perusic; Sekularac, Jerkovic, Galic, Matus, Kostic.
Scorers: Metreveli, Ponedelnik for Russia, Netto (own goal) for Yugoslavia.

EUROPEAN NATIONS CUP 1962-4

This time, England, Ireland and Wales competed, but Scotland inexcusably and inexplicably stayed out. England's performance was far from glorious. After struggling to draw with France at Sheffield, they played the return during the bitter winter of 1963, took a floundering team to Paris, poorly selected (no scheming inside-forward) and with a goalkeeper out of practice and form, to lose 5–2.

Ireland did better, playing gallantly to beat Poland, and exceedingly well to hold Spain to a draw, away. For the return, however, Spain recalled their Italian-based stars, Del Sol and Suarez, and just squeezed through, in Belfast. The Welsh, meanwhile, had already gone out to Hungary. Spain did not need Del Sol and Suarez to put out Eire, which they did with ease, while Hungary surprised France in Paris; a revitalised team.

The closing rounds, played in Spain, not surprisingly saw the home team prevail, though not without infinite trouble. After narrowly prevailing against Hungary, Spain ran up against a packed Russian defence, scored in five minutes, let in an eighth-minute equaliser, then inspired by Suarez, had enough of the play for Marcellino to give them the game with a brilliant opportunist goal. The Russians used Kornaev as an extra defender. Hungary took third place with a laborious win over Denmark.

Preliminary Round
Spain 6, *Rumania* 0
Rumania 3, *Spain* 1
Poland 0, *Northern Ireland* 2
Northern Ireland 2, *Poland* 0
Denmark 6, *Malta* 1
Malta 1, *Denmark* 3
Greece withdrew against Albania
East Germany 2, *Czechoslovakia* 1
Czechoslovakia 1, *East Germany* 1
Hungary 3, *Wales* 1

Wales 1, *Hungary* 1
Italy 6, *Turkey* 0
Turkey 0, *Italy* 1
Holland 3, *Switzerland* 1
Switzerland 1, *Holland* 1
Norway 0, *Sweden* 2
Sweden 1, *Norway* 1
Yugoslavia 3, *Belgium* 2
Belgium 0, *Yugoslavia* 1
Bulgaria 3, *Portugal* 1
Portugal 3, *Bulgaria* 1
Bulgaria 1, *Portugal* 0
England 1, *France* 1
France 5, *England* 2

Second Round
Spain 1, *Northern Ireland* 1
Northern Ireland 0, *Spain* 1
Denmark 4, *Albania* 0
Albania 1, *Denmark* 0
Austria 0, *Eire* 0
Eire 3, *Austria* 2
East Germany 1, *Hungary* 2
Hungary 3, *East Germany* 3
Russia 2, *Italy* 0
Italy 1, *Russia* 1
Holland 1, *Luxemburg* 1
Luxemburg 2, *Holland* 1
Yugoslavia 0, *Sweden* 0
Sweden 3, *Yugoslavia* 2
Bulgaria 1, *France* 0
France 3, *Bulgaria* 1

Quarter-finals
Luxemburg 3, *Denmark* 3
Denmark 2, *Luxemburg* 2
Denmark 1, *Luxemburg* 0
Spain 5, *Eire* 1
Eire 0, *Spain* 2
France 1, *Hungary* 3
Hungary 2, *France* 1
Sweden 1, *Russia* 1
Russia 3, *Sweden* 1

Semi-finals
Russia 3, *Denmark* 0 in Barcelona
Spain 2, *Hungary* 1 in Madrid

Third Place match:
Hungary 3, *Denmark* 1 after extra time

Final *Madrid*, June 21, 1964
Spain (1) 2, *Russia* (1) 1
Spain: Iribar; Rivilla, Calleja; Fuste, Olivella, Zocco; Amancio, Pereda, Marcellino, Suarez, Lapetra.
Russia: Yachin; Chustikov, Mudrik; Voronin, Chesternijev, Anitchkine; Chislenko, Ivanov, Ponedelnik, Kornaev, Khusainov.
Scorers: Pereda, Marcellino for Spain, Khusainov for Russia.

EUROPEAN NATIONS CUP 1966-8

Italy won a most unsatisfactory final series, on their own soil. In the semi-finals, they drew with Russia after extra time at Naples and won the toss: a competition rule which properly met with bitter criticism. In the final, a late goal from a free kick gave them a lucky draw against the superior Yugoslav side. The replay, two days later, found Yugoslavia exhausted, Italy reinforced by capable reserves, and the Italians won with some ease. Previously, in a brutally hard match, Yugoslavia had put out England in Florence through a late goal by Dzajic.

England had qualified for the quarter-finals by winning the home international championship. Beaten at Wembley by Scotland, they drew the vital match at Hampden in February, 1968. The Scots threw away points against weaker opposition. England went on to eliminate Spain in the quarter-finals, playing specially well in Madrid.

The competition was this time divided into eight qualifying groups, in which the results were as follows:

Group I
Eire 0, *Spain* 0
Eire 2, *Turkey* 1
Spain 2, *Eire* 0
Turkey 0, *Spain* 0
Turkey 2, *Eire* 1
Eire 0, *Czechoslovakia* 2
Spain 2, *Turkey* 0
Czechoslovakia 1, *Spain* 0
Spain 2, *Czechoslovakia* 1
Czechoslovakia 4, *Turkey* 0
Turkey 0, *Czechoslovakia* 0
Czechoslovakia 1, *Eire* 2

Group II
Norway 0, *Bulgaria* 2
Portugal 1, *Sweden* 2
Bulgaria 4, *Norway* 2

Sweden 1, *Portugal* 1
Norway 1, *Portugal* 2
Sweden 0, *Bulgaria* 2
Norway 3, *Sweden* 1
Sweden 5, *Norway* 2
Bulgaria 3, *Sweden* 0
Portugal 2, *Norway* 1
Bulgaria 1, *Portugal* 0
Portugal 0, *Bulgaria* 0

Group III
Finland 0, *Austria* 0
Greece 2, *Finland* 1
Finland 1, *Greece* 1
Russia 4, *Austria* 3
Russia 2, *Finland* 0
Finland 2, *Russia* 5
Austria 2, *Finland* 1
Greece 4, *Austria* 0
Austria 1, *Russia* 0
Greece 0, *Russia* 1
Austria 1, *Greece* 1
Russia 4, *Greece* 1

Group IV
Albania 0, *Yugoslavia* 2
West Germany 6, *Albania* 0
Yugoslavia 1, *West Germany* 0
West Germany 3, *Yugoslavia* 1
Yugoslavia 4, *Albania* 0
Albania 0, *West Germany* 0

Group V
Holland 2, *Hungary* 2
Hungary 6, *Denmark* 0
Holland 2, *Denmark* 0
East Germany 4, *Holland* 3
Hungary 2, *Holland* 1
Denmark 0, *Hungary* 2
Denmark 1, *East Germany* 1
Holland 1, *East Germany* 0
Hungary 3, *East Germany* 1
Denmark 3, *Holland* 2
East Germany 3, *Denmark* 2
East Germany 1, *Hungary* 0

Group VI
Cyprus 1, *Rumania* 5
Rumania 4, *Switzerland* 2

Italy 3, *Rumania* 1
Cyprus 0, *Italy* 2
Rumania 7, *Cyprus* 0
Switzerland 7, *Rumania* 1
Italy 5, *Cyprus* 0
Switzerland 5, *Cyprus* 0
Switzerland 2, *Italy* 2
Italy 4, *Switzerland* 0
Cyprus 2, *Switzerland* 1
Rumania 0, *Italy* 1

Group VII
Poland 4, *Luxemburg* 0
France 2, *Poland* 1
Luxemburg 0, *France* 3
Luxemburg 0, *Belgium* 5
Luxemburg 0, *Poland* 0
Poland 3, *Belgium* 1
Belgium 2, *France* 1

Poland 1, *France* 4
Belgium 2, *Poland* 4
France 1, *Belgium* 1
Belgium 3, *Luxemburg* 0
France 3, *Luxemburg* 1

Group VIII
Ireland 0, *England* 2
Wales 1, *Scotland* 1
England 5, *Wales* 1
Scotland 2, *Ireland* 1
Ireland 0, *Wales* 0
England 2, *Scotland* 3
Wales 0, *England* 3
Ireland 1, *Scotland* 0
England 2, *Ireland* 0
Scotland 3, *Wales* 2
Scotland 1, *England* 1
Wales 2, *Ireland* 0

Quarter-finals
England 1, *Spain* 0
Spain 1, *England* 2
Bulgaria 3, *Italy* 2
Italy 2, *Bulgaria* 0
France 1, *Yugoslavia* 1
Yugoslavia 5, *France* 1
Hungary 2, *Russia* 0
Russia 3, *Hungary* 0

Semi-finals (*Italy*)
Yugoslavia 1, *England* 0
Italy 0, *Russia* 0, *Italy won toss*

Third-place match (*Rome*)
England 2, *Russia* 0

Final (*Rome*)
Italy 1, *Yugoslavia* 1

Replayed Final *Rome*, June 10, 1968
Italy (2) 2, *Yugoslavia* (0) 0
Italy: Zoff; Burgnich, Facchetti; Rosato, Guarneri, Salvadore; Domenghini, Mazzola, Anastasi, De Sisti, Riva.
Yugoslavia: Pantelic; Fazlagic, Damjanovic; Pavlovic, Paunovic, Holcer; Hosic, Acimovic, Musemic, Trivic, Dzajic.
Scorers: Riva, Anastasi for Italy.

Chapter Fourteen
World Club Championship History

These matches began in 1960 – originally without the blessing of FIFA – between the winners of the European Cup and the winners of the more recently innovated South American Cup. They were to play one another at home and away, the championship to be decided not on goal average but on actual results. That is to say, were each team to win one match a play-off would be necessary, and that play-off would take place immediately, on the ground of the team playing at home in the second leg. Clearly this was monstrously unjust to the team playing away and, in view of the rules of the competition, the third match has twice been invoked. On each occasion, the team playing at home – a South American team – has duly won, by a goal.

In 1960 there was no need for such a play-off. Real Madrid, having drawn 0–0 in Montevideo on a day of pouring rain, easily crushed Penarol in Madrid – two full months later – though Penarol suffered from the lack of their brilliant linking half-back, Gonçalvez.

In 1961, Penarol had their revenge. Beaten 1–0 in Lisbon by Benfica, they thrashed the Portuguese club 5–0 in the return, although Benfica had to play without their two key men, Germano, centre-half and Aguas, centre-forward. For the third match, they flew out the 19-year-old coloured inside-forward, Eusebio. He scored a brilliant goal, but again Penarol prevailed.

In 1962, it was the turn of Santos. Once more, Benfica were the losers. There was nothing they could do against the astounding brilliance of Pelé who, if he was superb in the first leg in Brazil, reached supreme heights of virtuosity in Lisbon.

In 1963, Milan, who had already beaten Santos 4–0 earlier in the year in the Milan City Cup, beat them again 4–2 in the first leg, Amarildo, their new Brazilian star, playing superbly and scoring twice. But they fell badly to pieces in the return, after being two goals up, at the Maracana. Santos' recovery was all the more remarkable in that they lacked Zito and Pelé. Almir, who took Pelé's place, was their star.

The decider, a couple of days later, was bad tempered and violent Two players were sent off, Maldini of Milan – who gave away the penalty that won the match – and Ismael of Santos. There could scarcely have been a better example of the competition's misbegotten rules.

In 1964, it was Inter who beat Independiente in a third match; played in Madrid.

In 1965, for the second year in succession, Internazionale defeated Independiente of Buenos Aires; but this time, there was no need for a third match. In Milan, Inter majestically overwhelmed an Independiente side foolishly committed to playing them at their own game, of defence and breakaway. Inter demonstrated that they knew how to attack, and express themselves, just as well as defend.

In Buenos Aires, by contrast, they rose above intimidation in the streets and on the field – Herrera and at least four players were struck by missiles – to cling to the draw they had come for.

In 1966, Penarol and Real Madrid met for the title, the Uruguayan club scoring two surprisingly decisive victories. Just as in their meeting seven years earlier, it rained heavily in Montevideo, but this time Penarol scored twice, each time through Spencer, their coloured centreforward from Ecuador, to win. In the return, their fine defence and dazzling breakaways were too much for Real. With Leczano, of Paraguay, sweeping-up, the veteran Abbadie in midfield, Joya, from Peru, and Spencer brilliant strikers, they again won 2–0, the first goal coming from a penalty, Joya making the second with a clever backheel, for Spencer.

The finals of 1967 were a disgrace to the game. Violently provoked by the tactics of Racing Club of Buenos Aires, Glasgow Celtic eventually matched brutality with brutality, in the third game in Montevideo.

In Glasgow, they'd won a dull, bruising match through McNeill's header at a corner. Before the return, in Buenos Aires, could even begin, Ronnie Simpson, the goalkeeper, was hit by a stone on the back of the head, and had to leave the field. Cardenas scored the game's winning goal, three minutes after half-time.

In Montevideo, disgraceful scenes took place, involving culprits on both sides. Four Celtic and two Racing players were sent off. Celtic, on their return, fined each of their players £250. Racing gave theirs a new car. The only goal of the play-off was scored with a strong, high shot by Cardenas, in the second half.

The 1968 Finals were scarcely an improvement. Again, the disgraceful behaviour of an Argentinian team was at the root of it; this time, Estudiantes de la Plata. The first leg, in Buenos Aires, was preceded by an almost hysterical campaign against the little Manchester United and England half-back, Nobby Stiles. In the event, he was sent off for a mere gesture of disgust at a linesman who gave him wrongly offside this, after he himself had been deliberately back-headed in the face, early in the game, cutting his eye, while Bobby Charlton had to have three stitches in his shin, after being brutally kicked by Pachamé. No wonder such famous forwards as Law and Best stood virtually apart from the proceedings; won 1–0 by Estudiantes through a goal headed from a corner-kick by Conigliaro.

The return, in Manchester, was predictably rough and ill tempered. A good goal headed by Veron, from a free kick, after only five minutes, virtually decided matters. Best and Medina were sent off for brawling; Morgan eventually though uselessly equalised.

1960 *Montevideo*, July 3
Penarol (0) 0, *Real Madrid* (0) 0
Penarol: Maidana; Martinez, Aguerre; Pino, Salvador, Gonçalvez; Cubilla, Linazza, Hohberg, Spencer, Borges.
Real Madrid: Dominguez; Marquitos, Pachin; Vidal, Santamaria, Zarraga; Canario, Del Sol, Di Stefano, Puskas, Bueno.

Madrid, September 4
Real Madrid (4), 5 *Penarol* (0) 1
Real Madrid: Dominguez; Marquitos, Pachin; Vidal, Santamaria, Zarraga; Herrera, Del Sol, Di Stefano, Puskas, Gento.
Penarol: Maidana; Pino, Mayewki, Martinez; Aguerre, Salvador; Cubilla, Linazza, Hohberg, Spencer, Borges.
Scorers: Puskas (2), Di Stefano, Herrera, Gento for Real, Borges for Penarol.

1961 *Lisbon*, September 4
Benfica (0) 1, *Penarol* (0) 0
Benfica: Costa Pereira; Angelo, Joao; Netto, Saraiva, Cruz; Augusto, Santana, Aguas, Coluna, Cavem.
Penarol: Maidana; Gonzales, Martinez, Aguerre; Cano, Gonçalvez; Cubilla, Spencer, Cabrera, Sasia, Ledesma.
Scorer: Coluna for Benfica.

Montevideo, September 17
Penarol (4) 5, *Benfica* (0) 0
Penarol: Maidana; Gonzales, Martinez, Aguerre; Cano, Gonçalvez; Cubilla, Ledesma, Sasia, Spencer, Joya.
Benfica: Costa Pereira; Angelo, Joao; Netto, Saraiva, Cruz; Augusto, Santana, Mendes, Coluna, Cavem.
Scorers: Sasia penalty, Joya (2), Spencer (2) for Penarol.

Montevideo, September 19
Penarol (2) 2, *Benfica* (1) 1
Penarol: Maidana; Gonzales, Martinez, Aguerre; Cano, Gonçalvez; Cubilla, Ledesma, Sasia, Spencer, Joya.
Benfica: Costa Pereira; Angelo, Cruz; Netto, Humberto, Coluna; Augusto, Eusebio, Aguas, Cavem, Simoes.
Scorers: Sasia (2) (1 penalty), for Penarol, Eusebio for Benfica.

1962 *Rio*, September 19
Santos (1) 3, *Benfica* (0) 2
Santos: Gilmar; Lima, Calvet; Zito, Mauro, Dalmo; Dorval, Mengalvio, Coutinho, Pelé, Pepé.
Benfica: Costa Pereira; Jacinto, Raul, Humberto, Cruz; Cavem, Coluna; Augusto, Santana, Eusebio, Simoes.
Scorers: Pelé (2), Coutinho for Santos, Santana (2) for Benfica.

Lisbon, October 11
Benfica (0) 2, *Santos* (2) 5
Benfica: Costa Pereira; Jacinto, Raul, Humberto, Cruz; Cavem, Coluna; Augusto, Santana, Eusebio, Simoes.
Santos: Gilmar; Olavo, Calvet; Dalmo, Mauro, Lima; Dorval, Zito, Coutinho, Pelé, Pepé.
Scorers: Pelé (3), Coutinho, Pepé for Santos, Eusebio, Santana for Benfica.

1963 *Milan*, October 16
Milan (2) 4, *Santos* (0) 2
Milan: Ghezzi; David, Trebbi; Pelagalli, Maldini, Trapattoni; Mora, Lodetti, Altafini, Rivera, Amarildo.
Santos: Gilmar; Lima, Haroldo, Calvert, Geraldino; Zito, Mengalvio; Dorval, Coutinho, Pelé, Pepé.
Scorers: Trapattoni, Amarildo (2), Mora for Milan, Pelé (2) (1 penalty) for Santos.

Rio, November 14
Santos 4, *Milan* 2 (0–2)
Santos: Gilmar; Ismael, Dalmo, Mauro, Haroldo; Lima, Mengalvio; Dorval, Coutinho, Almir, Pepé.
Milan: Ghezzi; David, Trebbi; Pelagalli, Maldini, Trapattoni; Mora, Lodetti, Altafini, Rivera, Amarildo.
Scorers: Altafini, Mora for Milan, Pépe (2), Almir, Lima for Santos.

Rio, November 16
Santos (1) 1, *Milan* (0) 0
Santos: Gilmar; Ismael, Dalmo, Mauro, Haroldo; Lima, Mengalvio; Dorval, Coutinho, Almir, Pepé.
Milan: Balzarini (Barluzzi); Pelagalli, Trebbi; Benitez, Maldini, Trapattoni; Mora, Lodetti, Altafini, Amarildo, Fortunato.
Scorer: Dalmo (penalty) for Santos.

1964 *Buenos Aires*, September 9
Independiente (0) 1, *Internazionale* (0) 0
Independiente: Santoro; Ferreiro, Rolan; Acevedo, Guzman, Maldonado; Bernao, Mura, Prospitti, Rodriguez, Savoy.
Internazionale: Sarti; Burgnich, Facchetti; Tagnin, Guarneri, Picchi; Jair, Mazzola, Peirò, Suarez, Corso.
Scorer: Rodriguez for Independiente.

San Siro, September 23
Internazionale (2) 2, *Independiente* (0) 0
Internazionale: Sarti; Burgnich, Facchetti; Malatrasi, Guarneri, Picchi; Jair, Mazzola, Milani, Suarez, Corso.
Independiente: Santoro; Acevedo, Decaria; Maldonado, Ferreiro, Paflik; Suarez, Mura, Prospitti, Rodrigues, Savoy.
Scorers: Mazzola, Corso for Inter.

Madrid, September 26
Internazionale (0) 1, *Independiente* (0) 0 *(After extra time)*
Internazionale: Sarti; Maletrasi, Facchetti; Tagnin, Guarneri, Picchi; Domenghini, Peirò, Milani, Suarez, Corso.
Independiente: Santoro; Guzman, Decaria; Acevedo, Paflik, Maldonado; Bernao, Prospitti, Suarez, Rodrigues, Savoy.
Scorer: Corso for Inter.

1965 *Milan*, September 8
Internazionale (2) 3, *Independiente* (0) 0
Internazionale: Sarti; Burgnich, Facchetti; Bedin, Guarneri, Picchi; Jair, Mazzola, Peirò, Suarez, Corso.
Independiente: Santoro; Pavoni, Navorro; Acevedo, Guzman, Ferreiro; Bernao, De La Mata, Avallay, Rodriguez, Savoy.
Scorers: Peirò, Mazzola (2) for Internazionale.

Buenos Aires, September 15
Independiente (0) 0, *Internazionale* (0) 0
Independiente: Santoro; Navarro, Pavoni; Rolan, Guzman, Ferreiro; Bernao, Mura, Avallay, Mori, Savoy.
Internazionale: Sarti; Burgnich, Facchetti; Bedin, Guarneri, Picchi; Jair, Mazzola, Peirò, Suarez, Corso.

1966 *Montevideo*, October 12
Penarol (1) 2, *Real Madrid* (0) 0
Penarol: Mazurkiewicz; Forlan, Gonzales; Conçalves, Lezcano, Varela; Abbadie, Cortes, Spencer, Rocha, Joya.
Real Madrid: Betancort; Pachin, Sanchis; Ruiz, De Felipe, Zoco; Serena, Amancio, Pirri, Velasquez, Bueno.
Scorer: Spencer (2) for Penarol.

Madrid, October 26
Real Madrid (0) 0, *Penarol* (2) 2
Real Madrid: Betancort; Calpe, Sanchis; Pirri, Del Felipe, Zoco; Serena, Amancio, Grosso, Velasquez, Gento.
Penarol: Mazurkiewicz; Gonzales, Caetano; Gonçalves, Lezcano, Varela; Abbadie, Cortes, Spencer, Rocha, Joya.
Scorers: Rocha (pen.), Spencer for Penarol.

1967 *Glasgow*, October 18
Celtic (0) 1, *Racing Club* (0) 0
McNeill
Celtic: Simpson; Craig, Gemmell; Murdoch, McNeill, Clark; Johnstone, Lennox, Wallace, Auld, Hughes.
Racing: Cejas; Perfumo, Diaz; Martin, Mori, Basile; Raffo, Rulli, Cardenas, Rodrigues, Maschio.

Buenos Aires, November 1
Racing Club (1) 2, *Celtic* (1) 1
Raffo, Cardenas   Gemmell (penalty)
Racing: Cejas; Perfumo, Chabay; Martin, Rulli, Basile; Raffo, Cardoso, Cardenas, Rodrigues, Maschio.
Celtic: Fallon; Craig, Gemmell; Murdoch, McNeill, Clark; Johnstone, Wallace, Chalmers, O'Neill, Lennox.

Montevideo, November 4
Racing Club (0) 1, *Celtic* (0) 0
Cardenas
Racing: Cejas; Perfumo, Chabay; Martin, Rulli, Basile; Raffo, Cardoso, Cardenas, Rodrigues, Maschio.
Celtic: Fallon; Craig, Gemmell; Murdoch, McNeill, Clark; Johnstone, Lennox, Wallace, Auld, Hughes.

1968 *Buenos Aires*, September 25
Estudiantes (1) 1, *Manchester United* (0) 0
Estudiantes: Poletti; Malbernat, Suarez, Madero, Medina; Bilardo, Pachamè, Togneri; Ribaudo, Conigliaro, Veron.
Manchester United: Stepney; Dunne, Burns; Crerand, Foulkes, Stiles; Morgan, Sadler, Law, Charlton, Best.

Manchester, October 16
Manchester United (0) 1, *Estudiantes* (1) 1
Morgan   Veron
Manchester United: Stepney; Dunne, Brennan; Crerand, Foulkes, Sadler; Morgan, Kidd, Charlton, Law (Sartori), Best.
Estudiantes: Poletti; Malbernat, Suarez, Madero, Medina; Bilardo, Pachame, Togneri; Ribaudo, Conigliaro, Veron (Echecopar).

San Siro, October 8, 1969
    Milan (2) 3, *Estudiantes de la Plata* (0) 0
    Sormani 2, Combin
Milan: Cudicini; Malatrasi; Anquilletti, Rosato, Schnellinger; Lodetti, Rivera, Fogli; Sormani, Combin (Rognoni), Prati.
Estudiantes: Poletti; Aguirre, Suarez, Manera, Madero, Malbernat; Bilardo, Togneri, Echecopar; Flores, Conigliaro, Veron.

Buenos Aires, October 22
    Estudiantes de la Plata (2) 2, *Milan* (1) 1
    Aguirre Suarez, Conigliaro   Rivera
Estudiantes: Poletti; Manera, Aguirre Suarez, Madero, Malbernat; Bilardo (Echecopar), Romeo, Togneri; Conigliaro, Taverna, Veron.
Milan: Cudicini; Matatrasi (Fogli); Anquilletti, Maldera, Rosato, Schnellinger; Lodetti, Rivera; Sormani, Combin, Prati (Rognoni.)
    Milan, under the new dispensation whereby goal aggregate is decisive, won by 4 goals to 2.

Chapter Fifteen
The European Cup History

The European Cup was the brainchild of the veteran French journalist, selector and international player, Gabriel Hanot, and his Parisian newspaper, *L'Equipe*. Confined to clubs which have won their national League championship (though the holders' country may enter a second team), matches preceding the Final are decided on a home and away goal aggregate basis.

Though Scotland entered at once when the tournament began in 1955, England did not. The Football League refused Chelsea, then the English champions, permission to take part, and the following season advised Manchester United not to enter. Fortunately United would have no truck with such negative counsel, and duly took part, but in 1958, when the organisers generously invited them to take part again, as a token of sympathy for the Munich air crash disaster, they were meanly frustrated. The League forbade them to enter, maintaining that this was a competition for national champions, and United had not won the League title (thus claiming to make EUFA's rules for them). United appealed successfully to the Football Association but the League, in turn, were upheld in their decision by a joint F.A.–F.L. body. It was a thoroughly shabby episode.

The feature of the first five European Cups was the extraordinary dominance of Real Madrid. Off the field, the credit belonged to their vigorous President, Santiago Bernabeu; but on it, to the great Argentinian centre-forward, Alfredo Di Stefano. Long before the coming of Puskas, Di Stefano had inspired his team to bestride Europe. Not until 1960–1 did Barcelona at last become the first team to knock Real out of the European Cup.

EUROPEAN CUP 1955-6

With no entry from England, Hibernian of Edinburgh were the sole representatives of Britain and they reached the semi-finals with an excellent team which included Tommy Younger in goal, and a forward-line of Gordon Smith, Combe, Reilly, Turnbull and Ormond. A brilliant 4–0 away win against Rot Weiss Essen took them through the first round; Djurgarden of Sweden were twice beaten on Scottish soil in the second, but Reims proved too strong for them in the semi-final. The return match, at Easter Road, was a brilliant one, with Kopa and Bob Jonquet in splendid form for Reims, but Hibernian having most of the play – and failing to score.

The Final, in Paris, provided a splendid match between Reims and Real, in which Di Stefano and Kopa reached great heights of technique and organisation. Leblond and Templin gave Reims a 2–0 lead in the first ten minutes, it was 2–2 at half-time, Hidalgo restored the lead for Reims, but a remarkable individual goal by the Real centre-half Marquitos equalised, and Rial, the Argentinian-born inside-left, scored the winner, 11 minutes from time.

First Round
Sporting Club Lisbon 3, Partizan Belgrade 3
Partizan Belgrade 5, Sporting Club 2
Voros Logobo 6, Anderlecht 3
Anderlecht 1, Voros Logobo 4
Servette Geneva 0, Real Madrid 2
Real Madrid 5, Servette 0
Rot Weiss Essen 0, Hibernian 4
Hibernian 1, Rot Weiss Essen 1
Aarhus 0, Reims 2
Reims 2, Aarhus 2
Rapid Vienna 6, Eindhoven 1
Eindhoven 1, Rapid 0
Djurgarden 0, Gwardia Warsaw 0
Gwardia 1, Djurgarden 4
Milan 3, Saarbrücken 4
Saarbrücken 1, Milan 4

Quarter-finals
Hibernian 3, Djurgarden 1
Djurgarden 0, Hibernian 1 (Edinburgh)
Reims 4, Voros Logobo 2
Voros Logobo 4, Reims 4

Real Madrid 4, Partizan Belgrade 0
Partizan Belgrade 3, Real Madrid 0
Rapid Vienna 1, Milan 1
Milan 7, Rapid Vienna 2

Semi-finals
Reims 2, Hibernian 0
Hibernian 0, Reims 1
Real Madrid 4, Milan 2
Milan 2, Real Madrid 1

Final *Paris*, June 13, 1956
Real Madrid (2) 4, Reims (2) 3
Real: Alonso; Atienza, Lesmes; Munoz, Marquitos, Zarraga; Joseito; Marchal, Di Stefano, Rial, Gento.
Reims: Jacquet; Zimny, Giraudo; Leblond, Jonquet, Siatka; Hidalgo, Glovacki, Kopa, Bliard, Templin.
Scorers: Leblond, Templin, Hidalgo for Reims, Di Stefano, Rial (2), Marquitos for Real Madrid.

EUROPEAN CUP 1956-7

Manchester United now entered the lists for England, and put up an excellent performance, reaching the semi-finals with a dazzling young team among whose stars were Roger Byrne, Duncan Edward and Tommy Taylor – all to die at Munich. Their ten-goal win over Anderlecht, at Maine Road, was a remarkable one. Denis Viollet, their inside-left, scored four of the goals. The third round, in Bilbao, saw United beaten 5-3 on a very heavy pitch, but they recovered for a splendid 3-0 victory in the return, and went through to the semi-finals, where the power of Real was just too much for them.

Rangers, Scotland's entry, went out ingloriously to Nice.

In the Final, Italy's gifted Fiorentina side, which had splendid South American forwards in Julinho and Montuori, succumbed to Real, on Real's own ground.

First Round (*Preliminary*)
Dortmund Borussia 4, Spora Luxemburg 3
Spora Luxembourg 2, Dortmund Borussia 1
Dortmund Borussia 7, Spora Luxemburg 0
Dynamo Bucharest 3, Galatassaray 1
Galatassaray 2, Dynamo Bucharest 1
Slovan Bratislava 4, CWKS Warsaw 0
CWKS Warsaw 2, Slovan Bratislava 0
Anderlecht 0, Manchester United 2
Manchester United 10, Anderlecht 0
Aarhus 1, Nice 1
Nice 5, Aarhus 1
Porto 1, Atletico Bilbao 2
Atletico Bilbao 3, Porto 2

First Round Proper
Manchester United 3, *Dortmund Borussia* 2
Dortmund Borussia 0, *Manchester United* 0
CDNA Sofia 8, *Dynamo Bucharest* 1
Dynamo Bucharest 3, *CDNA Sofia* 2
Slovan Bratislava 1, *Grasshopper* 0
Grasshopper 2, *Slovan Bratislava* 0
Rangers 2, *Nice* 1
Nice 2, *Rangers* 1
Rangers 1, *Nice* 3
Real Madrid 4, *Rapid Vienna* 2
Rapid Vienna 3, *Real Madrid* 1
Real Madrid 2, *Rapid Vienna* 0
Rapid Juliana 3, *Red Star Sofia* 4
Red Star Sofia 2, *Rapid Juliana* 0
Fiorentina 1, *Norrköping* 1
Norrköping 0, *Fiorentina* 1
Atletico Bilbao 3, *Honved* 2
Honved 3, *Atletico Bilbao* 3

Quarter-finals
Atletico Bilbao 5, *Manchester United* 3
Manchester United 3, *Atletico Bilbao* 0
Fiorentina 3, *Grasshoppers* 1
Grasshoppers 2, *Fiorentina* 2
Red Star 3, *CDNA Sofia* 1
CDNA Sofia 2, *Red Star* 1
Real Madrid 3, *Nice* 0
Nice 2, *Real Madrid* 3

Semi-finals
Red Star 0, *Fiorentina* 1
Fiorentina 0, *Red Star* 0
Real Madrid 3, *Manchester United* 1
Manchester United 2, *Real Madrid* 2

Final *Madrid*, May 30, 1957
Real Madrid (0) 2, *Fiorentina* (0) 0
Real: Alonso; Torres, Lesmes; Munoz, Marquitos, Zarraga; Kopa, Mateos, Di Stefano, Rial, Gento.
Fiorentina: Sarti; Magnini, Cervato; Scaramucci, Orzan, Segato; Julinho, Gratton, Virgili, Montuori, Bizzarri.
Scorers: Di Stefano (penalty), Gento for Real Madrid.

EUROPEAN CUP 1957–8

For British football, this was the European Cup which was cruelly overshadowed by the Munich disaster, when the Elizabethan carrying

Manchester United back from their match in Belgrade crashed on take-off, killing seven players. United had already qualified for the semi-finals, and their patched-up team made a brave show against Milan, winning the first leg in Manchester 2-1, Ernie Taylor getting the winner from a penalty, but losing the return 4-0. Rangers, who knocked out St. Etienne, had been comfortably despatched by Milan in the eighth-finals.

Real, who now had Santamaria at centre-half were lucky to get the better of Milan in a really thrilling Final. Real survived when a shot by Cucchiaroni hit the bar, to go on and win in extra-time with a 107th-minute goal by Gento. It was a fine day for the Milan inside-forwards, Nils Liedholm and Argentina's Ernesto Grillo.

Preliminary Round
*Rangers 3, St. Etienne 1
St. Etienne 2, Rangers 1
CDNA Sofia 2, Vasas 1
Vasas 6, CDNA Sofia 1
Red Star 5, Stade Dudelange 0
Stade Dudelange 1, Red Star 9
Aarhus 0, Glenavon 0
Glenavon 0, Aarhus 3
Gwardia Warsaw 3, Wismut Karl-Marx-Stadt 1
Wismut Karl-Marx-Stadt 2, Gwardia Warsaw 0
Wismut Karl-Marx-Stadt 1, Gwardia Warsaw 1 (Wismut won the toss)
Seville 3, Benfica 1
Benfica 0, Seville 0
Shamrock Rovers 0, Manchester United 6
Manchester United 3, Shamrock Rovers 2
Milan 4, Rapid Vienna 1
Rapid Vienna 5, Milan 2
Milan 4, Rapid Vienna 2
Antwerp 1, Real Madrid 2
Real Madrid 6, Antwerp 0*

First Round Proper
*Norrköping 2, Red Star 2
Red Star 2, Norrköping 1
Wismut Karl-Marx-Stadt 1, Ajax Amsterdam 3
Ajax Amsterdam 1, Wismut Karl-Marx-Stadt 0
Manchester United 3, Dukla Prague 0
Dukla Prague 1, Manchester United 0
Young Boys Berne 1, Vasas 1
Vasas 2, Young Boys Berne 1
Rangers 1, Milan 4
Milan 2, Rangers 0
Seville 4, Aarhus 0
Aarhus 2, Seville 0*

Dortmund Borussia 4, CCA Bucharest 2
CCA Bucharest 3, Dortmund Borussia 1
Dortmund Borussia 3, CCA Bucharest 1

Quarter-finals
Manchester United 2, Red Star 1
Red Star 3, Manchester United 3
Real Madrid 8, Seville 0
Seville 2, Real Madrid 2
Ajax Amsterdam 2, Vasas 2
Vasas 4, Ajax Amsterdam 0
Dortmund Borussia 1, Milan 1
Milan 4, Dortmund Borussia 1

Semi-finals
Real Madrid 4, Vasas Budapest 0
Vasas 2, Real Madrid 0
Manchester United 2, Milan 1
Milan 4, Manchester United 0

Final *Brussels*, May 28, 1958
Real Madrid (0) 3, Milan (0) 2 after extra time
Real Madrid: Alonso; Atienza, Lesmes; Santisteban, Santamaria, Zarraga; Kopa, Joseito, Di Stefano, Rial, Gento.
Milan: Soldan; Fontana, Beraldo; Bergamaschi, Maldini, Radice; Danova, Liedholm, Schiaffino, Grillo, Cucchiaroni.
Scorers: Schiaffino, Grillo for Milan, Di Stefano, Rial, Gento for Real Madrid.

EUROPEAN CUP 1958-9

After the champagne of Manchester United, the rather flat beer of the Wolves, who were put out, somewhat obscurely, by Schalke 04 in their first time. As for Hearts, the coloured Liège centre-forward, quaintly named Bonga-Bonga, tore their defence to shreds. Real proved more majestic than ever, especially in the crushing of Wiener Sportklub. But the all-Madrid semi-final with Atletico turned out to be a frighteningly close affair, in which Atletico (led by Brazil's Vavà) fought with magnificent spirit, forcing a third match. The final, against Reims, was anti-climax; a dull match in which Real won despite an injury to Kopa, playing against his old club.

Preliminary Round
Boldklub Copenhagen 3, Schalke 04 0
Schalke 04 5, Boldklub Copenhagen 2
Schalke 04 3, Boldklub Copenhagen 1
Standard Liège 5, Hearts 1
Hearts 2, Standard Liège 1

Dynamo Zagreb 2, *Dukla Prague* 2
Dukla Prague 2, *Dynamo Zagreb* 1
Esch 1, *Gothenburg* 2
Gothenburg 0, *Esch* 1
Gothenburg 5, *Esch* 1
Wismut Karl-Marx-Stadt 4, *Petrolul Ploesti* 2
Petrolul Ploesti 2, *Wismut Karl-Marx-Stadt* 0
Wismut Karl-Marx-Stadt 4, *Petrolul Ploesti* 0
Polonia Bytom 0, *MTK Budapest* 3
MTK Budapest 3, *Polonia Bytom* 0
Atletico Madrid 8, *Drumcondra* 0
Drumcondra 1, *Atletico Madrid* 5
DSO Utrecht 3, *Sporting Lisbon* 4
Sporting Lisbon 2, *DSO Utrecht* 1
Ards 1, *Reims* 4
Reims 6, *Ards* 2
Juventus 3, *Wiener SK* 1
Wiener SK 7, *Juventus* 0

First Round Proper
Sporting Lisbon 2, *Standard Liège* 3
Standard Liège 3, *Sporting Lisbon* 0
MTK 1, *Young Boys Berne* 2
Young Boys Berne 4, *MTK* 1
Wiener SK 3, *Dukla Prague* 1
Dukla Prague 1, *Wiener SK* 0
Atletico Madrid 2, *CDNA* 1
CDNA 1, *Atletico Madrid* 0
Atletico Madrid 3, *CDNA* 1 after extra time
Gothenburg 2, *Wismut Karl-Marx-Stadt* 2
Wismut Karl-Marx-Stadt 4, *Gothenburg* 0
Wolverhampton Wanderers 2, *Schalke 04* 2
Schalke 04 2, *Wolverhampton Wanderers* 1
Real Madrid 2, *Besiktas Istanbul* 0
Besiktas Istanbul 1, *Real Madrid* 1
Reims 4, *Helsinging Palloseura* 0
Reims 3, *Helsinging Palloseura* 0

Quarter-finals
Standard Liège 2, *Reims* 0
Reims 3, *Standard Liège* 0
Atletico Madrid 3, *Schalke 04* 0
Schalke 04 1, *Atletico Madrid* 1
Wiener SK 0, *Real Madrid* 0
Real Madrid 7, *Wiener SK* 1
Young Boys Berne 2, *Wismut Karl-Marx-Stadt* 2
Wismut Karl-Marx-Stadt 0, *Young Boys Berne* 0
Young Boys Berne 2, *Wismut Karl-Marx-Stadt* 1

Semi-finals
Young Boys Berne 1, *Reims* 0
Reims 3, *Young Boys Berne* 0
Real Madrid 2, *Atletico Madrid* 1
Atletico Madrid 1, *Real Madrid* 0
Real Madrid 2, *Atletico Madrid* 1

Final *Stuttgart*, June 2, 1959
Real Madrid (1) 2, *Reims* (0) 0
Real Madrid: Dominguez; Marquitos, Zarraga; Santisteban, Santamaria, Ruiz; Kopa, Mateos, Di Stefano, Rial, Gento.
Reims: Colonna; Rodzik, Giraudo; Penverne, Jonquet, Leblond; Lamartine, Bliard, Fontaine, Piantoni, Vincent.
Scorers: Mateos, Di Stefano for Real Madrid.

EUROPEAN CUP 1959-60

The year 1960 produced one of the greatest and most spectacular Finals, a match in which Real – who now had the great Puskas in the side, with tireless Del Sol at inside-right – easily rode an early goal by Eintracht, to crush them 7-3. The immense Hampden crowd gave them a memorable ovation after the match. Di Stefano and Puskas were peerlessly brilliant, Puskas getting four of the goals, his left foot as ferocious as ever, with Di Stefano, tirelessly inventive, scoring the other three.

But Eintracht must not be written off; their progress to the Final was splendid, not least their contemptuous home and away thrashing of Rangers. Their veteran inside-left, Pfaff, was a major star.

Nor must one forget the virtuosity of Barcelona and their polyglot team, under the flamboyant Herrera – who was attacked by fans and sacked, after the elimination by Real in two awe-inspiring matches. Previously, they had killed the legend that Continentals cannot play in thick mud by humiliating Wolves on just such a pitch at Molineux. Of all the European Cups played, this was so far the most exciting and glittering.

Preliminary Round
Nice 3, *Shamrock Rovers* 2
Shamrock Rovers 1, *Nice* 1
CDNA Sofia 2, *Barcelona* 2
Barcelona 6, *CDNA Sofia* 2
Linfield 2, *IFK Gothenburg* 1
IFK Gothenburg 6, *Linfield* 1
Esch-sur-Alzetta 5, *Lodz* 1
Lodz 2, *Esch-sur Alzetta* 1
Wiener SK 0, *Petrolul Ploesti* 0
Petrolul Ploesti 1, *Wiener SK* 2

Olympiakos 2, Milan 2
Milan 3, Olympiakos 1
Fenerbachce 1, Csepel 1
Fenerbachce 2, Csepel 3
Rangers 5, Anderlecht 2
Anderlecht 0, Rangers 2
Red Star 2, Porto 1
Porto 0, Red Star 2
Vorwärts Berlin 2, Wolverhampton Wanderers 1
Wolverhampton Wanderers 2, Vorwärts Berlin 0

First Round
Real Madrid 7, Esch 0
Esch 2, Real Madrid 5
BK Odense 0, Wiener SK 3
Wiener SK 2, BK Odense 2
Sparta Rotterdam 3, IFK Gothenburg 1
IFK Gothenburg 3, Sparta Rotterdam 1
Sparta Rotterdam 3, IFK Gothenburg 1
Milan 0, Barcelona 2
Barcelona 5, Milan 1
Young Boys Berne 1, Eintracht Frankfurt 4
Eintracht Frankfurt 1, Young Boys Berne 1
Red Star 1, Wolverhampton Wanderers 1
Wolverhampton Wanderers 3, Red Star 0
Rangers 4, Red Star Bratislava 3
Red Star Bratislava 1, Rangers 1
Fenerbachce 2, Nice 1
Nice 2, Fenerbachce 1
Nice 5, Fenerbachce 1

Quarter-finals
Nice 3, Real Madrid 2
Real Madrid 4, Nice 0
Barcelona 4, Wolverhampton Wanderers 0
Wolverhampton Wanderers 2, Barcelona 5
Eintracht 2, Wiener SK 1
Wiener SK 1, Eintracht 1
Rangers 3, Sparta 2
Sparta 1, Rangers 0
Rangers 3, Sparta 2

Semi-finals
Eintracht 6, Rangers 1
Rangers 3, Eintracht 6
Real Madrid 3, Barcelona 1
Barcelona 1, Real Madrid 3

Final *Glasgow*, May 18, 1960
Real Madrid (3) 7, *Eintracht Frankfurt* (1) 3
Real Madrid: Dominguez; Marquitos, Pachin; Vidal, Santamaria, Zarraga; Canario, Del Sol, Di Stefano, Puskas, Gento.
Eintracht: Loy; Lutz, Hoefer; Wellbaecher, Eigenbrodt, Stinka; Kress, Lindner, Stein, Pfaff, Meier.
Scorers: Di Stefano (3), Puskas (4) for Real, Kress, Stein (2) for Eintracht.

EUROPEAN CUP 1960–1

At long last, the reign of Real Madrid was brought to an end. But the team that eliminated them – Barcelona, taking revenge for the previous year – did not win the Cup. Instead, it went, against all expectation, to Benfica, the Portuguese club, managed with immense shrewdness by the veteran Hungarian, Bela Guttmann. Benfica may have had a little luck in the Final, when the sun dazzled Ramallets, and he let in a couple of simple goals, but they undoubtedly had a splendid team. Germano, the centre-half, was the best and most mobile in Europe, Coluna a superb midfield player, and Aguas a mature centre forward.

Burnley, England's representatives, played skilful football, but failed badly against Hamburg in their return quarter-final, when they had enough of the play to have won. Hearts were unfortunate enough to meet Benfica in the first round.

Preliminary Round
Frederikstadt 4, *Ajax Amsterdam* 3
Ajax Amsterdam 0, *Frederikstadt* 0
Limerick 0, *Young Boys* 6
Young Boys 4, *Limerick* 2
Kamraterna 1, *IFK Malmö* 3
IFK Malmö 2, *Kamraterna* 1
Reims 6, *Esch* 1
Esch 0, *Reims* 5
Rapid Vienna 4, *Besiktas Istanbul* 0
Besiktas Istanbul 1, *Rapid Vienna* 0
Juventus 2, *CDNA Sofia* 0
CDNA Sofia 4, *Juventus* 1
Aarhus GF 3, *Legia Warsaw* 0
Legia Warsaw 1, *Aarhus GF* 0
Red Star Belgrade 1, *Ujpest* 2
Ujpest 3, *Red Star Belgrade* 0
Barcelona 2, *Lierse SK* 0
Lierse SK 0, *Barcelona* 3
Hearts 1, *Benfica* 2
Benfica 3, *Hearts* 0
Forfeited: Glenavon and CCA Bucharest.

First Round
Aarhus GF 3, *Frederikstadt* 0
Frederikstadt 0, *Aarhus GF* 1
IFK Malmö 1, *CDNA Sofia* 0
CDNA Sofia 1, *IFK Malmö* 1
Young Boys Berne 0, *SV Hamburg* 5
SV Hamburg 3, *Young Boys Berne* 3
Spartak Kralove 1, *Panathanaikos* 0
Panathanaikos 0, *Spartak Kralove* 0
Benfica 6, *Ujpest* 2
Ujpest 2, *Benfica* 1
Real Madrid 2, *Barcelona* 2
Barcelona 2, *Real Madrid* 1
Rapid Vienna 3, *Wismut Karl-Marx-Stadt* 1
Wismut Karl-Marx-Stadt 2, *Rapid Vienna* 0
Rapid Vienna 1, *Wismut Karl-Marx-Stadt* 0
Burnley 2, *Reims* 0
Reims 3, *Burnley* 2

Quarter-finals
Burnley 3, *Hamburg* 1
Hamburg 4, *Burnley* 1
Barcelona 4, *Spartak Kralove* 0
Spartak Kralove 1, *Barcelona* 1
Benfica 3, *Aarhus* 1
Aarhus 2, *Benfica* 4
Rapid Vienna 2, *IFK Malmö* 0
IFK Malmö 0, *Rapid Vienna* 2

Semi-finals
Barcelona 1, *Hamburg* 0
Hamburg 2, *Barcelona* 1
Barcelona 1, *Hamburg* 0
Benfica 3, *Rapid Vienna* 0
Rapid Vienna 1, *Benfica* 1

Final *Berne*, March 31, 1961
Benfica (2) 3, *Barcelona* (1) 2
Benfica: Costa Pereira; Joao, Angelo; Netto, Germano, Cruz; Augusto, Santana, Aguas, Coluna, Cavem.
Barcelona: Ramallets; Foncho, Gracia; Verges, Garay, Gensana; Kubala, Kocsis, Evaristo, Suarez, Czibor.
Scorers: Aguas, Ramallets (own goal), Coluna for Benfica, Kocsis, Czibor for Barcelona.

EUROPEAN CUP 1961–2

It was now the turn of the brilliant Spurs team to represent England. They played some memorable matches, not least the one in which they crushed Gornik of Poland 8–1 in a frenzied atmosphere of partisan passion, after losing the first leg. But over-emphasis on defence in Lisbon, mistakes by the backs, and a little bad luck in a frenetic return, against Benfica, cost them the semi-finals. Benfica went on to win a marvellous Final against Real, in Amsterdam, proving that their success the season before had been no fluke. They survived a fine early goal worked out by Di Stefano and Puskas, and the shooting in this match from Puskas, Coluna, Eusebio, Cavem, really had to be seen to be believed.

Rangers, once again representing Scotland, had a creditable passage, but failed sadly and surprisingly in Liège against Standard.

Preliminary Round
Nuremberg 5, Drumcondra 0
Drumcondra 1, Nuremberg 4
Vorwärts 3, Linfield 0
(Linfield gave Vorwärts a walkover in the second leg when the East Germans were refused visas.)
Spora Luxemburg 0, Odense 6
Odense 9, Spora Luxemburg 2
Monaco 2, Rangers 3
Rangers 3, Monaco 2
Vasas 0, Real Madrid 2
Real Madrid 3, Vasas 1
CDNA Sofia 4, Dukla 4
Dukla 2, CDNA Sofia 1
Standard Liège 2, Frederikstadt 1
Frederikstadt 0, Standard Liège 2
IFK Gothenburg 0, Feyenoord 3
Feyenoord 8, IFK Gothenburg 2
Servette 5, Valetta 0
Valetta 1, Servette 2
Gornik 4, Tottenham Hotspur 2
Tottenham Hotspur 8, Gornik 1
Sporting Lisbon 1, Partizan Belgrade 1
Partizan Belgrade 2, Sporting Lisbon 0
Panathanaikos 1, Juventus 1
Juventus 2, Panathanaikos 1
Bucharest 0, FK Austria 0
FK Austria 2, Bucharest 0

First Round
Odense 0, Real Madrid 3
Real Madrid 9, Odense 0
Fenerbachce 1, Nuremberg 2
Nuremberg 1, Fenerbachce 0
Standard Liège 5, Valkeakosken 1
Valkeakosken 0, Standard Liège 2

FK Austria 1, *Benfica* 1
Benfica 5, *FK Austria* 1
Servette 4, *Dukla* 3
Dukla 2, *Servette* 0
Feyenoord 1, *Tottenham Hotspur* 3
Tottenham Hotspur 1, *Feyenoord* 1
Partizan 1, *Juventus* 2
Juventus 5, *Partizan* 1
Vorwärts Berlin 1, *Rangers* 2
Rangers 4, *Vorwärts Berlin* 1

Quarter-finals
Nuremberg 3, *Benfica* 1
Benfica 6, *Nuremberg* 0
Standard Liège 4, *Rangers* 1
Rangers 2, *Standard Liège* 0
Dukla 1, *Tottenham Hotspur* 0
Tottenham Hotspur 4, *Dukla* 1
Juventus 0, *Real Madrid* 1
Real Madrid 0, *Juventus* 1
Real Madrid 3, *Juventus* 1

Semi-finals
Benfica 3, *Tottenham Hotspur* 1
Tottenham Hotspur 2, *Benfica* 1
Real Madrid 4, *Standard Liège* 0
Standard Liège 0, *Real Madrid* 2

Final *Amsterdam*, May 2, 1962
Benfica (2) 5, *Real Madrid* (3) 3
Benfica: Costa Pereira; Joao, Angelo; Cavem, Germano, Cruz; Augusto, Eusebio, Aguas, Coluna, Simoes.
Real Madrid: Araquistain; Cassado, Miera; Felo, Santamaria, Pachin; Tejada, Del Sol, Di Stefano, Puskas, Gento.
Scorers: Puskas (3) for Real Madrid, Aguas, Cavem, Coluna, Eusebio (2) for Benfica.

EUROPEAN CUP 1962-3

For the third successive time, Benfica reached the Final, but this one was to end in their defeat. Milan beat them at Wembley in a slightly disappointing game. Managed now by the Chilean, Riera, instead of Guttmann, Benfica had gone over to 4-2-4 and a more defensive outlook, partly dictated by the loss of Germano through injury, Aguas through form. Milan, well generalled by the precocious young Rivera, hit back with two goals by Brazil's Altafini (the second of which looked offside) after Eusebio had put Benfica ahead. But an injury to Coluna, who had to go off in the second half, badly affected them.

Ipswich, England's representatives, and Dundee both went out to Milan. Ipswich floundered in heavy rain in Milan, played more briskly in the return – and won – but Dundee were a revelation. Clever breakaway tactics and a defence splendidly marshalled by Ian Ure enabled them to become the dark horse of the tournament. For Real, knocked out in Belgium by a goal from Jef Jurion, this was a season of relative twilight.

Preliminary Round
Linfield 1, Esbjerg 2
Esbjerg 0, Linfield 0
Real Madrid 3, Anderlecht 3
Anderlecht 1, Real Madrid 0
Floriana Malta 1, Ipswich Town 4
Ipswich Town 10, Floriana Malta 0
Dundee 8, Cologne 1
Cologne 4, Dundee 0
Shelbourne 0, Sporting Lisbon 2
Sporting Lisbon 5, Shelbourne 1
Vorwärts 0, Dukla 3
Dukla 1, Vorwärts 0
Norrköping 9, Partizan Tirana 2
Partizan Tirana 1, Norrköping 1
Dynamo Bucharest 1, Galatassaray 1
Galatassaray 3, Dynamo Bucharest 0
Polonia 2, Panathanaikos 1
Panathanaikos 1, Polonia 4
Frederikstadt 1, Vasas 4
Vasas 7, Frederikstadt 0
FK Austria 5, Kamraterna 3
Kamraterna 0, FK Austria 2
CDNA Sofia 2, Partizan Belgrade 1
Partizan Belgrade 1, CDNA Sofia 4
Milan 8, US Luxemburg 0
US Luxemburg 0, Milan 6

First Round
FK Austria 3, Reims 2
Reims 5, FK Austria 0
Sporting Lisbon 1, Dundee 0
Dundee 4, Sporting Lisbon 1
Norrköping 1, Benfica 1
Benfica 5, Norrköping 1
Galatassaray 4, Polonia Bytom 1
Polonia Bytom 1, Galatassaray 0
Esbjerg 0, Dukla 0
Dukla 5, Esbjerg 0

Feyenoord 1, *Vasas* 1
Vasas 2, *Feyenoord* 2
Feyenoord 1, *Vasas* 0
Milan 3, *Ipswich Town* 0
Ipswich Town 2, *Milan* 1

Quarter-finals
Anderlecht 1, *Dundee* 4
Dundee 2, *Anderlecht* 1
Galatassaray 1, *Milan* 3
Milan 5, *Galatassaray* 0
Benfica 2, *Dukla* 1
Dukla 0, *Benfica* 0
Reims 0, *Feyenoord* 1
Feyenoord 1, *Reims* 1

Semi-finals
Milan 5, *Dundee* 1
Dundee 1, *Milan* 0
Benfica 3, *Feyenoord* 1
Feyenoord 0, *Benfica* 0

Final *Wembley Stadium*, May 22, 1963
Milan (0) 2, *Benfica* (1) 1
Milan: Ghezzi; David, Trebbi; Benitez, Maldini, Trapattoni; Pivatelli, Sani, Altafini, Rivera, Mora.
Benfica: Costa Pereira; Cavem, Cruz; Humberto, Raul, Coluna; Augusto, Santana, Torres, Eusebio, Simoes.
Scorers: Eusebio for Benfica, Altafini (2) for Milan.

EUROPEAN CUP 1963-4

Britain's challenge disappeared with depressing speed. Rangers, somewhat unlucky to lose to a late goal by Puskas, at Ibrox, in a breakaway, were torn apart in Madrid, where Puskas showed much of his old form. It must be said in Rangers' defence that they lacked several experienced forwards. Everton were baffled by the reinforced Inter defence, at Goodison, though many feel they did breach it, when a goal by Vernon was narrowly judged offside. In Milan, they themselves employed massive defence, and it was only a freak goal from near the by-line, scored by Jair, which beat them.

Benfica, lacking Costa Pereira and Eusebio, were thrashed in their return match with Borussia Dortmund who went on to eliminate Dukla. A superb display in Madrid enabled Real to eliminate Milan, while Inter's massive defence and breakaway attacks accounted for Monaco, Partizan and Borussia. In the Final, Inter left out their extra defender, Szymaniak, gambled on a genuine leader in Milani, blotted out Real's attack, and exploited the mistakes of their defence. Mazzola scored from long range just before half-time Poor goalkeeping gave

Milani a second, Felo headed in from a corner, but an incredible blunder by Santamaria presented Mazzola with the third.

Preliminary Round
Galatassaray 4, Ferencvaros 0
Ferencvaros 2, Galatassaray 0
Partizan Belgrade 3, Anorthosis 0
Anorthosis 1, Partizan Belgrade 3
Dundalk 0, FC Zürich 3
FC Zürich 1, Dundalk 2
Lyn Oslo 2, Borussia Dortmund 4
Borussia Dortmund 3, Lyn Oslo 1
Dukla 6, Valetta 0
Valetta 0, Dukla 2
Everton 0, Internazionale 0
Internazionale 1, Everton 0
Gornik 1, FK Austria 0
FK Austria 1, Gornik 0
Gornik 2, FK Austria 1
Monaco 7, AEK Athens 2
AEK Athens 1, Monaco 1
Dynamo Bucharest 2, Motor Jena 0
Motor Jena 0, Dynamo Bucharest 1
Valkae Kosken 4, Jeunesse Esch 1
Jeunesse Esch 4, Valkea Kosken 0
Standard Liège 1, Norrköpping 0
Norrköpping 2, Standard Liège 0
Tirania 1, Spartak Plovdiv 0
Spartak Plovdiv 3, Tirania 1
Eindhoven 7, Esbjerg 1
Esbjerg 3, Eindhoven 4
Distillery 3, Benfica 3
Benfica 5, Distillery 0
Rangers 0, Real Madrid 1
Real Madrid 6, Rangers 0

First Round
Benfica 2, Dortmund Borussia 1
Dortmund Borussia 5, Benfica 0
Internazionale 1, Monaco 0
Monaco 0, Internazionale 3
Norrköpping 1, Milan 1
Milan 5, Norrköpping 2
FC Zürich 3, Galatassaray 0
Galatassaray 2, FC Zürich 0
Gornik 2, Dukla 0
Dukla 4, Gornik 1
Jeunesse Esch 2, Partizan Belgrade 1

Partizan Belgrade 6, Jeunesse Esch 2
Spartak Plovdiv 0, *Eindhoven* 1
Eindhoven 0, *Spartak Plovdiv* 0
Dynamo Bucharest 1, *Real Madrid* 3
Real Madrid 5, *Dynamo Bucharest* 3

Quarter-finals
Real Madrid 4, *Milan* 1
Milan 2, *Real Madrid* 0
Partizan Belgrade 0, *Internazionale* 3
Internazionale 2, *Partizan Belgrade* 1
Eindhoven 1, *FC Zürich* 0
FC Zürich 3, *Eindhoven* 1
Dukla 0, *Borussia Dortmund* 4
Borussia Dortmund 1, *Dukla* 3

Semi-finals
Borussia Dortmund 2, *Internazionale* 2
Internazionale 2, *Borussia Dortmund* 0
FC Zürich 1, *Real Madrid* 2
Real Madrid 6, *FC Zürich* 0

Final *Vienna*, May 27, 1964
Internazionale 3, *Real Madrid* 1
Internazionale: Sarti; Burgnich, Facchetti; Tagnin, Guarneri, Picchi; Jair, Mazzola, Milani, Suarez, Corso.
Real Madrid: Vicente; Isidro, Pachin; Muller, Santamaria, Zocco; Amancio, Felo, Di Stefano, Puskas, Gento.
Scorers: Mazzola (2), Milani for Internazionale, Felo for Real Madrid.

EUROPEAN CUP 1964–5

Once again, Inter won the tournament, though not without considerable difficulty on the way. Much of this was gallantly provided by Liverpool who, three days after a bruising Cup Final, involving extra time, and playing without two key men, brilliantly defeated them at Anfield. Inter, however, recovered to win in Milan, though Peiró's goal, after a challenge on the goalkeeper, Lawrence, is still a subject of dispute. Previously, Liverpool had had a notable success against an Anderlecht team till then in splendid form. A clever tactical plan, using Smith as a second centre-half, was their chief weapon, but they were very lucky indeed to win the toss in Rotterdam against a brave 10-man Cologne team, which fought back from 0–2.

Rangers also did well, and might have done better still, had not Jim Baxter broken a leg, while helping materially to get them through, in Vienna.

In the Final, Inter won laboriously and unconvincingly against a brave Benfica side, naturally reluctant to play it on Inter's own ground. Benfica lost Costa Pereira, their goalkeeper, half-an-hour from time, but the score remained unchanged. And the goal, by Jair, was really owed to the appalling, rainy conditions; a shot which slipped under Costa Pereira's body.

Preliminary Round
Anderlecht 1, *Bologna* 0
Bologna 2, *Anderlecht* 1
Anderlecht 0, *Bologna* 0 (in Barcelona)
Anderlecht won toss
Rangers 3, *Red Star* 1
Red Star 4, *Rangers* 2
Rangers 3, *Red Star* 1 (Highbury)
Chemie Leipzig 0, *Vasas Gyoer* 2
Vasas Gyoer 4, *Chemie Leipzig* 2
Dukla 4, *Gornik* 1
Gornik 3, *Dukla* 0
Gornik 0, *Dukla* 0 (Duisburg)
Dukla won toss
Reipas 2, *Lyn* 1
Lyn 3, *Reipas* 0
Tirania 0, *Cologne* 0
Cologne 2, *Tirania* 0
St. Etienne 2, *Chaux de Fonds* 2
Chaux de Fonds 2, *St. Etienne* 1
Glentoran 2, *Panathanaikos* 2
Panathanaikos 3, *Glentoran* 2
Odense 2, *Real Madrid* 5
Real Madrid 4, *Odense* 0
Aris 1, *Benfica* 5
Benfica 5, *Aris* 1
DWS Amsterdam 3, *Fenerbachce* 0
Fenerbachce 0, *DWS Amsterdam* 1
Rapid Vienna 3, *Shamrock Rovers* 0
Shamrock Rovers 0, *Rapid Vienna* 2
Lokomotiv Sofia 8, *Malmö* 3
Malmö 2, *Lokomotiv Sofia* 0
Reykjavic 0, *Liverpool* 5
Liverpool 6, *Reykjavic* 1
Dynamo Bucharest 5, *Sliema Wanderers* 0
Sliema Wanderers 0, *Dynamo Bucharest* 2

First Round
Panathanaikos 1, *Cologne* 1
Cologne 2, *Panathanaikos* 1
Internazionale 6, *Dinamo Bucharest* 0
Dinamo Bucharest 0, *Internazionale* 1

Vasas Gyoer 5, Lokomotiv Sofia 3
Lokomotiv Sofia 4, Vasas Gyoer 3
Rangers 1, Rapid Vienna 0
Rapid Vienna 0, Rangers 2
Real Madrid 4, Dukla 0
Dukla 2, Real Madrid 2
Liverpool 3, Anderlecht 0
Anderlecht 0, Liverpool 1
DWS Amsterdam 5, Lyn 0
Lyn 1, DWS Amsterdam 3
Chaux de Fonds 1, Benfica 1
Benfica 5, Chaux de Fonds 0

Quarter-finals
Cologne 0, Liverpool 0
Liverpool 0, Cologne 0
Liverpool 2, Cologne 2 (Rotterdam)
Liverpool won toss
Internazionale 3, Rangers 1
Rangers 1, Internazionale 0
Benfica 5, Real Madrid 1
Real Madrid 2, Benfica 1
DWS Amsterdam 1, Vasas Gyoer 1
Vasas Gyoer 1, DWS Amsterdam 0

Semi-finals
Vasas Gyoer 0, Benfica 1
Benfica 4, Vasas Gyoer 0
Liverpool 3, Internazionale 1
Internazionale 3, Liverpool 0

Final *Milan,* May 27, 1965
Internazionale (1) 1, *Benfica* (0) 0
Internazionale: Sarti; Burgnich, Facchetti; Bedin, Guarneri, Picchi; Jair, Mazzola, Peiró, Suarez, Corso.
Benfica: Costa Pereira; Cavem, Cruz; Netto, Germano, Raul; Augusto, Eusebio, Torres, Coluna, Simoes.
Scorer: Jair for Inter.

EUROPEAN CUP 1965-6

Once again, Manchester United reached the semi-finals – and folded up. Once again Real Madrid, for the sixth time in their history, took the Cup. The virtual Final was composed by their two matches against Inter, the holders and favourites, who made the mistake of fielding a defensive formation against them in the first leg of the semi-finals, in Madrid. Real got through by the only goal and, at San Siro, virtually settled matters when they took the lead through Amancio. Inter equalised; but never seemed likely to win.

In the Final, Real, a young, vigorous side with none of the high quality of the Di Stefano days, duly beat Partizan, the Belgrade dark horses, despite falling behind to a goal by Vasovic, 10 minutes after half-time.

Previously, Partizan had beaten a sloppy Manchester United side in Belgrade, and held them to a single, rather lucky, goal by Stiles, at Old Trafford, where United were without Best, Partizan without their midfield schemer, Kovacevic – and without Galic, doing his military service but recalled for the Final, in Brussels. United had the consolation of putting up perhaps the finest display of the competition, when they brilliantly thrashed Benfica in Lisbon, in the return leg of the quarter-finals. George Best, irresistible, scored the two opening goals in the first 12 minutes.

Preliminary Round
Lyn 5, Derry City 3
Derry City 5, Lyn 1
Feyenoord 2, Real Madrid 1
Real Madrid 5, Feyenoord 0
Kevflavik 1, Ferencvaros 4
Ferencvaros 9, Kevflavik 1
Fenerbachce 0, Anderlecht 0
Anderlecht 5, Fenerbachce 1
Tirania 0, Kilmarnock 0
Kilmarnock 1, Tirania 0
Djurgarden 2, Levski 1
Levski 6, Djurgarden 0
Drumcondra 1, Vorwärts 0
Vorwärts 3, Drumcondra 0
Linz 1, Gornik 3
Gornik 2, Linz 1
Partizan 2, Nantes 0
Nantes 2, Partizan 2
HIK 2, Manchester United 3
Manchester United 6, HIK 0
Lausanne 0, Sparta Prague 0
Sparta Prague 4, Lausanne 0
Dundelange 0, Benfica 8
Benfica 10, Dundelange 0
Panathanaikos 4, Sliema 1
Sliema 1, Panathanaikos 0
Hapoel Nicosia 0, Werder Bremen 5 (Bremen)
Werder Bremen 5, Hopoel Nicosia 0
Dynamo Bucharest 4, Odense 0
Odense 2, Dynamo Bucharest 3

First Round
*Partizan 3, Werder Bremen 0
Werder Bremen 1, Partizan 0
Levski 2, Benfica 2
Benfica 3, Levski 2
Ferencvaros 0, Panathanaikos 0
Panathanaikos 1, Ferencvaros 3
Kilmarnock 2, Real Madrid 2
Real Madrid 5, Kilmarnock 1
Vorwärts 0, Manchester United 2
Manchester United 3, Vorwärts 1
Sparta 3, Gornik 0
Gornik 1, Sparta 2
Dynamo Bucharest 2, Internazionale 1
Internazionale 2, Dynamo Bucharest 0
Anderlecht 9, Derry City 0* (no return match)

Second Round
*Manchester United 3, Benfica 2
Benfica 1, Manchester United 5
Anderlecht 1, Real Madrid 0
Real Madrid 4, Anderlecht 2
Sparta 4, Partizan 1
Partizan 5, Sparta 0
Internazionale 4, Ferencvaros 0
Ferencvaros 1, Internazionale 1*

Semi-finals
*Partizan 2, Manchester United 0
Manchester United 1, Partizan 0
Real Madrid 1, Internazionale 0
Internazionale 1, Real Madrid 1*

Final *Brussels*, May 11, 1966
*Real Madrid (0) 2, Partizan (0) 1
Real Madrid:* Araquistain; Pachin, Sanchis; Pirri, De Felipe, Zoco; Serena, Amancio, Grosso, Velazquez, Gento.
Partizan: Soskic; Jusufi, Mihailovic; Becejac, Rasovic, Vasovic; Bakic, Kovacevic, Hasanagic, Galic, Primajer.
Scorers: Amancio and Serena for Real, Vasovic for Partizan.

EUROPEAN CUP 1966-7

To the general surprise, and delight, the Cup was won by a Celtic team competing in it for the first time; one, moreover, which overwhelmed a weary and pathetically negative Inter in the Final, at Lisbon. Shrewdly and forcefully managed by their old centre-half, Jock Stein Celtic's football was (with the exception of a cautious holding action away to Dukla) fast, muscular and attacking, Gemmell overlapped powerfully at left-back, scoring a magnificent, half-volleyed goal in the Final, Auld was a fine midfield player, little Johnstone a superb outside-right.

Inter reached their zenith in the quarter-finals, when they took an ample revenge on Real Madrid for the previous year's elimination. Cappellini, then, looked an impressive new centre-forward. Then the bubble burst, and they made pitifully heavy weather disposing, in three matches, of the honest, modest CSK Sofia, previously much troubled by Linfield.

Liverpool were thrashed by a splendid Ajax forward-line, in Amsterdam; finely led by Cruyff; but Dukla knew too much for Ajax. Torpedo, Russia's first entrants, put up a sturdy fight against Inter, in Milan, but went out by the only goal – Voronin's own goal – of the tie.

In the Final, Inter, without their midfield general, Suarez, and with Mazzola not fully fit, took the lead from a penalty when, in the eighth minute, Craig tripped Cappellini, then bolted back into defence, to be besieged for the rest of the game. Gemmell equalised after 63 minutes, and Chalmers got the winner five minutes from time.

Extra Preliminary Round
Sliema Wanderers 1, *CSK Sofia* 2
CSK Sofia 4, *Sliema Wanderers* 0
Waterford 1, *Vorwärts Berlin* 6
Vorwärts Berlin 6, *Waterford* 0

First Round
Reykjavik 2, *Nantes* 3
Nantes 5, *Reykjavik* 2
Aris Bonnevoie 3, *Linfield* 3
Linfield 6, *Aris Bonnevoie* 1
Admira 0, *Vojvodina* 1
Vojvodina 0, *Admira* 0
Anderlecht 10, *Valkeakovski* 1
Valkeakovski 0, *Anderlecht* 2 (*Brussels*)
Munich 1860 8, *Nicosia* 0
Nicosia 1, *Munich 1860* 2 (*Munich*)
Liverpool 2, *Petrolul Ploesti* 0
Petrolul Ploesti 3, *Liverpool* 1
Liverpool 2, *Petrolul Ploesti* 0 (*Brussels*)
Celtic 2, *Zurich* 0
Zurich 0, *Celtic* 3
Malmö 0, *Atletico Madrid* 2
Atletico Madrid 3, *Malmö* 1
Ejsberg 0, *Dukla Prague* 2
Dukla Prague 4, *Ejsberg* 0
Ajax Amsterdam 2, *Besiktas* 0
Besiktas 1, *Ajax Amsterdam* 2
Vasas 5, *Sporting Lisbon* 0

Sporting Lisbon 0, Vasas 2
CSK 3, Olimpiakos Piraeus 1
Olimpiakos Piraeus 1, CSK 0
Gornik 2, Vorwärts 1
Vorwärts 2, Gornik 1
Gornik 3, Vorwärts 1 (Budapest)
Internazionale 1, Torpedo 0
Torpedo 0, Internazionale 0

Second Round
Valerengen Oslo 1, Linfield 4
Linfield 1, Valerengen Oslo 1
Inter 2, Vasas 1
Vasas 0, Inter 2
Dukla 4, Anderlecht 1
Anderlecht 1, Dukla 2
Munich 1860 1, Real Madrid 0
Real Madrid 3, Munich 1860 1
CSK 4, Gornik 0
Gornik 3, CSK 0
Vojvodina 3, Atletico Madrid 1
Atletico Madrid 2, Vojvodina 0
Atletico Madrid 2, Vojvodina 3 (Madrid)
Nantes 1, Celtic 3
Celtic 3, Nantes 1
Ajax 5, Liverpool 1
Liverpool 2, Ajax 2

Quarter-Finals
Inter 1, Real Madrid 0
Real Madrid 0, Inter 2
Linfield 2, CSK 2
CSK 1, Linfield 0
Ajax 1, Dukla 1
Dukla 2, Ajax 1
Vojvodina 1, Celtic 0
Celtic 2, Vojvodina 0

Semi-Finals
Celtic 3, Dukla 1
Dukla 0, Celtic 0
Inter 1, CSK 1
CSK 1, Inter 1
Inter 1, CSK 0 (Bologna)

Final *Lisbon,* May 25, 1967
Celtic (0) 2, Internazionale (1) 1

Celtic: Simpson; Craig, Gemmell; Murdoch, McNeill, Clark; Johnstone, Wallace, Chalmers, Auld, Lennox.
Inter: Sarti; Burgnich, Facchetti; Bedin, Guarneri, Picchi; Bicicli, Mazzola, Cappellini, Corso, Domenghini.
Scorers: Gemmell, Chalmers for Celtic, Mazzola (penalty) for Inter.

EUROPEAN CUP 1967-8

For the first time, the European Cup was won by an English club; most fittingly, Manchester United, who had been semi-finalists on three previous occasions. The final, at Wembley, was remarkable. United dominated the first half, but couldn't turn their advantage into goals, flagged badly, late in the second half, when Benfica equalised Charlton's goal, and were ultimately galvanised by a superb goal, early in extra time, scored by George Best. The young forwards, Aston and Kidd, made an unexpectedly large contribution to their success. The injured Law didn't play.

Previously, they'd had little trouble with the Maltese – though they surprisingly drew 0–0 in Malta – had overcome a rough, determined Sarajevo, and beaten Real Madrid after an astonishing revival at Bernabeu Stadium, Foulkes, centre-half, getting the equaliser. There was also a memorable quarter-final versus Gornik, when brilliant goalkeeping defied them at Old Trafford, and they kept the score down to 1–0 on an impossibly Arctic pitch, in Poland.

Celtic, the holders, surprisingly went out to Dynamo Kiev in the first round. Bychevetz was their destroyer in Glasgow, but they were rather unlucky in the return, when Murdoch was sent off, and fighting broke out late in the game. Glentoran, the Irish champions, gave Benfica a terrible fright in the same round, going out only on the newly and dubiously introduced rule whereby away goals, in case of equality, count double. Benfica did not really find form, and recover from their manager's, Riera, resignation, till the semi-finals, when Vasas were overcome. At Wembley, they lost many friends with their rough treatment of Best.

This was the first European Cup to be seeded.

First Round
Glentoran 1, *Benfica* 1
Benfica 0, *Glentoran* 0
Besiktas 0, *Rapid Vienna* 1
Rapid Vienna 3, *Besiktas* 0
Celtic 1, *Dynamo Kiev* 2
Dynamo Kiev 1, *Celtic* 1
Olimpiakos 0, *Juventus* 0
Juventus 2, *Olimpiakos* 0
Dundalk 0, *Vasas* 1
Vasas 8, *Dundalk* 1

Manchester United 4, Hibernian (Malta) 0
Hibernian 0, Manchester United 0
St. Etienne 2, Kuopio 0
Kuopio 3, St. Etienne 0
Karl-Marx-Stadt 1, Anderlecht 3
Anderlecht 2, Karl-Marx-Stadt 1
Basel 1, Hvidovre 2
Hvidovre 3, Basel 3
Skeid Oslo 0, Sparta Prague 1
Sparta Prague 1, Skeid Oslo 1
Olimpiakos Nicosia 2, Sarajevo 2
Sarajevo 3, Olimpiakos Nicosia 1
Ajax 1, Real Madrid 1
Real Madrid 2, Ajax 1
Valur 1, Jeunesse Esch 1
Jeunesse Esch 3, Valur 3
Gornik 3, Djurgarden 0
Djurgarden 0, Gornik 1
Plovdiv Traka 2, Rapid Bucharest 0
Rapid Bucharest 3, Plovdiv Traka 0
Eintracht bye, Tirania scr.

Second Round
Sarajevo 0, Manchester United 0
Manchester United 2, Sarajevo 1
Hvidovre 2, Real Madrid 2
Real Madrid 4, Hvidovre 1
Rapid Vienna 1, Eintracht Brunswick 0
Eintracht Brunswick 2, Rapid Vienna 0
Benfica 2, St. Etienne 0
St. Etienne 1, Benfica 0
Vasas 6, Reykjavik 0
Reykjavik 1, Vasas 5
Dynamo Kiev 1, Gornik 2
Gornik 1, Dynamo Kiev 1
Juventus 1, Rapid Bucharest 0
Rapid Bucharest 0, Juventus 0
Sparta Prague 3, Anderlecht 2
Anderlecht 3, Sparta Prague 3

Quarter-finals
Eintracht Brunswick 3, Juventus 2
Juventus 1, Eintracht Brunswick 0
Juventus 1, Eintracht Brunswick 0 (play-off)
Manchester United 2, Gornik 0
Gornik 1, Manchester United 0
Real Madrid 3, Sparta Prague 0
Sparta Prague 2, Real Madrid 1

Vasas 0, *Benfica* 0
Benfica 3, *Vasas* 0

Semi-finals
Manchester United 1, *Real Madrid* 1
Real Madrid 3, *Manchester United* 3
Benfica 2, *Juventus* 0
Juventus 0, *Benfica* 1

Final *Wembley Stadium*, May 29, 1968
Manchester United (0) (1) 4, *Benfica* (0) (1) 1 (after extra time).
Manchester United: Stepney; Brennan, Dunne; Crerand, Foulkes, Stiles; Best, Kidd, Charlton, Sadler, Aston.
Benfica: Henrique; Adolfo, Humberto, Jacinto, Cruz; Graça, Coluna; Augusto, Eusebio, Torres, Simoes.
Scorers: Charlton (2), Best, Kidd for Manchester United. Graça for Benfica.

EUROPEAN CUP 1968-9

Milan won their second European Cup, gathering strength and momentum as the competition progressed, knocking out both Celtic and Manchester United, finally overwhelming Ajax in a one-sided final. Pierino Prati established himself as one of the game's most dangerous finishers, ruthlessly exploiting a slip by McNeill, at a throw-in, to put out Celtic, in Glasgow, scoring three times, with much help from Gianni Rivera, in the Final, in Madrid.

Mistaken selection and sloppy defensive play helped to put out Manchester United, after they had comfortably accounted for Rapid – Best showing superb form. Surprisingly, in the first leg of the quarter-final in Milan, they chose the veteran Foulkes for centre-half; Sormani was thus allowed his best game for months. The inexperienced Rimmer played in goal. United lost 2–0, and though they won an ill-tempered return in Manchester – during which Cudicini was felled by a missile from the notorious Stretford End – they properly went out; once again gifted but maddening.

Ajax, with Cruyff a dazzling centre-forward, were first astonished by Benfica, before astonishing them in their turn. A poor first game by Spartak Trnava's goalkeeper assisted their passage into the Final, but there, they were simply outclassed.

All the Iron Curtain teams but the Czech withdrew in protest against a decision to re-draw the First Round.

First Round
St. Etienne 2, *Celtic* 0
Celtic 4, *St. Etienne* 0
Waterford 1, *Manchester United* 3
Manchester United 7, *Waterford* 1

Manchester City 0, Fenerbachce 0
Fenerbachce 2, Manchester City 1
Anderlecht 3, Glentoran 0
Glentoran 2, Anderlecht 2
AEK 3, Jeunesse Esch 0
Jeunesse Esch 3, AEK 2
Nuremberg 1, Ajax 1
Ajax 4, Nuremberg 0
Malmo 2, Milan 1
Milan 4, Malmo 1
Steaua 3, Spartak Trnava 1
Spartak Trnava 4, Steaua 0
Zurich 1, AB Copenhagen 3
AB Copenhagen 1, Zurich 2
Trondheim 1, Rapid Vienna 3
Rapid Vienna 3, Trondheim 3
Valetta 1, Reipas Lahti 1
Reipas Lahti 2, Valetta 0
Real Madrid 6, Limassol 0
Real Madrid 6, Limassol 0 (played in Madrid)
Valur Reykjavik 0, Benfica 0
Benfica 8, Valur Reykjavik 0

Second Round
Manchester United 3, Anderlecht 0
Anderlecht 3, Manchester United 1
Celtic 5, Red Star 1
Red Star 1, Celtic 1
Rapid Vienna 1, Real Madrid 0
Real Madrid 2, Rapid Vienna 1
Reipas Lahti 1, Spartak Trnava 9
Spartak Trnava 7, Reipas Lahti 1
AEK Athens 0, AB Copenhagen 0
AB Copenhagen 0, AEK Athens 2
Ajax 2, Fenerbachce 0
Fenerbachce 0, Ajax 2

Quarter-finals
Ajax 1, Benfica 3
Benfica 1, Ajax 3
Ajax 3, Benfica 0
Milan 0, Celtic 0
Celtic 0, Milan 1
Manchester United 3, Rapid Vienna 0
Rapid Vienna 0, Manchester United 0
Spartak Trnava 2, AEK 1
AEK 1, Spartak Trnava 1

Semi-finals
Milan 2, *Manchester United* 0
Manchester United 1, *Milan* 0
Ajax 3, *Spartak Trnava* 0
Spartak Trnava 2, *Ajax* 0

Final *Madrid* May 28, 1969
Milan (2) 4, *Ajax Amsterdam* (0) 1
Milan: Cudicini; Anquilletti, Schellinger; Maldera, Rosato, Trapattoni; Hamrin, Lodetti, Sormani, Rivera, Prati.
Ajax: Blas; Suurbier (Nuninga), Vasovic, Van Duivenbode, Hulshoff; Pronk, Groot; Swart, Cruyff, Danielsson, Keizer.
Scorers: Prati 3, Sormani for Milan. Vasovic (penalty) for Ajax.

EUROPEAN CUP 1969-70

Feyenoord, the second consecutive Dutch team to reach the Final of the European Cup, most unexpectedly won it with a fine victory over Celtic. Their superiority in the second half in Milan was such that the game should never have gone to extra time; let alone the closing minutes of extra time, when Kindvall got away to score the winner. Feyenoord's performance was all the more meritorious in that it included a deserved victory over the holders, Milan; much scarred, admittedly, by their harsh encounters with Estudiantes in the world championship.

The peak of Celtic's achievement was their splendid double over Leeds United, whom they deservedly beat in the semi-finals at Elland Road with an early, deflected goal by Connelly, then overwhelmed in front of an immense, frenzied crowd at Hampden Park, despite Bremner's early goal, against the play. Leeds, however, were tired and depleted by their efforts in three major competitions.

Feyenoord's performance in Milan was a marvel of flexibility, severe *catenaccio* modulating in the second half to lively attack, with Hasil brilliant in midfield. Gemmell gave Celtic a rather fortunate lead with a pulverising free kick. From another free kick, Israel, Feyenoord's sweeper, came up to head the equaliser. Kindvall's belated winner followed a break down the left when McNeill misjudged and handled the ball. It was a curiously flaccid and disappointing performance by Celtic, a dazzling one by Feyenoord, accompanied by a myriad of honking Dutch horns.

Preliminary Round
Turku Palloseura 0, *KB Copenhagen* 1
KB Copenhagen 3, *Turku Palloseura* 0

First Round
Milan 5, *Avenir Beggen* 0
Avenir Beggen 0, *Milan* 3

Leeds United 10, Lyn Oslo 0
Lyn Oslo 0, Leeds United 6
Red Star (Belgrade) 8, Linfield 0
Linfield 2, Red Star 4
Basel 0, Celtic 0
Celtic 2, Basel 0
Hibernians (Malta) 2, Spartak Trnava 2
Spartak Trnava 4, Hibernians 0
Galatassaray 2, Waterford 0
Waterford 2, Galatassaray 3
CSKA Sofia 2, Ferencvaros 1
Ferencvaros 4, CSKA Sofia 1
Arad 1, Legia Warsaw 2
Legia Warsaw 8, Arad 0
Vorwaerts 2, Panathinaikos 0
Panathinaikos 1, Vorwaerts 1
Bayern Munich 2, St. Etienne 0
St. Etienne 3, Bayern Munich 0
Standard Liège 3, Nendori Tirana 0
Nendori Tirana 1, Standard Liège 1
Feyenoord 12, Reykjavik 0
Reykjavik 0, Feyenoord 4
FK Austria 1, Dynamo Kiev 2
Dynamo Kiev 3, FK Austria 1
Fiorentina 1, Oester 0
Oester 1, Fiorentina 2
Benfica 2, KB Copenhagen 0
KB Copenhagen 2, Benfica 3
Real Madrid 8, Olimpiakos (Cyprus) 0
Olimpiakos 1, Real Madrid 6

Second Round
Leeds United 3, Ferencvaros 0
Ferencvaros 0, Leeds United 3
Celtic 3, Benfica 0
Benfica 3, Celtic 0 (Celtic won toss)
Dynamo Kiev 1, Fiorentina 2
Fiorentina 0, Dynamo Kiev 0
Milan 1, Feyenoord 0
Feyenoord 2, Milan 0
Spartak Trnava 1, Galatassaray 0
Galatassaray 1, Spartak Trnava 0 (Galatassaray won toss)
Legia Warsaw 2, St. Etienne 1
St. Etienne 0, Legia Warsaw 1
Vorwaerts 2, Red Star 1
Red Star 3, Vorwaerts 2
Standard Liège 1, Real Madrid 0
Real Madrid 2, Standard Liège 3

Quarter-finals
Standard Liège 0, *Leeds United* 1
Leeds United 1, *Standard Liège* 0
Celtic 3, *Fiorentina* 0
Fiorentina 1, *Celtic* 0
Galatassaray 1, *Legia Warsaw* 1
Legia Warsaw 2, *Galatassaray* 0
Vorwaerts 1, *Feyenoord* 0
Feyenoord 2, *Vorwaerts* 0

Semi-finals
Leeds United 0, *Celtic* 1
Celtic 2, *Leeds United* 1
Legia Warsaw 0, *Feyenoord* 0
Feyenoord 2, *Legia Warsaw* 0

Final *San Siro, Milan*, May 6, 1970
Feyenoord (1) 2, *Celtic* (1) 1 after extra time
Feyenoord: Pieters Graafland; Romeyn (Haak), Israel, Laseroms, Jansen, Van Duivenbode; Hasil, Van Hanegem; Wery, Kindvall, Moulijn.
Celtic: Williams; Hay, Gemmell; Murdoch, McNeill, Brogan; Johnstone, Wallace, Hughes, Auld (Connelly), Lennox.
Scorers: Gemmell for Celtic; Israel, Kindvall for Feyenoord.

Chapter Sixteen

The European Cup Winners' Cup History

This Cup is something of a poor relation to the European Cup, if only because relatively few countries have a *bona fide* Cup competition. Italy, who play theirs off obscurely in midweek, are a notable instance. On the other hand, the decisive matches have drawn mammoth crowds and evinced huge enthusiasm, while Tottenham's performance in winning the 1963 tournament was of high quality.

EUROPEAN CUP WINNERS' CUP 1960-1

This was really Glasgow Rangers' finest hour to date in a European competition. Their appetite whetted by the European Cup, their fans took wholeheartedly to the new tournament, and virtually invaded Wolverhampton, on the occasion of the floodlit tie there.

In the Final, however, Fiorentina were a little too well balanced and experienced. Above all, they had in Kurt Hamrin, their Swedish international outside-right, one of the greatest match winners in Europe.

Qualifying Round
Vorwärts 2, Red Star Brno 1
Red Star Brno 2, Vorwärts 0
Rangers 4, Ferencvaros 2
Ferencvaros 2, Rangers 1

Quarter-finals
Red Star Brno 0, Dynamo Zagreb 0
Dynamo Zagreb 2, Red Star Brno 0
FK Austria 2, Wolverhampton Wanderers 0
Wolverhampton Wanderers 5, FK Austria 0
Borussia Dusseldorf 0, Rangers 3
Rangers 8, Borussia Dusseldorf 0
Lucerne 0, Fiorentina 3
Fiorentina 6, Lucerne 2

Semi-finals
Fiorentina 3, Dynamo Zagreb 0
Dynamo Zagreb 2, Fiorentina 1
Rangers 2, Wolverhampton Wanderers 0
Wolverhampton Wanderers 1, Rangers 1

Final
1st Leg. *Glasgow*, May 17, 1961
Rangers (0) 0, Fiorentina (1) 2
Rangers: Ritchie; Shearer, Caldow; Davis, Paterson, Baxter; Wilson, McMillan, Scott, Brand, Hume.
Fiorentina: Albertosi; Robotti, Castelletti; Gonfiantini, Orzan, Rimbaldo; Hamrin, Micheli, Da Costa, Milan, Petris.
Scorer: Milan (2) for Fiorentina.

2nd Leg. *Florence*, May 27, 1961
Fiorentina (1) 2, Rangers (1) 1
Fiorentina: Albertosi; Robotti, Castelletti; Gonfiantini, Orzan, Rimbaldo; Hamrin, Micheli, Da Costa, Milan, Petris.
Rangers: Ritchie; Shearer, Caldow; Davis, Paterson, Baxter; Scott, McMillan, Millar, Brand, Wilson.
Scorers: Milan, Hamrin for Fiorentina, Scott for Rangers.

EUROPEAN CUP WINNERS' CUP 1961–2

Leicester City took the place of Spurs, who had beaten them in the Final but, having also won the League, were committed to the European Cup. Spain, entering for the first time in the imposing shape of Atletico

Madrid, won the tournament, beating Leicester on the way and ultimately defeating Fiorentina in a replayed Final – no longer a two-legged affair.

Preliminary Round
Glenavon 1, Leicester City 4
Leicester City 3, Glenavon 1
Dunfermline 4, St. Patrick's 1
St. Patrick's 0, Dunfermline 4
Swansea Town 2, Motor Jena 2
Motor Jena 5, Swansea Town 1
Chaux de Fonds 6, Leixoes 2
Leixoes 5, Chaux de Fonds 0
Sedan 2, Atletico Madrid 3
Atletico Madrid 4, Sedan 1
Rapid Vienna 0, Spartak Varna 0
Spartak Varna 2, Rapid Vienna 5
Floriana 2, Ujpest 5
Ujpest 10, Floriana 2

First Round
Fiorentina 3, Rapid Vienna 1
Rapid Vienna 2, Fiorentina 6
Leicester City 1, Atletico Madrid 1
Atletico Madrid 2, Leicester City 0
Dunfermline 5, Vardar 2
Vardar 2, Dunfermline 0
Werder Bremen 2, Aarhus 0
Aarhus 2, Werder Bremen 3
Ajax 2, Ujpest 1
Ujpest 3, Ajax 1
Olympiakos 2, Dynamo Zilina (Czech.) 3
Dynamo Zilina 1, Olympiakos 0
Leixoes (Portugal) 1, Progresul 1
Progresul 0, Leixoes 1
Motor Jena 7, Alliance 0
Alliance 2, Motor Jena 2

Quarter-finals
Atletico Madrid 3, Werder Bremen 1
Werder Bremen 1, Atletico Madrid 1
Ujpest 4, Dunfermline 3
Dunfermline 0, Ujpest 1
Fiorentina 2, Dynamo Zilina 3
Dynamo Zilina 0, Fiorentina 2
Motor Jena 1, Leixoes 1
Leixoes 1, Motor Jena 3

Semi-finals
Fiorentina 2, Ujpest 0
Ujpest 0, Fiorentina 1
Atletico Madrid 1, Motor Jena 0
Motor Jena 0, Atletico Madrid 4

Final *Glasgow*, May 10, 1962
Fiorentina (1) 1, Atletico Madrid (1) 1
Scorers: Peirò for Atletico Madrid, Hamrin for Fiorentina.

Replay *Stuttgart*, September 5, 1962
Atletico Madrid (2) 3, Fiorentina (0) 0
Atletico Madrid: Madinabeytia; Rivilla, Calleja; Ramirez, Griffa, Glaria; Jones, Adelardo, Mendonça, Peirò, Collar.
Fiorentina: Albertosi; Robotti, Castelletti; Malatrasi, Orzan, Marchesi; Hamrin, Ferretti, Milani, Dell'Angelo, Petris.
Scorers: Jones, Mendonça, Peirò for Atletico Madrid.

EUROPEAN CUP WINNERS' CUP 1962-3

This was most impressively won by the Spurs. Invincible at home, they played brilliant football to humiliate Rangers, and recovered impressively after a poor performance in Bratislava. OFK, after losing in Belgrade, never had much of a chance of survival. In the Final, though robbed at the last moment of the dynamic Mackay with a stomach injury, the Spurs played some magnificent football to defeat Atletico Madrid, dominated the first half, survived a sticky patch at the beginning of the second, and at last turned the game with a surprising long-range goal by outside-left Terry Dyson.

One must not leave this Cup without recording the brave achievement of the little Welsh non-League club, Bangor City, who actually beat the expensive Naples team and forced them to a third, decisive, game.

Preliminary Round
Lausanne 3, Sparta 0
Sparta 4, Lausanne 2
St. Etienne 1, Vitoria 1
Vitoria 0, St. Etienne 3
Alliance 1, Odense 1
Odense 8, Alliance 1
Rangers 4, Seville 0
Seville 2, Rangers 0
OFK Belgrade 2, Chemie 0
Chemie 3, OFK Belgrade 3
Steaua 3, Botev 2
Botev 5, Steaua 1
Ujpest 5, Zaglebie 0
Zaglebie 0, Ujpest 0

Bangor City 2, Naples 0
Naples 3, Bangor City 1
Naples 2, Bangor City 1 (at Highbury)

First Round
St. Etienne 0, Nuremburg 0
Nuremburg 3, St. Etienne 0
Atletico Madrid 4, Hibernian Malta 0
Hibernian Malta 0, Atletico Madrid 1
Botev 4, Shamrock Rovers 0
Shamrock Rovers 0, Botev 1
Graz 1, Odense 1
Odense 5, Graz 3
Tottenham Hotspur 5, Rangers 2
Rangers 2, Tottenham Hotspur 3
OFK Belgrade 5, Portadown 1
Portadown 3, OFK Belgrade 2
Lausanne 1, Slovan Bratislava 1
Slovan Bratislava 1, Lausanne 0
Ujpest 1, Naples 1
Naples 1, Ujpest 1
Naples 3, Ujpest 1

Quarter-finals
Slovan 2, Tottenham Hotspur 0
Tottenham Hotspur 6, Slovan 0
Odense 0, Nuremburg 1
Nuremburg 6, Odense 0
Botev 1, Atletico Madrid 1
Atletico Madrid 6, Botev 0
OFK Belgrade 2, Naples 0
Naples 3, OFK Belgrade 1
Play off: OFK Belgrade 3, Naples 1

Semi-finals
OFK Belgrade 1, Tottenham Hotspur 2
Tottenham Hotspur 3, OFK Belgrade 1
Nuremburg 2, Atletico Madrid 1
Atletico Madrid 2, Nuremburg 0

Final
Rotterdam, May 15, 1963
Tottenham Hotspur (2) 5, Atletico Madrid (0) 1
Spurs: Brown; Baker, Henry; Blanchflower, Norman, Marchi; Jones, White, Smith, Greaves, Dyson.
Atletico Madrid: Madinabeytia; Rivilla, Rodrigues; Ramiro, Griffa, Glaria; Jones, Adelardo, Chuzo, Mendonça, Collar.
Scorers: Greaves (2), White, Dyson (2) for Spurs, Collar (penalty) for Atletico Madrid.

EUROPEAN CUP WINNERS' CUP 1963-4

Tottenham's success in 1963 meant that England were able to enter two teams, and as luck would have it, Spurs and Manchester United were quickly drawn together. A dour first leg at Tottenham saw Spurs get through with great difficulty, 2-0. But in the return the unhappy Mackay fractured a leg, and Manchester United took the game 4-1 and qualified. It was the first time the holders had been eliminated before the final. United, who should have had a bigger lead in their first leg against Sporting, lost the return in Lisbon a few days after an exhausting F.A. Cup semi-final. Glasgow Celtic were the splendid surprise of the tournament. Qualified only because Rangers, the Scottish Cupholders, were in the European Cup, they sailed through Europe, before falling to MTK in the semi-final. Celtic put up a brave fight, but were overwhelmed in the reply when MTK got their international stars, Sandor and Nagy, back. Sporting won a tremendously tight semi-final series in a third, deciding match; Lyon had a man sent off in the second half. In the Final, the opportunism of Sandor enabled MTK to hold their own in Vienna, but the better-balanced Sporting team defeated them in Antwerp. The winning goal was scored by Morais, direct from a corner, in the twentieth minute.

Preliminary Round
Fenerbachce 4, Petrolul 1
Petrolul 1, Fenerbachce 0
Basel 1, Celtic 5
Celtic 5, Basel 0
Tilburg Holland 1, Manchester United 1
Manchester United 6, Tilburg 1
SV Hamburg 4, US Luxemburg 0
US Luxemburg 2, SV Hamburg 3
Olympiakos 2, Zaglebie 1
Zaglebie 1, Olympiakos 0
Olympiakos 2, Zaglebie 0
Shelbourne 0, Barcelona 2
Barcelona 3, Shelbourne 1
Lyon 3, Odense 1
Odense 1, Lyon 3
MTK Budapest 1, Slavia 0
Slavia 1, MTK Budapest 1
Linz 1, Dynamo Zagreb 0
Dynamo Zagreb 1, Linz 0
Dynamo Zagreb 1, Linz 1
   (Linz lost the toss, Dynamo Zagreb w.o.)
Sliema Wanderers 0, Borough United 0
Borough United 2, Sliema Wanderers 0
Atalanta 2, Sporting Lisbon 0
Sporting Lisbon 3, Atalanta 1

Apoel (Cyprus) 6, *Gjoevik (Norway)* 0
Gjoevik 1, *Apoel* 0
Hellsingin Palloseura 1, *Slovan Bratislava* 4
Slovan Bratislava 8, *Hellsingin Palloseura* 1

First Round
Tottenham Hotspur 2, *Manchester United* 0
Manchester United 4, *Tottenham Hotspur* 1
Fenerbachce 4, *Linfield* 1
Linfield 2, *Fenerbachce* 0
Barcelona 4, *SV Hamburg* 4
SV Hamburg 0, *Barcelona* 0
SV Hamburg 3, *Barcelona* 2
Sporting Lisbon 16, *Apoel* 1
Apoel 0, *Sporting Lisbon* 2
Lyon 4, *Olympiakos* 1
Olympiakos 2, *Lyon* 1
Motor Zwickau 1, *MTK Budapest* 0
MTK Budapest 2, *Motor Zwickau* 0
Celtic 3, *Dynamo Zagreb* 0
Dynamo Zagreb 2, *Celtic* 1
Borough United 0, *Slovan Bratislava* 1
Slovan Bratislava 3, *Borough United* 0

Quarter-finals
Manchester United 4, *Sporting Lisbon* 1
Sporting Lisbon 5, *Manchester United* 0
SV Hamburg 1, *Lyon* 1
Lyon 2, *SV Hamburg* 0
Celtic 1, *Slovan Bratislava* 0
Slovan Bratislava 0, *Celtic* 1
Fenerbachce 1, *MTK Budapest* 1
MTK Budapest 1, *Fenerbachce* 0

Semi-finals
Celtic 3, *MTK Budapest* 0
MTK Budapest 4, *Celtic* 0
Lyon 0, *Sporting Lisbon* 0
Sporting Lisbon 1, *Lyon* 1
Lyon 0, *Sporting Lisbon* 1

Final *Brussels*, May 13, 1964
MTK Budapest 3, *Sporting Lisbon* 3 after extra time (full-time 3-3)
MTK Budapest: Kovalik; Keszei, Dansky; Jenei, Nagy, Kovaks; Sandor, Vasas, Kuti, Bodor, Halapi.
Sporting Lisbon: Carvalho; Gomez, Peridis; Baptista, Carlos, Geo;

Mendes, Oswaldo, Mascarenhas, Figueiredo, Morais.
Scorers: Sandor (2), Kuti for MTK Budapest, Figueiredo (2), Dansky (own goal) for Sporting Lisbon.

Replay *Antwerp,* May 15, 1964
MTK Budapest 0, *Sporting Lisbon* 1
Scorer: Morais for Sporting Lisbon.

EUROPEAN CUPWINNERS' CUP 1964-5

For the second time in three years, a London team was the winner, and West Ham's splendid performance at Wembley, in an exciting Final, was a memorable one. Hammers' achievement was the more impressive as they lost Johnny Byrne, their outstanding forward, injured while playing for England against Scotland. This caused him to miss the second leg of the semi-final, in Saragossa, and the Final itself. Saragossa were probably the second best team in the competition, with outstanding forwards in Lapetra, on the left wing, and the centre-forward, Marcelino. Mention must also be made of the astonishing achievement of Cardiff City, a Second Division club, in knocking out the holders, Sporting Lisbon. They did almost as well by pulling back two goals to draw in Saragossa, but a defensive slip cost them the return match.

Munich 1860 were a physically strong, direct, intelligent side, thwarted in the Final by Standen's splendid goalkeeping. Late in the game, after a rash of missed chances, Alan Sealey scored twice for West Ham, to settle the match.

Preliminary Round
Admira Vienna 1, *Legia Warsaw* 3
Legia Warsaw 1, *Admira Vienna* 0
Lausanne 2, *Honved* 0
Honved 1, *Lausanne* 0
US Luxemburg 0, *Munich 1860* 4
Munich 1860 6, *US Luxemburg* 0
Valetta 0, *Saragossa* 3
Saragossa 5, *Valetta* 1
AEK Athens 2, *Dynamo Zagreb* 0
Dynamo Zagreb 3, *AEK Athens* 0
Dinamo Bucharest 3, *Derry City* 0
Derry City 0, *Dinamo Bucharest* 2
Magdeburg 1, *Galatassaray* 1
Galatassaray 1, *Magdeburg* 1
Magdeburg 1, *Galatassaray* 1 (*Vienna*)
Galatassaray won toss
Esbjerg 0, *Cardiff City* 0
Cardiff City 1, *Esbjerg* 0

Skeid Oslo 1, *Haka Finland* 0
Haka Finland 2, *Skeid Oslo* 0
Porto 3, *Lyon* 0
Lyon 0, *Porto* 1
Sparta Prague 10, *St. Anorthosis (Cyprus)* 0
St. Anorthosis 0, *Sparta* 6
La Gantoise 0, *West Ham United* 1
West Ham United 1, *La Gantoise* 1
Torino 3, *Fortuna Geelen* 1
Fortuna Geelen 2, *Torino* 2
Slavia Sofia 1, *Cork Celtic* 1
Cork Celtic 0, *Slavia Sofia* 2

First Round
Dundee 2, *Saragossa* 2
Saragossa 2, *Dundee* 1
Slavia 1, *Lausanne* 0
Lausanne 2, *Slavia* 1
Lausanne 3, *Slavia* 2 (Rome)
Legia 2, *Galatassaray* 1
Galatassaray 2, *Legia* 1
Legia 2, *Galatassaray* 1
West Ham United 2, *Sparta* 0
Sparta 2, *West Ham United* 1
Porto 0, *Munich 1860* 1
Munich 1860 1, *Porto* 1
Dinamo Bucharest 1, *Dynamo Zagreb* 1
Dynamo Zagreb 2, *Dinamo Bucharest* 0
Sporting Lisbon 1, *Cardiff City* 2
Cardiff City 0, *Sporting Lisbon* 0
Torino 5, *Haka* 0
Haka 0, *Torino* 1

Quarter-finals
Saragossa 2, *Cardiff City* 2
Cardiff City 0, *Saragossa* 1
Legia 0, *Munich 1860* 4
Munich 1860 0, *Legia* 0
Torino 1, *Dynamo Zagreb* 1
Dynamo Zagreb 1, *Torino* 2
Lausanne 1, *West Ham United* 2
West Ham United 4, *Lausanne* 3

Semi-finals
West Ham United 2, *Saragossa* 1
Saragossa 1, *West Ham United* 1
Torino 2, *Munich 1860* 0

Munich 1860 3, *Torino* 1
Munich 1860 2, *Torino* 0 (*Zurich*)

Final *Wembley Stadium*, May 19, 1965
West Ham United (0) 2, *Munich 1860* (0) 0
West Ham United: Standen; Kirkup, Burkett; Peters, Brown, Moore; Sealey, Boyce, Hurst, Dear, Sissons.
Munich 1860: Radenkovic; Wagner, Kohlars; Bena, Reich, Luttrop; Heiss, Kuppers, Brunnenmeier, Grosser, Rebele.
Scorer: Sealey (2) for West Ham United.

EUROPEAN CUPWINNERS' CUP 1965-6

Despite getting three of their four entrants into the semi-finals, Britain failed to retain the Cup, which went to Borussia and Germany – on merit. The Dortmund team, astoundingly fit and very incisive, broke wonderfully well from defence, despite the fact that they used Paul as sweeper-up behind four backs. Sigi Held, later to play so well in the World Cup, was a splendid striker, powerfully abetted by the Bundesliga's top scorer, Lothar Emmerich, the nominal left-winger.

Defending powerfully and breaking rapidly, Borussia surprisingly took all West Ham, the holders, could hurl at them, at Upton Park, and won on a couple of counter-attacks. In the Final, they deserved to beat a disappointing Liverpool team, terribly vulnerable through the middle and lucky to equalise when the ball had so clearly crossed the goal line. Celtic, beaten by Liverpool in the semi-final, had an excellent run, and showed how their manager and former centre-half, Jock Stein, had tempered them for major competition.

First Round
Reykjavik 1, *Rosenberg Trondheim* 3
Rosenberg Trondheim 3, *Reykjavik* 1
Wiener Neustadt 0, *Stintza Cluj* 1
Stintza Cluj 2, *Wiener Neustadt* 0
Reipas Lahti 2, *Honved* 10
Honved 6, *Riepas Lahti* 0
Coleraine 1, *Dynamo Kiev* 6
Dynamo Kiev 4, *Coleraine* 0
Sion 5, *Galatassaray* 1
Galatassaray 2, *Sion* 1
Atletico Madrid 4, *Dynamo Zagreb* 0
Dynamo Zagreb 0, *Atletico Madrid* 1
Dukla 2, *Rennes* 0
Rennes 0, *Dukla* 0
SC Magdeburg 1, *Spora* 0
Spora 0, *SC Magdeburg* 2
Go Ahead Deventer 0, *Celtic* 6
Celtic 1, *Go Ahead Deventer* 0

Juventus 1, *Liverpool* 0
Liverpool 2, *Juventus* 0
Limerick 1, *CSKA Sofia* 2
CSKA Sofia 2, *Limerick* 0
Floriana 1, *Borussia Dortmund* 5
Borussia Dortmund 8, *Floriana* 0
Omonia Nicosia 0, *Olympiakos* 1
Olympiakos 1, *Omonia Nicosia* 1
Aarhus 2, *Vitoria Setubal* 1
Vitoria Setubal 1, *Aarhus* 2

Second Round
Dukla 2, *Honved* 3
Honved 1, *Dukla* 2
Honved won on away goals rule
Borussia Dortmund 3, *CSKA* 0
CSKA 4, *Borussia Dortmund* 2
SC Magdeburg 8, *Sion* 1
Sion 2, *SC Magdeburg* 2
Stintza Cluj 0, *Atletico Madrid* 2
Atletico Madrid 4, *Stintza Cluj* 0
Aarhus 0, *Celtic* 1
Celtic 2, *Aarhus* 0
West Ham United 4, *Olympiakos* 0
Olympiakos 2, *West Ham United* 2
Liverpool 3, *Standard Liège* 1
Standard Liège 1, *Liverpool* 2
Rosenberg 1, *Dynamo Kiev* 4
Dynamo Kiev 2, *Rosenberg* 0

Quarter-finals
Celtic 3, *Dynamo Kiev* 0
Dynamo Kiev 1, *Celtic* 1
Atletico Madrid 1, *Borussia Dortmund* 1
Borussia Dortmund 1, *Atletico Madrid* 0
Honved 0, *Liverpool* 0
Liverpool 2, *Honved* 0
West Ham United 1, *SC Magdeburg* 0
SC Magdeburg 1, *West Ham United* 1

Semi-finals
West Ham United 1, *Borussia Dortmund* 2
Borussia Dortmund 3, *West Ham United* 1
Celtic 1, *Liverpool* 0
Liverpool 2, *Celtic* 0

Final *Glasgow*, May 5, 1966
Borussia Dortmund (0) 2, *Liverpool* (0) 1

Borussia: Tilkowski; Cyliax, Redder; Kurrat, Paul, Assauer; Libuda, Schmidt, Held, Sturm, Emmerich.
Liverpool: Lawrence; Lawler, Byrne; Milne, Yeats, Stevenson; Callaghan, Hunt, St. John, Smith, Thompson.
Scorers: Held, Yeats (own goal) for Borussia, Hunt for Liverpool.

EUROPEAN CUPWINNERS' CUP 1966-7

After a fine passage to their second Cupwinners' Cup Final, Rangers found the luck of the (German) venue and Bayern's all-round accomplishment just too much for them.

The competition was played under the highly suspect dispensation of away goals counting double, in the event of two teams finishing level on aggregate. Rangers put out the holders, Borussia Dortmund, beating them in Glasgow more easily than the score suggests, and holding them in Munich, despite an injury to Watson. But they were lucky to get through against Saragossa, on the toss of a coin. Bayern scraped through against a brave Shamrock Rovers, and recovered from defeat in Vienna to beat Rapid in a rough second leg, to take the other semi-final. Muller, their young centre-forward, scored the winner in extra time.

In the Final, played at Nuremberg, Rangers dominated the first half, Bayern the second and extra time was again needed. It produced the decisive goal, by Roth.

Preliminary Round
Valur Reykjavik 1, *Standard Liège* 1
Standard Liège 8, *Valur Reykjavik* 1

First Round
Skeid Oslo 3, *Saragossa* 2
Saragossa 3, *Skeid Oslo* 1
Rapid Vienna 4, *Galatassaray* 0
Galatassaray 3, *Rapid Vienna* 5
Servette 1, *Kamraterna Turku* 1
Kamraterna Turku 1, *Servette* 2
Glentoran 1, *Rangers* 1
Rangers 4, *Glentoran* 0
Swansea Town 1, *Slavia Sofia* 1
Slavia Sofia 4, *Swansea Town* 0
Tatan Presov 1, *Bayern Munich* 1
Bayern Munich 3, *Tatan Presov* 2
AEK Athens 0, *Braga (Portugal)* 1
Braga 3, *AEK Athens* 2
Shamrock Rovers 4, *Spora Luxemburg* 0
Spora 1, *Shamrock Rovers* 4
Aalborg 0, *Everton* 0

Everton 2, Aalborg 1
OFK Belgrade 1, Spartak Moscow 3
Spartak Moscow 3, OFK Belgrade 0
Fiorentina 1, Vasas Gyoer 0
Vasas Gyoer 4, Fiorentina 2
Chemie Leipzig 3, Legia Warsaw 0
Legia Warsaw 2, Chemie Leipzig 2
Strasbourg 1, Steau Bucharest 0
Steaua Bucharest 1, Strasbourg 1
Floriana Valetta 1, Sparta Rotterdam 1
Sparta Rotterdam 6, Floriana Valetta 0
Standard Liège 5, Limassol 1
Limassol 0, Standard Liège 1

Second Round
Saragossa 2, Everton 0
Everton 1, Saragossa 0
Shamrock Rovers 1, Bayern Munich 1
Bayern Munich 3, Shamrock Rovers 2
Vasas Gyoer 3, Sporting Braga 0
Sporting Braga 2, Vasas Gyoer 0
Spartak Moscow 1, Rapid Vienna 1
Rapid Vienna 1, Spartak Moscow 0
Servette 2, Sparta Rotterdam 0
Sparta Rotterdam 1, Servette 0
Rangers 2, Borussia Dortmund 1
Borussia Dortmund 0, Rangers 0
Strasbourg 1, Slavia Sofia 0
Slavia Sofia 2, Strasbourg 0
Chemie Leipzig 2, Standard Liège 1
Standard Liège 1, Chemie Liepzig 0

Quarter-finals
Rapid Vienna 1, Bayern Munich 0
Bayern Munich 2, Rapid Vienna 0
Rangers 2, Saragossa 0
Saragossa 2, Rangers 0
Vasas Gyoer 2, Standard Liège 1
Standard Liège 2, Vasas Gyoer 0
Servette 1, Slavia Sofia 0
Slavia Sofia 3, Servette 0

Semi-finals
Bayern Munich 2, Standard Liège 0
Standard Liège 1, Bayern Munich 3
Slavia Sofia 0, Rangers 1
Rangers 1, Slavia Sofia 0

Final *Nuremberg, May 31*
Bayern Munich (0) 1, Rangers (0) 0

Bayern: Maier; Nowak, Kupferschmidt; Roth, Beckenbauer, Olk; Nafziger, Ohlhauser, Muller, Koulmann, Brenninger.

Rangers: Martin; Johansen, Provan; Jardine, McKinnon, Greig; Henderson, Smith, A., Hynd, Smith, D., Johnston.

Scorer: Roth *After Extra Time*

EUROPEAN CUPWINNERS' CUP 1967-8

Milan, who in the meantime were comfortably carrying off the Italian Championship, added to it the European Cupwinners' Cup, on their first appearance in the tournament. Their victory over Hamburg in the Final, at Rotterdam, was a mere canter. Both goals were scored by the veteran Swedish right-winger, Kurt Hamrin, the second a brilliant individual affair. It was far easier for Milan than their painfully hard qualifications against Vasas Gyoer and Standard Liège.

Cardiff City were Britain's most impressive competitors, doing wonderfully well. Shamrock Rovers and Breda were no great problem, and in the quarter-finals, they belied recent poor League form by knocking out Torpedo, Moscow. They won at home with a fine, late headed goal by Barrie Jones, went down 1–0 in Tashkent then, with five reserves, won the play-off, in Augsburg, 1–0, Toshack heading down for Dean to score. In the semi-finals, still fighting relegation in the League, they held Hamburg (without Seeler and Schulz) to a draw, away, then lost unluckily at home.

Spurs went out feebly to Lyon, after a brawl in the away match, and some dismal defence at home. Aberdeen went down to Liège, though they played well at home in the return leg. Liège went on to draw twice with Milan, but lost the play-off, while Milan then knocked out the holders, Bayern, in the semi-finals.

First Round
FK Austria 0, *Steaua Bucharest* 2
Steaua Bucharest 2, *FK Austria* 1
Hamburg 5, *Randers Freja* 3
Randers Freja 0, *Hamburg* 2
Milan 5, *Levski* 1
Levski 1, *Milan* 1
Hajduk 0, *Tottenham Hotspur* 2
Tottenham Hotspur 4, *Hajduk* 3
Shamrock Rovers 1, *Cardiff City* 1
Cardiff City 2, *Shamrock Rovers* 0
Lausanne Sports 3, *Spartak Trnava* 2
Spartak Trnava 2, *Lausanne* 0
Aberdeen 10, *Reykjavik* 0
Reykjavik 1, *Aberdeen* 4
Valencia 4, *Crusaders* 0

Crusaders 2, Valencia 4
Torpedo Moscow 0, Motor Zwickau 0
Motor Zwickau 0, Torpedo Moscow 1
Izmir 2, Standard Liège 3
Standard Liège 0, Izmir 0
Aris Bonnevoie 0, Lyon 3
Lyon 2, Aris Bonnevoie 1
Fredrikstadt 1, Setubal 5
Setubal 2, Frederikstadt 1
Vasas Gyoer 5, Apollon Limassol 0
Apollon Limassol 0, Vasas Gyoer 4
Bayern Munich 5, Panathanaikos 0
Panathanaikos 1, Bayern Munich 2
JHK Helsinki 1, Wislaw Cracow 4
Wislaw Cracow 4, JHK Helsinki 0
Floriana Malta 1, NAC Breda 2
NAC Breda 1, Floriana Malta 0

Second Round
Bayern Munich 6, Vittoria Setubal 2
Vittoria Setubal 1, Bayern Munich 1
Wislaw 0, Hamburg 1
Hamburg 4, Wislaw 0
NAC Breda 1, Cardiff City 1
Cardiff City 4, NAC Breda 1
Vasas Gyoer 2, Milan 2
Milan 1, Vasas Gyoer 1
Lyon 1, Tottenham Hotspur 0
Tottenham Hotspur 4, Lyon 3
Standard Liège 3, Aberdeen 0
Aberdeen 2, Standard Liège 0
Torpedo Moscow 3, Spartak Trnava 1
Spartak Trnava 1, Torpedo Moscow 3
Steaua Bucharest 1, Valencia 0
Valencia 3, Steaua Bucharest 0

Quarter-finals
SV Hamburg 2, Lyon 0
Lyon 2, SV Hamburg 0
SV Hamburg 2, Lyon 0
Standard Liège 1, Milan 1
Milan 1, Standard Liège 1
Milan 2, Standard Liège 0
Torpedo Moscow 1, Cardiff City 0
Cardiff City 1, Torpedo Moscow 0
Cardiff City 1, Torpedo Moscow 0 (Augsberg)
Valencia 1, Bayern Munich 1
Bayern Munich 1, Valencia 0

Semi-finals
SV Hamburg 1, Cardiff City 1
Cardiff City 2, SV Hamburg 3
Milan 2, Bayern Munich 0
Bayern Munich 0, Milan 0

Final *Rotterdam*, May 23, 1968
Milan (2) 2, SV Hamburg (0) 0
Milan: Cudicini; Anquilletti, Schnellinger; Trappatoni, Rosato, Scala; Hamrin, Lodetti, Sormani, Rivera, Prati.
SV Hamburg: Ozcan; Sondemann, Kurbjohn; Dieckemann, Horst, Schulz, H.; Dorfel II, Kramer, Seeler, Hornig, Dorfel I.
Scorer: Hamrin (2) for Milan.

EUROPEAN CUPWINNERS' CUP 1968-9

For the first time, one of the two major European club competitions was won by an Iron Curtain country; more precisely by the Czech team, Slovan Bratislava. It was, in a way, especially appropriate, given that the other Iron Curtain clubs had withdrawn in protest against the decision to "zone" the first round, so many West European clubs having refused to play Iron Curtain teams in protest against the invasion of Czechoslovakia the previous summer.

Dunfermline, cleverly managed by the old Blackpool goalkeeper, George Farm, did best of the British entry, surviving until the semi-final. After a rough second leg, in which they had a player sent off, they protested at the way they were treated in Bratislava.

West Bromwich Albion, the F.A. Cup holders, were surprisingly among Dunfermline's victims. After conceding a draw at home, Dunfermline adjusted better to the icy circumstances at The Hawthorns, and won by Gardner's headed goal scored after only 90 seconds.

Barcelona, if anybody, looked favourites for the Final, especially after their fine 4-1 victory over Cologne, in the second leg of the semi-finals. But for the second time they lost a European final on Swiss soil. Cvetler, Slovan's clever winger, put them ahead in the second minute, and by half-time discomfited Barcelona was 3-1 behind. Though Rexach proceeded to score straight from a corner kick, the Czechs held on to win.

Cardiff, veteran of so many brave battles in this tournament, alas went out at the first hurdle.

First Round
Bruges 3, West Bromwich Albion 1
West Bromwich Albion 2, Bruges 0
Dunfermline 10, Apoel Nicosia 1
Apoel Nicosia 0, Dunfermline 2
Crusaders 2, Norrköpping 2
Norrköpping 4, Crusaders 1

Cardiff City 2, *Porto* 2
Porto 2, *Cardiff City* 1
Bordeaux 2, *Cologne* 1
Cologne 3, *Bordeaux* 0
Slovan Bratislava 3, *Bor* 0
Bor 2, *Slovan Bratislava* 0
Partizan Tirana 1, *Torino* 0
Torino 3, *Partizan Tirana* 1
Rumelange 2, *Sliema Malta* 1
Sliema Malta 1, *Rumelange* 0
Izmir 3, *Lyn Oslo* 1
Lyn Oslo 4, *Izmir* 1
Freja 1, *Shamrock Rovers* 0
Shamrock Rovers 1, *Freja* 2
Lugano 0, *Barcelona* 1
Barcelona 3, *Lugano* 0
Olympiakos 2, *Frem Reykjavik* 0
Frem Reykjavik 0, *Olympiakos* 2
ADO 4, *Graz* 1
Graz 0, *ADO* 2

Second Round
Dinamo Bucharest 1, *West Bromwich Albion* 1
West Bromwich Albion 4, *Dinamo Bucharest* 0
Dunfermline 4, *Olympiakos* 0
Olympiakos 3, *Dunfermline* 0
Porto 1, *Slovan Bratislava* 0
Slovan Bratislava 4, *Porto* 0
Randers Freja 6, *Sliema Malta* 0
Sliema Malta 0, *Randers Freja* 2
ADO 0, *Cologne* 1
Cologne 3, *ADO* 0

Quarter-finals
Barcelona 3, *Lyn Oslo* 2
Barcelona 2, *Lyn Oslo* 2 (played in Barcelona)
Cologne 2, *Randers Freja* 1
Randers Freja 0, *Cologne* 3
Torino 0, *Slovan Bratislava* 1
Slovan Bratislava 2, *Torino* 1
Dunfermline 0, *West Bromwich Albion* 0
West Bromwich Albion 0, *Dunfermline* 1

Semi-finals
Dunfermline 1, *Slovan Bratislava* 1
Slovan Bratislava 1, *Dunfermline* 0
Cologne 2, *Barcelona* 2
Barcelona 4, *Cologne* 1

Final *Basel*, May 21, 1969
Slovan Bratislava (3) 3, *Barcelona* (1) 2
Slovan: Vencel; Filo, Hrivnak; Jan Zlocha, Horvarth, Hrdlicka; Cvetler, Moder, Josef Capkovic, Jokl, Jan Capkovic.
Barcelona: Sadurni; Franch, Eladio; Rife, Olivella, Zabalza; Pelicer, Castro, Zaldua, Fuste, Rexach, subs: Pereda, Mendonça.
Scorers: Cvetler, Hrivnak, Jan Capkovic for Slovan; Zaldua, Rexach for Barcelona.

EUROPEAN CUPWINNERS' CUP 1969-70

Manchester City added the Cupwinners' Cup to the various honours they had won since 1968, decisively beating Gornik in the Final, despite some rough treatment by the Polish defenders On their way to Vienna, they beat Atletico Bilbao in the first round, after being at one stage 3-1 down in the first leg, in Spain, but rallying to draw, 3-3. Their League form in mid-season was poor, but they were always able to produce something extra for their Cupwinners' Cup matches. Slovan, the holders, went out in the very first round, to Dynamo Zagreb. Lierse were thoroughly thrashed in the second round by Manchester City, Academica Coimbra narrowly beaten in the third. Schalke won the first leg of the semi-finals thanks to a characteristic individualist's goal by Libuda, but City annihilated them at Manchester. Francis Lee, Colin Bell and Mike Summerbee, till he was hurt, were ebullient.

Gornik beat Roma to reach the Final on the toss of a coin. In heavy rain, Lee had another fine match, and City comfortably overcame the loss of Doyle, through injury. Gornik's goal, made by Lubanski for Oslizlo, came too late to matter. Young and Lee - a penalty when Young was fouled - got City's goals.

Preliminary Round
Rapid Vienna 0, *Torpedo Moscow* 0
Torpedo Moscow 1, *Rapid Vienna* 1

First Round
Atletico Bilbao 3, *Manchester City* 3
Manchester City 3, *Atletico Bilbao* 0
Ards 0, *Roma* 0
Roma 3, *Ards* 1
Rangers 2, *Steaua* 0
Steaua 0, *Rangers* 0
Mjoendalen 1, *Cardiff City* 7
Cardiff City 5, *Mjoendalen* 1
Shamrock Rovers 2, *Schalke 04* 1
Schalke 04 3, *Shamrock Rovers* 0

Magdeburg 1, *MTK* 0
MTK 1, *Magdeburg* 1
Dukla 1, *Marseilles* 0
Marseilles 2, *Dukla* 0
Rapid Vienna 1, *PSV* 2
PSV 4, *Rapid Vienna* 2
Frem 2, *St. Gallen* 1
St. Gallen 1, *Frem* 0
Norkopping 5, *Sliema* 1
Sliema 1, *Norkopping* 0
Dynamo Zagreb 3, *Slovan Bratislava* 0
Slovan Bratislava 0, *Dynamo Zagreb* 0
Lierse 10, *Apoel Cyprus* 0
Apoel Cyprus 0, *Lierse* 1
Olimpiakos 2, *Gornik* 2
Gornik 5, *Olimpiakos* 0
Goeztepe Izmir 3, *Union Luxemburg* 0
Union Luxemburg 2, *Goeztepe Izmir* 3
IBV Reykjavik 0, *Levski* 4
Levski 4, *IBV Reykjavik* 0
Academica 0, *Palloseura* 0
Palloseura 0, *Academica* 1

Second Round
Lierse 0, *Manchester City* 3
Manchester City 5, *Lierse* 0
Gornik 3, *Rangers* 1
Rangers 1, *Gornik* 3
Goeztepe Izmir 3, *Cardiff City* 0
Cardiff City 1, *Goeztepe Izmir* 0
Roma 1, *PSV* 0
PSV 1, *Roma* 0 (Roma won toss)
Norkopping 0, *Schalke 04* 0
Schalke 04 1, *Norkopping* 0
Levski 4, *St. Gallen* 0
St. Gallen 0, *Levski* 0
Magdeburg 1, *Academica* 0
Academica 2, *Magdeburg* 0
Marseilles 1, *Dynamo Zagreb* 1
Dynamo Zagreb 0, *Marseilles* 0

Quarter-finals
Academica 0, *Manchester City* 0
Manchester City 1, *Academica* 0
Roma 2, *Goeztepe Izmir* 0
Goeztepe Izmir 0, *Roma* 0
Levski 3, *Gornik* 2
Gornik 2, *Levski* 1

Dynamo Zagreb 1, *Schalke 04* 3
Schalke 04 1, *Dynamo Zagreb* 0

Semi-finals
Schalke 04 1, *Manchester City* 0
Manchester City 5, *Schalke 04* 1
Roma 1, *Gornik* 1
Gornik 2, *Roma* 2
Gornik 1, *Roma* 1 (at Strasbourg. Gornik won toss)

Final *Vienna* April 29, 1970
Manchester City (2) 2, *Gornik* (0) 1
Manchester City: Corrigan; Book, Booth, Heslop, Pardoe; Doyle (Bowyer), Oakes, Towers; Bell, Lee, Young.
Gornik: Kostka; Gorgon, Oslizlo, Latocha, Florenski (Deja), Olek, Szoltysik, Wilczek (Skowronck), Banas, Lubanski, Szarynski.
Scorers: Young, Lee for Manchester City; Oslizlo for Gornik.

Chapter Seventeen

The European Inter-Cities Fairs Cup History

This competition, which made a creaking start, taking an unconscionable time a-playing, has since gathered prestige and popularity. It is nominally open to cities which put on trade fairs, and initially, London entered a representative team, later falling into line and putting out club sides. Home and away aggregate decides.

1955–8
London eliminated Basel, Frankfurt and Lausanne, but lost in the Final to Barcelona. Birmingham City knocked out Inter and Zagreb, but lost (4–3, 0–1, 1–2 at Basel) to Barcelona.
London 2, *Barcelona* 2 *(Chelsea)*
Barcelona 6, *London* 2

1958–60
Chelsea, representing London, went out in the second round (1–0, 1–4) to Belgrade. Birmingham eliminated Cologne (2–2, 2–0), Zagreb (2–0, 3–3) and Union St. Gilloise (4–2, 4–2) but lost to Barcelona in the Final.
Birmingham 1, *Barcelona* 1
Barcelona 4, *Birmingham* 1

1960–1
By now the competition had been properly stabilised, and played off within one season. Hibernian, representing Scotland, put out Barcelona

in the second round. The match at Edinburgh which decided produced violent scenes, as the Barcelona players ran riot. Hibernian, having drawn 4–4 in Barcelona, won this 3–2.

Birmingham City eliminated BK Copenhagen (4–4, 5–0), having previously put out Ujpest of Hungary, while Hibernian had a walkover against Lausanne.

In the semi-finals, Birmingham maintained their fine record in this contest by defeating Inter 2–1 both at home and away. But Hibernian, having drawn 2–2 and 3–3 with Roma, crashed 6–0 in the play-off.

In the Final, Roma beat Birmingham.
Birmingham City 2, Roma 2
Roma 2, Birmingham City 0

1961–2

The Spaniards now succeeded in getting the entry temporarily increased to three clubs per country; and one of their own clubs, Valencia, was successful.

Of the British clubs, Sheffield Wednesday knocked out Lyon and Roma, but were eliminated by Barcelona, on 4–3 aggregate, in the quarter-finals. Valencia crushed Nottingham Forest on 7–1 aggregate in the first round, but Hearts eliminated Union St. Gilloise (5–1 aggregate). In the next round, however, Inter put them out, 5–0 on aggregate.

In the Final, Valencia, having accounted for Inter in the quarter-finals, won an all-Spanish clash with Barcelona, most convincingly.
Valencia 6, Barcelona 2
Barcelona 1, Valencia 1

1962–3

Valencia, their teeth now well into this trophy, won it again. Everton, coming in for the first time, were surprisingly knocked out (1–0 and 0–2) by the compact Dunfermline side. Hibernian had another excellent run, eliminating Staevnet, Copenhagen, 4–0 and 3–2, Utrecht of Holland 1–0 and 2–1, and finally going out, 0–5, 2–1, to Valencia who had beaten Dunfermline in a third match decider in the second round. Dunfermline lost away, 4–0, but won gallantly at home, 6–2.
Dynamo Zagreb 1, Valencia 2
Valencia 2, Dynamo Zagreb 0

1963–4

In an all-Spanish final at Barcelona, Saragossa narrowly got home against Valencia.

First Round
(Results of British Teams only)
Copenhagen 1, Arsenal 7
Arsenal 2, Copenhagen 3
Utrecht 1, Sheffield Wednesday 4
Sheffield Wednesday 4, Utrecht 1

Glentoran 1, *Partick Thistle* 4
Partick Thistle 3, *Glentoran* 0
Lausanne 2, *Hearts* 2
Hearts 2, *Lausanne* 2
Lausanne 3, *Hearts* 2

Second Round
Cologne 3, *Sheffield Wednesday* 2
Sheffield Wednesday 1, *Cologne* 2
Arsenal 1, *Royal Liegois* 1
Royal Liegois 3, *Arsenal* 1
Partick Thistle 3, *Spartak Brno* 2
Spartak Brno 4, *Partick Thistle* 0
Lausanne 1, *Saragossa* 2
Saragossa 3, *Lausanne* 0
Juventus 1, *Atletico Madrid* 0
Atletico Madrid 1, *Juventus* 2
Roma 2, *Belenenses* 1
Belenenses 0, *Roma* 1
Valencia 0, *Rapid Vienna* 0
Rapid Vienna 2, *Valencia* 3

Quarter-finals
Roma 3, *Cologne* 1
Cologne 4, *Roma* 0
Saragossa 3, *Juventus* 2
Juventus 0, *Saragossa* 0
Royal Liegois 2, *Spartak Brno* 0
Spartak Brno 2, *Royal Liegois* 0
Royal Liegois 1, *Spartak Brno* 0
Valencia 5, *Ujpest* 2
Ujpest 3, *Valencia* 1

Semi-finals
Valencia 4, *Cologne* 1
Cologne 2, *Valencia* 0
Royal Liegois 1, *Saragossa* 0
Saragossa 2, *Royal Liegois* 0

Final
Saragossa 2, *Valencia* 1

EUROPEAN INTER-CITIES FAIRS CUP 1964–5

A tournament surprisingly and meritoriously won by Ferencvaros of Budapest; very much the outsiders from the semi-finals onward, despite a forward-line which included the internationals Albert, Rakosi and Fenyvesi, whose goal beat Juventus in the Final. Manchester

United, England's hopes, who had won an all-English clash with Everton on the way, slipped badly in the semi-finals, confirming the fears of those who believed their organisation hardly matched their talent. The first of their two matches in Budapest, won by Ferencvaros with a disputed penalty, was bad tempered and unpleasant; a man from each side was sent off. Juventus, after making a very laborious way to the semi-final, suddenly found some form, to recover against Atletico Madrid, but in the end went down at home to Ferencvaros – and Dr. Fenyvesi.

Preliminary Round
Eintracht 3, Kilmarnock 0
Kilmarnock 5, Eintracht 1
Wiener Sportklub 2, S.C. Leipzig 1
S.C. Leipzig 0, Wiener Sportklub 1
Strasbourg 2, Milan 0
Milan 1, Strasbourg 0
Basel 2, Spora Luxemburg 0
Spora Luxemburg 0, Basel 1
Bilbao 2, OFK Belgrade 2
OFK Belgrade 0, Bilbao 2
Ferencvaros 2, Spartak Brno 0
Spartak Brno 1, Ferencvaros 0
Goztep Smyrna 0, Petrolul Ploesti 1
Petrolul Ploesti 2, Goztep Smyrna 1
Odense 1, VfB Stuttgart 3
VfB Stuttgart 1, Odense 0
Betis Seville 1, Stade Francais 1
Stade Francais 2, Betis Seville 0
Dynamo Zagreb 3, Grazer A.K. 2
Grazer A.K. 0, Dynamo Zagreb 6
Borussia Dortmund 4, Bordeaux 1
Bordeaux 2, Borussia Dortmund 0
Union St. Gilloise 0, Juventus 1
Juventus 1, Union St. Gilloise 0
Valencia 1, Liège 1
Liège 3, Valencia 1
Vojvodina 1, Lokomotiv 1
Lokomotiv 1, Vojvodina 1
Lokomotiv 2, Vojvodina 1 (Sofia)
Djurgaarden 1, Manchester United 1
Manchester United 6, Djurgaarden 1
Valerenger 2, Everton 5
Everton 4, Valerenger 2
Leixoes 1, Celtic 1
Celtic 3, Leixoes 0
Barcelona 0, Fiorentina 1
Fiorentina 0, Barcelona 2

Aris 0, Roma 0
Roma 3, Aris 0
Belenenses 1, Shelbourne 1
Shelbourne 0, Belenenses 0
Shelbourne 2, Belenenses 1 (Dublin)
Dunfermline 4, Oergryte 2
Oergryte 0, Dunfermline 0
Hertha Berlin 2, Antwerp 1
Antwerp 2, Hertha Berlin 0
BK Copenhagen 3, DOS Utrecht 4
DOS 2, BK Copenhagen 1
Servette 2, Atletico Madrid 2
Atletico Madrid 6, Servette 1

First Round
Dynamo Zagreb 1, Roma 1
Roma 1, Dynamo Zagreb 0
Stade Francais 0, Juventus 0
Juventus 1, Stade Francais 0
Basel 0, Strasbourg 1
Strasbourg 5, Basel 2
Kilmarnock 0, Everton 2
Everton 4, Kilmarnock 1
Petrolul 1, Lokomotiv Plovdiv 0
Lokomotiv Plovdiv 2, Petrolul 0
Borussia Dortmund 1, Manchester United 6
Manchester United 4, Borussia Dortmund 0
Dunfermline 1, VfB Stuttgart 0
VfB Stuttgart 0, Dunfermline 0
Bilbao 2, Antwerp 0
Antwerp 0, Bilbao 1
Barcelona 3, Celtic 1
Celtic 0, Barcelona 0
Utrecht 0, Liège 2
Liège 2, Utrecht 0
Ferencvaros 1, Wiener S.K. 0
Wiener S.K. 0, Ferencvaros 0
Shelbourne 0, Atletico Madrid 1
Atletico Madrid 1, Shelbourne 0

Second Round
Torino 1, Dynamo Zagreb 1
Dynamo Zagreb 1, Torino 2
Strasbourg 0, Barcelona 0
Barcelona 2, Strasbourg 2
Barcelona 0, Strasbourg 0 (Barcelona)
Strasbourg won toss

Manchester United 1, *Everton* 1
Everton 1, *Manchester United* 2
Juventus 1, *Lokomotiv* 1
Lokomotiv 1, *Juventus* 1
Juventus 2, *Lokomotiv* 1 (*Turin*)
Bilbao 1, *Dunfermline* 0
Dunfermline 1, *Bilbao* 0
Bilbao 2, *Dunfermline* 1 (*Bilbao*)
Roma 1, *Ferencvaros* 2
Ferencvaros 1, *Roma* 0
Liège 1, *Atletico Madrid* 0
Atletico Madrid 2, *Liège* 0

Quarter-finals
Ferencvaros 1, *Bilbao* 0
Bilbao 1, *Ferencvaros* 0
Ferencvaros 3, *Bilbao* 0 (*Budapest*)
Strasbourg 0, *Manchester United* 5
Manchester United 0, *Strasbourg* 0

Semi-finals
Manchester United 3, *Ferencvaros* 2
Ferencvaros 1, *Manchester United* 0
Ferencvaros 2, *Manchester United* 1 (*Budapest*)
Atletico Madrid 3, *Juventus* 1
Juventus 3, *Atletico Madrid* 1
Juventus 3, *Atletico Madrid* 1 (*Turin*)

Final *Turin*
Juventus (0) 0, *Ferencvaros* (0) 1; Fenyvesi, M.

EUROPEAN INTER-CITIES FAIRS CUP 1965–6

A tournament which produced a rash of violent matches ended in anticlimax, the two Spanish finalists being ordered by their Federation to postpone the two-legged Final till the following season. When it was at last played, it turned out thoroughly dramatic; winning on Barcelona's ground, Saragossa proceeded to lose on their own, three of Barcelona's goals being scored by a young newcomer to the attack, Pujol.

Chelsea's young team did well, none better than the brilliant young forward, Peter Osgood. Their three ties with Milan were memorable, above all the game at Stamford Bridge, when Schnellinger gave a performance for Milan which was matchlessly combative. Memorable for more sinister reasons was the previous round's game in Rome, where the players were bombarded with missiles. Leeds' home game against Valencia gave rise to a disgraceful brawl. But it was Saragossa who eventually eliminated them, with surprising ease, in a decider played at Leeds.

First Round
Union Luxembourg 0, Cologne 4
Cologne 13, Union Luxembourg 0
Hibernian 2, Valencia 0
Valencia 2, Hibernian 0
Valencia 3, Hibernian 0
F.C. Liège 1, Zagreb 0
Zagreb 2, F.C. Liège 0
Red Star 0, Fiorentina 4
Fiorentina 3, Red Star 1
Stade Francais 0, Porto 0
Porto 1, Stade Francais 0
Malmö 0, Munich 1860 3
Munich 1860 4, Malmö 0
Bordeaux 0, Sporting Lisbon 4
Sporting Lisbon 6, Bordeaux 1
Milan 1, Strasbourg 0
Strasbourg 2, Milan 1
Milan 1, Strasbourg 1
(Milan won toss)
Chelsea 4, Roma 1
Roma 0, Chelsea 0
Spartak Brno 2, Lokomotiv Plovdiv 0
Lokomotiv Plovdiv 1, Spartak Brno 0
Nuremberg 1, Everton 1
Everton 1, Nuremberg 0
Antwerp 1, Glentoran 0
Glentoran 3, Antwerp 3
Wiener S.K. 6, PAOK Salonika 0
PAOK Salonika 2, Wiener S.K. 1
Leeds United 2, Torino 1
Torino 0, Leeds United 0
DSO Utrecht 0, Barcelona 0
Barcelona 7, DSO Utrecht 1
Valerengen 1, Hearts 3
Hearts 1, Valerengen 0

Second Round
Aris 2, Cologne 1
Cologne 2, Aris 0
Goztepe Izmir 2, Munich 1860 1
Munich 1860 9, Goztepe Izmir 1
Ujpest 3, Everton 0
Everton 2, Ujpest 1
Dunfermline 5, BK Copenhagen 0
BK Copenhagen 2, Dunfermline 4
Hanover 86 5, Porto 0

Porto 2, Hanover 86 1
Sporting Lisbon 2, Espanol Barcelona 1
Espanol Barcelona 4, Sporting Lisbon 3
Espanol Barcelona 2, Sporting Lisbon 1
Zagreb 2, Red Star Brasov 2
Red Star Brasov 1, Zagreb 0
Antwerp 2, Barcelona 1
Barcelona 2, Antwerp 0
Shamrock Rovers 1, Saragossa 1
Saragossa 2, Shamrock Rovers 1
Wiener S.K. 1, Chelsea 0
Chelsea 2, Wiener S.K. 0
Leipzig 1, Leeds United 2
Leeds United 0, Leipzig 0
C.U.F. Setubal 2, Milan 0
Milan 2, C.U.F. Setubal 0
Milan 1, C.U.F. Setubal 0
Basel 1, Valencia 3
Valencia 5, Basel 1
Fiorentina 2, Spartak Brno 0
Spartak Brno 4, Fiorentina 0

Third Round
Hearts 3, Saragossa 3
Saragossa 2, Hearts 2
Saragossa 1, Hearts 0
Leeds United 1, Valencia 1
Valencia 0, Leeds United 1
Hanover 96 2, Barcelona 1
Barcelona 1, Hanover 96 0
Hanover 96 1, Barcelona 1
(Barcelona won toss)
Cologne 3, Ujpest 2
Ujpest 4, Cologne 0
Dunfermline 2, Spartak Brno 0
Spartak Brno 0, Dunfermline 0
Espanol 3, Red Star Brasov 1
Red Star Brasov 4, Espanol 2
Espanol 1, Red Star Brasov 0
Milan 2, Chelsea 1
Chelsea 2, Milan 1
Milan 1, Chelsea 1
(Chelsea won toss)

Fourth Round
Leeds United 4, Ujpest 1
Ujpest 1, Leeds United 1
Munich 1860 2, Chelsea 2
Chelsea 1, Munich 1860 0

Dunfermline 1, Saragossa 0
Saragossa 4, Dunfermline 2

Semi-finals
Saragossa 1, Leeds United 0
Leeds United 2, Saragossa 1
Leeds United 1, Saragossa 3
Barcelona 2, Chelsea 0
Chelsea 2, Barcelona 0
Barcelona 5, Chelsea 0

Final
Barcelona 0, Saragossa 1
Saragossa 2, Barcelona 4

EUROPEAN INTER-CITIES FAIRS CUP 1966-7

Postponed for the second time until the following season, the final of the 1966-7 competition was ultimately won by Dynamo Zabreg, at the expense of Leeds United. In Zagreb, they deservedly won, both goals being scored by their 18-year-old outside-right, Cercer. At Elland Road, their defence, with Skoric excellent in goal, massed to keep out the Leeds attack. Two other well-known internationals, Belin, the right-half, and Zambata, the striker, also increased their reputations.

Barcelona, the holders, had gone out only a matter of weeks after winning the postponed 1966 Final, to Dundee United, who shocked them by beating them on their own ground. Seemann and Perssonn, their Scandinavian wingers, playing splendidly. Juventus, however, were too strong for them in the Third Round, even though they won the return, in Dundee.

Burnley had a very good run, beating VfB Stuttgart, Lausanne and Naples – where, in the return match, they had to survive a short and vicious riot, involving Naples players and spectators.

Burnley's own robust tactics provoked a brawl late in the home game against Eintracht, which they surprisingly lost – thus going out of the competition.

Leeds United did very well to beat Valencia away from home, got through against Bologna on the toss of a coin, and competently disposed of Kilmarnock, on their way to the Final. But Benfica, on their first appearance in the tournament, surprisingly went out to Leipzig in the Third Round. Dynamo Zagreb had a splendid 3-0 home win to put out Juventus in the quarter finals, then turned a 3-0 deficit into a 4-3 aggregate win over Eintracht, in the semis.

First Round
VfB Stuttgart 1, Burnley 1
Burnley 2, VfB Stuttgart 0

Frigg Oslo 1, *Dunfermline Ath.* 3
Dunfermline Ath. 3, *Frigg Oslo* 1
Red Star 5, *Bilbao* 0
Bilbao 2, *Red Star* 0
Valencia 2, *Nuremberg* 1
Nuremberg 0, *Valencia* 2
Drumcondra 0, *Eintracht* 2
Eintracht 5, *Drumcondra* 1
Naples 3, *Wiener S.K.* 1
Wiener S.K. 1, *Naples* 2
Porto 2, *Bordeaux* 1
Bordeaux 2, *Porto* 1
(Bordeaux won toss)
Nice 2, *Oergryte* 2
Oergryte 2, *Nice* 1
Djurgaarden 1, *Lokomotiv Leipzig* 3
Lokomotiv Leipzig 2, *Djurgaarden* 1
Dynamo Pitesti 2, *Seville* 0
Seville 2, *Dynamo Pitesti* 2
Spartak Brno 2, *Dynamo Zagreb* 0
Dynamo Zagreb 2, *Spartak Brno* 0
(Dynamo won toss)
U.S. Luxemberg 0, *Antwerp* 1
Antwerp 4, *U.S. Luxemberg* 0
Bologna 3, *Goeztepe* 1
Goeztepe 1, *Bologna* 2
DWS 1, *Leeds United* 3
Leeds United 5, *DWS* 1

Second Round
Lokomotiv Leipzig 0, *Liège* 0
Liège 1, *Lokomotiv Leipzig* 2
Lausanne 1, *Burnley* 3
Burnley 5, *Lausanne* 0
La Gantoise 1, *Bordeaux* 0
Bordeaux 0, *La Gantoise* 0
Oergryte 0, *Ferencvaros* 0
Ferencvaros 7, *Oergryte* 1
Toulouse 3, *Dynamo Pitesti* 0
Dynamo Pitesti 5, *Toulouse* 1
Dunfermline 4, *Dynamo Zagreb* 2
Dynamo Zagreb 2, *Dunfermline* 0
Barcelona 1, *Dundee United* 2
Dundee United 2, *Barcelona* 0
Odense b. 1909 1, *Naples* 4
Naples 2, *Odense b. 1909* 1
Antwerp 1, *Kilmarnock* 1
Kilmarnock 7, *Antwerp* 2

Valencia 1, Red Star 0
Red Star 1, Valencia 2
Sparta Prague 2, Bologna 2
Bologna 2, Sparta Prague 1
Spartak Plovdiv 1, Benfica 1
Benfica 2, Spartak Plovdiv 0
DOS Utrecht 1, West Bromwich Albion 1
West Bromwich Albion 5, DOS Utrecht 2
Juventus 3, Setubal 1
Setubal 0, Juventus 2
Eintracht 5, BK Copenhagen 1
BK Copenhagen 2, Eintracht 2

Third Round
Lokomotiv Leipzig 3, Benfica 1
Benfica 2, Lokomotiv Leipzig 1
Kilmarnock 1, La Gantoise 0
La Gantoise 1, Kilmarnock 2
Burnley 3, Naples 0
Naples 0, Burnley 0
Leeds United 1, Valencia 1
Valencia 0, Leeds United 2
Bologna 3, West Bromwich Albion 0
West Bromwich Albion 1, Bologna 3
Juventus 3, Dundee United 0
Dundee United 1, Juventus 0
Dynamo Zagreb 1, Dynamo Pitesti 0
Dynamo Pitesti 0, Dynamo Zagreb 0
Eintracht 4, Ferencvaros 1
Ferencvaros 2, Eintracht 1

Quarter-finals
Bologna 1, Leeds United 0
Leeds United 1, Bologna 0
(Leeds won toss)
Juventus 2, Dynamo Zagreb 2
Dynamo Zagreb 3, Juventus 0
Eintracht 1, Burnley 1
Burnley 1, Eintracht 2
Lokomotiv Leipzig 1, Kilmarnock 0
Kilmarnock 2, Lokomotiv Leipzig 0

Semi-finals
Leeds United 4, Kilmarnock 2
Kilmarnock 0, Leeds United 0
Eintracht 3, Dynamo Zagreb 0
Dynamo Zagreb 4, Eintracht 0

Final
August 30, 1967   *Dynamo Zagreb* (1) 2   *Leeds United* (0) 0
                   Cercer 2
September 6, 1967 *Leeds United* (0) 0   *Dynamo Zagreb* (0) 0

EUROPEAN INTER-CITIES FAIRS CUP 1967–8

This time, Leeds United, in another postponed final – or finals – consoled themselves for the previous year's disappointment by defeating Ferencvaros, to win. They were two hard games, each on the same pattern; an away team clamming up in defence and allowing the home team to come at them. Leeds won the first game and scored the only goal of the finals in controversial circumstances; Jackie Charlton standing on the goal line at a corner and blocking the goalkeeper's path, Jones thumping the ball home.

On their way to the Final, Leeds had tough opposition from Partizan of Belgrade and Hibernian – who had rallied superbly in their return match with Naples, winning 5–0 after losing 4–1 away – but didn't concede a goal against Rangers.

Ferencvaros, winners of the trophy in 1965, played beautiful football at Liverpool, where Munich had crashed – and were cheered off the field by the Kop. Bologna, in the semi-finals, pushed them very hard.

Dundee had a splendid run into the semi-finals, but Leeds, again, were too good for them, defeating a Scottish side for the third time in the competition. They won the return, at Elland Road, nine minutes from time through a goal by Gray, during an accumulation of postponed matches.

First Round
Spora Luxemburg 0, Leeds United 9
Leeds United 7, Spora Luxemburg 0
PAOK Salonika 0, Liège 2
Liège 3, PAOK Salonika 2
Wiener S.K. 0, Atletico Madrid 5
Atletico Madrid 2, Wiener S.K. 1
St. Patrick's 1, Bordeaux 3
Bordeaux 6, St. Patrick's 3
Utrecht 3, Saragossa 2
Saragossa 3, Utrecht 1
Naples 4, Hanover 0
Hanover 1, Naples 1
Bologna 2, Lyn Oslo 0
Lyn Oslo 0, Bologna 0
Nice 0, Fiorentina 1
Fiorentina 4, Nice 0
Dresden Dynamo 1, Rangers 1
Rangers 2, Dresden Dynamo 1

Argesul Pitesti 3, Ferencvaros 1
Ferencvaros 4, Argesul Pitesti 0
Malmö 0, Liverpool 2
Liverpool 2, Malmö 1
Hibernian 3, Porto 0
Porto 3, Hibernian 1
Eintracht 0, Nottingham Forest 1
Nottingham Forest 4, Eintracht 0
Dynamo Zagreb 5, Petrolul Ploesti 0
Petrolul Ploesti 2, Dynamo Zagreb 0
Atletico Bilbao 1, Frem 0
Frem 0, Atletico Bilbao 1
Bruges 0, Sporting Lisbon 0
Sporting Lisbon 2, Bruges 1
Frem 0, Atletico Bilbao 1
Atletico Bilbao 3, Frem 2
Zurich 3, Barcelona 1
Barcelona 1, Zurich 0
Lokomotiv Leipzig 5, Linfield 1
Linfield 1, Lokomotiv Leipzig 0
DWS Amsterdam 2, Dundee 1
Dundee 3, DWS Amsterdam 0
Partizan 5, Lokomotiv Plovdiv 1
Lokomotiv Plovdiv 1, Partisan 1
Vojvodina 1, CUF 0
CUF 1, Vojvodina 3
Cologne 2, Slavia Prague 0
Slavia Prague 2, Cologne 2
Royal Antwerp 1, Goeztepe Izmir 2
Goeztepe Izmir 0, Royal Antwerp 0

Second Round
Nottingham Forest 2, Zurich 1
Zurich 1, Nottingham Forest 2
Bordeaux 1, Atletico Bilbao 3
Dundee 3, Liège 1
Liège 1, Dundee 4
Vojvodina 0, Lokomotiv Leipzig 0
Lokomotiv Leipzig 0, Vojvodina 2
Saragossa 2, Ferencvaros 1
Ferencvaros 3, Saragossa 0
Liverpool 8, Munich 1860 0
Munich 1860 2, Liverpool 1
Rangers 3, Cologne 0
Cologne 3, Rangers 1
Bologna 0, Dynamo Zagreb 0
Dynamo Zagreb 1, Bologna 2
Naples 4, Hibernian 1

Hibernian 5, Naples 0
Partizan 1, Leeds United 2
Leeds United 1, Partizan 1
Fiorentina 1, Sporting Lisbon 1
Sporting Lisbon 2, Fiorentina 1

Third Round
Ferencvaros 1, Liverpool 0
Liverpool 0, Ferencvaros 1
Leeds United 1, Hibernian 0
Hibernian 1, Leeds United 1
Vojvodina 1, Goeztepe Izmir 0
Goeztepe Izmir 0, Vojvodina 1
Zurich 3, Sporting Lisbon 0
Sporting Lisbon 1, Zurich 0

Quarter-finals
Ferencvaros 2, Bilbao 1
Bilbao 1, Ferencvaros 2
Rangers 0, Leeds United 0
Leeds United 2, Rangers 0
Dundee 1, F.C. Zurich 0
F.C. Zurich 0, Dundee 1
Bologna 0, Vojvodina 0
Vojvodina 0, Bologna 2

Semi-finals
Dundee 1, Leeds United 1
Leeds United 1, Dundee 0
Ferencvaros 3, Bologna 2
Bologna 2, Ferencvaros 2

Final
Leeds United 1 (Jones), Ferencvaros 0
Ferencvaros 0, Leeds United 0

EUROPEAN INTER-CITIES FAIRS CUP 1968-9

For the second successive year, an English club won the Fairs Cup; suprisingly and laudably, Newcastle United, on their first entry into European competition. After a somewhat erratic beginning, in which they played irresistibly at home, indifferently away, they reached a brilliant crescendo in the two-legged Final against Ujpest – conquerors of the holders, Leeds United.

Having soundly beaten them at Gallowgate, thanks to two goals by their normally defensive half-back, Bobby Moncur, they rode a two-goal deficit in Budapest to win dramatically, 3–2.

Leeds might have done rather better had they not become so intensely engaged with the League Championship. They put out Standard Liège, were lucky to eliminate Naples on the iniquitous toss of a coin (Naples must be getting used to it; a similar expedient decided the 1960 Olympic semi-final and the 1968 European Nations semi-final, at Fuorigrotta), annihilated Hanover, but were well beaten, home and away, by Ujpest.

Newcastle overcame Feyenoord, Sporting Lisbon, Saragossa, Vitoria Setubal, then Rangers. "Away goals" allowed them to scrape through against the Spanish team, but Rangers couldn't score a goal against them. Their failure provoked a barbaric invasion of the Newcastle pitch by Rangers' fans, and a prolonged stoppage of the game.

Thus to the Final, in which Moncur got yet another fine goal in Budapest, and young Foggon, coming on as substitute, raced splendidly through alone to score the winner.

First Round
Chelsea 5, Morton 0
Morton 3, Chelsea 4
Newcastle United 4, Feyenoord 0
Feyenoord 2, Newcastle United 0
Slavia Sofia 0, Aberdeen 0
Aberdeen 2, Slavia Sofia 0
Atletico Bilbao 2, Liverpool 1
Liverpool 2, Atletico Bilbao 1
Rangers 2, Vojvodina 0
Vojvodina 1, Rangers 0
Ljubljana 0, Hibernian 3
Hibernian 2, Ljubljana 1
OFK Belgrade 6, Rapid Bucharest 1
Rapid Bucharest 3, OFK Belgrade 1
Wiener Sportklub 1, Slavia Prague 0
Slavia Prague 5, Wiener Sportklub 0
Skied Oslo 1, AIK Stockholm 1
AIK Stockholm 2, Skied Oslo 1
Trakia Plovdiv 3, Real Saragossa 1
Real Saragossa 2, Trakia Plovdiv 0
Dynamo Zagreb 1, Fiorentina 1
Fiorentina 2, Dynamo Zagreb 1
Legia Warsaw 6, Munich 1860 0
Munich 1860 2, Legia Warsaw 3
Daring Brussels 2, Panathanaikos 1
Panathanaikos 2, Daring Brussels 0
Wacker Innsbruck 2, Eintracht Frankfurt 2
Eintracht Frankfurt 3, Wacker Innsbruck 0
Sporting Lisbon 4, Valencia 0
Valencia 4, Sporting Lisbon 1
Bologna 4, Basel 1

Basel 1, Bologna 2
Aris Salonika 1, Hibernian Malta 0
Hibernian Malta 0, Aris Salonika 6
DOS Utrecht 1, Dundalk 1
Dundalk 2, DOS Utrecht 1
Atletico Madrid 2, Waregem 1
Waregem 1, Atletico Madrid 0
Goztepe Izmir 2, Marseilles 0
Marseilles 2, Goztepe Izmir 0
Metz 1, Hamburg S.V. 4
Hamburg S.V. 3, Metz 2
Lyon 1, Academica Coimbra 0
Academica Coimbra 1, Lyon 0
Lausanne 0, Juventus 2
Juventus 2, Lausanne 0
Beerschot 1, DWS Amsterdam 1
DWS Amsterdam 2, Beerschot 1
BK Odense 1, Hanover 96 3
Hanover 96 1, BK Odense 0
Vitoria Setubal 3, Linfield 0
Linfield 1, Vitoria Setubal 3
Standard Liège 0, Leeds United 0
Leeds United 3, Standard Liège 2
Naples 3, Grasshoppers 1
Grasshoppers 1, Naples 0

Second Round
Hibernian 3, Lokomotiv Leipzig 1
Lokomotiv 0, Hibernian 1
Leeds United 2, Naples 0
Naples 2, Leeds United 0
Rangers 6, Dundalk 1
Dundalk 0, Rangers 3
Aberdeen 2, Real Saragossa 1
Real Saragossa 3, Aberdeen 0
Chelsea 0, DWS Amsterdam 0
DWS Amsterdam 0, Chelsea 0
Sporting Lisbon 1, Newcastle United 1
Newcastle United 1, Sporting Lisbon 0
Vitoria Setubal 5, Lyon 0
Lyon 1, Vitoria Setubal 2
Goztepe Izmir 3, Argesul Pitesti 0
Argesul Pitesti 3, Goztepe Izmir 2
Hansa Rostock 3, Fiorentina 2
Fiorentina 2, Hansa Rostock 1
Hamburg SV 4, Slavia Prague 1
Slavia Prague 3, Hamburg SV 1
Panathanaikos 0, Bilbao 0

Bilbao 1, Panathanaikos 0
OFK Belgrade 1, Bologna 0
Bologna 1, OFK Belgrade 1
Aris Salonika 1, Ujpest 2
Ujpest 9, Aris Salonika 1
AIK Stockholm 4, Hanover 96 2
Hanover 96 5, AIK Stockholm 2

Third Round
Leeds United 5, Hanover 96 1
Hanover 96 1, Leeds United 2
Hamburg S.V. 1, Hibernian 0
Hibernian 2, Hamburg S.V. 1
Legia Warsaw 0, Ujpest 1
Ujpest 2, Legia Warsaw 2
Real Saragossa 3, Newcastle United 2
Newcastle United 2, Real Saragossa 1
OFK Belgrade 3, Goztepe Izmir 1
Goztepe Izmir 2, OFK Belgrade 0
Eintracht Frankfurt 1, Atletico Bilbao 1
Atletico Bilbao 1, Eintracht Frankfurt 0
DWS Amsterdam 0, Rangers 2
Rangers 2, DWS Amsterdam 1
Vitoria Setubal 3, Fiorentina 0
Fiorentina 2, Vitoria Setubal 1

Quarter-finals
Newcastle United 5, Vitoria Setubal 1
Vitoria Setubal 3, Newcastle United 1
Rangers 4, Atletico Bilbao 1
Atletico Bilbao 2, Rangers 0
Leeds United 0, Ujpest 1
Ujpest 2, Leeds United 0
Goztepe Izmir v. Hamburg. S.V. Hamburg scr.

Semi-finals
Goztepe Izmir 1, Ujpest 4
Ujpest 4, Goztepe Izmir 0
Rangers 0, Newcastle United 0
Newcastle United 2, Rangers 0

Final

Newcastle United (0) 3   *Ujpest (0) 0*
Moncur (2), Scott
Ujpest (2) 2   *Newcastle United (0) 3*
Bene, Gorocs   Moncur, Arentoft, Foggon

Newcastle United's team in both matches: McFaul; Craig, Clark; Gibb, Burton, Moncur; Scott, Robson, Davies, Arentoft, Sinclair. Substitute in each match: Foggon.

EUROPEAN FAIRS CUP 1969–70

Yet again, this now bloated, slightly amorphous competition had an English winner. Though there were moments in the course of the tournament when an Arsenal victory seemed the unlikeliest of outcomes, the North London club finally and impressively prevailed, to win their first major honour since 1954.

They began modestly, actually losing to Glentoran in the first round's return leg. A flaccid Sporting Lisbon team were easily crushed at Highbury, a hardly more impressive Rouen side gave a startling amount of trouble.

In the quarter-finals, Newcastle United, the holders, were bitterly unlucky to be squeezed out by Anderlecht on a late away goal, while Arsenal thrashed Dynamo Baku. In the semi-finals, they played vigorously to trounce Ajax 3–0 at home, Cruyff and all, lost the return only 1–0, and so met the powerful Anderlecht in the Final.

The Belgians, who had rallied surprisingly to beat Inter at San Siro, after losing at home, were much too good for Arsenal in Brussels. But again Arsenal proved formidable at home, breaking down Anderlecht's defence with a marvellous first half goal by young Kelly, scoring two more in the second half.

First Round

Arsenal 3, Glentoran 0
Glentoran 1, Arsenal 0
Dundee United 1, Newcastle United 2
Newcastle United 1, Dundee United 0
Liverpool 10, Dundalk 0
Dundalk 0, Liverpool 4
Partizan 2, Ujpest 1
Ujpest 2, Partizan 0
Sabadell 2, Bruges 0
Bruges 5, Sabadell 1
Las Palmas 0, Hertha Berlin 0
Hertha Berlin 1, Las Palmas 0
Wiener Sportklub 4, Ruch Chorzow 2
Ruch Chorzow 4, Wiener Sportklub 1
Rouen 2, Twente 0
Twente 1, Rouen 0
Vitoria Guimaraes 1, Banik 0
Banik 1, Vitoria Guimaraes 1
Sporting Lisbon 4, Linz 0
Linz 2, Sporting Lisbon 2

Jena 1, Altay Izmir 0
Altay Izmir 0, Jena 0
Lausanne 1, Vasas Gyor 2
Vasas Gyor 2, Lausanne 1
Trondheim Rosenborg 1, Southampton 0
Southampton 2, Trondheim Rosenborg 0
Hansa Rostock 3, Panionios 0
Panionios 2, Hansa Rostock 0
Baku Dynamo 6, Floriana 0
Floriana 0, Baku Dynamo 1
Slavia Sofia 2, Valencia 0
Valencia 1, Slavia Sofia 1
Internazionale 3, Sparta Prague 0
Sparta Prague 0, Internazionale 1
Juventus 3, Lokomotiv 1
Lokomotiv 1, Juventus 2
VfB Stuttgart 3, Plazs Malmo 0
Plazs Malmo 1, VfB Stuttgart 1
Hanover 96 1, Ajax 0
Ajax 3, Hanover 96 0
Aris Salonika 1, Cagliari 0
Cagliari 3, Aris Salonika 0
Metz 1, Naples 1
Naples 2, Metz 1
Barcelona 4, Odense 0
Odense 0, Barcelona 2
Gwardia Warsaw 1, Vojvodina 0
Vojvodina 1, Gwardia Warsaw 1
Dunfermline 4, Bordeaux 1
Bordeaux 2, Dunfermline 0
Zurich 3, Kilmarnock 2
Kilmarnock 3, Zurich 1
Munich 1860 2, Skeid Oslo 2
Skeid Oslo 2, Munich 1860 1
Valur Reykjavik 0, Anderlecht 6
Anderlecht 2, Valur Reykjavik 0
Charleroi 2, Zagreb 1
Zagreb 1, Charleroi 3
Hvidovre 1, Porto 2
Porto 2, Hvidovre 0
Jeunesse d'Esch 3, Coleraine 2
Coleraine 4, Jeunesse d'Esch 0
Vitoria Setubal 3, Rapid Bucharest 1
Rapid Bucharest 1, Vitoria Setubal 4

Second Round

Sporting Lisbon 0, Arsenal 0
Arsenal 3, Sporting Lisbon 0

Anderlecht 6, Coleraine 1
Coleraine 3, Anderlecht 7
Vitoria Setubal 1, Liverpool 0
Liverpool 3, Vitoria Setubal 2
Porto 0, Newcastle United 0
Newcastle United 1, Porto 0
Ajax 7, Ruch Chorzow 0
Ruch Chorzow 1, Ajax 2
Hansa Rostock 2, Internazionale 1
Internazionale 3, Hansa Rostock 0
Karl Zeiss Jena 2, Cagliari 0
Cagliari 0, Karl Zeiss Jena 1
Hertha Berlin 3, Juventus 1
Juventus 0 Hertha Berlin 0
Vasas Gyor 2 Barcelona 3
Barcelona 2 Vasas Gyor 0
VfB Stuttgart 0 Naples 0
Naples 1 VfB Stuttgart 0
Kilmarnock 4 Slavia Sofia 1
Slavia Sofia 2, Kilmarnock 0
Bruges 5, Ujpest Dosza 2
Ujpest Dosza 3, Bruges 0
Skeid Oslo 0, Baku Dynamo 0
Baku Dynamo 2, Skeid Oslo 0
Charleroi 3, Rouen 1
Rouen 2, Charleroi 0
Vitoria Guimaraes 3, Southampton 3
Southampton 5, Vitoria Guimaraes 1
Dunfermline 2, Gwardia Warsaw 1
Gwardia Warsaw 0, Dunfermline 1

Third Round

Newcastle United 0, Southampton 0
Southampton 1, Newcastle United 1
Anderlecht 1, Dunfermline 0
Dunfermline 3, Anderlecht 2
Rouen 0, Arsenal 0
Arsenal 1, Rouen 0
Kilmarnock 1, Dynamo Baku 1
Dynamo Baku 2, Kilmarnock 0
Karl Zeiss Jena 1, Ujpest 0
Ujpest 0, Karl Zeiss Jena 3
Barcelona 1, Internazionale 2
Internazionale 1, Barcelona 1
Vitoria Setubal 1, Hertha Berlin 1
Hertha Berlin 1, Vitoria Setubal 0
Naples 1, Ajax 0
Ajax 4, Naples 0

Quarter-finals

Karl Zeiss Jena 3, *Ajax* 1
Ajax 5, *Karl Zeiss Jena* 1
Hertha 1, *Internazionale* 0
Internazionale 2, *Hertha* 0
Anderlecht 2, *Newcastle United* 0
Newcastle United 3, *Anderlecht* 1
Dynamo Baku 0, *Arsenal* 2
Arsenal 7, *Dynamo Baku* 1

Semi-finals

Anderlecht 0, *Internazionale* 1
Internazionale 0, *Anderlecht* 2
Arsenal 3, *Ajax* 0
Ajax 1, *Arsenal* 0

Final

First leg *Brussels*, April 22, 1970
Anderlecht (2) 3, *Arsenal* (0) 1
Anderlecht: Trappeniers; Heylens, Velkeneers, Kialunda, Cornelis (Peeters), Desengher, Nordahl; Devrindt, Mulder, Van Himst, Puis.
Arsenal: Wilson; Storey, McNab; Kelly, McLintock, Simpson; Armstrong, Sammels, Radford, George, Graham.
Scorers: Devrindt, Mulder 2 for Anderlecht; Kennedy for Arsenal.

Second leg *Highbury*, April 28, 1970
Arsenal (1) 3, *Anderlecht* (0) 0
Arsenal: Wilson; Storey, McNab; Kelly, McLintock, Simpson; Armstrong, Sammels, Radford, George, Graham.
Anderlecht: Trappeniers; Heylens, Velkeneers, Kialunda, Martens; Nordahl, Desanghere; Devrindt, Mulder, Van Himst, Puis.
Scorers: Kelly, Radford, Sammels for Arsenal.

Chapter Eighteen

South American Championship History

		Winners	Runners-up
1917	Montevideo	Uruguay	Argentina
1919	Rio	Brazil	Uruguay
1920	Valparaiso	Uruguay	Argentina
1921	Buenos Aires	Argentina	Brazil
1922	Rio	Brazil	Paraguay

		Winners	**Runners-up**
1923	Montevideo	Uruguay	Argentina
1924	Montevideo	Uruguay	Argentina
1925	Buenos Aires	Argentina	Brazil
1926	Santiago	Uruguay	Argentina
1927	Lima	Argentina	Paraguay
1929	Buenos Aires	Argentina	Uruguay
1937	Buenos Aires	Argentina	Paraguay
1939	Lima	Peru	Brazil
1942	Montevideo	Uruguay	Argentina
1947	Guayaquil	Argentina	Paraguay
1949	Rio	Brazil	Paraguay
1953	Lima	Paraguay	Brazil
1955	Santiago	Argentina	Chile
1957	Lima	Argentina	Brazil
1959	Buenos Aires	Argentina	Brazil
1963	La Paz	Bolivia	Paraguay
1967	Montevideo	Uruguay	Argentina

Chapter Nineteen

South American Libertadores Cup History

The South American Cup, or Copa de Los Libertadores, was founded in 1960 to provide a South American team to play the winners of the European Cup, for the unofficial championship of the world. It was initially confined, like the European Cup, to champions of various countries – Brazil organised a new cup tournament to find one – but when, in the later 60s, it was enlarged to include two teams per country, Brazilian and Argentinian clubs objected and, on various occasions, withdrew. Thus, no Brazilian clubs competed in 1965, or 1969, a year in which Argentina were represented only by the South American Cup-holders and world champions, Estudiantes. The clubs now qualify in "mini-league" groups, in two stages, for a final played at home and away, with goal average irrelevant.

1960
Penarol 1, *Olimpia Paraguay* 0
Olimpia Paraguay 1, *Penarol* 1

1961
Penarol 1, *Palmeiras* 0 *(Sao Paulo)*
Palmeiras 1, *Penarol* 1

1962
Santos 2, Penarol 1
Penarol 3, Santos 2
Santos 3, Penarol 0

1963
Santos 3, Boca Juniors 2
Boca Juniors 1, Santos 2

1964
Nacional 0, Independiente 0
Independiente 1, Nacional 0

1965
Independiente 1, Penarol 0
Penarol 3, Independiente 1
Independiente 4, Penarol 1

1966
Penarol 2, River Plate 0
River Plate 3, Penarol 2
Penarol 4, River Plate 2

1967
Racing Club 0, Nacional 0
Nacional 0, Racing Club 0
Racing Club 2, Nacional 1

1968
Estudiantes 3, Palmeiras 1
Palmeiras 3, Estudiantes 1
Estudiantes 2, Palmeiras 0

1969
Nacional 0, Estudiantes 1
Estudiantes 2, Nacional 0

1970
Estudiantes 1, Penarol 0
Penarol 0, Estudiantes 0

Chapter Twenty

Olympic Football

The Olympic Games football tournament, a knock-out affair, goes back to the London Olympics of 1908, and has been held at every subsequent Olympiad except Los Angeles, in 1932. Beyond doubt, its most brilliant and notable winners were the Uruguayan teams of 1924 and 1928, at a time when Uruguayan football was quite new to Europe. Indeed, it remained unknown to Britain for another twenty-five years. Even then, the thin, sometimes non-existent, line between amateurism and professionalism flawed the tournament, and in 1924 Britain withdrew over the question of "broken time" payments, not to return until 1936.

Though frequently interesting, this blemish has made the competition increasingly unsatisfactory, as the amateur footballer – at high level – became more and more a figure of the past. Several members of the alleged "student" team with which Italy won in Berlin, in 1936, went straight into the full national side. Indeed, the full-backs, Foni and Rava, were the World Cup Final pair two years later.

In the 1960 Olympic football tournament, no player who had taken part in the 1958 World Cup was allowed to be chosen, a rule which still exists, with dubious effect. On that occasion it led to the elimination of Russia (who had reached the 1958 Finals and could not field their full international team) and by Bulgaria, who could. Italy got round the problem, and still do, by deciding that, since their players could not *officially* be professional till 21, they must in the meantime be amateurs. Thus they were able to field a brilliant young side, almost every member of which has since been fully capped.

The 1908 tournament was won by a very powerful United Kingdom side, including the Rev. K. R. G. Hunt, of Wolves, and the brilliant Spurs and England inside-forward, Vivian Woodward. France entered two teams in a knock-out tournament, each of which was annihilated, but the Swedes, Dutch and, above all, the Danes, greatly impressed. Denmark, in fact, lost only by 2–0 to the United Kingdom in the Final, and had more of the play.

In 1912, at Stockholm, the United Kingdom again beat Denmark in the Final 4–2, but the Danes were reduced to ten men by injury.

In 1920, in Antwerp, Britain surprisingly went out 3–1 to Norway in the first round. The Belgians won the tournament, after the Czechs walked off the field in the Final, in protest against the sending off of one of their players. Thus, second position was awarded to the rising Spanish team, who had beaten Denmark.

The year 1924 saw the first triumph of Uruguay, bringing such brilliant forwards to Paris as Petrone and Scarone. A crowd of 60,000 watched Uruguay beat Switzerland in the Final. Four years later, in Amsterdam, Argentina entered for the first time, losing 2–1 to Uruguay in a replayed Final.

In 1936, a less powerful field, in Berlin, saw the victory of the Italians, Britain, with Bernard Joy at centre-half, beat China 2–0 then lost 4–5 to Poland. The Italians won the Final, 2–1, against Austria, coached by Jimmy Hogan.

The 1948 tournament, again held in London, was a fine one. The Swedish, Danish and Yugoslav teams were among the strongest of the day, while the British amateur side put up a very fine display. After beating the powerful Dutch team in a gruelling match at Highbury, they knocked out France 1–0 at Fulham, with a goal by Bob Hardisty; lost in the semi-final to the powerful Yugoslavs; and again – with honour – in the third match with Denmark.

The Swedes, who beat Yugoslavia 3–1 at Wembley in the Final, included all three famous Nordahl brothers, and had Nils Leidholm, Gunnar Gren and Garvis Carlsson in attack.

The year 1952 saw the entry into the lists of a still greater team – Puskas and his Hungarians. Britain were ingloriously knocked out 4–5 in the first match, by little Luxemburg. Russia competed, coming out of splendid isolation, and fought out a remarkable 5–5 draw with Yugoslavia, after being four behind, but lost the replay 3–1. In the Helsinki Final, Hungary beat the Slavs 2–0, but not without hard labour.

In 1956 it was Russia's turn. Britain, though knocked out in the eliminators, were invited to Australia to make up the complement, but, without their regular goalkeeper, were thrashed by Bulgaria. The Russians (who had to replay to beat the Indonesians) plodded to an unsatisfying success, against the Yugoslavs. India were the surprise, taking fourth place.

In 1960, the Yugoslavs at last had their victory, in Rome, but it was a lucky one; they won their Naples semi-final against Italy on the toss of a coin. A fine Danish team, having knocked out Hungary, played wearily in the final and went down 3–1, even though the Slav forward, Galic, was sent off.

In 1964 Britain, after eliminating Iceland, were defeated by Greece, 5–3 on aggregate, thus failing to qualify for Tokyo. Hungary, with Bene superb, beat the Czechs 2–1 in a splendid final.

OLYMPIC FOOTBALL

The Mexican tournament, in 1968, was convincingly won by Hungary, even though the over-rigorous officiating of Diego De Leo, the referee, reduced the Final to farce, three Bulgarians and a Hungarian being sent off. By and large, the sea level teams adapted themselves very well to the high altitude; three of them, France, Bulgaria and

Japan, in fact defeated Mexico. The Japanese, their attack superbly led by Kamamoto, were the revelation of the tournament.

OLYMPIC WINNERS

1908 London: United Kingdom 2, Denmark 0
1912 Stockholm: United Kingdom 4, Denmark 2: 3rd, Holland
1920 Antwerp: Belgium 2, Czechoslovakia 0 (match abandoned) 2nd place awarded to Spain
1924 Paris: Uruguay 3, Switzerland 0: 3rd, Sweden
1928 Amsterdam: Uruguay 2, Argentina 1 (after 1–1 draw): 3rd, Italy
1936 Berlin: Italy 2, Austria 1: 3rd, Norway
1948 London: Sweden 3, Yugoslavia 1: 3rd Denmark
1952 Helsinki: Hungary 2, Yugoslavia 0: 3rd, Sweden
1956 Melbourne: Russia 1, Yugoslavia 0: 3rd, Bulgaria
1960 Rome: Yugoslavia 3, Denmark 1: 3rd, Hungary
1964 Tokyo: Hungary 2, Czechoslovakia 1: 3rd, E. Germany
1968 Mexico City: Hungary 4, Bulgaria 1: 3rd, Japan

Chapter Twenty-one

England and Great Britain versus The Rest

October 26, 1938. *Arsenal Stadium*
England (2) 3, *Rest of Europe* (0) 0
England: Woodley (Chelsea); Sproston (Spurs), Hapgood (Arsenal); Willingham (Huddersfield Town), Cullis (Wolves), Copping (Arsenal); Matthews (Stoke), Hall (Spurs), Lawton (Everton), Goulden (West Ham), Boyes (Everton).
Europe: Olvieri; Foni, Rava (Italy); Kupfer (Germany), Andreolo (Italy), Kitzinger (Germany); Aston (France), Braine (Belgium), Piola (Italy), Szengeller (Hungary), Brustad (Norway).
Scorers: Hall, Goulden, Lawton for England.

May 10, 1947. *Hampden Park, Glasgow*
Great Britain (4) 6, *Rest of Europe* (1) 1
Britain: Swift (England); Hardwick (England), Hughes (Wales); Macaulay (Scotland), Vernon (Ireland), Burgess (Wales); Matthews (England), Mannion (England), Lawton (England), Steel (Scotland), Liddell (Scotland).
Europe: Da Rui (France); Petersen (Denmark), Steffen (Switzerland);

WORLD CUP 1974

European Qualifying Groups

GROUP I: Sweden, Hungary, Austria, Malta.
GROUP II: Italy, Switzerland, Turkey, Luxembourg.
GROUP III: Belgium, Netherlands, Norway, Iceland.
GROUP IV: Rumania, East Germany, Albania, Finland.
GROUP V: England, Poland, Wales.
GROUP VI: Bulgaria, Portugal, Northern Ireland, Cyprus.
GROUP VII: Yugoslavia, Spain, Greece.
GROUP VIII: Czechoslovakia, Denmark, Scotland.
GROUP IX: Russia, France, Republic of Ireland.

Winner of Group IX to play-off against winner of South American Group III.

Carey (Ireland), Parola (Italy), Ludl (Czechoslovakia); Lambrecht (Belgium), Gren (Sweden), Nordahl (Sweden), Wilkes (Holland), Praest (Denmark).
Scorers: Mannion (2), Lawton (2), Steel, Parola (own goal) for Britain, Nordahl for Europe.

October 21, 1953. *Wembley*
England (2) 4, *Rest of Europe (FIFA)* (3) 4
England: Merrick (Birmingham); Ramsey (Spurs), Eckersley (Blackburn R.); Wright (Wolves), Ufton (Charlton Athletic), Dickinson (Portsmouth); Matthews (Blackpool), Mortensen (Blackpool), Lofthouse (Bolton Wanderers), Quixall (Sheffield Wednesday), Mullen (Wolves).
Fifa: Zeman (Austria) [Beara (Yugoslovia)], Navarro (Spain), Hanappi (Austria); Cjaicowski (Yugoslavia), Posipal (Germany), Ocwirk (Austria); Boniperti (Italy), Kubala (Spain), Nordahl (Sweden), Vukas, Zebec (Yugoslavia).
Scorers: Mullen (2), Mortensen, Ramsey (penalty) for England, Boniperti (2), Kubala (2) (1 penalty) for FIFA.

August 15, 1955. *Belfast*
Great Britain (1) 1, *Rest of Europe* (1) 4
Britain: Kelsey (Wales); Sillett, P. (England), MacDonald (Scotland); Blanchflower (Ireland), Charles (Wales), Peacock (Ireland); Matthews (England), Johnstone (Scotland), Bentley (England), McIlroy (Ireland), Liddell (Scotland).
Europe: Buffon (Italy); Gustavsson (Sweden), Van Brandt (Belgium); Ocwirk (Austria), Jonquet (France), Boskov (Yugoslavia); Soerensen, (Denmark), Vukas (Yugoslavia), Kopa (France), Travassos (Portugal), Vincent (France).
Scorers: Johnstone for Britain, Vincent, Vukas (3) for Europe

October 23, 1963. *Wembley.* Centenary International
England (0) 2, *Rest of the World* (0) 1
England: Banks (Leicester City); Armfield (Blackpool), Wilson (Huddersfield Town); Milne (Liverpool), Norman (Spurs), Moore (West Ham United; Paine (Southampton), Greaves (Spurs), Smith, R. (Spurs), Eastham (Arsenal), Charlton (Manchester United).
Fifa: Yachin (Russia) [Soskic (Yugoslavia)]; Santos, D. (Brazil) (Eyzaguirre (Chile)]; Schnellinger (Germany); Pluskal, Popluhar (Czechoslovakia), Masopust (Czechoslovakia) [Baxter (Scotland)]; Kopa (France) [Seeler (Germany)], Law (Scotland), Di Stefano (Spain), Eusebio (Portugal) [Puskas (Spain)], Gento (Spain).
Scorers: Paine, Greaves for England, Law for FIFA.